FLYING
CLOSE
TO THE SUN

FLYING CLOSE TO THE SUN

MY LIFE AND TIMES
AS A WEATHERMAN

CATHY WILKERSON

Seven Stories Press

New York • Toronto • London • Melbourne

A Seven Stories Press First Edition

Seven Stories Press
140 Watts Street
New York, NY 10013
http://www.sevenstories.com

In Canada: Publishers Group Canada, 559 College Street, Suite 402, Toronto, ON M6G 1A9

In the UK: Turnaround Publisher Services Ltd., Unit 3, Olympia Trading Estate, Coburg Road, Wood Green, London N22 6TZ

In Australia: Palgrave Macmillan, 15-19 Claremont Street, South Yarra, VIC 3141

College professors may order examination copies of Seven Stories Press titles for a free six-month trial period. To order, visit http://www.sevenstories.com/textbook or send a fax on school letterhead to (212) 226-1411.

Book design by Jon Gilbert

Library of Congress Cataloging-in-Publication Data

Wilkerson, Cathy.
  Flying close to the sun : my life and times as a weatherman / Cathy Wilkerson.
    p. cm.
  ISBN-13: 978-1-58322-771-8 (hardcover)
  1. Wilkerson, Cathy. 2. Women revolutionaries--United States--Biography. 3. Weatherman (Organization) 4. Youth--United States--Political activity. I. Title.
  HQ1413.W55A3 2007
  322.4'2092--DC22
                                    2007020900
Printed in the U.S.A.

9 8 7 6 5 4 3 2 1

This book is dedicated to
Ted Gold
Diana Oughton
Terry Robbins

and all the others who gave their lives during
the upheavals of the 60s and 70s

The people will live on.
The learning and blundering people will live on.
They will be tricked and sold and again sold
And go back to the nourishing earth for rootholds,
The people so peculiar in renewal and comeback,
You can't laugh off their capacity to take it.
The mammoth rests between his cyclonic dramas.

• • •

This old anvil laughs at many broken hammers.
There are men who can't be bought.
The fireborn are at home in fire.
The stars make no noise.
You can't hinder the wind from blowing.
Time is a great teacher.
Who can live without hope?

—*Carl Sandburg, from "Where to? what next?"*

We forget that the necessary ingredient needed to make the past work for the future is our energy in the present, metabolizing one into the other.

—*Audre Lorde*

CONTENTS

■ ■

INTRODUCTION

..

On the morning of March 6, 1970, in the subbasement of 18 W. 11th Street in Greenwich Village, a piece of ordinary water pipe, filled with dynamite, nails, and an electric blasting cap, ignited by mistake. Seconds later, the shock waves from this pipe bomb set off a secondary explosion of dynamite sticks in a nearby packing box. The whole townhouse rose up a foot or two, shattering bricks and splintering wooden beams, and then was transformed into dust and rubble, shuddering in a deep pit in which a ruptured gas main burst into flame. The narrow four-story structure, which was completely demolished by these two explosions, had been the home of my father and stepmother. I had been staying there briefly with some friends while my parents were away on vacation. Only two of us survived.

This book is an investigation of how my friends and I came to be there at that moment and what I believed we were trying to do. Because the explosion in the townhouse has become somewhat iconic in 60s lore, a piece of my own story has been incorporated into the narratives of countless others. Women's voices, however, have been noticeably absent in those narratives, although in the past few years this has begun to change. My efforts now to be part of the public discourse are an extension of the story itself in which, as a young person, I struggled to define my humanity independently of the public expectations of my class, gender, and race.

Many in my generation were deeply moved by the post–World War II rhetoric of liberal Christianity, Judaism, and democracy. As we came of age, the civil rights movement allowed us to see that our horizons did not need to be limited by the constraints handed down by our families and schools. For young women especially, the movement offered opportunities unavailable almost anywhere else; there we could learn about the political configurations of our world and take part in the public discourse about our collective future.

1

Those of us in Students for a Democratic Society (SDS) and, later, Weatherman, saw ourselves as part of a worldwide uprising of young people working for freedom and equality. By the late 60s, a great many young people were reeling from the rapid bombardment of many ideas—about feminism, national liberation, black nationalism, environmental destruction, and the apparent impotence of our electoral system. We ricocheted from event to event: violent attacks against buses of school children; US incursions into the Dominican Republic and Laos, as well as Vietnam; the assassinations of activists; and FBI dirty tricks. Presented with both national and world events that were emotionally overwhelming, and ill-prepared to make the choices that lay in front of me, I made a series of decisions, from a standpoint of rage, hopelessness, and fear, in which I accepted the same desanctification of human life practiced by Richard Nixon, Henry Kissinger, and William Westmoreland. I accepted their supposition that, in the end, violence is the only effective strategy for social change; that might makes right, despite the fact that treasuring humanity—and each life within it—was one of the values that I had fought for. I abandoned myself to the sanctimoniousness of hating my enemies.

Actions had been planned for that March of 1970, some details of which I had only cursory knowledge. What I felt deep down, but did not allow myself to acknowledge or express, was that this plan was so ill-conceived on so many levels that the chance of an accident happening somewhere along the way was almost inevitable. The intention, as far as I know, was not to cause carnage but chaos, the disruption of life as usual. It is a characteristic of rage and despair, however, that consequences are not thought through with any clarity beyond the immediate, desperate need to make a subjective statement. In my imagination, I saw splintered wood and a jumble of table and chairs and wounded soldiers. I saw Vietnam. But mostly I thought about the political impact, not about individual lives. In reality, if we had succeeded in our early phase of the plan, the damage could well have been more deadly than it was.

The violence of the era I discuss here was not significantly worse than that of earlier times, when feudalism, slavery, religious or tribal tyranny, and natural disasters devastated whole populations. The centralized political structures and powerful technologies that have helped contemporary society to moderate the impact of floods and epidemics, however, have provided us with the capacity to inflict significantly more damage in the ceaseless warring for dominance that has characterized much of humanity's sojourn on the planet.

How do young people today make sense of the violence all around them? How do they construct a coherent view of the world amid conflicting messages, many of which use the language of rights, addiction, entitlements, and fear? I hope that my story from the past will shed some light on the urgency young people feel to seek coherence in an incoherent world.

I dedicate this book to the three people killed in the townhouse. Each of these people was motivated, like I was, primarily by the passionate wish that the privileges of family, friends, adequate food, housing, education, and relative safety be accessible to all of the billions of people on the planet who were desperately trying to climb out of poverty and dislocation. Each of them also believed that the only moral choice was to act, despite a host of unanswered questions; to be passive was to acquiesce in the diminishment of their humanity. Their deaths led me, and many others, to begin to turn away from responding to violence with violence and self-sacrifice, and to search for a different paradigm for change.

The fifth person in the townhouse that day was Kathy Boudin. While Kathy and I had both been in SDS for years, I had not spoken with her before until the previous summer in Cleveland, and did not know her well. Kathy is still on parole after twenty-two years in prison on an unrelated charge incurred more than ten years after the townhouse explosion. I have chosen not to speak for her at all, so that she can elaborate on her own story should she ever chose to do so. Consequently, she appears in this book only at the moment of the explosion and in a few references to public documents.

During the telling of this story, I have tried to maintain the immediacy of my consciousness. I trust that readers will remember that other characters who appear are people with their own complicated stories, which I cannot know and whose stories I have not attempted to tell.

Mine is not an absolute, factual record. I have tried to tell the story as accurately as I can, as I remember it forty years later. In a few instances, for reasons of my own, I have used pseudonyms for people who appear only briefly in the story.

While I made peace in the late 70s and early 80s with most of the big issues in this story, I would never have been able to articulate my thinking with any clarity or completeness then. In my work as an educator I have learned a language of change that has helped me analyze what happened and that has guided me in the telling of my story. I have been influenced by twenty years of teaching and working with young people who are grappling with their own fury at the injustices they have seen around them and the doublespeak of official society. I felt I owed this story to them and to all young people trying to face these challenges.

CHAPTER ONE

NEW ENGLAND SOIL

■ ■

My ancestors settled on North American soil so long ago that any family memories of an earlier time and life on European shores had faded by the time of my parents' birth. Some branches of the family have been traced back to the Revolution and even to the Mayflower. The only stories of a culture of origin concerned a great-great-grandfather on my mother's side, Theophilus Olena, a descendant of French settlers in Canada named Oligny. Theophilus followed the markets of his family's small imported wine and liquor business down the Hudson, and settled in Brooklyn, New York, in the early 1800s, the family name now anglicized to Olena. Theophilus Olena eventually became a Brooklyn alderman, and was present at the ribbon cutting of the Brooklyn Bridge in 1883. Many of the men in the family worked in the business, supervising the loading of barges at the docks and finding new outlets as the business grew and spread westward along the Erie Canal to Buffalo. Some of the women helped with the business as well, but mostly they tended the home and the children, many of whom succumbed to diphtheria, flu, or some form of accident.

They were proper folks, salesmen, inventors, and shopkeepers. After thriving in Brooklyn, they felt entitled to prosperity and assumed that the future would continue to offer opportunities for each new generation. When Prohibition ended the family business, the remaining inventory was sold, and a small piece of the proceeds went to my grandfather. He invested it in a lumber mill in the South and promptly lost it all, incurring a large debt in the process.

My grandfather was a lawyer working in Manhattan, and he was able to keep his job throughout the Depression. He married my grandmother (after waiting eight years while she cared for her ailing father) and had two children with her, my mother and her younger brother.

When my mother Audrey Olena reached school age, the family moved from Brooklyn to Garden City, Long Island, a new suburb that excluded both Jews and people of color. There, my grandmother carried on the traditions of earlier times, which strictly limited the horizons for women of her class. Having been raised in a family that offered little warmth, she had little to share with her two children, but she attended to their physical and intellectual needs with religious thoroughness. She argued constantly with her husband about his generous impulses, as the family continued to struggle with debt. These loud and bitter altercations terrified my mother, engendering in her a lifelong belief that the expression of anger was cruel and destructive and could never serve any purpose. Strong emotions were to be distrusted, contained, and hidden if at all possible.

My mother attended public school and, like my father, had the security and freedom of an adventurous childhood filled with neighborhood games such as bicycle polo, cards, dolls, and the exploration of undeveloped lots. At home, however, she and her younger brother lived by a rigid set of rules generated by their mother's sense of propriety. At the end of eighth grade, she was sent to a nearby Quaker boarding school to complete her education.

Here, my mother was exposed to a completely different set of values and challenges. The Quakers used silence as a way to explore and resolve conflict and believed in the power of community to help people divine God's will. The quiet orderliness and intellectual rigor of the Friends Academy became a haven of new possibilities after the tensions at home. The Quakers valued the thinking and potential of women as well as men, kindling a deep intellectual ambition in my mother's imagination. Her love of reading developed into a passion for literature, and her love of and commitment to music deepened, as she studied both voice and piano.

The Quaker ideas my mother brought home about pacifism and tolerance, however, remained a complete mystery to her parents, who had come of age during the Spanish–American War at the end of the nineteenth century. The United States had been busy pursuing international economic interests, backed by the military, while within its own country, the US government continued to usurp land from native peoples, in violation of earlier treaties, and Jim Crow maintained the rule of white economic interests in the South, enforced by the established norm of lynching.

Comfortably insulated from the dramas of politics and commerce beyond their immediate sphere, my grandparents never troubled themselves with the underlying economic dynamics responsible for their well-being, however precarious. Accepting the status quo, they embraced its values, which justified the reality that hard work by those of European stock paid better than the same work done by others. The violence of this system remained politely hidden from their everyday life. With industry and hard work, my grandparents expected their family's station in life to hold steady and gain increasing security.

A superior upbringing that guaranteed their children a place above the rabble would be the family's bequest to the next generation, and so a good deal of the family resources were devoted to it. As my mother approached the end of high school, her mother considered her education complete. Now, she needed to prepare herself for marriage, perhaps by attending a finishing school. My mother's piano teacher, however, who had become a mentor in her life, argued that my mother go on to college, and suggested Smith College in particular. Hungry now to pursue her intellectual interests, my mother pleaded to be allowed to go. Her father stepped in and said that if she wanted to go to college, she, as well as her brother, should have the opportunity. He was proud of her achievements in high school, and even though he expected her to be a wife and mother, he believed she would benefit from expanding her horizons, her circle of friends, and her interests. Despite growing debt, he agreed to send her.

On my father's side, his grandmother, Miriam Wampler, also traveled on the Erie Canal, moving as a small child with her parents, in the mid-1800s, from a village in Maine to a farm just outside Dayton, Ohio. She remembered watching the funeral train that bore President Lincoln's body back to Illinois.

To supplement the farm's income, much of the family moved into town to take up whatever jobs were available in the mercurial economy. Miriam's daughter married a young man named Oscar Wilkerson, a man with an irrepressible sense of humor and a good job as a fireman on the railroad. When his wife was bedridden upstairs after the very difficult birth of their only child, my grandfather, she was startled by a noisy commotion on the wooden staircase. Oscar appeared at the bedroom doorway with a newly purchased horse to present for her inspection.

Oscar died twelve years later in an accident on the job, and Oscar Jr. had to leave school to help support himself and his mother. His newspaper route, which he kept through an assortment of jobs, including a stint as a semipro baseball player, led to a job with the National Cash Register Company, where he studied to be a secretary. During the next ten years, he took on added responsibilities and changed companies. At twenty-seven he married his sweetheart—who was only fifteen or sixteen at the time— and began a family.

Soon after the birth of his second son, my father James, Oscar relocated for his job at an office furniture company when it moved to Rahway, New Jersey. The family, including Grandmother Wilkerson, followed, eventually settling in Colonia, New Jersey. Here my father grew up with his two brothers in a house full of merriment and adventure. A constant stream of games—word games, board games, math games, card games, and outdoor games like horseshoe and croquet—filled their days. Despite his parents' determination to give him the best education by sending him to private school (especially as neither of them had gone past grade school), my father was an indifferent student, and instead put his energy into his friends, pets, and pranks.

My father did not apply to college, preferring instead to go to work. However, it was still the heart of the Depression, and jobs were hard to come by. In the fall of 1933 he went to visit a high school friend who was entering Amherst College in Massachusetts. My father's friend encouraged him to come, and upon investigation, it turned out that if my father could pay the fees, there was still room in the freshman class. With a phone call home to his father, now a manager at the furniture company, my father was suddenly a college student, beginning what would become a lifelong love affair with Amherst College.

James, soon given the nickname Joe, was inspired by Amherst's professors to extend the range of his knowledge, and he worked hard to make up for his academic deficits. His real interests, however, remained outside of class. He managed the debate society, the football team, and the band, forming close friendships that stayed with him throughout his entire life. His upbringing had prepared him to be a creative problem solver, and the challenge of getting people to work together efficiently interested him. His managerial experiences taught him that what was needed was not another expert debater or football player or musician, but someone who could listen to all the experts, find out what was required, and devise a creative way to provide it. He also developed self-confidence, finding that anything he developed an interest in he was able to learn about. With his ability to savor experience, life was ahead of him, waiting to be enjoyed.

My father graduated in 1937, the first in the family to complete college. His father Oscar recommended that he learn sales because, as my father later reported, "it was his philosophy, and is now mine, that if a person has the ability to sell, he, or she, could always find a job. . . ."[1]

After a year of selling office equipment, my father joined a new company where he sold pots and pans. During this time, he had been courting my mother, still a senior at Smith College. When my mother graduated, she worked for a year in Manhattan as a student teacher under the supervision of Bank Street School for Education. There she was exposed to ideas about teaching and learning that transformed many of her beliefs about working with children. Soon after, she and my father married and moved to New Orleans, where my father had found a job driving a soft-drink truck, selling his wares store to store. Two years and two jobs later, however, my father had been unable to find a position with possibilities for advancement, and they went back to New York where, at the recommendation of a college friend, my father applied for and got a job as a messenger at Young & Rubicam, an up-and-coming advertising agency.

In December 1941, the Japanese attacked Pearl Harbor, and the war quickly intruded into the lives of young people, with the prospect of an imminent draft. Like many educated young men, my father searched out a wartime job that required special training rather than waiting to be drafted into the infantry. He studied to be a navigator and joined the

Naval Air Transport Service. He then spent the remainder of the war flying supply missions, largely from the east coast of the US to Africa.

My older sister Ann was born while my father was away in May 1943. Twenty months later, I came along during a January snowstorm. In 1945, a few months after I was born and the war in Europe had ended, my father was discharged from the navy and he rejoined the media department at Young & Rubicam. He had a wife, two children, and a steady job with a bright future. We were somewhat cramped in the small one-bedroom garden apartment in Hartsdale, New York, but housing was difficult to find, as many returning servicemen were starting new families. Finally, we moved in with friends of friends, a young couple as yet childless, in a rambling old house in Yorktown, New York.

My earliest memories of Yorktown are of sunlight. Less than three feet tall, I was looking across the small snow-covered field into the woods behind our house. Tall orange-brown stalks of grass, still capped with heavy seed heads, stood erect despite the thick blanket of snow. As I peered into the little hills and valleys made by the drifts in among the stalks, I imagined myself a tiny figure wandering through this forest of grasses. I was exhilarated by the beauty of the sunshine on the snow and the delicate designs in white, dramatically framed by the tall gray and dark browns of the trees rising up high in the actual woods beyond. A dazzling sense of excitement and possibility flooded the first years of my life.

My father pushed me on the swing, my hands barely large enough to grip the thick rope that came down from high up in an old sugar maple. In the mornings, he filled the sink, lathered his face with soap, put in a fresh razor blade, and went to work on his whiskers. My sister Ann and I sat on the edge of the tub and sang to keep him company, occasionally pushing the soap back into the water and laughing heartily as we did so.

The shared house pleased my mother because she could now have adult conversation during the day with Beth Vanderlyn, the home's owner, as well as another pair of eyes to help keep watch over me. I was nonstop energy and got into everything, completely different from my older sister, who was more thoughtful and reflective even as a small child.

By 1948, with help from the GI bill and my father's family, my parents were prepared to buy a small piece of land and build a house. At first they looked in New Canaan and Westport, towns in Connecticut that were popular with the ambitious men in my father's office. But, after several exploratory trips my parents discovered that both communities had a policy of excluding anyone but WASPs. My parents were especially dismayed to find that this policy held true for Jews, after the entire country had been involved in an effort to defeat Hitler. They agreed that they did not want to raise their children in such a community.

North Stamford was just across the border from New Canaan, and it had not yet been developed. The land there was considerably cheaper, and my parents bought a five-acre plot and began construction on a new house. In the spring of 1948, when my younger sister Robin was six months old, we moved in, even though it was not finished. My childhood explorations continued unabated. The grey-stained clapboard house was built in a clearing of hundred-year-old woods that had grown up on pastureland that had once been painstakingly cleared by seventeenth- and eighteenth-century farmers. The borders of their rocky fields were still marked with carefully constructed stone walls, which now ran among the trees, like old fish nets rotting in the sand.

In the winter, the bird feeder that hung from an old dogwood tree was always filled with chickadees, nuthatches, and cardinals. From my father I learned the names of the birds and their habits. My parents took us for a walk along the walls that bordered our five-acre lot. We were expected to stay inside that border, but my mother, somewhat overwhelmed, gave Ann and me tremendous freedom to explore, and we often ranged much deeper into the woods, which went on for miles in three directions.

My mother established an orderly routine in our lives, which she believed was essential for our good character and her sanity. We were pre–Dr. Spock children. As infants we were fed on a rigid schedule and left to cry when we were hungry or afraid of the dark. Our daily schedule developed a religious sanctity. I couldn't sleep during the day because I could not stop generating energy, but naps were required so I was put in my room for the requisite two hours every afternoon. Rest was not acceptable; only sleep would do. I learned at this young age to slip my picture books under the covers and feign sleep when I heard my mother's footsteps.

I was finally relieved of this nap ritual when my mother took me the following fall to enroll in kindergarten at the local elementary school. This was the first year of the baby boomers, however, and the kindergarten was full, so they placed me in the first grade, where there was still room.

The Martha Hoyt School in North Stamford was an old, three-story stone building. While I chaffed under the rules at home, I mostly understood and accepted them. At school, both the official rules given by teachers and the social rules among the children were completely foreign to me, and the punishment of choice in both cases seemed to be humiliation, far more terrifying than my mother's frustrated anger. I retreated into a painful shyness. Over time I learned the rules and began to make friends, but I remained wary.

Gradually the opportunities for learning pulled me in. I loved the smell of books, yet I struggled through *Dick and Jane*, and so remained in the lower reading groups. I failed spelling and handwriting every term. I wanted to be a good reader like my sister Ann, but my progress was slow. My hunger for stories was satisfied at home when my mother read us stories by E. B. White, J. R. R. Tolkien, and C. S. Lewis.

On Sundays, we dressed in our party clothes and went with my mother to church. I liked getting dressed up for Sunday school and there was something very comforting about the little wooden church with red carpets, bright white paint and beautiful stained-glass windows. Everyone at the church was very friendly.

Almost every day after school, regardless of the weather, Ann and I changed from the mandatory school dresses into pants to go outside to play. When she got old enough, Robin joined us. Two other girls who lived on our road and who were in my grade at school, Haven and Karla, rounded out our pack. We developed an ongoing world of fantasy in several different forums, encouraged by a box of old-fashioned child-sized clothing—capes, vests, hats and scarves that my mother had collected, a legacy of her time at Bank Street. One of our favorite games was Cowboys and Indians, a subject extensively covered in children's books of the day. We had all been given toy guns with holsters, Indian-style headbands, and toy bows and arrows.

It was clear to me that the Indians were the defenders of the land and the cowboys were the invaders, albeit possessed of a wild and romantic character of their own. But I felt no urgency to resolve this contradiction because it happened a long time ago, and I thought that there were no more cowboys or Indians. When I started studying American history in the sixth grade, and realized that there were still Indians (and cowboys) and that Indians had to live on tiny reservations and were very poor, I began to ask more questions and to pay attention to any information about this that came my way.

Social justice was at the heart of another favorite game, Robin Hood. I was usually relegated to the role of Friar Tuck because I was slightly on the chubby side, and the older girls got to play Robin Hood and Maid Marian.

While the outdoors represented almost unlimited freedom, indoors there were a lot of rules. We each had daily chores. At various times my father made charts to organize our chores and invented systems of different colored stars and rewards to encourage us. We were not exceptionally bright students, however, and the charts had many blank spaces without stars.

The most confusing rules for me were those about how to behave with adults who were not part of our family. Different adults seemed to have different rules and I couldn't figure out what made some adults be one way and others another. Why did I shake hands and be quiet as a mouse with some, shake hands and answer questions with others, "Be friendly!" with these ones, not shake hands but be polite with those, hug these. Especially when my father brought clients home from work, we could not assault him with our normal tumultuous greetings, but instead were to make a good impression. It was bewildering. I responded to my confusion with shyness.

It was in these greetings toward the adults outside of my family, it seems to me now, that as children we were taught our station in life—our perception of our place in the world—whether that position is high or low, benevolent or alienated. Most often the messages were subtle because adults themselves were not actively aware that they were transmitting a message, but sometimes—as in the case of Sammy Young Jr., who was murdered because of his choice of salutation to a white woman, or in the case of the very rich who are being groomed to inherit vast fortunes— the messages were explicit. Like most middle-class children in the 50s, I received mixed messages from church, school, parents, and peers. And like many children, I noticed. The contradictions stayed with me, an irritant fueling a need to understand, and, later, to change the rules.

My mother picked out our clothes and we were to accept her choices. For school, we each had three dresses. My mother expected us to be able to wear each one for two or three days, which we usually managed to do by changing out of our school clothes the second we came home and by wiping out spills with a washcloth. My mother believed that women should do their own housework, but she was not enthusiastic about it and she particularly hated ironing. She occasionally hired a woman named Catherine, a large black woman, to help with the ironing. Catherine also did general housework for several families nearby.

Other than Catherine I only knew one other black person, Annie Mae, who lived with my best friend Kricki's family and who did much of the cooking and cleaning there. Kricki, Annie Mae, and I had enjoyed many adventures in the kitchen. But when adults or even Kricki's siblings were around I sensed a subtle shift in Annie Mae's presentation. I discerned that relationships with black women who helped cook and clean involved yet another set of rules, but I was unable to decode it.

One day my mother drove Catherine home after she had missed the last bus into downtown Stamford. When my mother returned, she commented with some dismay that although Catherine lived in a torn-up tenement, she had to pay approximately the same amount of money in rent that we paid in mortgage payments for our wonderful house in the woods. As she turned her attention to fixing our dinner, I mulled over her words. Like most children, I had a fierce belief in fairness, and this didn't sound fair. I wondered if the fact that Catherine was a Negro had some-thing to do with it. Then I wondered why my mother didn't do something about it. How could she tell us to play fair, when the world wasn't play-ing fair and she wasn't doing anything about it? After that, I avoided Catherine, because I was too embarrassed to talk to her.

For the first time, I looked at my parents differently. I realized they were players in a larger drama beyond the family and I began to pay more atten-tion to this world. I noticed that my mother got upset while watching the McCarthy hearings on TV. I listened when she talked about how stupid she thought it was that we still had atomic-bomb drills in our school. Like many children in the 50s, I found the idea of the atomic bomb terrifying. If the bomb came, my mother said, hiding under the stairs wouldn't help.

All my life my parents and my teachers had exhorted me to stay away from matches. This had instilled in me a deep fear of fire. Yet my mother used fire to light her cigarettes and once in awhile to light candles on the table, and my father occasionally burned piles of brush that he had cleared from the woods. As a child I understood that I was not considered trustworthy to do these things.

I had recurring nightmares about fire. My house was on fire. The walls around me were consumed with angry red and orange flames. The hot air was burning my skin. I had only seconds to consider possible escape routes. Sometimes there were complications involving rescuing family members. I always awoke before the drama was resolved. Perhaps it was because of these dreams, or an attraction to powerful forces, that at age 7 or 8 I was driven to conduct my experiment. I was curious and also driven to tame this force. Since no one would show me, I would find out myself.

It was mid-August, but not too hot. A breeze caught the earth smells from the rich loam carried up by the last of the evaporating dew. Being close to the ground as I squatted in dusty sneakers, cotton shorts, and tee shirt, I could smell the rotting leaves as I cleared off a patch of earth.

I had constructed my experiment to test the boundaries of my confi-dence, and this is what made it exciting. Nonetheless, the excitement lay in the learning, not in any sense of danger, and so I positioned myself in view of the kitchen window where my mother might see me should I need to call for help.

I had taken a book of matches from the drawer where my mother kept her cigarettes, and now I pulled this out of my pocket and placed it on the ground. In the middle of the cleared patch of dirt I piled several dried, brown leaves. The breeze picked up the top leaf and lifted it slightly. I felt a wave of anxiety rise inside me until the breeze stopped.

I rubbed the red match tip along the strip on the bottom of the matchbook the way I had seen my mother do a thousand times. I scraped it slowly at first and then faster, nervous that the flame would burn my soft fingertips, which is exactly what happened the first time I was successful. I dropped the match quickly on the bare ground. On the next try, the match caught again, but before the flame finished consuming the top leaf it died. With a few more match strikes I had another successful flame, which I placed next to the bottom leaf this time. Again the flame ran around the edge of the leaf, but as it did so the leaf above began to smoke and quickly the flames jumped up. The smell of the burning leaves joined with the musky odors of the earth and I felt the excitement of fall.

This time, the fire continued to spread until all of the leaves were burning and the flames rose the height of my outstretched hand above the pile. The breeze held its breath. Then, just as quickly, the flame descended again as the ashy skeletons of the leaves collapsed into the dust. My eyes darted up to the kitchen window and then over to the door. No movement; I had gone undetected. I ran my hand over the pile of ashes and began to mix them into the dirt. While in part I was erasing the traces of my experiment, I also needed sensory affirmation that this power had taken me into its confidence.

By the end of third grade, I was still the shortest kid in class, but I had learned how to stand up for myself. When my teacher asked us to make a collage that represented what we would be when we grew up, mine showed me standing at a clothesline hanging up the wash like my mother. I imagined myself married to a farmer, raising lots of children.

I had learned to read competently and was working my way through dozens of Landmark biographies, the beginning of my lifelong fascination with American history. I began to take piano lessons with my sister Ann; only after I had practiced was I allowed to watch the one TV show we were permitted each night.

In the spring of my third-grade year, on a warm, clear Saturday, my mother called us all into her bedroom. We sat with her on my parents' big double bed and my mother explained to us that a wonderful thing was going to happen. My father had agreed to send us all to live in Switzerland for most of the next year. He would stay here to work, but the four of us would take a boat over and go to school in Lausanne. In the winter my father would come over to visit. We should be grateful to my father for arranging this, my mother said.

We were amazed. This sounded like the greatest adventure of all time, yet, while my mother was telling us this wonderful news, I notice she seemed to be fighting off tears. When I asked her about this, she said that she wanted to cry from happiness and that we should all run out to the woods, where my father was clearing brush, and thank him. Though I accepted this, I was not convinced.

Years later my sisters and I realized that this trip was the result of my father's growing dissatisfaction with his marriage. My mother had been chafing at the loss of the independence she had experienced while at college. She had been unprepared for the monotony of her marriage's demands—her children's constant needs, the household management, and the entertainment required by her husband. She missed the intellectual life of her years at school, and she wanted to work. My father, however, wanted a wife at home who enjoyed performing the social functions that were part of his rising career, and who could care for the children, whom he loved.

Since my mother had always longed to go back to Europe, this trip was a way to soften the blow of my father's growing disengagement from the relationship. Because of the stigma associated with separation and divorce at the time, the trip to an inexpensive postwar Europe was a way to disguise what was going on, and, perhaps, to give my parents another chance.

In August, my mother began to pack a great trunk. She had bought all kinds of strange things, like knee-length long underwear to go under our skirts, and woolen tights. She also had a year's supply of toothpaste and stockings for her, and new shoes for all of us. This heightened our sense that we were going somewhere very different. Because our house was to be rented, we had to pack up everything but the furniture and put it in the attic. My father drove us to New York City, where the boat we would take, the *Maasdam*, owned by the Holland American Line, was moored in the Hudson River.

We discovered that there were three classes on the boat, first, second, and tourist class. We were tourist class, which meant we were not allowed to go into the other areas. Of course, Ann and I saw this as a challenge, not a limitation. After two days of the eight-day journey we had discovered back stairways that allowed us to penetrate everywhere, to take in the view from the top deck and enjoy the pastries in first class.

When we arrived in France we took the train to Paris and then on to Lausanne. My mother had forgotten to buy water, and there was no water on the train. At the next stop, she opened the train window and leaned out to buy mineral water from a vendor on the platform. I was amazed that we could only drink bottled water. There was also a vendor selling glass bottles of Coca-Cola. My mother was horrified that American products were spreading to Europe and she was afraid they would ruin the local character of European villages and make everywhere the same.

The trip took all night. The next morning in Lausanne, we went up the side of the mountain that rose from the majestic Lac Léman to the pension where we would be staying. At one end of the lake we could see the massive snow-covered Alps rising to the west, even though it was still summer in Lausanne. We were introduced to "Madame," who ran the pension, and two of the other guests who happened to be in the living room when we arrived. We had two of the four rooms on the second floor, all of which shared a toilet off the main foyer.

My mother found a local kindergarten for my sister Robin and a school for Ann and me to attend. Everything was different. First of all, we left our shoes at the front door of the school and put on slippers, which we left at school. Second, our only classes were French and embroidery. There were other classes, but since we didn't speak French we could not attend them yet. I found it all new and interesting, and I worked hard to learn some French. My sister Robin reportedly sat alone all day in her kindergarten without talking, and then one day, she started speaking in French. After that, even though she was lonely, she knew the most of any of us. While we were in school, my mother took French lessons. At lunch we went home and my mother tutored us on the other subjects.

My mother told us that we should not tell strangers we were Americans because too many people didn't like Americans. It had something to do with the way American troops had acted during the occupation of Europe after the war. She said we should tell people we were German, which was really puzzling. Since the war was still very much a part of everyday consciousness, I was aware by that time that Germany had been on the other side, and I knew my mother didn't want to travel to Germany. Only later did I understand that the sympathies of many Swiss lay more with the Germans than the United States.

As the air turned colder, we donned the new soft wool long underwear under our skirts, and the new wool sweaters. My mother began preparations for us to go up into the Alps for the winter months, where we were to be placed in a boarding school for several weeks while she traveled. My father met us in Villars just before Christmas, and my parents went off to tour Italy and attempt a reconciliation. After several weeks of travel and one more quick visit with us, my father returned to New York. My mother returned to Lausanne thinking all was well, and picked us up a few weeks later. In the spring we began our way home, stopping to visit several towns in France, Holland, and Scotland.

On our return to the United States, we went back to school for the final month of classes, where I was now aware of the parochialism of the familiar places and rituals of my old life. I loved it no less. The next fall, I started fifth grade at the Emma Willard public middle school in North Stamford. I read a lot that year because I didn't make many new friends. Our gang at home still got together, but the older girls were less eager to play Cowboys and Indians or the other outside games. Haven was beginning to get interested in boys and gossiping with her friends from school, which held no interest for me.

After the first couple of months of school, my mother called us all together again one day to tell us that my father was moving out because my parents were having a trial separation. She reassured us that they both loved all three of us very much and that we would continue to see him on visits and hopefully he would move back. I couldn't imagine my father not living with us; I adored him. Even though he often came home after we were asleep, his sense of fun and mischief had made our lives wonderful and had shaped my boundless curiosity. My sense of loss was compounded by my mother's complete devastation when the trial separation led, a few months later, to the decision to get a divorce.

Once or twice a month on Friday, now, my mother took the three of us to the train station after school, and we went to New York City, where my father waited at the platform in Grand Central Station to meet us. He was renting an apartment on 37th Street, near the station and his office, and we stayed there, sleeping on the couches in the living room or on the twin beds in the second bedroom. He fed us cereal for breakfast, yogurt for lunch, and for dinner we usually got takeout or he cooked hamburgers. He took us to the movies and to see some of the New York landmarks. We all loved New York City but it didn't take the strangeness out of the visits. Often he took us out to Colonia to visit our cousins and my grandparents who were now getting older.

Released from the constraint of not working, my mother volunteered at a private school in New Canaan, called New Canaan Country School (NCCS) in the hopes of getting a job. She liked the school for its progressive educational philosophy and she especially admired the Principal, Henry Wells. She hoped her short experience student teaching in New York would help her in her effort to get a job. We had never before seen her so interested and focused on anything other than the family.

That summer we were sent for two months to a sleepaway camp in northern Vermont called Camp Hanoum. In groups of four to six girls we lived in old army tents on wooden platforms. We wore uniforms and took arts and crafts classes, swimming, canoeing, riding, archery, riflery, and theater. My shyness kept me from making any close friends, but I wasn't bothered by this. As always, my sister Ann was around if I really needed to confide anything, but otherwise, I was used to being independent and self-reliant. I kept my sadness about my father silently. He wrote often, usually funny postcards and letters written in spirals, or cut up like a puzzle, or written in code. My mother wrote excitedly that, as she had hoped, she had been offered a full-time job teaching at NCCS and that we had all been accepted to attend the school the following year at no cost. My father had always felt strongly that we should attend public school, that all children should have an equal start to life. The previous year, however, Robin had had a particularly cruel teacher who had locked her in a closet as punishment, and my mother was determined to move her to a better situation.

Our friend Haven had also come up to camp with us. While we had been in Europe, she had spent a year in bed with nephritis, and the following year, her mother, a heavy smoker, had died of breast cancer, leaving Haven alone at home with her father. My mother had started looking out for her and convinced Haven's father that Haven should also come to the school in New Canaan because she would get more support there.

My mother talked so favorably about the school that I was open to it, although I was completely unprepared for how different it was. There were only two sixth-grade classes, and the majority of the children had already been together for several years. My classmates seemed so comfortable in their surroundings, adept at field hockey, tennis, and softball, sports I had never played, and dismissive of the music and art classes I loved. It was my first exposure to a ruling clique of girls who dripped contempt on those they rejected. They were meticulous about their clothes and hair, and they had a different style than girls in public school. The excluded girls, those of us with less developed social skills, looked enviously at the in-crowd who seemed to be able to generate an aura of coolness and self-importance about them, with their internal dramas and exclusive social events outside of school. Many of the girls were already focused on boys and on developing a social life. I was still only ten, however, and couldn't see what the fuss was about. Even the friendship with my best friend Kricki, who was ecstatic that I had moved to her school, began to be pulled apart as I struggled to define my own way in this foreign environment.

The schoolwork, too, was challenging. For the first time, I had at least two to three hours of homework every night. I was expected to write a paper in social studies, something I had never done before. I loved singing in music class, however, and found that I was good at it. When my mother decided that I should take violin, I agreed. She saw to it that I practiced almost every day.

The other thing that changed after my father left was that we stopped going to the Episcopal church and instead began to attend a Quaker meeting. The Sunday school was not all that different, but in the adult meeting, everyone sat quietly on benches in a semicircle, until someone was moved to speak, after which silence resumed. I found it boring and missed the rituals and familiarity of our old church.

The one thing that did catch my attention was the Quakers' program that paid for young women from Hiroshima and Nagasaki to come to the United States to receive plastic surgery on burns caused by the atomic bomb. The women stayed with members of the meeting while they were going through the surgery, and some of them attended the meeting. The one or two women I saw had brutally scarred faces. I realized that after all our air-raid drills in school and our fear of Russian bombs, we were the only ones who had actually used the atomic bomb, and I was ashamed. I thought that the Quakers were very good to help these women.

One morning, as I left the house with my two sisters to walk down the hill to the school-bus stop, I complained to Ann that I had stayed up almost all night finishing my social studies assignment. I had been looking for sympathy, but instead Ann taunted me, as she often did: "Exaggerator! Exaggerator! Exaggerator!" She used her full authority as my older sister to heap contempt on my complaint because it was not quite literally true. When she dragged out her challenge two and then three times I stooped down, picked up a small stone from the dirt driveway, pivoted and hurled it at her. My intention was to come close and scare her, but I was a miserable shot and by mistake, I hit my target smack in the middle of her forehead.

"I'm hurt!" She wailed. I heard fear and surprise in her cry. She dropped her books to rub her forehead and saw a profusion of blood on her hand. I looked at the blood coming from her eye with rising panic, fearing that I had hit her in the eye. When I ran up to her to look more closely, however, I saw the wound was higher up and actually quite small. My mother rushed out in response to Ann's wail. She saw that the wound was not serious, but called her into the house to stop the bleeding.

In our school, kids did not fight—especially girls. After Robin and I boarded the school bus, a wide-eyed Robin first told her friends, and then the story traveled from seat to seat on the bus as we wound through the twisted back roads. Soon I felt stares turning me into a monster. I imagined the others inching away from me, afraid that some of my grotesqueness would rub off, or worse, that I would attack them. All morning the story traveled. During lunch, I sat down with my lunch box on one of the long lunch-table benches. The other seventh- and eighth-graders filed in, but the spaces all around me remained empty as the other girls crowded together away from me.

I stubbornly ate my baloney sandwich. I didn't raise my eyes, but I stayed; I didn't retreat. My sisters had not looked at me with this loathing. Even Ann, when I saw her at school, felt badly for me because she knew I was in a lot of trouble. She had reacted as if this eruption had occurred on familiar ground.

Mysteriously, I was spared a big scene at home that evening. Even my mother seemed cowed by the enormity of my transgression. I was lectured only briefly on how close I had come to causing permanent blindness to my sister and I was given Ann's share of the dishwashing chores for two weeks. Ann seemed to be impressed, sensing that these attacks on my emerging sense of self-expression, however imperfect, exposed my deeper vulnerabilities. For a while, at least, she stopped teasing me.

The next morning, I had another altercation at the bus stop, this time with Haven, who had stayed over the night before, as she often did. She picked that morning to taunt me about looking sexy, which she knew was about the last thing I wanted to hear. Haven's teasing cut deeply because the whole subject of sexuality felt so dangerous to me. I had been an adventurous, independent child. I had carried my weight around the house. I had the beginnings of my own intellectual life thinking and wondering about things on my own terms. When my breasts started to grow, however, my mother seemed to feel that my body was something to be ashamed of, to be shaved, contoured by bras, and restricted to modest activity. My manners, the clothes I wore, and the way I wore my hair all had to contribute to the final goal, securing a worthy husband. I was definitely too old, my mother said, to continue wandering around in the woods, as I still did after school.

Unlike many of my peers at school, who seemed eager to rush headlong into this narrowly prescribed 1950s image of femininity, I found it humiliating. Never was there a discussion about sexuality—at home or at school. I learned about the basics of sex from my friend Kricki when we were younger and we both had found it shocking. It was hard to figure out how the obsession with manners and morals went with taking your clothes off and letting a man put his penis in you. We were a little short on details, and both of us had been completely shielded from sexual passion either around our parents or in the films we were allowed to see. Sex, as far as we knew, was about reproduction, something men did to women when they were married. Marriage was the end of a woman's life as her own and the beginning of a life lived through her Prince Charming, a time when she put her husband and children's needs first. I believed in Prince Charming and thought it would be wonderful to raise a family of my own, but I was in no hurry to do it.

Perhaps because I was a year younger than my peers I was less ready. Perhaps because of my mother's despair about the end of her marriage I was more tuned in to potential pitfalls of traditional definitions of womanhood and marriage. And perhaps because I hit adolescence at a time when what was socially acceptable was so rigidly defined, I made the connection between privilege and female passivity. But it was the humiliation that struck the deepest: I realized that my own mother thought I was ugly, as evidenced by her insistence that my strong and developing body conform to rigid norms of propriety. As of yet, I had no basis to understand her fears about what might happen when I came into the full power of my sexuality, my intellect, and my inborn impulses to nurture. While she had encouraged both intellectual and economic independence for her daughters, she still believed the prevailing wisdom that a woman was not strong enough to control the combined power of her body, mind, and spirit moving together. I felt that my own internal life no longer seemed of value and that suddenly I had to subdue my passions, let go of my own self-direction, and submit to social expectations. I would find another way to grow up, I decided.

My mother, struggling to get through her first years of teaching with three and sometimes four girls at home, insisted that we not mope or complain, so I tried to develop an impassive front. Ann, Haven and I, each shut off in our private adolescent distress, became separate from each other. The next couple of years I focused by default on my schoolwork, spending hours at work every night. On the weekends, there were tests to study for, reports to write, and trips to visit my father. I still spent time out in the woods by myself, exploring further and further back into previously unexplored areas, seeking solace in the quiet and beauty. I read, losing myself in novels whose characters struggled against enormous difficulties to make sense of their lives and find a way to their humanity: *Jane Eyre*, *How Green Was My Valley*, *All This and Heaven Too*, *Daddy Long Legs*, *The Good Earth*, *My Ántonia*, and *Gone with the Wind*. I wasn't alone with my trials; it seemed to my dramatic mind that the task of humans throughout history was to engage the forces of backwardness and cruelty and to try to create instead a world with light and gentleness. This great turmoil was so much more rich and interesting than life at home or at school.

I loved the summer, when we went to camp for two months. My father also took us traveling. For our first trip, about a year after the divorce, he asked us if we would rather go to Disneyland, in California, or spend five days with him on a ranch in Wyoming. He was flabbergasted when we all instantly answered that we would rather go the ranch. That week we lived in a bunkhouse and went riding through the Wyoming countryside, exploring canyons and plateaus. We were in heaven.

The next summer, my father bought a 37-foot motorboat, a Chris-Craft Cruiser. We all took to the water eagerly. My father taught us how to read nautical charts and the buoys that marked the channels, and to understand the signals of foghorns. Depending on the length of the trip, we visited various ports up and down Long Island Sound, and sometimes out to Martha's Vineyard and Nantucket. It seemed he knew people everywhere.

Once, on our way back from Cutty Hunk, a tiny island near the end of Long Island Sound, a strong storm came up. The waves were far higher than the boat. When we were down in the trough, we could only see steep grey mountains of water immediately around us, which would then crash down on top of us, filling the stern with water, until another swell carried us up and the water poured out the drain holes. He made us all go below and closed the door while he tied himself to the captain's chair. The boat was swept up by the surges of water and then left to free-fall through the air into the trough.

My father had spotted a fishing boat and did his best to keep it in sight, knowing that it would lead us to shore. Finally, we heard the baleful clanging of a bell buoy emerge from the persistent cacophony of wind and crashing waves, and little by little the waters began to get calmer. I was astonished to be alive. My father's example of coolness under pressure made an indelible impression on me. While holding on during the boat's crashing and spinning, I had found a place deep inside, where the acceptance of death allowed for the possibility of courage.

CHAPTER TWO

NORTH AMERICAN ROOTS

■ ■

When Haven and I were in eighth grade, she and Ann became aware that Haven's father and our mother were spending more and more time together. They speculated about a romantic involvement between our parents and wanted me to join in their spying to see if they could learn more. I wanted none of it. If my mother were to remarry, it would be the end of my dreams that she and my father get back together. Besides, I didn't especially like Haven's father, finding him pompous, formal, and somewhat scary.

The romance did progress, however, and in the springtime my mother called us three together and announced that they were engaged and she hoped their marriage would provide a family for us again. She wanted to know how we all felt about it. I started to cry and was unable to speak. I tried to hide my feelings enough to give my formal support to the union that my mother seemed to want.

That summer while we were at camp, they got married. When we returned, my mother had moved us all over to my stepfather's house. Our old house was empty and on the market. There were no woods around Haven's house, and the only place to retreat to when I was home was my room, where I spent enormous amounts of time that year.

By ninth grade, the outlines of a monumental struggle with my mother began to take shape. I was 13 years old and deeply unhappy. My mother seemed perpetually disappointed in me. I never seemed to try hard enough for her. She saw my shyness and social confusion as possible indications of rudeness and bad manners.

When I expressed an interest in becoming a veterinarian, I was informed that it was very hard to get into a veterinarian school, and not something I should aspire to. Science was off my mother's radar screen

completely. Science was not a female pursuit. Nor should I pursue being
an ambassador (you had to be rich), a missionary (Quakers didn't believe
in missionary work), or a farmer (how childish). In fact, being a teacher
seemed the only acceptable alternative, or a translator at the UN, which
my sister Ann was interested in.

My mother couldn't see the ways in which she had instilled in all of us
a sense of our own power and potential, so that we had the imagination
and strength to dream beyond the limited perspectives of her generation.
Even though my mother and I had locked horns, I always knew she cared
passionately about her children's future. In place of the corrosive childhood loneliness and neglect she had felt due to her own mother's
emotional disinterest, my mother, along with my father, had provided a
profound security for the formative years of my life. Far from being
detached, she had micromanaged every detail of our lives. For me the
hardest part of the years to come was knowing that my mother could not
feel pride or joy at the accomplishments that I valued the most.

New Canaan Country School only went through the ninth grade, and
most of the students continued on in boarding school. The previous year
Ann had started at George School, a Quaker school in Pennsylvania. For
me, my mother picked an academically challenging all-girls school in Massachusetts, Abbot Academy. In the spring, we received the acceptance
letter, and everyone was very happy and proud of me. I was just glad to be
leaving home.

The last contact with my old classmates came at a party the week after
our graduation. The party was at a student's home, and the parents left us
alone. I knew my mother would be angry if she knew this. With Johnny
Mathis crooning in the background, however, an overwhelming rush of
hormones melted me into Ward's arms. I was completely startled, and
pleasantly so, by my response. Ward and I danced several dances, progress-
ing rapidly through my first slow dance, my first caresses, and my first kiss.
I was swept off my feet, although I sensed that this was more about me
discovering my sexuality than any newfound love between Ward and me.
Finally, the lights came on. I was embarrassed to suddenly be so exposed

in front of my sister and the other girls. Ward and I managed a self-conscious good-bye.

At Abbot we were not allowed to leave the five-acre campus without permission. We ate meals at round tables seating eight to ten girls and a member of the staff. Seating was assigned and changed every three weeks. We stood around the white tablecloths before each meal to sing or recite grace in unison. Only after the presiding staff person at the table had been seated by the senior student assigned to sit next to her would the rest of us sit down. The food, served in large bowls on each table, was, to me, delicious and there was a lot of it. We were expected to maintain ladylike behavior throughout meals, hands in the lap, conversation muted, and please and thank-yous at every turn.

Each day hung on ritual. A bell woke us up at 6:45 am; at 7:00 those on table-setting shift went to work; at 7:15 we had breakfast, and at 8:00, after room inspection, we went to chapel. The formality of the school's culture was counterbalanced by the intensity generated by two hundred and fifty girls going through adolescence in close quarters. Released from the constraints of New Canaan and the immediacy of my mother's expectations, I felt freer to explore conflicting passions and ideas. Dorm living allowed me to learn a great deal about the lifestyles of a wide range of girls, some of whom came from more affluent and socially ambitious families than mine, while others came from small rural towns where the public high schools did not offer college-prep classes. Some, like me, were from somewhat dysfunctional families that were unable to cope with adolescence, but that genuinely desired the best education possible for their children.

In weekly letters to my sister Ann, now spending a year in France with American Field Service, I wrote dramatic stories of my attempts to form friendships with girls at Abbot and with boys I met at the occasional dances with boys' prep schools. By the end of the year, however, I was refusing to go to any "horrible" tea dance at all, even when there was a boy, a senior at Exeter, who currently had my attention. I was eager, even desperate, for a social life, but the tea dances were structured to generate a particular kind of social exchange. An official pageantry enforced by the chaperones, in which the boys demonstrated their manners, a sense of self-importance, and their right to compete for the "best" girls. The girls were judged on our appearance—our clothes, makeup, and hair; on our submissiveness and propriety; and on our sense of flair—a willingness and ability to stand out and shine.

As a 14- or 15-year-old it was hard to get past this official structure to actually have a human exchange with a boy. By eleventh and twelfth grade, my friends and I had learned how to get invited to other kinds of events like football games and concerts, which were still firmly on male turf but which allowed more informal exchanges under less scrutiny. No alternative to the official social life existed, so it was either find a way to participate or stay in your dorm for the whole time.

When my birthday came in January, I wrote Ann:

> This is the last Tuesday I'll be 14. It's very sad. I still don't want to grow up yet I want to grow up. It's very confusing. I want to get married and stuff yet I don't want to leave my childhood behind forever. It's very depressing and confusing.

My favorite class that first year was world history. As was the case with about a third of the faculty, my teacher was just a couple of years out of college. She challenged us to tell her why the Americas were in the middle of the world map up on our wall, and when we couldn't figure it out, she pointed out that the map had been published in the United States, so the mapmakers put themselves in the middle. By logical extension I understood that the textbooks, including our own history book, were published in the United States and would also "put the United States in the middle."

In English we read one challenging book after another and had to write a paper every week. My favorite was *John Brown's Body*, by Stephen Vincent Benét, a book-length epic poem about two struggling families, on opposite sides of the Civil War, whose lives come to be intertwined. For my mid-year paper, I chose to write about *Walden* by Henry David Thoreau. The idea of spending a year in a tiny cabin in the woods alongside a pond, observing nature, sharing survival chores with neighboring farmers, and reflecting on the meaning of it all, was enormously appealing to me. Thoreau drew his morals from the same thrifty Yankee mentality that my childhood had been saturated in, and his concerns about the impact of commerce on both the environment and on democracy seemed as eloquent in 1960 as they had almost a hundred years before.

Every weekday morning, I walked silently into the chapel at 8:00. Often someone was playing my favorite Bach piece, *Jesu, Joy of Man's Desiring*, on the piano. As I moved down the red-carpeted aisle with the long, delicate, white wooden benches on either side, my attention was drawn inward to my own center. I felt humbled by the complexities of the world and a yearning to find expression as a moral person within it. We sang a hymn together and then, twice a week, a teacher gave a brief summary of the news of the distant world at large, our only exposure to current national and world events.

That year, my father became a senior vice president in charge of the international division at Young & Rubicam. He maintained his small apartment on 37th Street in Manhattan, but his primary office was now in London. He traveled all over the world, sending postcards, often one or two a week, in which he told some historical story or funny anecdote, or he described his lunch, adding how hard he was working to eat so many courses.

He delighted in new products and in new ideas for promoting them. He teased me for being old-fashioned because I worried about losing the woods in Stamford to new developments, worried about fallout from nuclear weapons testing, and about the disappearance of small farms.

During our visits my father and I began to talk more frequently about his work. I raised my concerns about the gap between rich and poor, about the environmental cost of this "progress." I had watched North Stamford go from a rural area teeming with wildlife, through a building boom where more than a hundred homes were built just on our little stretch of road, within the twelve years I had lived there. The lady's slippers and ground pine were bulldozed into manicured lawns.

My father had an unbounded optimism in progress and believed that whatever problems progress created, progress would solve. When I argued with him, he listened carefully to what I raised and then poked devastating holes in my logic. He feared that I would miss out on all the excitement of the modern world if I did not embrace his passion. I wondered if this was true. I had always shared my father's enthusiasm for life. Still, I found it upsetting that my father was willing to accept existing inequalities among people and the growing damage to the earth.

By my second year at Abbot, in 1961, I had gone from the friendless world of junior high to several rich friendships with girls who were part of different circles. When I returned to school in the fall I moved in with a new roommate, Marthe Osborne. Her father was a doctor and her mother, from Guatemala, stayed at home with her two younger brothers. She was a serious musician, and also shared interests in politics and the natural world. My newest friends, whom I had gotten to know through Marthe, were interested in contemporary music, art, and writing. As eleventh grade progressed, one of them, Susan Mallory, introduced us to beatnik writers like Jack Kerouac and contemporary poets like Lawrence Ferlinghetti and Denise Levertov. I was fascinated. Another friend, Susie Niebling, was the first to encourage my own tentative attempts to write. We were determined to make contact with the real world that existed somewhere outside the restrictive boundaries of Abbot.

The idea that poetry could be an entry into investigations of the meaning of life took hold of me that year. In eleventh-grade English we started with Shakespeare's sonnets and moved through Wordsworth, Pope, Thomas Hardy, Amy Lowell, and Coleridge. I memorized "Patterns" by Amy Lowell, in which she protests against the constriction of her "brocade gown," and "Barbara Fritchie" by John Greenleaf Whittier—here was a woman who found a way to be a patriot without being a soldier. What *was* women's role in warfare, I wondered?

I also made a number of close friends in the class below me, including Muthoni Githungo, one of several foreign students and the first African at Abbot. Because Abbot was one of the first girls' boarding schools to accept a few nonwhite and Jewish students, in the late 50s Mrs. Crane received several letters from African leaders urging her to accept promising young African girls. According to a *Harper's Magazine* article that appeared years later, Muthoni was recommended by Tom Mboya, the leader of the newly independent nation of Kenya. Mrs. Crane had consulted with student leaders who not only agreed the school should accept her, but agreed to help raise some of the money for her passage and tuition.[1]

Muthoni was the first person I knew to speak openly about race and nationality. I met one other black person during that time. When I played in the Andover orchestra my senior year, Charlie Beard was the first violinist. Although Charlie was very sociable, he wasn't friends with anyone else in particular in the string section. In the many moments during rehearsals when the conductor was addressing other members of the orchestra, we were able to talk quietly. On Sundays, Abbot girls were allowed to invite a date to come visit, and we were allowed to sit in the formal parlor and talk or walk around—and around—the circle at the heart of the campus. On several occasions I invited Charlie so we would have more time to talk. I was happy when he accepted. We were just friends, but I enjoyed the fact that a few of the faculty and other girls squirmed when they saw us together. Among white people the argument heard over and over against school integration in the wake of the 1954 Supreme Court decision was that maybe integration could work in the classroom, but it would lead to other things; and the follow-up question inevitably appeared: "Would you want your daughter to go out with a Negro?" I had the sense that Charlie enjoyed this aspect of our association too, but neither one of us knew how to discuss it.

Despite my best efforts to make the honor roll, my grades hovered in the middle range in my class. To make matters worse, my teachers consistently wrote comments indicating that I wasn't working hard enough to live up to my potential, despite the fact that I felt I was working as hard as I possibly could. My logic and reasoning skills were strong, so I always performed well on standardized tests, but my short-term memory was weak, and most of my grades suffered as a result. The disparity between my test scores and my grades led my teachers to conclude that I was not working hard enough. This verdict angered me, but I knew of no other explanation other than that I was stupid.

As the next summer approached, I told my mother that I wanted to work. The previous summer I had worked as a live-in babysitter for a teacher at school. At sixteen I hoped I could now find a regular job. My mother suggested that I could get into a counselor-training program at a camp and then be hired as a counselor. She also told me she had heard about an interesting camp through the Quaker meeting, called Farm and Wilderness, a name that immediately appealed to me. In central Vermont, it included a boys' camp, a girls' camp, and a coed work camp for teenagers. I agreed to apply and was accepted as a counselor-in-training at the girls' camp.

By July, I was walking down a dusty dirt road with two other sixteen-year-old girls. It was our day off. I was part of a group of eleven counselors-in-training, and we were on our way to hang out at the coed work camp down the road. To our right lay rows of lettuce, tomatoes, squash, green beans, radishes, scallions, and other vegetables, which supplied much of the vegetable intake at the camps. On this day, there were about twelve young people from the work camp out in the garden hoeing and weeding, some definitely working harder than others. They all wore lace-up work boots and jeans or shorts. It was hot, and the boys were mostly bare-chested and the girls in tank tops or wearing only their bras, which I had come to see as a natural and sensible way to dress in hot weather. In addition to the garden, the work-campers were also working on a major construction project, a new dining hall, and they sometimes went out on the Appalachian trail to clear and maintain it.

In an old cabin that served as a recreation center for the camp, one of the girls put on a record. I had never heard folk music before. Miriam Makeba, Odetta, and the other performers sang about injustice in the world, and about the efforts of ordinary people to survive. The passion of the music, about the brave, sometimes funny and sometimes tragic efforts of people to change the world, grabbed me by the heartstrings. During that summer of 1961, I heard the music of Josh White, Joan Baez, The Weavers, Woody

Guthrie, Pete Seeger, Peggy Seeger, Harry Belafonte, Flatt and Scruggs, Johnny Cash, and Bill Watson, and I discovered *Folkways* magazine.

These days off provided me my first experience of an informal coed environment. I was glad to meet young men who cared about the issues of poverty, civil rights, and peace, and who felt comfortable talking in a group, without the need to pair off. While I wanted to meet someone with whom I could fall madly in love, I was beginning to feel disconnected from the Cinderella script I had grown up with because the woman's role seemed so passive. In the rugged environment of the camp, I was able to reaffirm the deep connection between the sensuality I had felt as an active child in the woods with the sexuality that I was now growing into. Still, after the social rejection at New Canaan, I found young men's interest in me to be reassuring about my options in the future. In that setting—with the emphasis on having fun at the square dances or cooking together on hikes—it didn't matter much that I was still awkward and undiscriminating.

One Sunday morning I sat on the grass with other counselors-in-training, in a huge circle on the lawn by the main lodge at the girls' camp. The only sound was the slight breeze softly rustling the thick foliage around the clearing. I felt the heat rising from the thick meadow grasses, enveloping me as I looked up at the clouds passing lazily across the sky. During the week, we had silent meetings in our own cabins, or sometimes the members of a cluster of three or four cabins would meet together. In these smaller meetings, campers often spoke up about some issue that had been on their minds. The meetings were occasions to express hurts or joys and know you would be heard. The young people used it with uncanny wisdom.

For the first time, the Quaker meeting made sense to me. I felt connected as part of the community. I began to think about the way leaders of organized religion used rituals as a device to help people stay together. But maybe, I thought, it was only in the freedom of the trees that people within a community could really feel God's presence. God represented our yearning to be good and to do good things. God was the power of the idea of love that was somehow more than each of our capacities to love. I gave up thinking of God as an entity with a human purpose. It made sense, as the Quakers said, that God was love.

A couple of times we were visited by people who had been working in the civil rights movement in the South. After Sunday meeting they talked for a little while about what was going on. I was impressed by these white people who defined their activism as a natural outcome of their belief in equality and their love of humanity.

That summer I worked hard to learn all the required skills so that when I returned the following summer I could be a camp-craft counselor. I worked to overcome my fear of axes to learn how to cut down a tree, how to split wood, how to replace an ax handle and sharpen the blade. There were knots to learn, and I was intrigued by their different effects and what they could achieve. We learned how to make shelters in the wild with ponchos, to dig trenches for drainage, to dig a latrine and a grease pit, and to disassemble the campsite so no one could tell we had been there. We learned how to judge if stream water was safe to drink and how to purify it if need be. We lit a one-match fire in the rain, using only material we could find in the woods. I soon adopted my friends' contempt for non-woodsmen who had to use paper to start a fire.

As he often had, my father had scheduled to see us for a week at the end of the summer. He had remarried, and his bride, Audrey Potter, was a woman in her early thirties who had never been married before. She was clearly an adventurer, like my father, even-tempered and slow to express judgment. This trip was to be an opportunity for us to get to know our new stepmother. When the time came, to ensure that all went well, my father surrounded us with the most spectacular of settings: He had chartered a sailboat, which came with a crew member, to take all of us, including my cousin Steve, on a trip up to Cape Cod.

We were to call our new stepmother Potter, due to the odd coincidence that she had the same first name as our mother. We all enjoyed Potter, though my sisters and I were intensely aware that she was closer in age to Ann than she was to my father.

I had a wonderfully enthusiastic English teacher, Mrs. Sisson, and for the first time I received encouragement and, finally, specific suggestions for how to improve my writing. I wrote a long paper comparing the poetry of Langston Hughes, Carl Sandburg, and Vachel Lindsay, poets I had loved so much the year before. Each month we also studied an article in the student edition of the *Atlantic Monthly* magazine. In October 1961, the article was "The Arabs of Palestine," by Martha Gellhorn, addressing the 1948 war and its aftermath. I thought I would like it because Marthe had given me *Exodus*, by Leon Uris, to read the previous year and I had loved it. As I remembered it, *Exodus* hadn't mentioned a problem with the Palestinians or anything about all these people who, I learned, were now refugees. Gellhorn started her article with a composite "Arab view" in order to refute it in the rest of the article. But as I read that the United States, United Nations, and Britain had forced hundreds of thousands of Arabs to leave their homes, killing many in the process, Gellhorn's explanation seemed far less convincing. Once again I felt this deep sense of betrayal that I had not been told the whole truth. I was also sad because the Jewish community painted in *Exodus* had been so wonderful. They knew what it was like to be refugees; how could they have done this to others after what they had been through?

While I had found nothing in the article to convince me that Palestinian anger was wrong, I still found comfort in Gellhorn's condescension: someone did understand this distressing situation, did have all the answers, even if I couldn't understand them. I held on to this comfort, despite my uneasiness about what had been done to the Palestinians. I thought I just had to read more to understand; it didn't occur to me that the argument didn't make sense, and that to thoroughly understand the situation I would have had to be aware of several other agendas that were operating in the Middle East at the time.

One of the ways I tried to work through these conflicting ideas was by giving a series of short talks during chapel. My senior year I had been elected treasurer of the Abbot Christian Society (ACS). One of the reasons I had chosen to run was that the four officers of the ACS took turns giving a short talk during chapel every other week. I wanted to find a way to share some of the big ideas that we were grappling with about religion, about the problems of the larger society as we perceived them, about the strengths that lay in poetry and friendship, and about how there was more to life than the manners and rituals and preordained expectations that surrounded us.

Over the course of the year I gave four of these talks, somewhat confused medleys of thoughts propelled by a sense of urgency that we, as human beings, had an obligation to make the world a better place, and as young people we needed to break away from the familiar and explore everything we could to understand what *was* better, what we should dream for. This was the first time I had stood up before an audience of people to say something that I thought was important, and it challenged me to think about leadership in a new way.

I had further support, in my intellectual grappling, from Blair Danzel, a Latin and Greek teacher who was new to the school my senior year. She organized a group of seven Abbot students to attend a three-day religious conference called the Northfield Conference in Pembroke, Massachusetts. The main speaker of the conference was Dr. John McGuire, chairman of the department of religion at Wesleyan University in Connecticut, and a recent participant in the freedom rides in Alabama. Dr. McGuire gave three talks about his experiences, all included in the title "Is God Dead? ("No matter what you or I think the majority of people live as though he were.") After each talk, the sixty young people from many different high schools, evenly divided between boys and girls, met in small discussion groups to talk about what had been said. Informal groups congregated late at night as well, staying up to talk about religion, civil rights, democracy, and morality. I could have stayed for weeks.

Miss Danzel also arranged for a group of us to participate in an American Friends Service Committee weekend work camp, during which we painted apartments at a public housing project in Roxbury, a predominantly black neighborhood in nearby Boston. With a few others, I was assigned to work on the apartment of a single mother who was a member of the Nation of Islam, the Muslim group in which Malcolm X worked. I had heard of Malcolm X from my friends at camp and knew that the Black Muslims, as they were also known, were very organized in New York. I had also heard that they lived very upright lives—no smoking, drinking or cursing. They encouraged everyone to read and study and they were always nicely dressed. I wondered why we, a Christian group, were doing social service in a Muslim household since I had heard that they were very self-reliant.

During this time, I continued to have conversations with my father about the role of advertising. Advertising was about selling, my father said. Without selling, the economy would come to a halt. Humans need very little to survive—a cave, a piece of meat, and a fire. The engine of civilization and wealth has been fueled by humans' desire to make life easier, to add beauty. My sister Ann and I both felt that this perspective was faulty. What about our responsibility to the well-being of our fellow citizens, of democracy, of the physical world around us? Much of what seemed intuitively obvious to me, Ann, and to many other young people of my generation, was not yet part of the public conversation. I could warn that progress couldn't correct all its consequences, but I couldn't yet provide examples or proof beyond the bulldozing of the woods beyond my house as the land was developed.

A chasm was opening up between my father and me. He grew increasingly perplexed at my growing disapproval of his work, but he continued to give honestly of his opinions. I was clearly the person pulling away, and my anger and frustration with his beliefs felt particularly distressing because I loved him so much.

My sister Ann, who had gained more political awareness and sophistication than I while attending a Quaker boarding school, continued to pursue her interests in peace and world affairs at Smith College. In January 1962, she sent me a long leaflet written by Todd Gitlin, a student at Harvard and member of an ad hoc committee of students and faculty calling for an end to the US nuclear development and deployment. The leaflet called for public involvement to try to stop nuclear proliferation. Here was my chance to act on the fear of nuclear destruction that had plagued me since childhood. The leaflet called for a demonstration in Washington in support of disarmament in February. Ann said she was going on a bus of Smith students.

I shared the leaflet with my friends, several of whom, like me, were eager to finally have a public voice about nuclear weapons. We discovered that there would be a local demonstration in Boston on the same day. Eight of us decided to go. As seniors we were allowed one unsupervised off-campus day a semester, and we signed up for that Saturday.

The day before the march we all received notes in our mailboxes that we were to go see Mrs. Crane, the principal, that afternoon. When we are all seated in folding chairs around her desk, she asked us about the demonstration. I wondered how she had found out, since we had only said on our permission requests that we were going shopping in Boston. It was clear that she was very anxious about our going. She asked us what we would say if we were questioned by reporters. Since the thought had never occurred to any of us, we were not prepared with an answer. One girl ventured that she would say that she was against nuclear weapons of any kind, and that the US should promote peace in the world. Mrs. Crane asked us if we planned to say that we were from Abbot Academy. No, we said, we didn't see any reason to say that. She seemed satisfied, though still not happy.

I found the whole conversation amazing. Although I felt Mrs. Crane's disapproval, I was more strongly aware that she had taken us seriously as human beings who were making an informed choice, even if it was one she didn't think was wise. This was a new experience for me: I was challenging authority and that challenge was heard and respected.

When the day came, we joined a few hundred people marching silently in front of the statehouse, leafleting passersby for a couple of hours. Nuclear weapons could not be a reasonable element of our foreign policy because they would just continue to provoke more and more weapons development, the leaflets said, and soon every large country would have the power to destroy the whole world. In the school newspaper I later wrote: "It is very simply time to wake up and assimilate what is going on in the world around us; to form a constructive opinion instead of always leaving the action to the other fellow.... The people cannot know what they want unless they are constantly aware and have an active concern for the world at large."[2]

The pressure to apply to college had begun my first year at Abbot. Each report card noted on the bottom that an average of B- or below would not be sufficient to enter a "quality" college. Since my average hovered there, I felt a certain amount of despair about my prospects. Over Christmas vacation, my mother had the idea that since Ann had such a good experience at George School and I had enjoyed the Quaker camp so much, I should apply to a Quaker college. We decided to look at Swarthmore, just outside of Philadelphia, and after New Year's, we drove down. I liked the informal atmosphere but didn't have any idea how else to judge a college. As it turned out, I didn't get in to the music conservatory at Oberlin, where I had also applied, but I was accepted at Swarthmore. I had no idea that Swarthmore was a prestigious school. Nor did I, or my mother, have any idea that many students came to Swarthmore then eager to act on progressive, intellectual ideas they had been exposed to in their families or schools.

CHAPTER THREE

DISCOVERING THE WORLD

. .

On a sunny day in June 1962, once again dressed in a white dress and walking two by two with my classmates, I traveled a quarter mile down a rural lane in Andover to the huge, bright, white Congregational church where the graduation ceremony was held. The Reverend William Sloan Coffin from Yale, an avid supporter of the freedom rides in the South, was the speaker, and he warned our parents about the complexities of the future we were stepping into and encouraged us to look closely at current issues.

Shortly after returning to Stamford, I attended Robin's graduation from New Canaan Country School. We were to spend the summer in England and Europe with my father and stepmother. Although I remembered the wonderful childhood trips together, I was ambivalent about this trip. I had no idea how to sort out or even talk about my feelings about my father and his second marriage. In the conflicts between my parents, I had chosen to ally myself with my mother, having seen her anguish at my father's departure and the difficulties she had had managing everything afterward. As a result, I had maintained a melodramatic sense of tragedy about the divorce, and myself as a victim. Now that she was remarried, however, I began to feel that it wasn't fair that we were supposed to celebrate her new marriage and still maintain the tragedy about the old. Even I was beginning to see that both of my parents were happier in their new lives.

As it turned out, this trip would be the last time I spent any significant amount of time with my family for twenty years. Shortly after our return, I was off to college. I was stunned to be around people who openly competed over college board scores or academic ability. Everywhere I went, in the hallways, the groups on the lawns, and in dorm rooms, everyone I heard seemed to be brilliantly discoursing on some weighty subject about which I knew next to nothing. I had landed on a different planet, and I fiercely wanted to be able to hold my own.

I threw myself into my classes, trying unsuccessfully to complete all the reading, especially in my introductory political science class. I continued with music theory, which I had taken in high school instead of 12th grade math, and wanted to pick up math again. My advisor, however, said that since I was not ready for calculus, I shouldn't bother with math since girls usually don't do well in it anyway. At the time I was only vaguely aware that this exclusion from math cut me off from the exploding fields of science and technology in a world profoundly influenced by both.

The campus buzzed with opportunities for all kinds of things: Friday night films; folk, jazz, and classical performances; and of course weekend parties. I made friends with girls in the dorm and found them less intimidating than many of the boys. Several were also interested in politics, especially the civil rights movement and the new local peace candidates. These friends were also grappling with new relationships, and by midwinter questions about sex and morality loomed large in our conversations. I had enjoyed dating when I first arrived, but was well aware that I didn't yet know the rules. By midyear I had succumbed to the pressure of a young man I was dating to see him exclusively. Although I hadn't really been ready for such a commitment, the exclusivity allowed me to give in more to my growing sexual feelings. Still, I resented the ambient pressure to have intercourse, a level of sexual engagement I still thought should wait until marriage.

By November, I started hanging out in Sommerville, the campus snack bar, because I had noticed frequent political conversations among the crowd of juniors and seniors that hung out there, and it was possible to sit around the edges and listen. They talked about attacks on James Meredith as he tried to register at the University of Mississippi, the first black student to do so. There were also stories about the Student Nonviolence Coordinating Committee (SNCC), which was registering Negro voters in the South, especially in Mississippi. They were being shot at, beaten up, and arrested in the process.

I began to pick up and read the *New York Times*, often left on the tables.

The front page featured stories about the new Strategic Hamlet Program in Vietnam that forced whole villages of Vietnamese peasants to abandon their homes to be housed in villages under the "protection" of US and South Vietnamese troops. *Times* reviewers of Helen Gurley Brown's new book, *Sex and the Single Girl*, expressed shock and outrage that the author had put the words "single girl" and "sex" in the same phrase, and that she asserted that sex could and should be pleasurable for women as well as men. I also read that the Supreme Court ruled that mandatory prayer in the public schools was unconstitutional. Change was in the air.

The jukebox played in the background, alternating between Motown hits, rock and roll, and pop songs, the music that set us apart from our parents' generation.

One day I went to a meeting of the Swarthmore Political Action Club (SPAC). The room was packed. Of the forty or fifty students, three quarters were men, many of whom I recognized from Sommerville. There was apparently a disagreement between two of the leaders. Several young men spoke passionately. I noticed that no women spoke and that they all seemed to be with men. No one seemed particularly interested in whether I was there or not. I left with the impression that this was a very intellectual debating club. Perhaps I could hook up with a guy who was involved and find out about it that way.

At Thanksgiving, I went to visit my father and stepmother in New York City. They had recently bought a small townhouse on West 11th Street in Greenwich Village, once again making Manhattan their primary residence. That weekend, Jon, a young man I had been dating at school, came by with friends and took me up to the Apollo Theater in Harlem, for talent night. While it was even then a world-renowned showcase of black talent, I, of course, had never heard of it. When we climbed the subway stairs out onto 125th Street, the night lights in the stores and the many people on the street all seemed dazzling to me. Just as when I had first arrived in Paris, I was aware that I was in a different culture, with different foods, language cadences, and music.

As we walked down the street and found places in the theater, I was impressed by and curious about the fact that after all that white people had done to black people over the years these Harlem residents were so accepting of whites in their midst. I knew everyone didn't feel that way, because Malcolm X and the Nation of Islam, I'd learned, believed that white people were devils. Still, they did not advocate violence against whites, merely disengagement. Nonetheless, I assumed that anger and resentment must be in the air. How could they not be? I knew nothing of the many white people throughout US history who had devoted their lives to the struggle for equality and true democracy or of those who had formed interracial relationships at work, in the arts, and/or in personal relationships. They could have been role models.

Meanwhile, in my political science class, we were looking at different kinds of democracy and at the role of culture in democracy. My understanding of history up to that point mostly came from the novels, biographies, and poetry I had read. Now I was trying to understand how the writings of political theorists matched up to the experiences of ordinary people. The onslaught of information, however, was akin to a thirsty person trying to drink from a gushing fire hydrant with her hands tied behind her back.

In April, Carl Wittman, one of the seniors who sometimes joined the late-night gatherings in Sommerville, organized a weekend trip down to the eastern shore of Maryland, to support the local struggle against segregation in Cambridge. The eastern shore had been home to Harriet Tubman before her own escape, and was still considered to be more akin to the deep South than the middle states. Many local citizens lionized George Wallace, the Alabama governor who in January, at his inauguration speech, had proclaimed "Segregation now! Segregation tomorrow! Segregation forever!"[1]

Carl had worked with civil rights activists in Cambridge the previous summer, and had returned on several occasions since then. He was both passionate about politics and down to earth. While he was president of SPAC, when I chatted with him in Sommerville he spoke in engaging, anecdotal language, not the jargon of SPAC meetings. He seemed to genuinely care that I understood the ideas he was putting forward about the civil rights movement and was not contemptuous of me because I didn't already know them. When he told me about the trip to Cambridge, I signed up eagerly. We were to help local organizers challenge the whites-only hiring practices of the downtown stores and the segregation policy of the local movie theater and various restaurants.

We had been invited by Gloria Richardson, director of the Cambridge Nonviolent Action Group. We drove first to her home for a planning meeting. Richardson welcomed us warmly when we came into her living room where the sofa and all the chairs were already filled with local activists of all ages. We sat on the carpeted floor or stood around the edges of the gathering, careful not to knock over several delicate lamps on the end tables. With the exception of Carl, we were greenhorns walking into a scene full of battle-worn veterans. I was grateful that everyone there seemed to genuinely welcome us anyway. I quickly realized that each body meant another bit of strength in the fight against segregation.

Richardson, who had earlier been refused a job in the all-white social-work department in Cambridge despite her college degree and credentials, led the meeting with a no-nonsense but inclusive style. Local store owners, with the support of local politicians and much of the white population, had resisted the demands of the local NAACP to integrate their staffs. The resistance had been as ugly and violent as anywhere in the South. We were to join ongoing picket lines in front of some of the stores. We listened as actions and events of the previous week were reviewed and then we received our instructions about how to participate in a nonviolent way. As Richardson finalized the plan for the day's picketing, making sure everyone had a chance to contribute information, I felt myself being pulled into the determination and hopefulness of the moment.

Richardson's house was not far from Race Street, the street that divided the black and white communities. The street had originally been named after a man named Race, and, ironically, it only later became a racial boundary line. I knew that civil rights leaders were often shot at or had their homes firebombed, especially for holding meetings. I was deeply impressed by Richardson's commitment, despite the risks.

With my new firsthand feel for what the movement was like, I started to follow the civil rights news much more closely in the *New York Times*. At that moment, SNCC, the group I had first heard about at Farm and Wilderness, was conducting voter registration drives in Southwest Georgia and in Ruleville, Mississippi, reaching out to the rural residents of the county despite repeated threats of violence and retaliation against those who participated. Local police beat and jailed sharecroppers like Mrs. Fannie Lou Hamer, who dared to register to vote. Others were shot at and driven from their homes. In Birmingham, Alabama, mass meetings were attended almost daily by hundreds of people seeking to integrate the downtown businesses. Fred Shuttlesworth and others in the Southern Christian Leadership Conference (SCLC) had built a solid infrastructure of black leadership over the years, and in April they invited Martin Luther King to come lend his voice. After King was arrested marching on Good Friday, he wrote from jail:

> I must confess that over the last few years I have been gravely disappointed with the white moderate. I have almost reached the regrettable conclusion that the Negro's great stumbling block is not the White Citizen's Counciler or the Ku Klux Klanner, but the white moderate who is more devoted to "order" than to justice, who prefers a negative peace which is the absence of tension to a positive peace which is the presence of justice. . . . Shallow understanding from people of good will is more frustrating than absolute misunderstanding from people of ill will. Lukewarm acceptance is much more bewildering than outright rejection.[2]

When Dr. King's letter was passed around at school in a newsletter, I thought he was talking to me. I didn't know that King was frustrated with the Kennedy administration because they had not lived up to their initial promises of support. King was under pressure from young activists, especially in SNCC, to do more than rely on the goodwill of President Kennedy and other liberal federal officials. SNCC wanted to dig into specific locales in the South and build local organizations that were as self-reliant as possible, until they could wrest specific changes from the racist power structure. As far as I was concerned, however, white moderates were the people I had grown up around, even all the adults at Swarthmore who did not encourage our activism. I would have to include myself, I thought, if I didn't find a way to contribute directly.

Despite the passion of the civil rights movement, it was not at all clear that the business and political leaders of the South would not succeed in turning back this great initiative the way they had turned back others before. Shortly after the end of the school year, on June 11, Alabama governor George Wallace stood in the door of the University of Alabama and personally denied entrance to two black students, James Hood and Vivian Malone.[3] That night, Medgar Evers, a field secretary for the NAACP in Jackson, Mississippi, was assassinated in front of his family as he returned from an NAACP meeting.

After each incident of Southern violence, I heard the echo of the words of black leaders who urged black Americans to shun all contact with white economic and social spheres. Did this fight for integration have a chance? Or would the talk about white devils carry the day and define a different, angrier, and more impatient response to change? I could easily see where the rage was coming from.

The next summer I returned, now eighteen, to Farm and Wilderness as a senior counselor responsible for a cabin of ten eleven-year-old girls. They were enthusiastic participants in the camp activities. The daily twenty-minute Quaker meeting in the cabin after lunch affirmed the growing relationships between us as the campers used the time to comment on an emotional issue that had come up or to reflect on our values. During our cabin meetings we often discussed issues of peace and justice, how they applied to the world at large, and how they came up in our personal relationships.

During rest period I read out loud from *Hiroshima*, by John Hersey, in which he vividly describes the lives of five residents of Hiroshima before, during, and after the United States dropped the atom bomb on that city in August 1945. The campers were riveted. We talked about the bomb, about Hitler and the death camps, about discrimination. They were at an age when they were quick to identify the big moral issues and to frame them in the context of their young sense of fairness and of right and wrong.

We also talked about civil rights. We had several visitors who had been supporting SNCC in the South or working with SCLC. Over the course of the ten weeks of camp, 20,000 people were arrested in 800 demonstrations. Ten people were killed. We heard about a massive march for civil rights that was being planned for August 28th in Washington, DC.

Two of my campers were black, one from a middle-class family in Ohio and the other from Mississippi and brought up on the camp's scholarship program. This girl remained silent during our conversations. On the few occasions I asked her why, she evaded my questions. Only on the last day of camp did I realize that she had been intimidated by the other campers. She was as confused as anyone about what she thought about the dramatic events of the civil rights movement. She had not felt safe enough in the group of Northern middle-class kids to explore her feelings. I was ashamed that I had been so oblivious to this child's insecurity and realized that I had probably contributed to her stress and discomfort. For the first time it occurred to me that my own behavior could reinforce discrimination, without my meaning it to, and that inaction, or obliviousness, could actively hurt someone.

When camp was over, I returned home to Meriden, New Hampshire, hoping to travel to New York and then on to the March on Washington with my new friends. My mother, however, was uncompromisingly opposed to my attendance at the march, wanting me to stay home until I had to return to school. As it turned out, I was with her in Lebanon, New Hampshire, at the supermarket on the day of the march. As we walked toward the store, I heard a broadcast of the march coming from a car radio. I stayed outside to listen to Dr. Martin Luther King's "I Have Dream" speech, standing on the sun-baked asphalt.

My sophomore year I focused on doing better in school. I took classes in economics, history, philosophy, and American literature, and a seminar in

Asian political systems. I loved the seminar, in which we studied the village structure in India as a way to understand how culture and politics were interwoven in the last two hundred years of Indian history. I read Gandhi's autobiography and learned about satyagraha, his philosophy of nonviolent political resistance. I studied how Gandhi worked to build a movement, first in South Africa against apartheid, and then in India for independence from British colonialism. This was also my first explicit exposure to Hinduism, Islam, and Buddhism. I was most impressed by Gandhi's struggle to apply his political ideas to the minutest, most personal detail of his life. He, like Thoreau and Gloria Richardson, *lived* his beliefs.

That fall of 1963, four young black girls were killed in a bombing of a black church in Birmingham, a church that had allowed civil rights workers to meet there. The pictures of the rubble were sickening.

My room was still in Parish dorm, the huge old building that had served for more than a hundred years as the hub of the campus. One day in November, before climbing the stairs to return to my room after my last afternoon class, I stopped to look over the student bulletin board. My eyes fell on a pale orange sheet of paper on which someone had carefully written by hand "Franklin School Boycott, Come Support CFFN." The leaflet went on to explain: "The Committee for Freedom Now (CFFN) and parents of children at Franklin Elementary School are boycotting Franklin elementary school because of the dangerously poor conditions at the 95% Negro school in Chester." CFFN had decided to focus on the worst school in Chester, a nearby decaying industrial city. Now, parents and local community members had picketed and protested for three days at the school, the school board, and the City Council. They needed reinforcements to close the school down again the next morning. Picketers might face more arrests.

I looked away from the bulletin board, into the sunlight, to get my bearings. I tried to consider the possibility, indeed the likelihood, of arrest, but this idea was overwhelming. In my world only bad girls got arrested and by doing so I would become one. Once I started down this path, I knew I would never turn back. My arrest would make it public, especially to my family, and I knew that the terms of reconciliation would not be terms I wanted to accept.

I counterposed this image of the bad girl with the thought of Gloria Richardson and all the women sitting around in that living room. Even though they had jobs to lose and children to protect, they had gone to jail. They risked the firebombing of their homes. By comparison, I was risking little that I could think of except missing class and incurring my parents' wrath. I looked at the bottom of the leaflet to see where students were meeting to take the short bus ride to Chester. Then I turned and joined the clusters of young women climbing the stairs to their rooms. I had made a decision.

The next morning I abandoned my classes and took the bus with several to join the peaceful picket line in front of the school. Most of the picketers were members of the local school community, parents and children, and several students from Swarthmore, Bryn Mawr, and Haverford. The protesters from the day before were still in jail. We marched around in a circle, some people holding signs. I learned that Franklin School had been built to house five hundred students, but it now held twelve hundred. The library was just a single desk and a few books in the hallway. Only two working toilets served the whole building.[4]

On the picket line, we chanted and sang. Although lights were on in the school, no one entered while we were there. "Oh-oh freedom, oh-oh freedom . . ." Several policemen edgily watched the goings-on for about fifteen minutes, at which point several police cars and big, boxy paddy wagons suddenly pulled up to the curb. The police ordered us to disperse and in almost the same breath began to direct us toward the paddy wagons. Several of the women with small children started to move away from the line because they didn't want to get arrested. The police, however, with arms reaching out, insisted that they turn around, and pushed them into the wagons. I didn't see the police hit anyone but they were yelling intimidating orders and threats. Some of the children, as young as three and four, started to cry and there was a lot of confusion.

I stretched to reach the high step into the back of the paddy wagon along with a crowd of mostly women and children. Two benches had been attached to either side of the box, but those were already filled. The rest of us had to stand stooped over or sit on our haunches on the dirty floor. Even while everyone was trying to find a place to anchor themselves for the coming ride, the back doors slammed closed, and, with the bright sunlight suddenly shut out, we were in almost complete darkness. For a few seconds I took in the musty, metallic smells of the dirty truck bed, which was quickly beginning to mingle with the warm, sweet smells of women and children packed into the van. A confused cacophony of voices filled the space as people rushed to make sure the children were all present and secured on someone's knee or lap. Then we heard the song coming from another wagon and someone in our wagon picked up the tune. Soon that single, strong melody began to swell from our own jumble of bodies and transformed our spirits. The frightened cries of children quieted as the music gave us strength. I didn't know this song, but by the second chorus I could join in. The chord progressions of the music were familiar to me from my own years of church singing.

After a blessedly short ride, during which the people who were standing were thrown around dangerously, we arrived at the town jail. As we climbed down from the paddy wagon, the men were separated out. The women and children were packed into two small cells intended perhaps for no more than twelve people. Altogether, eighty-two people had been arrested. We continued to sing, matching the voices of the men, who we could hear next door.

After a long forty-five minutes, with the silences between songs growing longer because we were tired and thirsty, a large cop came up to the locked door of the cell to say that all the children should come out so they could get water and go to the bathroom. With considerable misgiving the mothers sent their children out to accompany the officer, and then, fulfilling their worst fears, the children did not return. A half hour passed. Mothers banged on the cell demanding to know what had happened to the children, but the police responded with silence. The mood of determination and community began to unravel as women became angry and anxious.

After nearly another hour, the police began to call us out in groups of five to sit at a big table and give our names and addresses. Many women refused to come until they received an explanation about what had happened to the children, and the police said that the children were being released. We had no choice but to believe them. Only one person had been allowed a phone call, though that had been right at the beginning. When our turn came, those of us in college were required to give our home addresses, which I gave reluctantly. We were then moved back into the paddy wagon, to be transported to the state prison.

When our wagon was filled, we were taken off on a trip that lasted almost an hour. The doors finally opened in front of a long, low, brick building out in the middle of farmland, with cows grazing serenely in the distance. Up on a low hill, I saw another, larger complex of brick buildings which I assumed to be a men's prison that was part of the same complex. Our guards herded us out of the vans, through the front doorway, and into a small lobby in the central hallway. In another room we saw women who had been arrested the day before, apparently ready to take the paddy wagons back to the county jail where they were to be released.

We were then herded forward into another hall, where we could see cell blocks stretching out on either side. I heard a commotion at the front of our group, and everyone began to sit down. Two uniformed white matrons were trying to direct black women down one cell block and whites down another. This was my first experience of an officially segregated space. I was shocked. We all quickly joined those in front and sat down and started singing. Someone negotiated with the officers, and, after a period of confusion, we were led straight ahead into the day room. It appeared that our refusal to go into the cell blocks meant that we would spend the night in this room.

The light was starting to fade, and we were famished when they brought out a big tray of baloney sandwiches and jugs of Kool-Aid. Tired, women sat around quietly talking in small groups. I, too sat quietly, trying to re-center myself. I stared out the window through bars, looking at the fences surrounding the building. It seemed so absurd for some human beings to lock others up in cages.

The gates to both wings were still open so that the regular inmates could come into the day room. Various members of the civil rights group wandered back into the cell blocks to talk with these women and explain why we were there. I wandered back and sat in on one of these conversations, learning more about the activities that had led up to the boycott.[5]

The sun was setting over the fields and the autumn leaves were beginning to drop in the evening breeze. The enforced idleness felt oppressive. Even animals, I thought, should not be in cages. That night we slept the best we could. In the morning, the matrons brought in Wonder Bread slices smeared with apple butter and an enormous metal coffee pot of lukewarm coffee, already mixed with tons of sugar and milk. Not long after breakfast, we were informed that we were to be shipped back to the county jail to be released.

While people from the first day's arrest had had to post $200 bail, we were released from the city jail with no bail. I returned to my dorm to shower and brush my teeth and process the last thirty-six hours. Many people on campus were talking about the arrests and I was proud to have taken part. My teachers, however, were silent on the subject and remained focused on their classes. I knew that, one way or another, my mother would find out about the arrest and there would be a scene.

As it turned out, the local police *had* called the police in Meriden, N.H., where there was only one part-time officer, and he had contacted my mother immediately. Word spread to the rest of the town within hours. My mother had called the college and been given the basic outline of what had happened and been assured that there would be no consequences as far as the college was concerned. She had been so upset that it took her weeks before she expressed her dismay. My choices would cut off opportunities for me in the future, she wrote, a future she had worked so hard to provide for me. Most notably, she said, some education jobs, because of the legacy of McCarthyism, might already be out of reach. She ended, as she so often did, by asking wasn't I aware of how deeply my actions had hurt her? Why was I being so cruel? I didn't want to disappoint her, but I also couldn't let her define who I was becoming.

The evening of our release, there was a mass meeting at which Stanley Branch, a leader of CFFN, announced that the school board had promised to reduce class size, provide better toilet facilities, and plan for the construction of a new school. This was a tremendous victory for the parents and children of the Franklin School and for the movement in Chester. It validated the organizers' promises that moral victories are to be had by those who risk and sacrifice. Justice will be done.

Of course the organizers knew that they must continue to build the movement and to maintain a momentum to put pressure on the school board to live up to its promises.[6]

During this time I was influenced by Carl's belief that the problem in the North was primarily a more general problem of entrenched poverty, within which racial discrimination was one additional, albeit critical, factor denying black people economic access. He saw Chester as an opportunity to draw northern students into civil rights work in the North modeled on the work being done by SNCC, and by Gloria Richardson in particular, while at the same time creating a broader radical presence in a poor community. That winter, Carl and Tom Hayden, wrote "An Interracial Movement of the Poor," to bring these thoughts to SDS and Northern civil rights activists. Others, however, feared that because corrupt politicians had convinced many poor whites that blacks would take away the few scarce jobs for unskilled or semi-skilled workers, organizers would have a hard time convincing poor white people to join integrated organizations.

After two days in jail, I returned to my regular schedule of classes, but I also began to attend the SPAC meetings, now largely devoted to updates and discussions of the work in Chester. On Friday, November 22, while I was fulfilling my gym requirement by playing tennis on an indoor court, another student came bursting into the gym to announce that President Kennedy had been shot. We all put down our rackets and left the gym in a state of numbness and disbelief. I returned to my dorm room to change clothes and walked down to Sommerville where many of my friends had gathered to listen to the radio.

By then, Kennedy had died, and Johnson was being sworn in as President on Air Force One on his way back to Washington. I felt like the lens through which I viewed the world had cracked. I must quicken the pace with which I was ready to disassemble my assumptions, question everything, and reconstruct a way to view the world that jibed more with reality. Because Kennedy, however belatedly, had publicly endorsed civil rights, he had been mythologized in many poor black households. His death was seen by many, in the immediate aftermath, as the martyrdom of a white ally to the civil rights movement. Within weeks, almost every household I entered in Chester had a picture of Kennedy on display.

CCFN had made plans to have a training session the next week over the Thanksgiving holiday, to train students and Chester residents who were active in the school fight how to work with the block organizing. I was assigned to a one-block area in a very poor section of Chester and sent with one other student to organize a block association. I, like the residents of Chester, had been filled with hope and was excited by the opportunity to participate actively. I was aware of my inexperience, but also felt welcome to make whatever contribution I could. In fact, I, like most of my fellow students, was far more ignorant than I could imagine.

Our block had been selected because one of the residents was part of the Franklin School struggle. Her apartment and her friendliness were the only resource we had to start with. Our first step was to leaflet the block to call a meeting to address local problems at Mrs. M.'s house. Several people, mostly women, came, mostly because our hostess was known and liked. We laid out our plan and started to collect issues that concerned the residents. The sidewalk, mostly dirt or mud, was one such issue, along with the problems of rats and roaches, unreliable garbage collection, and irregular heat and hot water. Most of the houses were in serious disrepair.

We researched the city government to find out who was responsible for different services. We found out the garbage pick-up schedule in the more affluent neighborhoods and then went with several residents down to the sanitation department for three days in a row, demanding that they pick up garbage in our neighborhood on the same schedule, until finally they agreed.

We found out that landlords were responsible for sidewalks. Most residents were afraid to challenge their landlords for fear of eviction, so we decided to pressure the city to enforce the city ordinance requiring landlords to maintain paved sidewalks. Groups of us went to the highway department several times, until they came to inspect the sidewalk. They then contacted the landlords. We kept the pressure on. As the weeks went by, I went to Chester more and more, often several times a week, occasionally during class time.

On days when I didn't go to Chester, I often took a late-afternoon study break at Sommerville, to listen to music on the jukebox and hang out with the regulars. One afternoon, several of us were sitting around a table, and Paul Booth, a SPAC officer and senior, said that he was having trouble following the war in Cyprus—on the front page of the *Times* for several days—because he found it tedious. I chimed in and said that I felt the same way about the battles in Vietnam, which were also beginning to appear regularly on the front page. Much to my astonishment, Paul leapt out of his chair crying "Noooo! Vietnam is different!" Vietnam was a war of national liberation, he said. The Vietnamese were fighting for the right to govern their own country. He explained about how the French used to claim Vietnam as a colony, but that after World War II, the Vietnamese had declared independence. When the French refused to acknowledge the Vietnamese government in Hanoi, the Vietnamese fought a long war with France and eventually won, installing their own national government, at which point the United States took up the fight.

He definitely had my attention. The Beatles sang their hearts out in the background, as the conversation continued. "So beside civil rights and nuclear disarmament, now there is a whole new issue," I said. "Noooo!" Paul leapt out of his seat again—he had a strong sense of the dramatic— "The issues are all connected!"

He explained that just as some people had seen easy money in slavery, others now saw easy money in the exploitation of resources in the undeveloped world. The United States wanted to extend its domination of trade and resources worldwide and didn't want to lose Vietnam or any other part of Southeast Asia to the socialist trade block. The United States believed its form of capitalism was the *only* feasible economic system and that if people chose other systems, they were wrong and, on pain of death, the United States would correct their error.

In November, Diem and Ngo Dinh Nhu, the president and vice president of South Vietnam, had been assassinated, only three weeks before Kennedy, and there were signs that the Central Intelligence Agency had set them up. The CIA saw itself as the protectorate of US manufacturing investments, which were then spreading steadily beyond US borders. Paul went on to say that there were now 15,000 so-called US military advisors in Vietnam. It was our country that was trying to prevent the Vietnamese effort to achieve independence and self-rule by whatever system they chose.

As often happened, this outpouring of information made me feel embarrassed: there was still so much I didn't know. Nonetheless, Paul's explanation helped me start to connect other things I had noticed. For the first time, I sensed that I could put together a coherent picture of the way the world worked—at least the most basic contending forces. The emerging patterns required me to rethink more assumptions. While I had disagreed with the government's decision to test and use nuclear weapons, I had never questioned the premises of US foreign policy. While I had believed that racial discrimination was wrong and that it should be corrected immediately, I had thought that prejudice was primarily the legacy of Southern racists. I didn't think that some people actually considered poverty to be an unfortunate byproduct of progress. For the first time I began to believe that there were more than superficial flaws in a basically good system.

How could it be that the United States was waging war on people who were genuinely fighting for independence, just as we had? Ho Chi Minh had been so impressed with the Declaration of Independence, I later learned, that he had included much of it in the current Vietnamese constitution. What was happening to the development of our ideas about freedom and democracy? Was there some flaw built into our democracy that meant it couldn't work anymore? Were we irrevocably on a path away from democracy? Again I felt deeply betrayed by the government and by all the adults who had acted like everything was on course, committed to "liberty and justice for all."

I also fell in love with Paul, or at least for a moment I thought I did.

He had enlightened me, helped me see the world in a clearer way so I would be better able to act intelligently. For years I confused this deep emotion with that of romantic love. We dated for a short time, until I realized that it wasn't a personal relationship I wanted to invest in; I was passionate about making a contribution to the movement. More than anything, I wanted to understand why things were the way they were.

Paul was not only a founder of the SPAC chapter, but vice president of an organization called Students for Democratic Society (SDS). Started by a handful of young people in 1960, SDS began as a youth group attached to an older, battle-scarred, and decaying progressive labor organization called League for Industrial Democracy. Several of these youths, including Carl and Paul, came from progressive families, but they had their pulse on a much broader wave of developing social consciousness among young whites. By 1962, this core of a few dozen gathered on the shores of Lake Huron to chart an independent political course, profoundly influenced by young people in the Southern civil rights movement. Their ranks included some newer members like Tom Hayden who came from more apolitical, mainstream families and who brought a sense of being children of the American Dream. The fusion of these two deeply rooted cultures turned out to be a high-energy coalescence, each group eager to learn from the other. Both groups were also ready to break from what they perceived to be the compromises embedded in the belief systems of their families.[7]

Tom Hayden, a journalism graduate student at Michigan, had recently returned from the South, where he had worked with and reported on SNCC for the *Michigan Daily*. He was the principal author of the draft document that was discussed, edited, and ratified by the 1962 SDS conference. It became known as the Port Huron Statement.

Historian Kirkpatrick Sale aptly described the Port Huron Statement as more a "shared view of the world" than a national program.[8] It eloquently championed the importance of equality and the dignity of all human beings. Genuine democracy was the only possible foundation for peace. The writers challenged current politicians to look at their policies to see why the problems of inequality, especially with regard to race and poverty in this country, had persisted so stubbornly, and why US foreign policy flew in the face of the values believed to be at the heart of political thought in the United States.

The way to fix these problems, the SDS document said, was to reactivate democracy—to make participation in decision making the center of social life in the United States Participatory democracy, as SDS called it, challenged the prevailing culture that encouraged political passivity. In the prevailing male-dominated language of the day, the Port Huron Statement said:

> We regard men as infinitely precious and possessed of unfulfilled capacities for reason, freedom, and love. . . . We oppose the depersonalization that reduces human beings to the status of things. . . . We oppose, too, the doctrine of human incompetence. . . . Men have unrealized potential for self-evaluation, self-direction, self-understanding, and creativity. It is this potential that we regard as crucial and to which we appeal. . . .[9]

My exams in January were difficult. With four survey courses and an intense seminar, I had an enormous amount of material to cover and review, especially since I had been spending so much time in Chester. I barely squeaked through.

The Swarthmore leadership was at odds with the local CFFN leadership over what issues to focus on and how to organize. The chapter leadership wanted to continue a direct-action approach to economic struggles, wanting to focus primarily on housing issues after the voter registration campaign was finished. The Chester leadership wanted, I thought, to focus on citywide campaigns directed at political power. CFFN also seemed to have disputes with the NAACP, just down the block. I began to see how complex political organizing was, how many different human factors were at work.

In the spring, CFFN organized a citywide campaign to pressure the city to discuss the rest of the demands regarding employment discrimination, employment opportunity, medical care, and housing. After briefly caving in to the Franklin School demands, the city's Republican machine steadfastly refused to acknowledge the movement. Finally, in April, CFFN called for another series of demonstrations at the public buildings and hundreds turned out.

The police responded by attacking, randomly clubbing, and arresting people, even chasing them into bars and stores to drag them out and beat them. The brutality of the assault was surprising and demoralizing, especially to the local leadership. This time, people were released only when they put up bail, so the strain of raising money interfered with all the other activities.

By May, some of the residents in the Chester neighborhood I worked in were ready to begin to challenge their landlords to make a number of basic repairs to plumbing and electricity. The first to do so was Mrs. M., in whose house we had our regular Sunday afternoon meetings. Sure enough, her landlord responded by threatening her with eviction. This knowledge intimidated many members of the organization, although Mrs. M. seemed unsurprised and unperturbed. I didn't know what to do. I felt at least partially responsible for her precarious position, and, to make matters worse, the term was ending and I was going to have to leave.

I tried to have a conversation about this dilemma with a friend in the SPAC chapter. "You're still working on a block organization?!" he responded with astonishment. It seemed that the discussion about strategy with CFFN had progressed to the point where the other Swarthmore students had shifted their work to the citywide political efforts, and all other work on the block organizations had ceased with the April demonstrations. Since I had not had time to keep up with the citywide meetings nor to attend the chapter meetings on campus regularly, I had missed that.

When I heard that no one else had maintained their block organizations I felt betrayed that no one had told me, and that no one seemed particularly concerned about the vulnerability of the people I had been working with. I had led people to go out on a limb, to take risks, without being able to back them up. I quickly went back to Mrs. M. and the others in the group and with great embarrassment and shame, told them that

I was going to have to leave, and I was not sure if there was anyone around to help them continue their efforts. Mrs. M. was less upset than I anticipated since she had assumed all along that I was going to leave at the end of the semester. I was, after all, a student.

It also turned out that a number of Swarthmore students had decided to move into Chester more permanently to continue working. They, like young people in several other cities—Philadelphia, Newark, Boston—were the pioneers in SDS's new Economic Research and Action Projects (ERAP). These community-organizing projects used the Cambridge and Chester experiences as a model, emphasizing economic concerns as much as racial discrimination. I considered joining them for the summer, but, after the disjointed end of my own work in Chester, I was unnerved by the students' lack of a coherent plan. With Carl and Paul both graduating, I no longer felt connected to anyone in leadership.

In June, SDS gathered delegates from each of the few dozen chapters that had sprouted up, for a national meeting in Pine Hill, New York. Carl and Paul, about to finish his second term as SDS vice president, both encouraged me to come. Despite my growing reservations about students working in poor communities, I was curious to know more about national SDS. At the meeting, Rennie Davis and Paul Potter, two leading members of SDS and architects of ERAP, encouraged me to write up my experiences with block organizing. I was flattered that someone was interested in what I thought, and set to work immediately. The result, a mimeograph under the title "Rats, Washtubs, and Block Organizing," was unfortunately a rather incoherent mix of contending views. I began by stating:

> In the process of starting a block organization, certain long term goals and objectives must constantly be kept in mind. This has been difficult in Block Organizations which have been started in the last year, because in most cases their long term purpose has not been clear. However, I will hope to set out certain general objectives which pertain to the organization of lower class people by this method as well as short term goals and strategies.

While I was home for spring vacation, my mother had informed me that she did not want me to return to Swarthmore, but instead to take my junior year abroad at the Sorbonne in France. She looked at my grades and, not unreasonably, blamed my activism for the generally low performance. While she mustered some support for my activities, she continued to fear that my passion would distract me from becoming the educated, refined young woman that was her own vision of success. It was one thing to help people who were poor, but quite another to identify with them or see them as mentors. The privilege of education and good breeding was my birthright *and* my birth obligation. She rose to the challenge of protecting me from the irreversible harm I might unknowingly cause both her and myself.

When she told me her decision, I didn't quite know how to respond. She was right that it was precisely the irreversibility of the direction of my life that I was seeking. I loved my mother deeply, but I could not accept her terms or her fear about my future. I was building an alternative life, one I loved, filled with the company of people who did not feel "better" than others. The clothes, the music, the homes that my mother considered "cheap" were what I liked. I wanted to grow up with those trying to change the world for the better, not with those who seemed to protect themselves with privileges and hide from the full richness of life.

By the end of May, however, my reservations about ERAP's strategies led me to decide that going to France might be a good way to step back and get some perspective on my political work. I wasn't sure how long I would stay, but I hoped the break would help me focus on the next stage of my life. My mother purchased my boat ticket, still cheaper than airfare.

Two weeks after the June 1964 SDS national council meeting, I was in Paris with a limited budget, every penny of which I was to account for. I was trying to find a way south to Grenoble, where I had enrolled in a summer language program, when I saw a chance for an adventure I couldn't resist. In front of the American Express office, someone was selling an old Vespa for the equivalent of $25. Although slightly intimidated by the prospect of learning to ride a scooter, I was able to enlist another hitchhiker who was going in the same direction to start the trip with me and teach me to drive it. With that plan, I bought the scooter, learned to drive it with a few turns around a traffic circle, and we set off. My co-rider quickly abandoned the Vespa, realizing it was too slow for his schedule, but as I continued on my own, I met other young people from Italy who helped me out. We had various breakdowns and adventures, but eventually made it to Grenoble late the next day, thanks to the hospitality and mechanical knowledge of various French farmers along the way.

On a university bulletin board, I found a notice for a room for rent at the Foyer de l'Aide de Meres de Famille. When I found the big stone building, I climbed to the second floor and was given a large double room to myself with two closets, a desk and a sink, with a window that looked out over a courtyard.

I was somewhat unclear about what kind of place I was staying in. It turned out to be a dorm of sorts for women who worked for the government as part of their maternal care program. In France, when a woman with children gave birth, she could request a worker to come in and help with the new baby and other children. This building was operated by the agency which employed the women workers, but since they had about twenty-five rooms and didn't always need that many, they rented a few out to students. I was delighted.

The next day I started attending classes, focused either on the French language or French history and culture. In the evenings I visited with the women at the Foyer. On the weekends, they introduced me to the dance hall that was the center of their social scene, and I soon made friends with a number of other young people in the city.

I was thriving in my adventures in France, but I was also trying to keep up with the presidential campaign between Goldwater and Johnson, and developments in the civil rights movement, both well covered in the French press, and getting increasingly frustrated not to be more in the middle of it. Johnson was at the nadir of his progressive support. He had just signed the Civil Rights Act and declared a "war on poverty". With all the voter registration activity I thought must be going on, the time was right for progressive candidates to get elected. I knew that a number of people, including a professor from Swarthmore, were running peace campaigns. SNCC had been concentrating its energy on registering people to vote in the South, with the hopes of electing change through local offices, since convincing those in office to give up their segregationist policies didn't seem to be working. It was frustrating to read about the Mississippi Freedom Democratic Party (MFDP) challenge to the all-white Mississippi delegation to the Democratic convention and know that many students had been in Mississippi all summer working, and I was so far away.

In Vietnam, the US destroyer *Maddox*, operating on the edges of North Vietnamese waters in the Gulf of Tonkin, was shot at by three small North Vietnamese patrol boats, which pursued the *Maddox*, each launching one torpedo, none of which hit the destroyer. The *Maddox* also opened fire, sinking one of the boats and disabling the other two. Johnson played down the incident, despite the fact that members of the Defense Department wanted to use it as an opportunity to retaliate with a lot of firepower, to boost the morale of South Vietnamese troops.

Two days later, the French headlines said, the *Maddox* was fired on again, this time by many boats, although it was not hit. Within three days Johnson had rushed through Congress a bill that authorized him to "take all necessary measures" to repel North Vietnamese forces, basically giving him a carte blanche to conduct the war. This opened the way to massive bombing of the North, which would begin the following February and the introduction of regular US ground troops weeks later in 1965. Only later did it come out that no one on the *Maddox* had ever seen any attacking boats, and that the images on radar had been confusing. In other words there was no evidence that the *Maddox* had indeed ever been fired on.

In any event, didn't the Vietnamese have a right to defend their country? The *Maddox* seemed to have knowingly gone into North Vietnamese sovereign waters. (This was verified years later when documents on the war became public.)

My trip had opened my eyes to a wide range of experience, strengthened my self-confidence and resolve, but I realized how much I didn't want to be away for a whole year. I wanted to fight against the war, to support civil rights. I thought that maybe I could lay the basis for a career in electoral politics after I graduated. Just as there were no black citizens in Congress there were few women, and it was time for a change.

I wrote a letter home to my mother arguing that I should come back. I said I would be happy either to return to school or to try to get a job. In the meantime, I continued to study French and spend more time with my friends from the Foyer and the dance hall. I began to go out with Christophe, a young carpenter, sometimes going to his family's house and sometimes to his apartment. Mostly, though, we explored the city on his scooter and visited his friends, who would gather at cafes or each other's apartments after work. I enjoyed him immensely, although I always worried in the back of my mind that in his attentiveness, he expected some reward. Christophe and the women from La Maison had given me the entrée I wanted into the daily life of how free young people live. I continued to enjoy the mutual feelings of desire, as long as it was in the context of a group social interaction. I wasn't, however, interested in casual sex. I had overridden the ban on intercourse by then, believing that full sexual passion was a healthy part of committed relationships–whether they were intended to be lasting or not. I had finally slept with a boyfriend my sophomore year, enjoying a relationship that was both warm and fun until he left to go off to college in the fall. I had also learned that sexuality was about vulnerability as well as desire, and I wasn't interested in having my body used by someone who had no deep interest in or respect for the rest of me.

The last week I was in Grenoble, we were listening to records at Christophe's apartment, and it became clear that he expected our casual fooling around to progress further. He finally admitted it when I confronted him and told him clearly that I was not interested in having sex with him. Christophe then switched tacks and aggressively tried to persuade me, showing a side I had never seen before. I got mildly alarmed, and since he was between me and the door, I retreated into the bathroom. There was a large window in there that opened into the courtyard five feet below. I climbed through it and jumped down, shouting goodbye.

When he realized I was outside he shouted for me to wait and rushed outside, joining me as I got to the sidewalk. He apologized profusely and begged me to forgive him his misunderstanding. He wanted to drive me back to my room and I accepted. There, we parted amicably. I had learned that I needed to be much more vigilant about clarifying my expectations from the start.

By this time I had heard back from my mother that she was completely opposed to my return to the States on any terms. She stressed that I had made a commitment, and anyone with any character followed through on commitments. I would not be effective helping the poor, she said, if I didn't get my own house in order first. Further, she argued that as a woman my primary responsibility was to prepare to be well-rounded so I could raise a family, and that I did not want to make mistakes now that would jeopardize my life. There were differences in the sexes, she argued, and I was not paying sufficient attention to my responsibilities as a woman. I was disappointed, but not surprised by her response.

A few days later, I hitched a ride to Paris and found a temporary job passing the hat for a street band that played to the long movie lines waiting to see *West Side Story* and *My Fair Lady*. I got ten percent of the take, and after a week or so I had enough to buy an airplane ticket home. I also had my first experience smoking marijuana while exploring the social scene around the youth hostel and a couple of very cheap hotels. The slight detachment from reality was no more intense than the effect of a couple of mild drinks, but I felt slightly less in control. Given the unfamiliarity with the setting and my few acquaintances, I worried about becoming too vulnerable, especially after the incident with Christophe.

I managed to come through these various encounters unscathed, but a new friend from the States, Esther, had not fared as well. At a soup kitchen that catered to young people, she and two friends had met some young men who offered to give them a ride to a party. Esther was the first to enter the car and one of the young men pushed his way in behind her and slammed the door. The other three men got in simultaneously. Before Esther's friends could react, they sped off. Esther was raped repeatedly and left in a park. She had found her way back to their hotel and her friends had taken her to a hospital. There she had been treated, but hospital personnel neglected to fill out any of the paper work necessary for her to press charges.

Nonetheless, she really wanted to have the men arrested and charged, even if she knew eventually they wouldn't be convicted. Her friends had recognized one of the men when they returned to the soup kitchen the next day, and they knew his first name. Despite this and other solid leads, it became clear over the following days that the police had no intention of pursuing the rapists. One gendarme even started to aggressively flirt with me to distract my attention. The police in France apparently supported the status quo on this issue, as did too many of the police in the States.

After that summer I remained considerably more conscious of the circle of violence, especially sexual violence, that enforced women's secondary status. Even though I had managed to parry several potentially threatening situations over the past year, I realized that I couldn't escape the overall coercive influence of this climate of violence.

I remained in Paris a few more days, plotting my trip back to the States. I had written my father that I was coming to New York to look for a job. He had sent a telegram back to American Express telling me I would be welcome to stay with him. When I finally left for the airport I was more than ready to leave France. My father received me warmly, without any overt judgment. He approved of work, so he was undaunted by my decision to leave school. He had made inquiries and had a lead to get me a job with the advertising firm that was handling President Johnson's campaign. He explained that this was the first time both candidates had hired ad agencies to run their campaigns. The ad agencies would figure out how to "sell" the candidates.

Despite the fact that my father had always voted Republican, he respected the fact that I did not, which he assumed meant that I was a Democrat. I, of course, was horrified at the thought of Madison Avenue taking over the political campaign process and substituting psychological manipulation for substantive or informative debate. Nonetheless, I did my best to refuse the offer without raising any political controversies.

I then called my mother to tell her that I had returned to the States. She was shocked, despite my letters, to find that I had actually disobeyed her instructions to remain in France. She expressed her extreme disappointment and then argued that since I was back I should return to

Swarthmore. Under no circumstances was I to drop out of school. Since it was already September, I was doubtful that she would be able to get me back in to school, but she insisted that she would inquire.

The next morning my mother called to say that she had arranged for me to return to Swarthmore and, since the dorms were already full, she had found a place for me to stay with a casual acquaintance of hers from college, who was now married to a mathematics professor and lived on the edge of campus with their two sons. My mother was on her way to pick me up and drive me there. I was stunned, but agreed, to avoid further drama. If I stayed in New York she clearly intended to impose herself on every decision I made, so going back to school was a way to gain some independence. Besides, if I stayed in New York, I would have to accept my father's hospitality and I knew that would be awkward, given my divergent path. At least at Swarthmore, I was away from direct observation.

That winter I resumed my school work—a disparate combination of music, literature, and political science—and participated in a wide range of on- and off-campus activities. I no longer regularly went to SPAC meetings. The Chester project was in a period of confusion, and the campus SPAC meetings had again become too insular for me. I began dating a classmate, Steve, and started sleeping with him over at his off-campus house a lot. Once again, I had found a comfortable relationship with someone interested in literature, film, and having fun together. He had similar political sympathies, but without my sense of urgency and with no impulse toward activism. Given my need to pull back from my headlong engagement with the fight for civil rights and peace, however, I wasn't looking for political or emotional depth. I needed to be able to hold my own in the world and to do so, I needed to know my strengths. We listened to a lot of jazz that year, went to movies and parties, and studied.

Instead of working with SPAC that spring, I explored why it was that Congress seemed to be so passive in the face of the administration's aggressive foreign policy, why they accepted blatantly false information about Vietnam. While a few senators had spoken out, no one in the House seemed able to do so. In one of my earlier class readings, however, I had come across a group in the House of Representatives called the Democratic Study Group (DSG). Maybe, I thought, there *was* an attempt to marshal accurate information and act on it. I received permission to write an independent thesis on the topic. I wrote letters to all the Congressmen involved requesting interviews. Most accepted and I planned to spend my next vacation in Washington.

On February 7, 1965, President Johnson authorized the first air raids into North Vietnam, and two weeks later he began sustained, daily bombing of North Vietnam. Later in February, Malcolm X was killed. Then on March 7, in Selma, Alabama, peaceful civil rights marchers setting off for Montgomery in their church clothes were beaten to the ground by local law enforcement personnel. Viola Liuzzo, a white supporter and mother from Michigan, was murdered in her car as she gave one of the marchers a ride home after the march. Because Viola Liuzzo was a white *woman*, she was maligned by the local police, who insisted on a fabricated sexual subtext to the incident. Incredibly, the Northern press that carried civil rights protests somewhat sympathetically went along with the Southern press on this matter. To me, the reports rang false. This was a mother of several young children who had driven down from Detroit to lend her support for a few days. The accusation, that she was having a tryst with the young black man in the car, was ridiculous. Nonetheless, only a faint voice of protest from Selma activists ever found its way into the mainstream press reports. Clearly, white women activists had to be on their toes on a number of levels, I noted. Even within the movement, we were not valued equally, and we were vulnerable to being used as pawns in other struggles.

On March 8, the first regular combat troops came ashore in Da Nang. Also in March, Johnson sent in 15,000 marines to the Dominican Republic to put down huge popular demonstrations calling for a reinstatement of the popularly elected president Juan Bosch, who had been overthrown by the brutal dictatorship of Trujillo thirty years before.

Sitting around in Sommerville, I learned more about the relationship between US foreign policy and corporate power. The US Ambassador to the Organization of American States was Ellsworth Bunker, a board member of the National Sugar Refining Company, which owned huge holdings of Dominican sugar cane fields. Roving Ambassador Averell Harriman owned about ten percent of National Sugar through his private investment house. Many other Washington officials, including Supreme Court Justice Abe Fortas, had heavy investments in Dominican sugar on an island where one hundred sixty-five individuals and corporations owned ninety-eight percent of the land. The average daily wage was one dollar. US troops put down the insurrections and, acknowledging that Trujillo was more expense than he was worth now, installed instead his right hand man, Joaquín Balaguer. It seemed like the US had decided to come out in force against democracy, in its bid to consolidate world power.

Despite this growing awareness of political and economic unfairness, my only activism that spring was to attend the antiwar march in Washington organized by SDS and featuring a speech by its president, Paul Potter. I drove down with Steve and many others. Like most of the 25,000 who were there, I was deeply moved by Paul's speech, in which he insisted that we had to name the system and then stand up to it. Paul began:

> Most of us grew up thinking that the United States was a strong but humble nation, that involved itself in world affairs only reluctantly, that respected the integrity of other nations and other systems, and that engaged in wars only as a last resort. . . .
>
> But in recent years. . . the development of a more aggressive, activist foreign policy has done much to force many of us to rethink attitudes that were deep and basic sentiments about our country. The incredible war in Vietnam has provided the razor, the terrifying sharp cutting edge that has finally severed the last vestige of illusion that morality and democracy are the guiding principles of American foreign policy.

Paul looked at some of the particulars of the war and of the repression that was already evident at home in response: "What kind of system is it that allows good men to make those kinds of decisions?" He continued, "What kind of system is it that justifies the United States or any country seizing the destinies of the Vietnamese people and using them callously for its own purpose?"

He concluded that in order to change it, we must create a social movement:

> By a social movement I mean more than petitions or letters of protest, or tacit support of dissident Congressmen; I mean people who are willing to change their lives, who are willing to challenge the system, to take the problem of change seriously.

Here was SDS's vision: so profoundly inspirational and yet, once again, lacking in specifics about how to do it. This weakness was overshadowed, however, by the energy generated by so many young people coming together who were passionate about the issues of poverty, civil rights, and peace. I was drawn powerfully toward this movement and toward these national SDS leaders who were so warm and eloquent.

As summer approached, I was anxious to get a full-time job that would give me more financial independence. My future aspirations in electoral politics made Washington a natural choice for a place to look. I figured I could at least get a typing job.

I had told my father of my desire to work and, weeks later, he informed me that through a friend in Washington he had found out about a summer clerical job at the International Bar Association, which was planning an international conference on world peace through world law. I went down to Washington on a Friday to interview for the position and was hired to work as a clerical assistant as soon as school let out. A friend, Julie Diamond, introduced me to a senior, Florence, who was looking for a roommate that summer in Washington. Florence was hoping to put together a group of other girls to share a house.

A few days before the end of the term Florence saw me on a pathway and told me that Julie was in a local hospital. She had apparently secretly gone down to Washington to have an abortion, which was illegal then.

With only local painkillers, she had received a D and C. On her way back to campus she felt sick and ended up in the local hospital. When I went to visit her a couple of days later, she told me that after she arrived in the emergency room, the hospital personnel had followed regulations, which required them to call the police for any suspected abortion. An armed police officer arrived, stood by her bed, and demanded the name of the man who had performed the abortion, his address, and the person who had referred her to him. She refused to tell. The hospital then called the college to summon a representative to authorize an IV. Soon after, she was told she would be denied the right to attend her graduation. Her diploma was mailed later.

I started my job immediately after my last exam in May. The American Bar Association was inviting the justices from the highest courts in each country to a weeklong conference, along with top legal authorities. From the United States, Chief Justice Earl Warren and several other Supreme Court judges would be attending. The conference would be in late August. My first task was to type the envelopes for the five thousand invitations. I think it took me six or seven thousand envelopes to get five thousand perfect ones, and they had to be perfect. After all those envelopes, my typing had improved significantly, and I graduated to correspondence, each sheet of which had carbon sets for five copies.

Florence rented a small furnished house on N Street in a slightly dilapidated neighborhood of Northwest Washington. My room was one of two on the third floor. A third roommate, Liza, had been Florence's friend in high school. Early on they introduced me to their favorite local nightspots, especially a neighborhood bar called Taso's. It was my first experience hanging out in bars, and I found the easy comradery with a range of people to be interesting and fun. I was aggressively courted by a young man in his mid to late twenties who had been an acquaintance of Florence. He was dramatic, passionate, and theatrical. I soon found out he was an out-of-work bartender who was recovering from a near-fatal car crash he had while driving drunk. His previous relationship had ended when his girlfriend had a baby, and it became clear the Geoffrey was not going to be able to support them.

Geoffrey loved poetry and music, especially jazz. I had not revisited the beat poets since I was in high school and was glad to find someone else who had been moved by them. He was not competitive the way so many guys at Swarthmore were, but shared himself freely and inclusively. Coincidently, his mother now lived in Stamford, Connecticut, where she worked in a motel.

Within a couple of weeks, Geoffrey had attached himself to me, becoming a regular resident of the house. I was vaguely alarmed, as I could tell he was a very dependent person, unemployed and somewhat at wits' end. It would never have occurred to me to move so quickly to sexual intimacy, but I gave in to his sense of urgency and did not regret it. He was kind and gentle and lots of fun. I enjoyed the intensity of the physical intimacy even while I had no desire to match that with emotional strings or any kind of commitment for a lasting relationship. I had only the summer to get to know him and be part of this interesting social scene around Taso's. Florence also had found a live-in boyfriend, who was working as an exterminator.

While those of us with jobs were attentive to them during the day, on the nights and weekends we indulged our curiosity to explore new psychic spaces by sampling a host of drugs that seemed to be available to anyone with a job and the money to pay for them. Until then, while I was used to drinking on weekends at Swarthmore, drugs had scared me. I knew that some drugs were very addictive, and, since I was already addicted to cigarettes, I appreciated the dangers. I also remembered my feeling of vulnerability as a woman the summer before when I had experimented with marijuana amongst strangers. In the safety of our house that summer, however, I experimented with almost everything, except heroine and cocaine. I reveled in the capacity of my body to feel awareness beyond the limits of everyday life, especially the few times I tried small doses of acid and mescaline. The alcohol was always good for getting past shyness and amphetamines allowed us to burn the candle at both ends for the last couple of weeks of the summer.

Even during that summer, I followed the progression of the civil rights movement in the South. In June, James Meredith was felled by three shotgun blasts soon after the start of his solo walk through Mississippi. In August the black neighborhood of Watts in Los Angeles erupted in rage over a police shooting, and dozens of blocks were burned to the ground; six hundred businesses were destroyed. Sixteen thousand police, highway patrol, and national guards invaded the neighborhood, killing most of the thirty-four people who died. Four thousand were arrested. These were staggering numbers.

The riots, as they were called in the press, shocked and outraged mainstream society, which saw them simply as criminal outbursts. Martin Luther King was heckled during efforts to calm the anger in L.A. Later he acknowledged that the rebellions, as they came to be called, as the anger spread to other cities, represented a challenge to the movement, both black and white, to take on the intractable and widespread urban problems of education, jobs, and housing discrimination. These were the people from the valleys of the unlevel playing field speaking up, the people who for generations had contributed energy, creativity, and determination to the growth of the United States and gotten nothing, at best, or lynchings and imprisonment, at worst, for their efforts.

In the stories of white businesses being burned down, I also heard scary echoes of Malcolm X's early beliefs about white devils. Is this what would happen if people, white and black, gave up on integration, I wondered? The uprising seemed like an attempt to make the bitterness and frustration of more than two hundred years part of the public discourse. Yet the people who were killed and arrested were poor people, and the community that was destroyed was their own. They had sacrificed a great deal to gain a voice, I thought, and I couldn't see how they might reap actual power to improve the lives of the survivors.

In August, Congress passed the Voting Rights Act to explicitly address the persistent difficulties Southern black citizens were having registering to vote due to barriers like poll taxes and literacy tests. The law also put in place legal mechanisms that the disenfranchised could use in their ongoing battles for access to political power.

In Vietnam, US troops were now completely engaged on the ground.

Operation Rolling Thunder's bombing raids into North Vietnam had continued since February. Young men who spoke out against the war and the draft were losing their student deferments and were being reclassified 1-A, meaning they could be called up at any time.

The Conference on World Peace Through Law took place in late August 1965 for five days at the Washington Hilton, and at the end of the conference I was free to go. I had never delved deeply into the actual content of the conference. The working papers for the conference were prepared and printed elsewhere, and I never saw them. What little I had heard confirmed that Vietnam was not to be discussed. How could a conference come together and discuss world peace and not focus on the war in Vietnam, I wondered? My growing cynicism as well as the preoccupations of my life outside of work diminished my interest in pursuing the answer.

Geoffrey wanted to continue our relationship past the summer. I was skeptical. I cared for him and found his generous, spontaneous approach to life refreshing. His emotional vulnerability was compelling to me. We were both alienated from the roles that had been prescribed for us and looking for alternatives. But he was a lot older than I was, he was emotionally volatile, he wasn't self-reliant, and he didn't play by the same set of rules as people in the rest of my world. I doubted that there was any way for me to integrate him into the social scene at Swarthmore and questioned his ability to create a scene of his own. His relentless insistence, however, increased my guilt until I gave in. We agreed he would come up to Philadelphia and get a place and find a job while I went home for a visit.

In my senior year, I continued to grapple with the ways in which our democratic system did not provide liberty and justice for all. Could political democracy and a so-called economic free market coexist? Which issues and decisions should be the province of government and which left to other authorities like religious or commercial institutions? My original assumption, that the government had a mission to lead the country toward its vision of equality in every sphere, now seemed naïve. The machine in Chester had shown me how hard it was to break the hold of the economic elite once they had a firm grip on government, but was it impossible? What *should* the relationship of government to the economy be?

A few weeks into the semester, I began to pay a price for neglecting sleep and regular meals. I was smoking a lot by then and a cold developed into bronchitis. I was going into Philadelphia to see Geoffrey on the weekends and still trying to go full blast at school. The bronchitis turned into pneumonia with a high fever. I went to the infirmary and they gave me antibiotics. Within a few hours, I started getting sick to my stomach. The nurse wondered if I was having a reaction to the antibiotics, but I knew that probably it was another problem: I was pregnant. Geoffrey and I had twice relied on the "rhythm method." I knew it had been irresponsible of me to take the chance. Now, it seemed that I was going to pay the price.

As soon as I was released from the infirmary, I went to Philadelphia to a gynecologist I was referred to by another girl. I considered whether or not to continue the pregnancy. The first set of consequences, automatic expulsion from school and the drama from my family, especially my mother, were fairly horrifying to contemplate, but I was not immediately sure that they justified an abortion. Other consequences were more serious. I was finally engaged in my classes; I wanted to be politically active when I left school. If I had a child either I would be dependent on my family or I would be working full time to support us. I knew that I couldn't be a very good mother at that point because I would be too angry and frustrated. I wanted to have children, but when I did, I wanted to give them the best possible start in life. I didn't think I could give the child up for adoption.

Most significantly, I knew that I had probably been pregnant for over two months and during that time I had consumed quite a bit of alcohol and probably several amphetamines. I had eaten little healthy food and I had smoked at least a pack of cigarettes a day. I knew that these behaviors would likely have permanent negative consequences for the fetus. Finally, I felt that with so many people in the world already, a parent had an urgent obligation to teach any child to be a responsible member of society. I had no idea yet how to do that.

These factors made it clear to me that I wanted an abortion and once I decided, I was no longer ambivalent. A friend in my class gave me the phone number for a man who performed illegal abortions in Philadelphia.

My friend thought that this man was a doctor, but she wasn't sure. She said it was in an office in a house, it was clean, and he had given her total anesthesia.

There was a special code you had to use when you called for an appointment. I did not have enough money to pay for it, after giving Geoffrey money to help him with his first month's rent, but I had some of it. I went to an old boyfriend and asked him if I could borrow the rest until Christmas and he agreed.

Then, I went into Philadelphia and saw Geoffrey and told him I had to end the relationship. I couldn't handle school and him. He hadn't gotten a job or built a life for himself there. I didn't want him to be so dependent on me. I also told him that I was having an abortion. He was very upset, but he didn't argue. He left soon after.

I returned to Swarthmore and arranged to have a friend with a car take me to the abortion. The house was in a poor neighborhood in Philadelphia. I had been told to come alone and to have someone come pick me up in four hours. My friend dropped me off in front of the house and agreed to come back at the appointed time. I walked into the building's front room, which was set up as a waiting room. As I didn't see any receptionist and there were several other women sitting in chairs, I sat down. Shortly thereafter a middle-aged woman in light khaki pants and a white overblouse came into the room, looked around at all the women, and came up to me. I told her my name and said that I had called for an appointment. She seemed to recognize my name and asked me to wait. Not too long after that, she called me to come into the back to a room with a standard examining table. He must be a practicing doctor, I thought, and probably many of the women in the room were there for routine appointments.

When the doctor came in, he confirmed that I went to Swarthmore and asked me if I was sure that I wanted to do this. I said I was. He then said he was going to put me under anesthesia temporarily, give me a D and C, and that when I woke up and could stand, I could leave at the appointed time as long as someone came in to get me. His nurse was in the room as well. I put on the gown, lay down on the table and he gave me a shot. I hoped he was legitimate, that I would not be mutilated or even raped, as happened to another friend at Swarthmore.

When I woke up everything seemed all right. My friend came in at the appointed time and we left. I was fortunate that I had found a dedicated and responsible doctor who took risks because he believed in a woman's right to choose. I had two other friends who had successful abortions that year, and these experiences, along with Julie's the year before, made it clear to me that extensive secret networks could and did exist and that they could be protected even in the face of challenge.

As I was recovering from the abortion, two longtime white SNCC activists, Casey Hayden and Mary King, were meeting together to talk and write about the ways women could support each other within the community of the movement. Casey Hayden grew up poor in Texas and first became socially active in an integrated Christian organization on campus at the University of Texas in the late 50s. She had found her way to SNCC almost at its inception through her postcollege job at the YWCA, where she had been hired to organize student seminars on race. Mary King, a Northern minister's daughter with Southern family roots, had joined two years later when she graduated from college, having been inspired by TV coverage of the early sit-ins at Woolworths.

They both had read *The Golden Notebook*, by Doris Lessing, and the work of other early feminist writers, and had been struck by the similarities between discrimination against women and blacks. They presented their thoughts anonymously at a major SNCC meeting in Waveland, Mississippi, in November 1964. They looked at ways SNCC had sometimes supported women who challenged traditional roles, starting with their participation in the first sit-ins, and sometimes reinforced those roles. The movement was a setting, they believed, in which women could join together to explore their status in the movement and in society. A year later, Hayden and King got together again to write a paper, called "Sex and Caste: A Kind of Memo," which they circulated among their friends, including several women active in ERAP.[11] While I was still a long way from articulating my experience, King and Hayden had already figured out that:

"All the problems between men and women and all the problems of women functioning in society as equal human beings are among the most basic that people face."

When I got back on my feet after the abortion, I refocused on my work in school and on the escalating war in Vietnam. In October, another national march, this one led by A Committee for a Sane Nuclear Policy (SANE), gathered tens of thousands in Washington to protest the war in Vietnam. On campus, one of the few activist professors, Thompson Bradley, and a coalition of students, including SDSers, organized a teach-in about the war that went all evening and into the night. Hundreds of students came, almost half the student body. I learned more about the actual facts of the war, and for the first time became familiar with the reports of Wilfred Burchett, an Australian journalist who was covering the war for a weekly newspaper called the *National Guardian*. The *Guardian* reported that the US had almost 200,000 combat troops. The teach-in, and the fact that I barely knew many of the people active in organizing it, revealed that the movement both on and beyond our campus had been growing, adding new organizations, resources, strategies, people, and ideas.

As I continued to immerse myself in my classes, I also began to think seriously about the future and what I would do after Swarthmore. Many of my classmates, including most of the males who faced the newly imposed draft, were applying to graduate school, medical school, or law school. A few were planning to work full time in the movement. I was also drawn to work for the movement, but I couldn't see how to do it .

That spring, Stokely Carmichael had been elected as chairman of SNCC, quickly becoming the most visible—to Northern whites at least—interpreter of the newly articulated slogan, "black power," as it evolved over the course of that year. Stokely had graduated from the elite Bronx High School of Science in New York, and he had moved in the sophisticated New York progressive scene. At Howard University, the flagship of the traditionally black colleges, he had joined the Non-Violent Action Group, an affiliate of SNCC, in 1960. He also traveled to Cambridge, Maryland, on weekends. By 1961 his commitment and leadership had earned him an invitation to attend a three-week leadership seminar for

SNCC in Nashville. After his graduation, he had become a trusted and respected full-time SNCC staff member. In May 1966, as the differences within SNCC over the models of social change began to reach the boiling point, Stokely ran for the position of SNCC chairman.

While the black power slogan was treated as a big deal by the press, the conversation in SNCC about power—and about how to achieve it—had been going on from the beginning of the organization. After the Democratic Party rebuffed the electoral challenge of the Mississippi Freedom Democratic Party in Atlantic City in 1964, the conversation had moved in a new direction. SNCC organizers argued over the role of black consciousness as a key strategic element in their fight to gain power. Inevitably, this raised questions about the form of the organization itself. By 1966, almost all whites had been encouraged to go organize other whites in other organizations. I understood few of the historical currents that had contributed to this formulation, but I did understand that the relationship between organizing around poverty and around racial identity was complicated and the role of whites unclear.

My reluctance to join the movement also came from my deep-rooted desire for financial independence. I knew that most movement jobs paid nothing or next to nothing. I had very little savings to tide me over while I investigated what work was out there. I was almost as uneasy about being financially dependent on a movement organization as on my parents, wondering how one maintained political and intellectual independence when one received a paycheck from a particular organization, however small.

I was still drawn to work in traditional politics, where I held out hope for the possibility of strong Congressional leadership. The potential prestige and excitement of being part of a new wave of women becoming active as elected representatives tempted me. I hadn't encountered any women staffers other than clerical workers when I did my interviews on Capital Hill, but I knew that some women had managed to get elected to Congress (eleven in the House of Representatives and two in the Senate at that time).

That spring, while I continued to concentrate on my classes and a few good friendships, SDS was growing by leaps and bounds. Like SNCC, it too was in the throes of a confusing debate about the future of the organization. Many young people had joined SDS after the March on Washington in April 1965.

In June 1965, five hundred SDS members had met in Kewadin, Michigan, to grapple with SDS's chaotic and ungainly growth. SDS's structure had been set up to enable an orderly coming together of like-minded students to talk about the issues of the day and to try to develop positions and programs to better the country's future. Now it was overwhelmed by the energy it had helped release. Some members wanted SDS to extend ERAP's reach by sponsoring full-fledged programs to develop participatory democracy among the country's poor; others, including many newer members, were energized by the SDS March on Washington and saw an opportunity for SDS to take leadership, at least among young people—of the rapidly emerging national antiwar movement; still others felt passionately that SDS should remain campus based. A small but growing segment thought SDS should take the lead in building a broad-based movement for social change encompassing students, the poor, and the antiwar movement, and allying closely with other labor and civil rights organizations.

Members thought very differently about *how* to bring change, as well. Some wanted to influence the Democratic Party, while others, outraged by repeated betrayals and inaction, wanted to reject all forms of electoral politics. A segment of newer members identified more with the counterculture. Some of these wanted to expose and disrupt the hypocrisy and bankruptcy of traditional culture and politics. Others sought to bring change by creating new kinds of institutions, communities that were governed by cooperation rather than competition. The Port Huron Statement's eloquent vision was so inclusive, it could be summoned to accommodate any one, or all, of these objectives.

Many of the people who went to Kewadin understood that if SDS didn't re-conceptualize itself, its structure it would soon blow apart at the seams. With the best of intentions, the organization's old guard expected new members to be initiated slowly into *their* conversation about the role of social change. Most of the newer members, however, felt that the moral clarity of the issues of the war, poverty, and discrimination, which the Port

Huron Statement spoke to so clearly, demanded immediate attention. They were less interested in building structures that might last than in speaking out and acting on what they knew. They were more likely to draw on the lyrics of contemporary rebel poets and musicians than old texts.

The energy in the meeting—representative of the awakening of young people all over the country—was already far beyond what some teenagers and twenty-somethings could conceivably harness into a lasting organization. In fact, SDS's function as a place where all these forces could come together at that moment, where there was a place for everyone, was its brilliant strength. This function alone provided much of its momentum for the next five years, while the organization itself did indeed come apart at the seams, creating or contributing to dozens, if not hundreds, of more focused projects in its wake, most of which would thrive on their own. While it was rarely able to forge agreements or to formally mobilize resources for coherent initiatives, for the time it lasted, SDS gave thousands of young people the opportunity to network, share ideas, and celebrate the great diversity of those willing to give at least part of their lives to making the US a more humane and rational place to live.

Although the meeting at Kewadin did not resolve the organizational dilemma, it did host a significant workshop entitled "Women in the Movement," presented by several of the women from ERAP who had read Casey Hayden and Mary King's paper "Sex and Caste" over the previous year. They wanted to share the paper and the ideas it had generated. Most of these women had been active for several years, some in SDS and others coming from SNCC or peace organizations. Many were several years out of college and in graduate school or working at jobs. Some were or had been wives or girlfriends of the old guard.[12]

Some of the most heated discussion was about whether or not women had the right to explore these ideas without the presence of men, a few of whom demanded the right to attend. The idea of women meeting together separately to work out their own understanding of their experience felt powerfully subversive to both women and men. For many of the women there, the workshop altered their sense of themselves and gave them a new sense of the possibilities of women thinking and working together. Heather Tobis noted that for many women it was their first experience of women validating the value of caring about other women. They shared "the feeling that women should organize women and that situations had to be developed so women could support other women."[13] Many of these women left Kewadin inspired to continue their exploration of women's issues. They would lead the conversation about women's rights and be in the forefront of developing strategies for change both within SDS and in the broader movement of women that soon erupted.

At the end of the meeting in Kewadin, the membership voted down the candidates of the old guard and elected Carl Oglesby president of SDS and Jeff Shero, vice president. Carl, a recent recruit, and his wife Beth, were the parents of three small children. He had been a scientific writer for Bendix Corporation and had been horrified to find out that the basic research he was working on was actually being used to more efficiently disperse Agent Orange in Vietnam. Over the course of the next year, Carl spoke convincingly and powerfully all over the country in opposition to the war, telling carefully researched stories about the causes of the war, who was benefiting from it, and who was being hurt by it.

Jeff Shero, an SDS organizer from Texas, was a committed student organizer with a sense of humor and a strong sense of participatory democracy. Unwilling to leave his ongoing work in Texas and believing the leadership should remain rooted in local struggles, Shero returned home after the election, leaving only when called upon to do national speaking or visit other chapters.

After the meeting, many of the old guard were befuddled by the failure of their easy intellectual intimacy to carry the day. They left the convention to focus on their own work, especially ERAP projects. Very few of the resources, culture or working knowledge of national SDS were passed on to the new volunteers who stepped up to work in the national office. By midwinter, the subsequent financial crisis came close to shutting down the organization. Some of the founders decided to try again to address the growing organization crisis in SDS by calling for a Rethinking Conference in December, 1965, before the National Council meeting at the University of Illinois in Champaign-Urbana.

Here many of the old-guard leadership attempted for one last time to find a single direction for SDS and to reaffirm its long-range goal of building a broad social movement to influence electoral politics. Even the original leadership, however, couldn't agree on how to move toward this goal, let alone draw any kind of consensus from the hundreds of new members who came to the meeting. While the old guard ran the conference, it was to be their last. Again, no decision on reorganization was reached despite hours of dogmatic, unfocused and unresolved debates.

After SDS's collapse in 1970, some have argued that later factions, especially Weatherman and/or women groups, "destroyed SDS," but this argument serves only personal bitterness and nostalgia.[16] It was true that there was little reverence for the original founders and that some of their individual visions of SDS's mission were dashed on the rocks as SDS evolved. All of us who grew up some in SDS cherished its empowering culture, but its very success lay in the way it churned out young people to other, more sustained efforts. The women's movement and then Weatherman were but two of many significant fragments of SDS. The founders of SDS gave their best effort to create a lasting structure for the organization, and failed completely and inevitably at this juncture. Repeated attempts would be made every year from 1966 on. These efforts were doomed from the start, however, because they were premised on the belief that this phenomenal uprising of young people could or should be corralled into a single, hierarchical, monolithic organization.

There were, however, a couple of noteworthy accomplishments at the 1965 meeting in Champaign-Urbana. One was an endorsement of Al Haber's idea to start a Radical Education Project in Ann Arbor, to continue the work of research and pamphlet writing, and to turn SDS's mimeographed monthly newsletter into a weekly newspaper, full of chapter news, theoretical discussion, and proposals for the organization. Jeff Shero finally left Texas to move to the national office, now on West Madison Street in Chicago, to assume responsibility for the new weekly newspaper, called *New Left Notes*.

New Left Notes (*NLN*) groped for an identity, responding to the need to spread the word about SDS's work while also continuing to serve the organization's need for internal debate. It carried stories about various campaigns in support of farm workers and the Mississippi Freedom Labor Union, and against apartheid in South Africa. News of the war in Vietnam became a regular feature. SDS led a number of small demonstrations around the country to protest the resumption of US bombing, from three to twelve hundred people in each. Students began to picket General Taylor whenever he spoke. *NLN* also published program proposals, for training chapters on the history of SDS, for more actions against the war in Vietnam, for power-structure research, civil rights, union insurgencies, church activism, and for a program to teach how to develop regional programs. Some proposals provoked ongoing debate. That spring, several people weighed in on the issue of student power. Some argued that SDS should organize students around issues that affected their own lives, believing that people only truly become radicalized by dealing with their own oppression. The student-power effort focused on giving students more freedom—from mandatory dorm hours, mandatory dress codes, restrictive rules governing social encounters, and mandatory participation in chapel or other traditional school functions. Many such freedoms, like an end to dress codes and curfews, were of particular interest to women. Others argued that many middle-class students came to college already feeling entitled to the bounty of the American Dream, and a fight against their restrictions could easily become a fight for more privilege, neglecting more urgent work to support the poor and the victims of war and racism.

There were also letters and articles about black power. The new Southern Student Organizing Committee, organized by Sue Thrasher and others, wrote an article on black consciousness, in an attempt to help SDS address questions that Southern white activists were exploring. In the weeks that followed several others also contributed to this discussion.[17] Many young white activists reacted sympathetically to the cry for self-definition coming from young black activists. Ann Braden, of the Southern Christian Education Fund, was one of the few to explicitly argue that while whites *should* focus on bringing more whites into the movement, the best way to do that was in interracial organizations, and young whites should not give up on the model so quickly.[18]

In February 1966, the draft was extended to college students, except those with the highest grades. Colleges and universities were now required to rank students. Campus protests against ranking sprang up across the country. Many professors, daunted that a lower grade might condemn a young man to death, began giving everyone As. That May, students at UC Berkeley occupied the administration building in their protest against student ranking for the purposes of the draft, setting a precedent that would be followed by hundreds of student groups.

Increasingly, the war seemed to be taking priority over everything else on Johnson's agenda. No more big new social programs were coming on line. The excitement and optimism generated by the civil rights movement in the South, and then the measured hopefulness generated by the War on Poverty, the Civil Rights Act and the Voting Rights Act were fading. Now, it seemed like we were digging in to defend the civil rights that had been won, in theory, and to end the war in Vietnam.

In the face of these events, I put off my plan to apply to law school for a year. I decided to try to find a job working on one of the campaigns of the many peace candidates running for state and federal office, a compromise between the movement and established politics. I thought that maybe my research in Congress would give me an in into the world of electoral politics. Like many young women at that time, I could only imagine winning my own liberation by competing fiercely with men to get the chance to show that I could do an equally good job. It also meant competing with other women, because if a woman came before me and tried and failed, then, I thought, the men would not be willing to give another woman a chance. I sent out letters and a résumé to all of the candidates I knew about and thought decent.

The other life event that happened that spring was that I fell in love for the first time. My past relationships had begun when a like-minded guy pursued me, and I responded to the physical chemistry. I saw relationships as purely recreational. But this relationship was different: It engaged my deepest thoughts and feelings. Mark felt like a soul mate. A casual conversation at lunch quickly turned into a series of meetings in which we shared fears, longings, and confessions. We talked about politics, science, and poetry. For all its intensity, we kept the relationship secret. He was two years behind me, a sophomore; I was about to graduate. Even more importantly, he was the class president and an acknowledged genius who was majoring in math and was a straight-A student. I was a controversial misfit, considered a hard partier, a political activist, and an uneven student with an uncertain future. He was the darling of the establishment, and I was an outsider. Besides, I was determined that my desire to make a contribution to a better world would come ahead of everything else. Neither one of us knew how to get past these barriers to nurture a sustained relationship.

The Swarthmore campus was also an arboretum and had a grove of magnolia trees behind the library. I had never seen magnolias before I came there, and had never really noticed them my first three years on campus. But, that spring, the magnolia grove became our spot, as the buds swelled and burst early in the spring, we sat under a tree on the grass and looked up into the maze of blossoms which surrounded us on all sides. I had no idea life could be so breathtakingly beautiful.

In early May I heard, much to my surprise, that Congressman Robert Kastenmeier had agreed to hire me as a campaign aide. I was relieved. While he was not one of the first to vote against appropriations for the war, he had written repeatedly of his dissatisfaction with US conduct and goals of the war, and he had stressed the need for elections and self-determination for all the Vietnamese people, one of Ho Chi Minh's early demands. Congressman Kastenmeier had also exposed and condemned the use of gas by US troops and of the US torturing of Vietnamese civilians.

In 1961, Kastenmeier had been one of a small number of congressmen to stand up to the remnants of McCarthyism and vote against appropriations for the House Un-American Activities Committee (HUAC), which was still trying to intimidate people who opposed government policies. In a public statement explaining his vote, Kastenmeier argued that anyone who investigated matters of internal security should take heed:

The highest degree of responsibility and objectivity is required, and a congressional committee violates its trust when it resorts to deception, abuse of witnesses and unwarranted attacks on those who disagree. The Congress must not condone such acts; in fact, it must express its disapproval.[19]

Kastenmeier's statement was typical of the way he merged moral clarity and political caution. He was always aware that, however unfounded, the charge of having communist sympathies could cost him an election.

I knew that this job would win me respect and independence from my family, who would now have to step back and let me go. Congressman Kastenmeier wanted me to start the Monday after graduation, so I would not even have to go home.

CHAPTER FOUR

THE LIMITS OF ELECTORAL POLITICS

■ ■

In Washington, I found a room in a boarding house near Dupont Circle, an easy commute by bus to Capitol Hill. The room was tiny, just large enough for a single bed and a dresser, with a small closet in the corner. I shared a large bathroom with two African students who each had a room on the same floor. Our main social interaction entailed negotiations over the use of the large old-fashioned bathtub, where, in the evenings, the cool water provided the only relief from the unrelenting heat with temperatures day after day in the high nineties.

My work at the office was largely supervised by the administrative assistant, Kaz Oshiki, whose tasks included being the office liaison with the campaign. I met with the congressman once or twice at the beginning of the summer but otherwise rarely saw him except as he came and went in attendance to meetings, roll-call votes, and an endless stream of visitors to his office. A tall man with a lankiness that was filling out in middle age, he had a quick, warm smile that would occasionally break through his usual worried, preoccupied look. His long, purposeful strides spoke of many tasks yet to be done.

I was to work on the campaign in the four rural counties that surrounded the main city of the district, Madison, Wisconsin. Kastenmeier had always carried Madison, even though most students at the large University of Wisconsin were too young to vote, but he had often lost the rural counties. It was made clear to me that I should stay away from Madison and the student movement there because the congressman was worried about being red-baited if his relationship with academic activists were not handled carefully.

Before I went to Wisconsin, Kaz set me to work to familiarize myself with the issues important to Kastenmeier's district. I started by reading through recent files of mail from the district. Mr. Walter Perry of Mount Horeb wanted to be appointed postmaster; Mrs. Wallace Piper of Watertown had a problem with the Department of Agriculture's definition of hay land and wanted her crop to be accepted into the Cropland Adjustment Program. Mr. Russell McIntyre of McIntyre Farms wrote to express his opposition to the recent bombings in Vietnam and wanted information on milking shorthorns and on federal programs in Dane County to help farmers. Mr. E. W. Berg of Dr. Scholl's Shoe Manufacturing wrote of his support for the imposition of licensing restrictions on the export of hides and leather. Mr. Dean Rider had been approached to lease the mineral rights on his lands and wanted information. There were many people struggling to obtain disability, unemployment, social security, or veteran's benefits who described various ways the bureaucracy had somehow malfunctioned. Others contested the assignment of agricultural subsidies, and, increasingly, families were contesting individual draft calls. I learned that the draft boards in Wisconsin sometimes consisted of economically powerful real estate, banking, and corporate interests. One farmer called in distress when, as the draft calls were increased, his young son was called up. The loss of this one pair of hands might mean the bankruptcy of the farm. Kastenmeier and his staff handled these conflicts between members of his constituency delicately.

I was surprised by how much Congressman Kastenmeier served as a problem solver for individual members of his constituency. Seeing the diversity and complexity of the issues the Congressman had to know and deal with momentarily humbled my frustration with Congress's lack of leadership regarding the war and US foreign policy.

I was also surprised to find out how important constituent opinion letters were. Sometimes I was asked to compile an analysis of incoming mail on different issues, to tally pros and cons and identify any new aspects to district responses. For Kastenmeier, these letters were one important indicator of how the district was feeling about an issue, both in intensity and content. He also paid attention to his relationship to the local Democratic Party and especially to his major donors of both money and time.

I couldn't quite figure out how this layer of political activity coexisted with the work in Chester. Both seemed focused on immediate personal problems, whether the inadequacy of garbage collection in Chester or veterans' benefits in Wisconsin. But the work in Chester was fueled by a larger perspective that explained why the problems existed, and a vision of bringing communities together to solve them; while in Washington, problems were seen in isolation from each other. Working with Kastenmeier did not seem to be about change, but about service. I knew I didn't want to loose touch with the movement and the ideas of social change, so when I arrived in Washington, I renewed my $5 membership in SDS, which came with a subscription to *New Left Notes*.

One of the first issues of *NLN* to arrive in June carried a joint statement on the draft issued by SDS and SNCC, condemning both the inequities within the draft and the draft itself. Later in June, I read that pacifists Mike Ferber from Swarthmore and Staughton Lynd, a history professor from Yale, had begun to circulate "We Won't Go" petitions, forming what later became an organization called Resistance. By giving up their educational deferments and choosing jail rather than the draft, these young men set a high standard for commitment in the antiwar fight, much as the freedom riders had for so many in the early 60s. They lived their beliefs, whatever the consequences.

After about six weeks in Washington, during June and July, I moved out to Wisconsin to begin work on the campaign. During the summer Kastenmeier's wife, Dorothy, lived in the family's home in the small town of Beaver Dam, Wisconsin, with their three small children. She found a family in Beaver Dam who had a spare bedroom and were willing to take me in as a boarder.

Dorothy Kastenmeier and her good friends, Dick and Barbara Minning, immediately took me under their wing, often inviting me to spend evenings with them over endless pots of coffee after Dorothy's children were in bed. I was fascinated both by Dorothy, who was originally from a small town in eastern Texas, and her friends. They were kind, humane people who worked hard to make the world a better place. Dick worked to retrain people who had been injured on their jobs. From him, I found out what operating a jackhammer does to the heart after a few years. Dick and Barbara chatted with Dorothy, filling her in about various local events during the past year that she had missed while in Washington. They helped explain various local issues to me that I came across during the day. But the conversation rarely touched on the war or on poverty—on the big issues, as I saw it. What was missing was the sense of urgency that I had felt around movement people, that things weren't changing fast enough and that the myths that maintained the status quo were not being dispelled or challenged openly. Increasingly, I thought the congressman should speak out more about the war and civil rights, and try to educate his constituency instead of being limited by their opinions, many of which were the result of faulty information. I could never figure out how to open the conversation, however, without offending these people who had been so good to me. So I never did.

At work I was more confident because I had thought about how to talk to different kinds of people and help them feel a part of an organization. I had learned how to listen and respond, rather than barge in with a message. I spent a lot of time driving around asking farmers if we could put posters up on their barns. I listened to their concerns and reported back to Kaz. I went to local support meetings and arranged for people to have signs put on top of their cars. I went to endless county festivals to work with volunteers to distribute bumper stickers and other campaign materials.

Political campaigns, I learned, were less about substantive discussions of the issues, and much more about convincing people that the candidate was trustworthy and would look out for voters' interests.

I stayed in touch with the movement by avidly poring over each issue of *New Left Notes*. By now, SDS had 172 chapters and 5,500 members, less than half of whom were college students. It wasn't only SDS that was growing by leaps and bounds; dozens of peace groups, alternative schools, research organizations, and theater groups were popping up and growing. As the summer progressed, *NLN* continued to feature articles debating the future direction of SDS and how the organization should focus all of its new growth. A convention was planned for August in Clear Lake, Iowa, and I really wanted to go to meet the people writing in the pages of the paper, many of whom seemed so different than the SDS I had known at Swarthmore. I felt an increasing urgency to participate in this debate and be part of this movement.

In mid-August, however, Kastenmeier turned down my request to attend the convention. I sensed his displeasure about my growing interest in SDS, an organization he was familiar with because of the growing number of antiwar demonstrations at the University of Wisconsin in Madison. I concluded that it was going to be hard, if not impossible, to keep a foot in both worlds, the movement and established politics. I would have to choose.

The 1966 SDS Clear Lake convention became known, in later years, as something of a watershed moment, when the old guard finally gave up the last pretense of leadership of SDS and newer members, mostly from the Midwest, shouldered the main responsibilities. Greg Calvert, who had been editing *New Left Notes* over the summer for interim national secretary Jane Adams, was elected as national secretary, so Jane could return to organizing, as she wanted. Greg, like Carl Oglesby, was several years older and had already spent time in graduate school.

Clear Lake was also attended by many young organizers from the Midwest who had worked with the civil rights movement in the South, or had come from the tradition of agricultural and mining movements led by the radical labor activists, the Wobblies. While several of them were well read in Marxism and other progressive belief systems, their political education had come primarily through the filter of personal experience. Greg had been a student both of Marxism and of Christian theology. He became a passionate spokesperson for the belief that young people could only become radicalized if they started with an examination of their own lives. Those who only wanted to help others were liberals, a derogatory word, who only wanted to put Band-Aids on the more unseemly aspects of the current system, rather than working for fundamental change, which could only come from disparate people working together toward a vision of a more just world. No one brought freedom to someone else. Greg's view was also meant as a criticism of the old left, which he felt had not worked to redefine relationships and community among themselves.

Many of the young people at the convention responded positively to these arguments, while some of the old guard looked down their noses at the admittedly somewhat out-of-control exuberance of these newcomers and their relatively unschooled, irreverent approach to social change. To the newcomers, the small-group, academic camaraderie of the old guard seemed stodgy and aloof.

Greg did agree with the old guard that SDS's structure was woefully inadequate, and he would attempt to bring a thorough restructuring proposal before the membership in December, but the majority would again refuse to put it on the agenda. They didn't want to take time away from responding to the immediate travesties of the war to prepare SDS for the long haul. Let the future hold what it would.

In 1964 SDS had adopted the slogan "Part of the Way with LBJ," supporting Johnson because of his campaign pledge not to further escalate the conflict in Vietnam. After Johnson agreed to use the Tonkin Gulf incident as a pretense to resume bombing only two months after his election, however, most SDS members turned away from the Johnson administration completely. With mounting draft calls, SNCC and other organizations called for draft resistance, but until Clear Lake, SDS had balked at openly advising young men to break the law. Instead, SDS had tried to organize college students by circulating an "alternative draft exam," a program that never caught on.[1]

Greg committed himself to shifting SDS's focus primarily to the war and, as he was soon to say, from "protest to resistance." He also encouraged young people to strive for SNCC-like "loving communities" in which members were supportive rather than competitive, and which valued transparency and cooperation. The programs and tactics generated by local chapters now began to reflect a broader swath of young people's rebellion.

As a parting contribution before he moved on from SDS to work in the adult world of union organizing, old-guard SDSer Paul Booth wrote one more very long article on the history of radical struggle in the United

States, placing SDS in the mainstream of abolitionism, progressivism, and socialist labor struggles. (Characteristic of the time, he left out struggles for women's equality.) Because so few of the veterans of these struggles were willing to speak out against the war, however, young people were in no mood to look to these traditions for strength or for lessons learned. This rejection was compounded when many unions actively fought against integration and supported racist political candidates. As a result, many newer recruits to the movement remained totally unaware of this past. This suspicion and/or ignorance of the past made it easier for thousands of young people to approach the challenges of change creatively. Without this history, however, the movement had little ballast with which to steady itself when faced with the assassinations of 1968 and 1969 and with the recalcitrance of Vietnam policy hardliners.

As the election drew near, I spent even more time at county fairs and harvest events. I continued my drives through corn fields, watched the Beatles on the Ed Sullivan show and, for the most part, enjoyed being immersed in this Midwestern farm culture, talking about milk prices and this year's corn crop. While many of these rural residents did not vote for Kastenmeier, I rarely ran into anyone who was rude or unpleasant. Most were deeply patriotic and therefore supported without question any foreign policy objective of the government. Farmers were willing to make sacrifices, and the anticommunist perspectives of local reporters deflected questions about the purpose of the war or the value of the sacrifices being made. As reports filtered in about the incompetence of the South Vietnamese leadership and the ineptness of the war efforts, however, many people did begin to pay attention.

By late September, I concluded that Congress was not a strategic place to work to change public opinion about the war because congressmen constantly had to worry about getting reelected. While they *could* attempt to educate their constituents by providing a reasonable analysis of, for instance, the war—and I didn't think Kastenmeier was doing that enough—they were battling an increasingly efficient mass-media campaign waged in the name of patriotism by proponents of the war. No, I thought, the energy and leadership required to get the facts out in the face of all this misinformation had to come from the movement, and SDS was one organization trying to do that. Ultimately the power to stop the war did rest in Congress, but Congress would only move as fast as the American people insisted it move.

I also realized that if I were to pursue a career in Congress, as I had considered for the past several years, I would have to pay my dues in these early years, especially since I was female. I would need to let the veterans decide what was important for now. While my job with Kastenmeier was a big feather in my cap, it would mean nothing if I didn't toe the line. I knew that by even asking to go to Clear Lake I had already cut off some of my chances. Likewise, unless I made a focused commitment to work in the field of legislation, I could hardly ask Kastenmeier to give me a reference for any other job on the hill.

The six months had satisfied my need for validation. I knew that I *could* do this job, and I could figure out the rules to play the game successfully, "despite" being a woman. I had proved to my family that I could successfully negotiate the mainstream, or straight, world if I wanted. I had learned much about the way Congress worked and who the players were, but I was ready to move on. I wanted to find a way to work where my life wasn't fragmented, where I could express myself without disguises and deception. Encouraged by the new tenor of *New Left Notes*, I decided to go by the SDS national office and give SDS another try.

CHAPTER FIVE

NEW LEFT NOTES

■ ■

After the election, in which Kastenmeier won three of the four rural counties, I retraced my steps from the summer and removed Kastenmeier posters from barns and fences as we had promised. I loaded up the station wagon, said good-bye to Doris and her family, the congressman, and their friends and headed east to the SDS national office in Chicago. I was looking for another adventure.

I imagined Chicago as the tough, gritty city like the one described in Carl Sandburg's vivid poem, where the prairie winds still snaked along the paved roads from time to time and where neighbors talked, shared chores, and sought out each other's company. Although the city turned out to be far more diverse than I had imagined, I was not disappointed by its earthy, unpretentious character. It was a city I quickly grew to love.

I found West Madison Street on a map and arrived in a shabby neighborhood about a mile west of downtown. The November sky was gray and any errant weeds or stubby trees in the vacant lots had long since faded in a cold frost, leaving no color to distract from the austerity of the aging commercial buildings. The office was on the second floor of a large, three-story commercial building complex that housed a Spanish theater at one end, operated by Spanish Civil War veteran and landlord, John Rossen. The building was flanked by a liquor store that was open late and by a luncheonette that served a good hot bowl of chili for sixty cents. The next block sported a rundown Woolworth's, a storefront church, and a junk store. Across from the national office building, empty fields filled with rubble left from Model Cities' bulldozers gave a view of a small public housing project further back. This was Chicago's near west side on the edge of a strip referred to as Skid Row.

On West Madison, the number "1608" was painted in white on a set of large, brown, metal double doors set in the middle of the building. I pushed open one of the doors onto a set of wide, metal-trimmed, gray linoleum stairs leading straight up into a second-floor hallway that ran perpendicular to the top of the stairs. Large dirty windows looked out from the hallway into an air shaft. I followed the sound of voices and walked past a small windowless office on the left into a large room with boxes piled along the sides, under a series of large windows. A number of disheveled desks were placed randomly around the room. Makeshift floor-to-ceiling shelves had been built along the full length of the far wall and held varying-sized piles of back issues of *New Left Notes*; to the right, more shelves held piles of pamphlets that may have once been neatly stacked but had clearly been pilfered by many hands and now were, in some cases, dripping off the shelves onto the floor.

A young man in his late twenties greeted me warmly. He remembered my name as perhaps the only SDS member who had responded to his plea in *New Left Notes* that summer for members with jobs to tithe ten percent of their salaries to SDS to help with office expenses. We began exchanging stories. I explained briefly my history in the Swarthmore chapter and my participation in the Chester project. He explained that he was national secretary Greg Calvert. With wavy sandy brown hair combed back from his forehead, his somewhat cherubic face belied the fact that he had abandoned a dissertation and a college teaching job to work for SDS. He seemed genuinely concerned, but also slightly bemused, by the chaos of the office and the financial and administrative crisis that had been ongoing since his arrival. I liked his sense of humor and the fact that he didn't appear to take himself too seriously. At the same time, as he explained the current mission of the national office, it was clear that he was passionate about SDS and about the potential of young people's political activism.

We sat talking at a long worktable used to fold and collate the occasional mountains of literature that were run off on the old A. B. Dick press. Greg related that the editor of the newspaper had left a week ago, burned out. Since they hadn't heard from him, Greg was assuming that he had taken a serious break and wouldn't be back.

In addition to the need for an editor for the weekly newspaper, there was a postal regulation that stated that as of January 1, no fourth-class mail could be sent out without a zip code. All newspapers had to be sorted, tied, and labeled by zip code. As yet, there were *no* zips for the five thousand plus names on the mailing list. We would have to look up all five thousand zip codes, and retype and sort all the addressograph cards by zip code, instead of by their current alphabetical order, a monumental job.

At the end of this conversation, Greg, having been satisfied that I was literate (no writing sample required), asked me if I would take over the job. I protested that I was hardly qualified to edit a newspaper. He responded by pointing out the obvious, that most of the work was clerical; the articles came in from elsewhere, and he would help with the editing.

This was my introduction to the world of journalism. I could not believe that this opportunity was falling in my lap purely because of the accident of my arrival at this particular moment. I agreed to take over and to stay a couple of weeks, putting out the next issues with Greg so I could learn how to do it. Greg also suggested that I should find a way to attend the next national council meeting in San Francisco. I told him that I had committed myself to being in New Hampshire for Christmas, as always, but that I would fly out to California from there.

Greg had been continuing his push, begun at Clear Lake, to redirect SDS's antiwar activity "from protest to resistance," calling on young people to refuse induction any way they saw fit. If already in the armed services, SDS encouraged GIs to refuse to serve in Vietnam. SDS leaders also encouraged students to reveal how funding from large corporations and the Department of Defense was shaping research priorities and bringing both the war and corporate priorities into their classrooms and labs.

In both draft resistance and campus organizing, Greg continued to believe that a radical understanding of the world had to be rooted in a quest for personal freedom and a moral center. Whether the quest was primarily driven by racial, gender-based, or economic oppression or by a rejection of the system's venal expectations (or some combination of these), the choice to redefine one's own life was critical. Free, however, in no way meant privileged, especially at other people's expense. Embedded in this idea was the belief that we could all be free as individuals only if we treasured the freedom of all people, and if we shouldered our share of social responsibilities. The assumption of responsibility for society's problems was at the heart of this new morality.[1]

While a few of the original SDS members worried that the flirtation with direct confrontations, on campus or on the streets, against the draft and the war, would alienate a broader constituency of liberals who might otherwise support us, Greg argued that it was the merging of personal rebellion and the rising of a morally based vision that fueled the activism of young people. Greg showed how intimately these two goals were connected, and he had an intuitive sense about how to embrace them both.

While Greg obviously knew considerably more than I, he seemed genuinely interested in what I thought and was willing to give me enormous responsibility. The national office appeared to be a community that included novices and oddballs as well as sophisticated political thinkers, and there were young women as well as men.

I believed I could contribute to *New Left Notes* because my experience living in a small town in Wisconsin for four months had heightened my sense of the role the paper could play for that segment of SDS that was not in the main intellectual centers and felt isolated and new to political work. The paper could be a vehicle for collective self-discovery as we explored the critical issues of the times: the war, civil rights, the draft, and repression. While the earlier mimeographed SDS bulletins had also been attentive to chapters, many of the pages carried lengthy theoretical debates that were incomprehensible to many of the newer, younger members like myself. I didn't know how to integrate theoretical debate—so critical to one aspect of participatory democracy—without losing the attention of new recruits, but I would learn. As inadequate as I felt, I now had some sense, from my last year at Swarthmore, about how to participate in a conversation about ideas.

One of the people to come through the office while I was still there in November 1966 was Peter Henig, a recent graduate of Earlham who was then working in Ann Arbor with the Radical Education Project. He was a freewheeling and impassioned thinker. Talking with Greg in the national office, we all came up with the idea of writing an article for *New Left Notes* about the Selective Service System, now in charge of drafting thousands of new soldiers every month. Since SDS was embarking on an ambitious antidraft program, SDS members should know who the people were who ran it and how it worked. As *NLN* editor-to-be I agreed to help research the article and agreed to meet Peter in Washington in a couple of weeks to try to interview General Hershey, the head of Selective Service.

Of course the general himself didn't have time for us, but we were provided with an interview with someone from the press office. We carefully prepared our questions, assembled respectable outfits, and off we went. When we entered the Selective Service building we were ushered in to a small waiting room for the press office and given a packet of materials called the Selective Service Orientation Kit. Later we sat in a coffee shop and read:

> Educators, scientists, engineers and their professional organizations, during the last ten years particularly, have been convincing the American public that for the mentally qualified man there is a special order of patriotism other than service in uniform—that for the man having the capacity, dedicated service as a civilian in such fields as engineering, the sciences, and teaching constitute the ultimate in their expression of patriotism.

We understood that "mentally qualified" really meant privileged, white, and middle or upper class. We came to realize that the Selective Service System was part of a broader system that existed to mobilize the whole country for war and for profit. The big universities were the privileged citadels within this system, educating the country's elite, especially in skills that furthered preparedness for war, while those without college degrees had to face the mud, the confusion, and the bullets of the actual war. So much for patriotism!

After our initial hit-or-miss exploration of the pamphlets, Peter went back home for more thorough study and to write the article. When I drove east, I stopped to work with Peter again. He also took me to meet a number of his friends, including Mike Locker, who like him was a graduate of Earlham, and who soon, with Peter and others, formed the North American Congress on Latin America (NACLA) to do ongoing research on government policy and corporate investments in Latin America. Peter also introduced me to his friend Marge Piercy, who was at that time living in New York City, writing poetry, and her first novel, and working with New York SDS.

At Christmas, I returned to New Hampshire for the family gathering. My mother had hoped that I would continue on Capitol Hill. Or, she thought, I should return home and become a teacher. My career in journalism with SDS scared her and reminded her of my arrest back in Chester. She was sure I was associating with unsavory people. It was a world that was incomprehensible to her, and I no longer tried to extract either her approval or her appreciation for my happiness. Instead I tried to present this new career move as a step forward into the world of political journalism. It was clear, however, that I continued to be an enormous disappointment to her and that she was angry at me for what she saw as my betrayal and rejection of her well-meaning attempts to control my future direction.

The day after Christmas I flew youth fare to San Francisco for the national council meeting in Berkeley. I knew almost none of the two or three hundred people there. I connected with the national office staff people and with Peter and some of his friends, and shared the same living-room floor in Berkeley at night. Someone took a carload of us across the bay to explore Golden Gate Park and I was completely overwhelmed by the beauty of it. It was late December, and the rainy season had already turned everything a brilliant green. Everywhere there were young people with bell-bottoms, bare feet, and beads.

Back in Berkeley, the council started with an agenda debate that went well into the night. The next two days took the form of one long meeting, with breaks to eat and sleep. I loved the freewheeling, fervent debate, and the fact that serious, intellectual students were arguing with long-haired hippies, both of which made way for representatives from small colleges in Montana and Oregon to be heard as well. Since I had been away from SDS for two years, I just listened. It was at this national council that the first strong official resolution on the draft was passed, explicitly urging young men to resist.

For the ride back, I joined Peter and two others to take a drive-away, a frequent form of travel that cost nothing except the gas. With four drivers we could drive around the clock if need be. We piled into a midsized Ford sedan belonging to a serviceman who had been transferred to the East Coast, and we set off across the Rockies. Early in the morning on January 1, I arrived back in the national office, where I grabbed a few hours sleep on the floor. Already two office staffers had started on the zip-code project, and some other people and I joined in. We kept at it for the next thirty-six hours.

The actual paper was thrown together hastily. According to our postal permit, every issue had to go out on time or we would lose our fourth-class permit. We knew that schedule variations in other papers would be routinely overlooked, but that ours would not be. The printer of *NLN* had already been harassed by the Chicago Red Squad, a detail of detectives, similar to ones in New York and Los Angeles, specializing in leftist and movement activists. Since the printing company was outside the city's boundaries, however, and because our account was a relatively large one for them, they had not yet succumbed to the pressure to reject our business.

We lived on peanut butter and jelly, an occasional bottle of wine, and coffee. Greg had invited me to stay at the apartment behind the national office, where he lived with Dee Jacobsen, the recently hired office manager from Salt Lake City, Utah. While I was grateful for the offer, I declined, wary of immersing myself headfirst in a work scene that was also my "family" scene. I was learning that I needed a space to call my own because, wherever I worked or lived, I was easily enmeshed in other people's lives. As I entered this very intense world of national SDS I wanted to be sure I didn't lose my bearings.

After the initial flurry of work of the first two weeks back after the national council, I found an old outbuilding behind a small two-family house, which had at one time been inhabited, but was now filled with junk. The landlord agreed to empty the space and install a gas space heater, while I was on my own to clean it up.

I scrubbed the floor and cleaned as best I could, bought a piece of foam to put on the floor for a bed, and moved in my few records and the old portable record player my mother had given me when I was in seventh grade. On the street I found some chairs and a few cardboard and wooden boxes for my few clothes. At the corner thrift shop I bought a couple of glasses, a plate, and a couple of silverware settings. The house was probably quite charming when first built, and comfortable in the summer. But in January it was freezing. I spent little time there, rarely cooked, and only went home late at night to sleep.

In addition to *New Left Notes*, the national office printed and distributed small, easy-to-read pamphlets on a variety of issues. The largest category of pamphlets concerned foreign policy, especially US support for apartheid in South Africa, and the war in Vietnam. The national office also made available buttons, posters, and stickers including one with a Bertolt Brecht poem:

> Those who take meat from the table
> teach contentment.
> Those for whom the taxes are destined
> demand sacrifice.
> Those who eat their fill speak to the hungry
> of wonderful times to come.
> Those who lean the country into the abyss
> call ruling too difficult
> For ordinary men.

In the middle of January, just as I was getting situated, Peter sent in his article, entitled "The Selective Service System: On the Manpower Channelers." The article explained how the SSS arranged for the most educated men to avoid the draft by using the threat of the draft to pressure them to take jobs needed by the military-industrial complex. "The psychology of granting wide choice under pressure to take action is the American or indirect way of achieving what is done by direction in foreign countries where choice is not permitted."[2]

Articles in *NLN* also exposed Dow Chemical, a frequent participant in college recruitment fairs and maker of the highly profitable and deadly napalm. Dow's corporate recruiters became a prime target of boycotts and demonstrations on campus.[3]

In the same issue as Peter's article in *NLN*, we ran Jane Adams's article "People's Power: On Equality for Women." Jane had returned to campus organizing work in southern Illinois after her stint as national secretary. She explained how gender inequality, like racism, was fundamentally built into our system—it was in factories, universities, schools, party politics, the military, churches, welfare, and other institutions. Most of us were affected by it in multiple ways. All of these "dominance-submission" characteristics got played out in the family, she noted, with men being at the top and children being at the bottom. She showed how some people in the economy profited from women's inferior position, the same as they did from racism. "So what do women want to be free to do?" Jane ended:

1) Find a few freed people and form a community . . .
2) . . . Become a career woman, doing all the hard things necessary to make it, or become a housewife, active in the League of Women Voters, Women for Peace, PTA, etc.
3) Begin working for a society based . . . on equality, demanding equality within organizations one's in . . .

I still had not yet heard about the ongoing conversations inspired by the Hayden/King "Sex and Caste" paper. Jane's article was the first thing I had seen that openly linked women's lack of equal treatment with other forms of inequality. Here it was, an explanation about how I had felt at Swarthmore, but instead of suggesting only that women compete to prove we were men's equals, she urged women to turn toward each other to get support. This was a new idea for me. I was wary of anything that suggested that women meet in all-women forums, fearing that this separation was too similar to the separation and trivialization of women characteristic of my mother's generation. Men were all too content to let us go off for "women's talk" while they ran the show. Besides, I wasn't sure what women had to offer each other that would help us gain a voice and power in the public discourse.

I assumed, like many women, that this new aspect of the movement would be accepted, with some bluster perhaps. The whole point of the movement was to help all people be free. Since the office staff readily accepted that women were not always listened to or adequately respected either in SDS or in the world, I assumed this was a precursor to a change in attitude in SDS as a whole. I had not heard the stories about how angry some men had been when women had first attempted to discuss the issue in SDS in 1965. Jane's suggestions about what to do seemed to assume that once men understood the problem, they would support women's full participation in the movement because it would make us all stronger.

Jane's article encouraged the conversations to continue, but in the context of the national office, I didn't know how to do that. For the first time since Chester, I felt like I had landed in a community supportive of both women and men. The day-to-day life in the office seemed free of gender stereotypes. *No one* did the dishes until they wanted a clean cup or plate, and the men were as likely to sweep as the women. I was being listened to with more respect than I had ever experienced. All of the women on the national administrative committee and in the office were strong, outspoken women. I'm not saying there weren't gross examples of sexism—of men ignoring women's voices, expecting women to do the grunt work, seeing women only as social rather than intellectual beings—only that I didn't notice them. Here, I was able to join in the conversation, and people argued with me when I said something that reflected a lack of knowledge, rather than ignore me or talk past me. Like at Swarthmore, these men knew stuff I didn't know, and I wanted them to teach me. I had no idea, yet, that political relationships with women could add a new dimension to my comprehension of the world.

In February, I went to a conference with Jane and was impressed when she cooked a tasty and nutritious soup, costing almost nothing, to feed everyone there. I asked Jane if she'd be willing to print the recipe in *NLN*. This information was as critical a part of building a movement as theory was, I thought! Bringing attention to the recipe would be a way to introduce so-called women's work into the common forum, and I thought it would be fun because I could imagine the theoretically oriented men rolling their eyes at a recipe, with graphics no less, in *NLN*.

Confident enough of her intellectual powers and reputation, especially since her article on sexism had been in the previous issue, Jane was willing share the recipe. As expected, I heard that many men, both new and seasoned members, expressed contempt, although no one ever directly confronted me. Interestingly, in years to come, the recipe was sometimes cited by feminists as an example of SDS's sexism, a charge I thought revealed some inattention to the challenges of supporting a low-budget movement in action. *NLN* in that period also carried many articles, both news and analysis, by women.

We devoted a lot of attention to fundraising, since the national office was always in debt. Unlike some of the civil rights organizations, SDS never had any consistent large donors. We depended on small donations and subscriptions.

In February, Carl Oglesby's book *Containment and Change* went on sale for $1.45 and became a major source of revenue, since Carl donated $0.85 per book to SDS. Carl's carefully researched and footnoted but easy-to-read book looked squarely at the corruption of US foreign policy. He wrote in detail about the case of Brazil and how US business interests had colluded with our government to threaten and bribe Brazilian officials to give away Brazil's rich mineral resources to US companies (or to Brazilian companies owned by US stockholders). Iron, oil, manganese, and niobium, a rich atomic ore, were mined with no safeguards for workers, using methods that polluted vast river systems with poisonous heavy metals, killing the fish that were the main staple food for over a million people.

These same corporations, backed by the US government, forced Brazil to restructure its debt to profit US banks. When the people of Brazil rebelled and elected officials opposed these tactics, one after the other they were deposed.

On March 16, 1964, President Johnson addressed a meeting of the Alliance for Progress, an international economic body whose members included officers of the World Bank and International Monetary Fund in Washington, and warned Brazilian leaders that their protection of their national economic interests were seen as a threat to the United States. In less than two weeks a Brazilian general, with the full backing of the United States, assumed power. He then proceeded to reopen the country, allowing a flood of resources and profits to flow from Brazil to international, primarily US, corporations. Oglesby detailed the specific economic mechanisms used to do this and the specific, blow-by-blow involvement by US corporate and government leaders at the ambassadorial level.

Oglesby also gave several other quick but heavily cited instances of direct CIA manipulation of foreign governments, including the successful conspiracy to overthrow Premier Mohammed Mossadeq in Iran in 1953 because he advocated Cold War neutralism and threatened to nationalize foreign oil holdings; the ouster of progressive and popularly elected President Arbenz in Guatemala in 1954, so that United Fruit, which owned a major segment of all arable land, would not be subjected to even the most minor land reform (then secretary of state John Foster Dulles's law firm had represented the company during the 30s); the US Marines' invasion of the Dominican Republic in 1965, where US administration leaders owned controlling interests in sugar companies dominating the Dominican economy; a coup against Nkrumah in Ghana in 1966 in order to prospect for oil and open up the local fishing industry to the US, decimating their fledgling national fishing fleet. There were many more examples of this sort of economic plunder.[4]

Carl's book pulled together many of the things I had been learning. While our political system valued equality, Carl noted that the economic system—free enterprise—valued initiative, aggression, and power. As a result, the most aggressive were rewarded and everyone else had to serve them, or at least find a way to coexist with the terms they set. Democracy and equality, including equal opportunity, had no place in this system. The phrase "free market" had always made it seem as if the economic system were democratic and free too. Carl's examples showed just how undemocratic it had become, with the public having access to fewer and fewer decisions; and how much it favored, through taxation, tariffs, patents, and subsidy policies, the rich getting richer, with nothing to stop them or allow for a more equitable distribution of the wealth.

My father was right, I thought, that competition does sometimes encourage creativity, initiative, and efficiency, but after three hundred years, many of the victors of each round had moved to consolidate control, using a host of extremely unfair, often violent, tactics. There still existed some real competition, and there were still opportunities for some new people to make their way to the top through the invention of new technology, luck, or aggressive investments, but the more dominant feature was the decrease in competition on the highest level, where access was difficult and the exchanges often brutal.

Carl's information about Guatemala, Brazil, and Iran showed how much the corporate winners now influenced US foreign policy. It also explained why such a system depended on expansion, war, and internal repression: violence was the ultimate weapon of a system in which physical power was the prime arbiter in the economic sphere. Besides, the arms industry had become fabulously profitable for many of the rich and powerful. Carl summed it up:

> [T]he expansionary dynamic of Western commercial culture has been the root, the denominating constant, of modern history. The grandeur of Western liberalism, its material abundance, the flourishing of its arts and sciences, its painful construction of constitutional democracy—these interconnected achievements have been financed by the sustained theft called imperialism.[5]

I failed, however, to notice the fuller meanings in Carl's observation that the "achievements" in the area of limited democracy had been financed by "theft." I focused only on the theft part—and had begun to think less and less about the achievement part. I had been fascinated with the origins of our secular, constitutional democracy in college, but the more I learned about the damage we had done, the easier it was to forget what an accomplishment it had been. The US system had cobbled together many of the most progressive ideas of the times in a powerful combination, ideas from Native American federalist government, from utopians, from the philosophers of emergent capitalism, and from advocates of religious tolerance. From the rapidly escalating power of invention and science, thinkers of the day understood that within both nature and mechanics forces worked in tension with each other. Could a system bought with such devastating consequences have a future in a just and peaceful world? By then, I could only see greed as the primary motivating force for the cruelties of the system. It was a ready explanation for how the wealthy could be so immune to the human costs of their work and their wealth. In my focus on the human frailties of these wealthy power brokers, their use of the language of democracy seemed bitterly hypocritical.

The fact was, *we* didn't know how to address the problems of the economy, beyond our intuition that participatory democracy might hold the key. We had encountered a host of problems already, trying to bring that vision to life in relatively small projects like ERAP, and within SDS itself. As imperfect as the system in the United States was, most people who were excluded did not want to destroy the system, only to join in. The problem was that the system in its current state depended on the economic exclusion of a great many people to survive. I certainly didn't know how to change that. Who decided who got to benefit and who didn't? Was that even the question a democracy should ask?

Carl did not advocate any economic model. Instead, he sidestepped this conversation about alternatives to capitalism by asserting that "the revolutionary's motivating vision of change is at root a vision ... not of something that *will* be there, but of something that will be there *no longer....* The fundamental revolutionary motive is not to construct a Paradise but to destroy an Inferno."[6]

Up until then, I had assumed that the way to bring about change in the United States was to use the democratic system. I thought that if people like Kastenmeier campaigned on a platform of issues that explicitly explained the way things ran and argued for value-based economic decisions, they could continue to educate after they were elected. Once rigorous discussion became routine, red-baiting would loose its power. To further that scenario, we had to build a great social movement to engage people in thinking about the issues and fighting for change. To organize meant to engage people in a conversation about an issue so they would open themselves up to new information about it, and could then reflect on the injustice or stupidity involved. Awareness could lead to a willingness to participate either in protest or in the creation of alternatives.

Carl Oglesby's picture of the intractability of imperialism, however, reinforced what I had begun to hear elsewhere, and it gave me my first doubts that massive social movements would be enough. In the coming year, I would consider several models for change that had roots both in the idea of participatory democracy and also in the increasingly ubiquitous idea of revolution.

I encountered the first of these ideas soon thereafter. Sometime in January, Greg suggested I go with him to meet with a number of New York SDSers to discuss a proposal to start a theoretical supplement to *New Left Notes*. Dick Flacks, at the Radical Education Project in Ann Arbor, had suggested such a supplement the previous summer, as a means to make the paper accessible to new members while serving the needs of the organization's growth. Greg had tried to raise the issue at the previous national council but it had been bumped off the agenda. Now, three graduate students at the New School for Social Research—Bob Gottlieb, David Gilbert, and Gerry Tenney—were working on a paper as part of New York SDS's regional effort for the Radical Education Project. They were trying to update the Marxist analysis of capitalism for the current conditions in the United States, and then use that analysis to devise a strategy for change. We agreed to use the paper as the lead article in the new supplement.

David Gilbert, a graduate of Columbia and past president of the SDS chapter there, had not grown up in the left, but had discovered Marxism in high school. Intrigued by the vastness of Marx's analysis, he had studied Marxism persistently through college. His goal was to search for ideas that would be immediately helpful, rather than aspiring to become a Marxist scholar.

Gilbert and the others believed that the most radical people in the United States were not factory workers, as the old model of traditional Marxists suggested, but the more educated members of the workforce. In the United States, the paper's authors argued, factory work was decreasing while those with skilled training and even college degrees were becoming "the new working class." Students were beginning to understand how the big universities were training them to be powerless cogs in a machine. In this respect the paper was similar to and drew on Peter Henig's article on workforce channeling, especially its focus on the new roles for the university.[7]

Much of the paper was hard for me to comprehend because it discussed issues that were within the framework of Marxist orthodoxy. Nonetheless, I found it stimulating to think about who in society would be most likely to fight for change. How did we become conscious of our place in society? How did different experiences determine the extent to which we were aware of how our existence compared to that of others? What about our lives made us determined to change the way things were?

I liked the way the paper debunked the traditional Marxist reliance on industrial workers as the agents for change because, from what I saw in the United States, they were among the highest paid, most privileged, and most loyal to the government. Many, like those working in defense industries, construction, and trucking, had opposed efforts to end discrimination and had supported the war. I liked that the idea of a new working class explained why students and other young people were in the center of the outcry for change.

In the long run, however, the most important part of this paper for me came from an assumption that was never explicitly discussed: the idea that change was oppositional. The different groups, or classes, as Marx referred to different sectors of society, had interests that were so opposed to each other that those with power would never change in a way that gave power to those without it. The only way the rest of us could affect meaningful change was to depose those with the power, the same way our government deposed those who opposed them around the world—by force.

Marx believed that since capitalism ruled by means of violence, change could only come about through violence, although he never developed specific models for this process. This paper seemed to assume an eventual violent confrontation of some sort. It referred to revolution, although it, too, didn't explore what that might mean.

I didn't think systematically about this assumption at the time. Revolution was in the air. The Beatles and the Rolling Stones were singing about it, and the word sprang up everywhere. I knew that historically revolution meant a rapid and total systemic change from one system, whether political, economic, or scientific, to another. I thought of the industrial revolution. National liberation was a form of revolution, as was a war of self-defense against outside economic and political intervention. That was happening in Vietnam.

The original SDS vision of participatory democracy, like the vision of the civil rights movement, had been inclusive—built on the assumption that the common interest in equality and democracy overcame conflicting interests. Most of the liberal Democrats dismissed this vision as either hopelessly naive or as a utopian vision rooted in past agrarian/village forms of local governance. The experiences of many of those who had fought for civil rights in the South, however, revealed that a mobilization based on people's deep aspirations could unleash tremendous power. When people were given the opportunity to take responsibility for the collective good of society, SDS asserted, most people would rise to the occasion. Only this active engagement of all the people could create a healthy democracy, one in which the major economic and political decisions of the day were accessible to everyone they affected.

This model for change had begun to wear thin, however, not only in the face of Vietnam, but also when applied to the problem of persistent economic inequality. Perhaps our goal was not just building a social movement that demanded change, but building one so big and broad that in a convulsive period of upheaval, we could sweep out the old government leadership ourselves and install one willing and able to wrestle corporate greed and irresponsibility to the ground. That was what a revolution would be. Still, my reading of the paper, as well as of the many conversations I was beginning to hear, suggested that any "sweeping out" would not be accomplished without a fight, given the violent nature of our government. I was realizing that I had to reconsider this question of change and violence.

The new supplement to *New Left Notes* was called *Praxis*, which the paper's authors explained meant the unity of theory and practice. In addition to the introduction to the "New Working Class" paper, it also carried an article by Staughton Lynd that looked at radical religious traditions in the United States as they evolved through abolitionism and later labor and social movements. A final article explored attitudes about racism in a white community.

I had just turned twenty-two, and had been at the paper for six weeks. I was in heaven. Along with everyone else I worked twelve to fourteen hours a day, constantly facing new challenges. I took it for granted that every day I'd be learning and doing something I never thought I could do before. We did our best; there was no time to be a perfectionist. Greg made fun of everyone in the office, including himself. He could have a sharp tongue when under attack. Within the office, however, while the engagements might be occasionally fierce, they were never unfriendly.

After working all day into the evening, we hung out together, usually in the national office or at the staff apartment on the block behind the office. We would buy cheap California wine at the liquor store downstairs and talk endlessly about poetry, music, and politics. Greg had a good collection of jazz, so we had access to Coltrane and Miles Davis albums. And of course we had a collective collection of Janis Joplin, Dylan, the Beatles, the Rolling Stones, Jimi Hendrix, and the Doors, as they came out. But mostly we worked, proud of what we accomplished with so few resources. Late at night I caught the bus back to my own home. As cold and desolate as it was, it was the first place of my own and I liked ending each day there.

I wrote to my mother every few weeks telling her stories about my work at the office, even occasionally sharing some political thoughts, and repeating how happy I was. I knew that she was very distressed, and I tried to reassure her, knowing all along that there was little I could write that was truthful that would be the slightest bit reassuring. Fortunately, she was busy at work herself, involved with forming a local library, teaching, and later directing a teacher-training program. She continued to send me the occasional package of cheese, or a dress for my birthday.

By the end of February, our financial crisis deepened, and we had to cut the paper down to four pages. Meanwhile, chapter reports continued to come in. SDS members were running and sometimes being elected for student government positions on platforms fighting against university war research. Chapters were supporting the United Farm Workers grape boycott now spreading across the country to the East Coast. In February, we carried word of another boycott, this time of Levi Strauss in support of a struggle by the workers, mostly in the South, to unionize. As a result, grapes and Levis disappeared from SDS culture. Another article gave the text of a joint statement by SNCC and the Movimiento Pro Independencia, and the University Federation for Independence in Puerto Rico, outlining their similar outlooks and agreeing to work together. Finally there was an article on a gathering of SDS and Student Peace Union activists in Colorado.

Using colorful language to poke fun at themselves, chapter members wrote many articles to celebrate the imaginative tactics they had thought up to identify and protest against war profiteers and, in the process, to organize more people to understand and join. Austin SDS wrote about their Gentle Thursdays, when they urged everyone to gather and talk with people they didn't know, amid music and balloons. These gatherings countered attempts by some to polarize the campus and instead facilitated discussions with jocks and engineering students who had been divided from the movement by culture as much as politics. I liked how we were becoming creative and reaching out rather than acting superior. I put the story on the front page and many other chapters started to have Gentle Thursdays as well.

Being confrontational and inclusive at the same time is a difficult balance to attain. On the one hand we were outraged when people, including fellow students, went along with the war and passively tolerated the violations of civil rights all around us. The outrage was a necessary and powerful context for organizing; it provided moral grounding. If our compatriots continued to screen out both the physical and moral consequences of public policy, then we would find ways to force them to look by disturbing the peace.

Yet we also needed to reach out to these same people and to those who agreed with them, to encourage them to open their eyes and ears to what was going on and to think deeply about it. We *were* angry when we confronted them, but as pacifists understood so well, our anger could not be personal. We were most effective when we overturned the tables of military recruiters or swept their literature into the garbage, but also tried to reason with them about why it was necessary.

I began to have an intuitive sense of the power of this approach and was vaguely aware that it was very different from the work in Chester. There, we had worked to facilitate the strengthening of the community, so that people who already knew the limitations of the system could again have enough hope to fight for access to that system, to fight to make the system work more fairly. Here, the essential task was broadening the perspective of those who had been protected from the consequences of public policy, so that they could see that these consequences would also affect them negatively. As members of a broader community with pretensions of morality, they had to look realistically at what was going on. In the not-too-distant future, the consequences could affect them personally as well, as in the case of the draft.

I had to wrestle with this tension because the underlying emotional issues *were* very personal. I agreed with the pacifists that our anger should not be personal, but I *was* angry—angry at all the people in my past whom I cared about and who seemed content to reap the comforts of the day with little thought to either the immediate or long-term consequences. I expected better of them. I was also angry at the individuals at the top, those who could recommend and order the bombing of civilian populations of North Vietnam, those who stood by while banks refused to give loans to black farmers in the South or black small businesses in the North. I was angry at those who fought school integration. These behaviors seemed to indicate an inhumanity I found hard to fathom. It's hard to muster the necessary empathy for inclusion when angry. On the other hand, collaboration without keeping the moral issues and hard facts front and center was hypocritical and even corrupt.

I wasn't the only one wrestling with these issues; the anger and outrage also began to affect the internal culture of SDS because it infused our deliberations with a growing sense of urgency. As SNCC had already discovered, it was very hard to be a loving community and, at the same time, air a wide range of different perspectives, personal issues, and visions of the future, especially in a world where people were dying on a daily basis. Like many, I felt we should quickly find the best way to proceed, discarding all opposing ideas. It seemed that our decisions had such tremendous consequences.

As I took on more of the work, I began to care more about my ability to influence others. Greg had convinced me that we had to confront the draft head on, advocating refusal or desertion. Those who argued less confrontational approaches, I came to believe, were holding back our efforts to stop the war. Greg, who had been attacked personally as well as politically by some of the old guard, was occasionally provoked to return the personal attacks with equally passionate condemnations. It was tempting to want to silence the opposition.

While a vision of participatory democracy had brought us together, most of us had thought little about the mechanisms that might maximize informed participation on the one hand and efficient decision making on the other. SDS relied on *Robert's Rules of Order* to administer meetings, but as the sense of urgency increased, more and more of us were drawn to the same kind of backroom deals and attempts at emotional vote manipulation that characterized mainstream politics. It was easy to forget that the goal was to *convince* one's opponents, not to humiliate them in order to decrease their power.

It was here, although imperceptible at first, that I began to lose my bearings. It's a direct line from abandoning hope for those close to you, to abandoning hope for the larger population. It wasn't easy to argue and respond to different ideas with clarity and creativity; it was hard to have the patience to change the way someone else perceived themselves and the world. Some changes came so easily to all of us. When other changes met resistance—emotional, intellectual, or in the form of simple inertia—it was easier to dismiss the opposition with contempt than win them over. Complexities would be increasingly glossed over in favor of urgently needed answers to life-threatening problems. Instead of being rich fodder for understanding, these subtleties and apparent contradictions became obstacles that I, along with many others, was eager to "rise above."

On March 27, we put out a twelve-page issue completely dedicated to the draft. I wrote my first piece for *NLN*. Updating Peter's article on the Selective Service System, I wrote about one possible explanation for the proposed SSS lottery system:

> ...the built-in inequalities of the current deferment system have received very clear public visibility [leading to] widespread indignation. [Furthermore]...government and corporate leaders have come to doubt whether the SSS is the best administrative structure to oversee manpower allocation.

The struggle to survive financially continued to cause unending anxiety. To help out, one of the other women who had recently arrived in Chicago introduced me to the art of shoplifting. Once, at seven years old, I circumvented our restricted access to candy by stealing a Three Musketeers bar from the local country store. Somehow I was discovered, and my mother asked my beloved Uncle Arnie, who visited shortly afterwards, to talk to me about the law and about stealing. She thought that as a lawyer, his opinion would carry extra weight. We went alone to the small room that served as a den, and he talked to me about how the laws of the land were what held us together as a people. Furthermore, he told me, Mr. Jones, who owned the store, was not a rich man and worked hard to support *his* family. What I had done was neither moral nor fair. Chastened, I took the money my uncle gave me, and the next time my mother went to the store I gave it to Mr. Jones with my confession and apology. Thoroughly chagrined, I had remained absolutely respectful of the law until my college years when my run-ins with abortion laws began to erode my respect for the law. Even so, I had disapproved of my classmates' shoplifting at the college bookstore.

Since then, I had run across many instances in which laws reinforced behaviors that were injurious to the public welfare. The fact that cigarettes were legal but marijuana, which was considerably less addictive to most people and nowhere near as injurious to their health, was not, further challenged my blind acceptance of laws. I had come to make exceptions regarding laws I believed were immoral or just stupid.

Still, the laws against stealing were neither immoral nor stupid. By 1967, however, after I had learned about the corporate role in national policy, I started to change my mind. They broke the law to undermine unions, pollute the environment, and obtain raw materials through unscrupulous methods abroad. Advertisements told deliberately misleading half-truths and preyed on our vulnerabilities to addiction, and on our insecurities and our fears. Corporations had shown that they were driven by the bottom line and guided by whatever they could get away with. The law only chastised corporations with mild financial penalties when they got caught breaking the regulations that did exist. Rarely did those companies and their officers pay. I was beginning to think that only chumps took the law seriously. If corporations were stealing from us and selling us products that killed, then we too could steal from them to support the movement. We would be modern-day Robin Hoods.

When I began to shoplift, I discovered that all the skills I had developed in learning the manners and mannerisms of a well-mannered young lady made me an excellent thief. I could blend in, mask my emotions, anticipate other's expectations, and project a presence of myself as absolutely acceptable. No one paid attention to me, and if I went to return an item without a receipt, no one thought to question me. Of course I was further assisted by the color of my skin.

Somewhere in the back of my mind, I wondered if matching corporate immorality with my own was the best idea. I knew that in the end, the odds of playing their game and winning were against me, and I only resorted to this tactic when we were desperate. While I took some pride in my skills, I never enjoyed it.

Despite my best efforts, by mid-April SDS was $7,000 in debt, $3,500 of it to the printer. This crisis pushed us further to develop self-sufficiency—both to lower cost in the long run and also to be less susceptible to government interference. Resourceful staffers found a used plate maker (for the metal plates that had to go on the printer) and an enormous, ancient copy camera, and installed it in the office. Through trial and error and a lot of wasted paper, they got it to work. It printed a smudgy four-page edition, but it came out.

By mid-May we had raised enough money to pay off the printer and decided to make a $2,500 down payment on used composition equipment. My subsequent investigation into the world of used office equipment required that I overcome the intimidation of technology that I had absorbed during my youth, and it whetted my appetite to learn more.

Meanwhile, SDS president Carl Oglesby attended the War Crimes Tribunal in Stockholm, along with Courtland Cox from SNCC, Dave Dellinger, Jean-Paul Sartre and Simone de Beauvoir, and North Vietnamese officials, among others. There, an international panel investigated the ongoing series of US violations of international law in Vietnam.

Our efforts to find a site for the June convention were hampered by suspected FBI intervention with Antioch College, the original site. Few places were willing to lease to SDS, by then well-known in the press and perhaps not always the most responsible tenants. Finally, the University of Michigan agreed to rent space, although they also tried to renege later, after being contacted by the FBI. Fortunately we had had the foresight to get a signed contract.

The Chicago winter softened and spring made inroads. My sweet little house, which had been freezing in the winter, began to develop a slightly moldy smell as the weather turned wet. My savings from Wisconsin, with which I had been paying my rent, were running very low. Ellie Brecher, the new literature secretary, needed a place to live so she came to share the tiny space and the rent. I continued hanging out at the staff apartment in the evenings with Ellie, John Veneziale, Jeanne Peak, Greg, Dee Jacobsen, and others who stayed for a week or more. I loved the far-ranging conversations. It was there that I learned more about Marxism and the Wobblies, and about anarchists. Jeanne taught me about brown rice and inexpensive wine.

On May 29, *NLN* printed a position paper authored by Paul Potter, Hal Benenson, and Sarah Eisenstein that continued the debate about student power. Noting the ease with which we could organize students to act regarding issues of their own infantilization by colleges, the authors observed that it was not a given that students would move from there to a willingness to put time into demonstrations and into organizing work on deeper social justice and peace issues. Another conversation that spring revolved around the ongoing debate about whether, and if so, how, SDS should include young people who had left the universities and were now wage earners in a wide range of professions and hourly positions. Many current SDS members were beginning to talk about forming "adult" branches of SDS, naming their groups Movement for a Democratic Society chapters.

The national office staff continued to prepare for the annual five-day convention, coming up in June. Each chapter had one vote for every five members, monitored by a credentials committee. With over five thousand SDS members, over a thousand young people might come. In between, decisions were made by the quarterly national council meetings where each chapter got one vote for every twenty-five members. Most national officers were so exhausted after a term in the national office that they were eager to move on to other projects. The national office staff, like much of SDS, believed that national leadership could quickly get out of touch with the membership if we didn't rotate frequently, so we prepared to move on just like the elected officers.

I thought about whether I wanted to stay and develop my skills on the paper, to learn how to edit and develop a network of reporters. I knew the position had the potential to be fascinating and that by pursuing it I could develop a career that would carry me beyond SDS. I also talked with

Peter Henig about coming to New York where several of the "power structure research" folks were congregating, working on various projects and publications. I deeply admired the work that he and others were doing, and thought that by working with them for a while I could deepen my knowledge of the world and how it was that our democracy had turned out so unfairly. I felt that I would have to spend years, however, reading, digesting, and doing more research before I had the skills and knowledge required to contribute to the theoretical work. Many scholars were already hard at work, such as Felix Greene, whom I had met briefly in California at the December 1966 national council, and Wilfred Burchett, not to mention people in SDS who were much more skilled than I— Greg, Pete, Carl Oglesby, Tom Hayden, Al Haber, Michael Klare, Carol Brightman of *Viet-Report*, Jane Adams, and the authors of the *Praxis* paper. I decided instead that I would rather be out on the front lines, on the campuses confronting Dow Chemicals, Defense Secretary Robert McNamara, and State Department Secretary Dean Rusk.

I wanted to try my own hand at educating about the war, the civil rights movement, farm workers, and the striking Levi Strauss workers. Helping people break through passivity caused by misinformation was the most exciting and important challenge for me. The newspaper played a role in helping people take control of their lives, but I wanted to design programs that reached out on the local level to engage people. I knew I had learned the most in concrete programs in Cambridge and Chester, and I wanted to help others—especially young people—become involved in the same kind of concrete efforts on campus.

Where would I go? I knew little about the West Coast still, and no place in the Midwest jumped off the map at me. I didn't want to go to New York, where I found the movement culture to be competitive and overly intellectual. Boston and Philadelphia were too close to the world of my childhood. Somewhat randomly, I thought about Washington, DC. I had worked there for two summers so I knew the city fairly well, or at least parts of it, and liked it. There were very few SDS members in Washington, and only a few chapters, at the University of Maryland, American University, and Georgetown University. There was no antidraft program at all. There were a few older SDS members, including Art Waskow, Lee Webb, and Marilyn Salzman Webb, but they were not out organizing on local campuses. One University of Maryland SDS member, Mark Steiner, had told Greg that he would help anyone coming from the national office.

As the national convention approached, I concentrated on putting out a major thirty-two page convention issue. I rarely left the office that week. The issue carried stories about the Provos in the Netherlands who did early political performance art like fixing up old bicycles, painting them purple, and setting them out around the city for people to ride and leave for others to ride as they needed, challenging the root value of individual property, and modeling the possibility of free public transportation. Michael Klare wrote about secret war-related research on campuses and in consortiums of universities. Several of the remaining ERAP projects sent in reports, as did many campus chapters. In April, Martin Luther King had called for a summer of organizing around Vietnam, envisioning a program modeled on the 1964 Mississippi Summer. Marilyn Salzman Webb wrote about how some SDS members had planned a Vietnam Summer, a project geared to engage students in educating and mobilizing people in small communities across the country to stand against the war.

At the convention, I worked with Peter, Greg, and others to pass a draft organizing resolution that reaffirmed SDS's opposition to conscription in any form and again encouraged the formation of draft resistance unions to disseminate information about all the ways, legal and illegal, to avoid conscription. The resolution also mandated SDS to support organizing within the military by disseminating information and providing support for all GIs who wanted to get out of the military. I decided that the creation of a draft resistance union in Washington should be one of my first tasks.

The other moment when I was most focused at the convention came during the Women's Liberation Workshop. Jane Adams, Jeanne Peak, Elizabeth Sutherland (who had also worked with SNCC), and Susan Cloke wrote a draft resolution, developing many of the ideas presented in 1965 by Hayden and King. Much as Malcolm X and some SNCC activists had popularized the idea that black people in the United States represented an internal colony with lower wages, fewer rights, and a legacy of brutality against those who protested, the women's resolution argued that women also were maintained in a colonial, exploitative relationship by men. While the resolution set a broad context for an analysis of women's position in society, most of the particulars focused on the experience of women in the movement. It called for communal child care and the equal sharing of housework between the adults. It called on men in SDS to acknowledge and give up the privileges bestowed on them by their gender and to join women in making sure that women had full access to responsibility and leadership. Finally, the resolution called for reproductive rights for all women. The authors also called for a committee to take up the task of developing a fuller analysis of the position of women in society and to generate programs dedicated to women's rights.

At the workshop, women debated the proposal and more than a dozen women helped write the final formulations. This was SDS's internal democracy at its best. The discussions raised many questions. How were women different than men? What differences were biological and which were rooted in culture? How had women been kept second-class citizens? While many of these women had been wrestling with these questions for the past two years, the issues were new to me. I was impressed that these women had thought so deeply about them, and that they were coming up with complex answers. I wondered why I had not thought about it more, especially after Jane's earlier article.

At the same time, I still reacted cautiously to the enthusiasm some women showed for concentrating their efforts on organizing women. I agreed with the resolution's conclusion that women could only find their freedom in the context of freedom for all people, and so it seemed important that women continue to work with everyone on all the big issues facing us. The issues that had originally brought me to participate in the movement were the issues of civil rights, poverty, and the war. I believed that these issues were the way to reach other young people, both women and men. Nonetheless, the examples given in the paper, about how women had been prevented access to all kinds of jobs, leadership positions, and the ability to chart their own futures, all rang true to me, and it seemed important that all of SDS agree that these practices, like racism, had to be urgently addressed and changed.

When the proposal was read to the assembled body, a man jumped up and wanted to open the analysis for discussion of the whole group, saying he disagreed with it. The woman who had read the resolution announced that the analysis was not open for debate in the whole body, that women had arrived at their own analysis and the whole body could pass it or not as it was. Pandemonium erupted.[8] Here it was again, the idea that the members of a group that was treated unfairly by another group had both the right and the need to analyze how that treatment worked and how it felt, without interference. When some men tried to bully women into submitting the analysis to the group, I, along with most women and a few of the men, was outraged. This disrespectful reaction by men convinced me that women *did* need to take on the issues of women's roles in the movement, as well as in the larger society. Despite a period of chaos, the debate was not opened up, and the resolution was finally passed.

That summer, after I left Chicago, many of the women who had led or participated in the workshop continued to meet. Heather Booth and Naomi Weisstein led a course on women at the Center for Radical Research, a radical think tank set up briefly by SDS graduates, while Marilyn Webb and Sue Thrasher analyzed women's work during their months together in the Vietnam Summer office in Boston. Jane called a meeting of women in the SDS national office.[9] These conversations continued the ferment, fueling the formation of more formal groups of women in the fall and winter. I would reconnect with their work later in the winter when Marilyn Webb started a group of women in Washington.

At the convention, I felt a tremendous sense of release. It was a time to celebrate my new community of friends and the hard work of the past six months. While I was fully engaged in many of the discussions, I also partied hard. On the second afternoon, I left one of the workshops with two or three people from the national office, and a regional traveler from the East Coast, and the four of us each took a tab of LSD and lay on the grass under the trees in a sparsely traveled section of the campus. I paired off with the regional traveler, and we swirled into an hours-long examination of how people communicate with each other, a topic of great importance in our lives as educators and organizers. We ended up lying head to head, while it seemed like ideas flowed back and forth from my brain to his and back again. How, I wondered, can another person possibly understand how I *feel*—or I them—because when the feeling is translated into words it loses the context within which it was born, cut adrift without anchor or mast. These explorations into consciousness, or unconsciousness, were heady and fascinating when they worked but they could also be equally fearful or humiliating when they didn't. For me, the critical determinant was the degree of trust. These infrequent explorations added a new dimension to the thinking many of us were doing about democracy, human nature, and freedom.

At the end of the convention, national officers were elected for the coming year. I was nominated for and elected to the national interim committee, the monthly advisory and interim decision-making body. I was proud to be elected, and I also thought I was a good candidate for the job. With this election and my impending move to Washington, I felt that my role as apprentice was changing into that of full participant and even, a little bit, into that of a leader.

That spring, on Madison Street, we had explored new ways of being with each other, new music and food, and new ways of imagining our futures. I found the process exhilarating, with my enormous abundance of energy finally allowed to run unchecked as I tried to engage with the problems of life and the world without the fear of constant humiliation. I found the continual self-analysis we did—of the world, of the movement, and ourselves—to be fascinating.

After the convention, I returned briefly to Chicago to help train the new editor of *NLN*. I then traveled east with several friends, including Tom Bell from Cornell, listening to Motown on radio stations along the way. We stayed briefly at his home in rural Massachusetts, where we all helped Tom and his wife put up a large crop of green beans while listening to Cream, The Band, and the Doors. This was the year of the summer of love in San Francisco. The Beatles transformed themselves, and the Rolling Stones hardened.

I left from there to visit my family briefly. Relations with my mother continued to be extremely strained, but I could think of no way to make her feel better. I then spent a couple of weeks in Boston, western Massachusetts, and New York, visiting friends, reading, and conferring with other organizers. During this period I read a recent issue of *Monthly Review* magazine, which contained a work by French writer Régis Debray called *Revolution in the Revolution*. Debray had traveled to Cuba to interview Che Guevara, Fidel Castro, and other new leaders of Cuba who had come to power in 1959, after many years of demonstrations, popular uprisings, and a short war.

Debray did not go into detail about the goals of the Cuban government headed by Castro, beyond celebrating the enormous achievements in literacy and child health that had been gained in just eight years, bringing the infant mortality rate *below* that of the United States. He, like most advocates for poor and working people, saw Cuba as an early example of the popular uprisings that were sweeping the world at the time. Poor farmers were seeking to repossess land that had been seized by large United States or European magnates with the help of corrupt, local elites. Without control of the land, either productive agricultural soils or mineral-rich subsoils, local people could not hope to become economically self-reliant.

Just as Oglesby had described the way the US manipulated the political and economic institutions in many countries in Latin America, Debray gave concrete examples of the devastating work of the CIA in Cuba. It had funded and trained intelligence and death squads that would identify and destroy both intellectual and peasant leaders of the opposition. Debray then analyzed the theoretical assumptions, the beliefs, and dreams of those who fought successfully to overthrow the Batista regime in Cuba, and the reasons their efforts had been successful.

Finally, Debray put forth his theory of how to pursue liberation struggles, as he believed Che understood it. This was Debray's famous *foco* theory. He believed that political consciousness sprang from action, and so political leadership should then necessarily spring from activists (as opposed to theorists). In guerrilla warfare, he wrote, the action would necessarily have to be carried out in small groups (as opposed to armies), and it was the community bonds within the small groups and their commitment to action that endowed them with the insight and right to lead.

Although Debray's Cuban activists eventually engaged in armed struggle, they had initially focused on public confrontations over local injustices, just as we were doing now in the United States. It was not the military aspect of Debray's work that excited me, but his organizational theory, because he gave those of us engaged in the actual outreach and organizing a new authority. The lessons from our experience should guide the movement, not a theoretical overview. Our local organizations had legitimacy in and of themselves. The idea of *foco* groups also made me think about the idea of "guerrilla propaganda," small groups engaging in creative, startling actions that had an element of fun or beauty, and that surprised people, challenged their assumptions, and made them think. It fit in with my desire to be confrontational, but I wasn't thinking our confrontations would involve violence.

I was riding on a bus from Boston to Albany, along the recently completed Massachusetts turnpike, part of the massive interstate highway system that was constructed during the 1960s and that contributed to our lightheaded sense of mobility. As the lush green of the local New England woods sped by, I read about guerrilla bands forming into small *focos* to fight a mobile war against neocolonial governments. I wondered if eventually our own popular attempts to fight against discrimination and to build a healthier economy would also be subverted by electoral fraud, bribery, and physical intimidation. Was it possible that eventually we too would be deprived of electoral alternatives, or have our leaders targeted by assassins? Would we too have to retreat to the hills and resort to guerrilla warfare? I could see how we might have to learn how to operate with some protection from the increasing surveillance and interference of the FBI. At this point, though, we were contending only with annoying, crackling phones at the national office, with FBI interference with convention sites and local chapter functions, and with missing and opened mail and misinformation from the press. It was hard to imagine guerrilla warfare in the US. My private speculations remained in the realm of fantasy, more guided by Robin Hood and Peter Pan than by contemporary revolutionaries.

While I was reading Debray, news came in of an eruption of pent-up anger and frustration in Newark, New Jersey, which became a three-day rebellion with more than two dozen killed and hundreds of structures burned. Not too long afterward, Detroit experienced a similar eruption. The emotions that had boiled over in Watts just two years before had enabled the poor in every city to imagine a new kind of voice. The specter of a race war, a fearful possibility if people were mobilized only by frustration, fear and despair, seemed all the more likely. There could be no winners in such a confrontation. It was urgent that we find ways to bring a political perspective to people who were suffering, but who did not have a coherent plan for change.

My other reading that summer was Franz Fanon's book *The Wretched of the Earth*, which looked at colonialism and its effect on the inhabitants of Africa as Oglesby and Debray had done in Latin America. Fanon came from Martinique, a French colony in the Caribbean, and had trained as a psychiatrist in France. After completing the requirements for his degrees, he was sent to a clinic in the French colony of Algeria, as part of the French administration.

After World War II, independence movements in colonies around the world argued that if the US and European powers believed in democracy and self-rule then it was hypocritical for them to maintain colonies by force. The difficulties of defending empire were clear: Britain had lost India to a massive independence movement immediately after the war; in 1949, China had ousted Japan, the United States, Britain, and all other colonial powers who intended to stake claims after the war; and by 1954 France had acknowledged defeat in Vietnam. In 1959, as Fanon had begun writing his book, the Cuban guerrillas had overthrown Batista.

These anticolonial wars added astronomical costs to colonial administration, making the whole enterprise unprofitable. In many instances, colonial powers ceded nominal political independence while holding on to economic holdings and ambitions. Fanon watched European governments and the United States cultivate ruling elites with an appetite for

Western wealth. These kings, emirs, and presidents allowed foreign investors to maintain control over water, land, and transportation routes and channeled almost all economic profits to go to Europe and the United States. Little was delegated for the development of indigenous economic structures. In payment these rulers received ample, sometimes fabulous sums for personal use.

Fanon titled his first chapter "Violence." In it he documented the extensive and varied kinds of violence employed by European powers in their competitive quest for control over African resources, and the effect it had on the people living in those countries. Fanon came to believe that the only way Africans—and he mainly concerned himself with men— could reassert their humanity, put back together their traumatized, fragmented selves, was to rise up against those who deprived them of their humanity. He was profoundly influenced by the experiences of the Viet- namese, whose victory in 1954 had given local independence movements all over the world great hope, hope that small, poorly armed and trained indigenous movements could in fact defend themselves against the most powerful military powers in the world.

Fanon's assertion that the act of taking up arms against an oppressor actually triggered and supported a healing process in hearts depressed and infantalized by oppression, was a dramatic new idea, at least for me. The act of taking up arms against a seemingly all-powerful oppressor could, he said, in and of itself, transform a person's despair and passivity into hope and a desire to live again. Furthermore, the *joint* commitment to take up arms against the settlers also helped, he said, to rebuild unity and a sense of community among people who had previously been feuding under colonial rule.

Fanon directly confronted pacifism as a strategy for change, identifying the pacifists as those who, in the end, were seeking to share power with the colonizers, looking for dialogue and compromise. The pacifists' assumption, that it was possible to *convince* their opponents, was false when it came to neocolonialists whose administrators were acting at the behest of a system that was *not* human, but which had absolute market require- ments. It was not possible to convince the system.

Fanon also argued that violence had recently become a viable political tactic because the developed countries now needed their colonies and neocolonies not only for raw materials and labor, but also for markets. Total destabilization caused by violence disrupted markets and the free flow of goods, just at a time when the big companies in these countries needed to expand beyond their own shores.

Finally, Fanon's careful study of the effects of colonial violence included not only Algerians and other Africans who came through his clinic, but those of his patients who were suffering as the result of supervising and executing the violence as part of the colonial administration. In the section on case studies at the end of the book, Fanon included stories of Europeans to show that colonial repression was also toxic to those who inflicted it.

Never did Fanon romanticize or glorify violence. He accepted the reality of colonial violence, and his research indicated that those who responded with anger, who determined to fight back by any means necessary, were emotionally the healthiest and most whole human beings. While I had embraced Debray's *foco* theory quickly, Fanon challenged my beliefs and assumptions on a much deeper level. His analysis seemed clear and indisputable, passionate and moral. Certainly by then I had already come to support the right of the Vietnamese to resist US incursions into their country. I was questioning pacifism as a political strategy, not so much to replace it, but to consider how it could be more effective. In the South, it had seemed very powerful, but it had not worked with the same moral persuasiveness in the antiwar movement or in the struggle for political and economic equality in the North. I didn't know why exactly.

After reading Fanon, I wondered how his analysis might apply to members of colonial powers who did not support their own governments, like those of us in the movement. Were we bound to support others' armed struggles, or would Fanon carry it a step further and argue that we too needed to engage in armed struggle to heal our own identities?

I was determined that women be understood to be full-fledged agents of change too, so how did the alleged healing aspect of violence apply to us? Was it especially important that women engage in armed struggle because we ourselves had been in a colonial relationship to men? By say-

ing that we too could respond to violence with violence, were we stepping up to be fully equal members of the community? Would it be
possible for men to rape women if we took up arms? Was it possible that
as long as men were the ones to take up arms to defend people they would
always hold a superior position vis à vis women? If women showed that
we could, and would, also sacrifice our lives to fight for freedom, could
we then turn to face our brothers on equal ground? All of the images of
patriotism instilled in me in grammar school and by the mud-splattered
soldiers in World War II movies fueled my deliberations. Rather than being
the passive girlfriend waiting to receive back her wounded hero, I now
wanted to take my own place in history.

I was not aware then of how profoundly Fanon's analysis was framed
by the male experience. In the case studies at the end of his book, Fanon
discussed the impotence of a man whose wife had been raped by a colonial soldier, but the effect of rape on the woman is not mentioned. Fanon
never looked at his assumed connection between his definition of mental
health and the ability of Algerian men to protect, and dominate, their own
women.

Fanon's argument about the elitism of pacifists was particularly trou-
bling. Was it true that we were up against Adam Smith's "invisible hand"
and not Paul Potter's good men who do bad things?

Despite my first considerations of violence, I still could not begin to
imagine what it would look like in this country. Malcolm X had said "by
any means necessary" and I had wondered what he meant. Debray argued
that reform was impossible without first destroying the state, or the government, as had happened in the 1917 revolution in Russia. Fanon argued
that not only was violence necessary to accomplish the goal of independence, it was essential to the healing of the emasculated victims of
colonialism. With all these questions framed in my head, and no easy
answers forthcoming, Fanon and Debray became critical touchstones as I
weighed further ideas, movement goals, and strategies during the next
couple of years.

CHAPTER SIX

WASHINGTON SDS

▪ ▪

By mid-August 1967, I was on the train to Washington, where I stayed temporarily in my sister Ann's small railroad flat across from the train station. She had just completed one year with VISTA,[1] working in rural eastern Kentucky, and was now working for the Quakers at the Washington office of the American Friends Service Committee. We shared a common opposition to the war, but we were wary of delving too deeply into our political thinking, sensing that many disagreements lay just below the surface. While the Quakers were some of the most active and creative of the early antiwar forces, they held steadfastly to their commitment to pacifism and did not openly support the National Front for the Liberation of South Vietnam (NLF) as I now did. Besides, what would Ann think of my experimentation, however minimal, with psychedelics, or with the communal living situations that had become standard for the movement? SDS had embraced alternative lifestyles far more than the Friends did.

Perhaps the most significant difference between us was her ability to maintain a cordial if not warm relationship with my parents, her friends from college, and her past. I was increasingly feeling like an outsider because I had come to identify with many sectors of society at odds with the social world of my upbringing. Ann's curiosity about people led her to reach across class and racial barriers to form friendships, while I needed to become part of a community before I knew how to reach out that way. I couldn't bear to have anyone assume, even for a moment, that I accepted the racism that was so inherent within the culture, yet I knew that my looks, my background, and my family history led people to make those assumptions unless I actively disassociated myself from the subtly racist jokes and disparaging comments about working people. When I spoke up in response, the social contract was shattered, leaving me to feel like an accuser, always the surly, hostile, ungrateful one. But if I didn't speak up, my silence lent power to the words of the dominant culture. Ann became one of the few people I talked with who was able to move easily between those worlds. Despite the growing gulf, she always welcomed me and affirmed our bond, and she never judged me overtly.

A vibrant, multifaceted community of activists lived in Washington, including those who worked at community centers, the Institute for Policy Studies, the beginnings of an alternative clinic, a bookstore, and coffee shop. The underground newspaper, the *Washington Free Press* (*WFP*), started the previous year, covered a wide range of topics: the antiwar and student movements, with reports from each of the five major campuses in the area; the dozen or so existing or new peace and antiwar organizations; the black community's concerns about welfare, housing, and police brutality; black political organizations; and the growing youth culture. Reporters passed on medical advice about drugs and venereal disease, and wrote about the fight for legalized abortion. Right from the start, *Free Press* reporters insisted on their place in the large Washington press corps. They obtained press passes, and when denied entry to briefings or other events, they protested and threatened court action until they were admitted.

Sheila Ryan wrote about the connections between Democratic Party leaders and the Institute of International Labor Research, an organization that designed and set up "left" parties in seventeen Latin American countries, supporting them with funds from the CIA. The leaders of these parties then helped the United States to orchestrate the installation of politicians loyal to the United States, like Bosch in the Dominican Republic, without showing their hand too obviously. *WFP* writers also researched connections between local political people, including a few in the peace movement, and CIA-funded foundations and institutes. Through these articles, and others published in *Ramparts* magazine during the same period, I learned to search for the funding behind any foundation, organization, or institute and to stay suspicious of the hidden hand of the CIA, which in the name of democracy often sought to undermine local grassroots forces.

Along with this diverse fare of news and opinion, the newspaper was full of photographs and graphics, many of them psychedelic drawings or re-creations of art nouveau drawings by Beardsley and others. The look of the paper was distinctly different than the traditional political publication, and it drew young people like flypaper. The generally excellent quality of the writing allowed young people with little initial interest in politics to gain access to information and opinion that helped them make sense of their world.

The day I arrived I got on the phone and set up meetings with various contacts I had gotten from the national office and friends of friends, including Mark Steiner and his partner Debbie Stone, from the University of Maryland; Art Waskow from the Institute for Policy Studies; and Peter Henig's friend from Earlham, Marilyn McNabb. Marilyn, an SDS member, had come to Washington to work with the Friends Committee on National Legislation. She, like Peter and Sheila, was drawn to the task of teasing apart the connections between the various circles of power in the country, and in so doing, showed how these circles knowingly served each other. I soon met several people from the *Free Press* as well. Everyone was friendly and receptive to the idea of setting up an SDS region.

I needed a permanent place to live, and I wanted to set up an office for a draft resistance union. Several of those I had met, including Marilyn, were open to getting a place together where we could minimize expenses for all of us. Without much trouble we were able to rent a large house in Northwest Washington with six (or seven if you counted the front parlor) bedrooms for $250 a month, which came out to only about $40 a month per bedroom. If couples shared a room, it would be only $20 each. I used up the last of my savings and borrowed money from the national office to make the initial payment.

We had no furniture to speak of except a large empty cable spool we had found on the street and rolled back to deposit in the dining room. It became our collective table where we often shared the evening meal, sitting around it on the floor. The kitchen had a small back staircase leading up to the second and third floors, each of which had three bedrooms and a bath. Like everyone else, I worked a series of part-time jobs and kept my expenses to a bare minimum, subsisting on oatmeal and peanut butter, living in a noncash world. This income and the occasional birthday and Christmas cash presents from my family sufficed.

On Labor Day weekend, I flew standby youth fare to Chicago for one of the regular monthly meetings of the national interim committee. Also that weekend in Chicago was the National Conference on New Politics (NCNP), a coalition that had been laying the groundwork for a new electoral party representing those wanting social change. Although Art Waskow and others from the Institute for Policy Studies were heavily involved in the work, SDS stayed aloof, now firmly believing electoral politics to be a black hole absorbing energy that could better be spent organizing more people to work on specific issues, especially the draft.

Wanting their effort to have the backing of blacks as well as whites, the NCNP organizers had invited James Forman and H. Rap Brown from SNCC to speak. Forman, an important veteran and leader of SNCC, had just returned from a trip to Africa, reaffirming his perception that the liberation movements in South Africa, Mozambique, Angola, and Zimbabwe were following the example of Vietnam and were leading change in the world. He saw the efforts to achieve civil rights and to address the root causes of poverty in the United States as part of this worldwide movement. Forman and other black leaders were frustrated by the slow pace of change, especially the interminable setbacks in addressing poverty. They had come to believe that movements that addressed the issue of power and that committed themselves to acquiring the power to govern, were more advanced than those attempting only to convince existing governments to change. All of the movements in southern Africa had mobilized to form armed guerrilla bands once they became convinced the existing governments would not submit to any form of popular, democratic change. Forman had a long track record working with nonviolent movements in the South, but unlike SNCC leaders like James Lawson and Diane Nash, or SCLC's Martin Luther King, he saw nonviolence only as a necessary tactic in a volatile, violent environment; it had never been part of a spiritual belief or a way of life for him.

Forman's speech to the NCNP startled most white participants. He demanded that regardless of the composition of the new party, black participants should control fifty percent of the votes as a way of acknowledging the leadership of national liberation movements in world change. As the leading movement of people of color in the US, Forman claimed that black people were the local representatives of this worldwide struggle. He went on to demand that unless the new party denounced Israel's aggression against the Palestinians, no blacks would participate at all in the NCNP. These were two enormous issues injected into a gathering of people with no preparation and with few of the skills necessary to take them on in this diverse setting. Needless to say, the ensuing acrimonious debate led quickly to chaos and a collapse of the effort to form a new political party.

While few people today remember or have heard of this event, it affected all further efforts to form a progressive electoral party for decades. Before any strong alliances or unity could be forged, the full complexity of issues involved would have to be acknowledged, and a widespread conversation generated to explore them. How could we recognize the unique history of black–white relations in the United States and the multiple voices and perspectives on that history? How should people in the United States relate to movements for national independence? Was military engagement the ultimate form of contesting power? What were the legitimate criteria upon which a people could claim a homeland, whether it be Jewish refugees from pogroms and the Holocaust, displaced Palestinians, black citizens of the United States, or brutalized ethnic minorities around the world? What was the relationship between religious fundamentalism and oppression? Can church and state ever be combined without causing a massive abrogation of the individual rights? On what basis should contested claims for land and resources be negotiated, especially when there was a history of oppression (and there almost always was)?

These critical and difficult questions remain at the center of world events. It was no wonder that activists at that time were in way over our heads. Just to name these questions and put them squarely on the agenda was challenging, and rarely were such challenges executed gracefully. This one certainly was not. The demand for leadership from black activists, and their attempts to imagine organizational and programmatic implementation of this demand would distract the black movement and divide it within itself and from other movements for years to come. At the same time, the conversations that flowed from this demand challenged activists of all races and backgrounds to explore and negotiate new terms of discourse between those who had suffered extreme consequences of collective exploitation and those who had not. We continue to grapple with this discourse today.

Significantly, the other issue that erupted at the NCNP concerned the voices of women. Several of the women who had been meeting together decided that without a concerted effort by women, the issue of women's equality would be ignored at the conference, and women themselves largely excluded from positions of leadership in the new party. They prepared a statement of analysis and a program, and won a slot to speak to the gathering. Their presentation, scheduled to come after Forman's, however, was silenced by the furor over Forman's speech. The session ended with women's voices unheard yet again.

The experience left many women angry but with no consensus about a way to grapple with the issues raised by Forman. Nor could they agree on a strategy to insist that Forman hear the silenced women's voices and recognize them as critical allies. Even though I was in Chicago at the time, and I did not hear about the women's efforts until later, I did hear about the uproar over Forman's speech. Clearly, I thought, there was not sufficient consensus on the local level to allow for a national political party truly founded on a democratic basis. I was still soured on electoral politics and thought that the way to engage people to think and care about the issues was to concentrate on the local work against the war and poverty. There, we could explore the ways that racism and sexism affected us on societal, organizational, and individual levels. I accepted the necessity of divisions for the time being. Clearly something positive was happening as black activists separated out and explored their history, identity, and voice. I didn't see any urgency for working it all out. If the dialogue was sharp and at times accusatory, well, we were still learning how to listen. My own personal fascination was now directed to new organizational forms like the *focos*, which seemed to have so much more potential.

At the national interim committee meeting I made a proposal to apply Debray's *foco* theory to student organizing: to see campus SDS chapters as small, mostly self-reliant, and self-generating activist groups taking on the broadest responsibilities for organizing other young people. Greg, also on the interim committee, had deepened this idea, talking about how this was a forum for students to see how their own liberation was interrelated with that of others. While the national interim committee did not do anything with the idea, it remained my vision for how I wanted to organize in Washington. I didn't see any immediate contradiction between Forman's insistence on black leadership and my own ideas about organizing white people on campus. Black activists should get to argue about the terms with which white and black related. I saw none of the complexities in the argument. I considered the idea of nationalism primarily in the context of national liberation, not connecting it to my earlier reading on the history of nationalism in Europe and its positive and negative impacts.

By mid-September we were settled into the house. Marilyn, who was now working as a researcher for *Ramparts* magazine, had brought in two friends, Margie Stamberg, who was working for the *Washington Free Press*, and Elaine Fuller, from the Friends Committee on National Legislation. Another room was taken by a biracial couple from Howard University. I was busy traveling to the five major campuses in the area: University of Maryland in College Park, American University, George Washington University, Georgetown University, and DC Teachers College. I was looking up people who subscribed to *New Left Notes* and learning about the history of SDS work in the area. Maryland, George Washington, and Georgetown already had small functioning chapters. I set about trying to meet the members of those chapters and to set up regular meetings on the other campuses.

At that time, many campuses were challenging their colleges' ROTC programs, arguing that the university was not the place to train people to kill. SDS chapters were also organizing opposition to military recruiters and to war research that they had exposed, mobilizing both student and faculty opposition. I continued to grapple with the tension between confrontations and education. Was it a violation of free speech to challenge the right of recruiters and war researchers to work on campus? Were there limits to free speech when the speech resulted in people being killed? While there was little consensus on the details, our goal was to make it harder for people to continue going about their lives without addressing the questions of war, poverty and race. People were suffering and dying, and it was immoral to pretend it wasn't so and to pretend that our own tax dollars and leaders weren't a major part of the problem.

In keeping with my original plan, I also went to work setting up a draft resistance union to support opposition to the draft in the Washington area. While I focused on these tasks, others around the country were mobilizing with dizzying momentum. Hundreds of demonstrations that fall included several major confrontations. On October 17, police attacked a few hundred University of Wisconsin students demonstrating against Dow Chemical recruiters. The ensuing melee—dozens of students were bloodied, two were unconscious, and local hospitals were under instructions not to send ambulances—provoked thousands of students to shut down the campus. Also in early October, radical Catholic pacifists broke into a Selective Service office and poured blood over all the files. The newly formed Vietnam Veterans Against the War began organizing other veterans to speak out publicly against the war. Young black activists in Oakland, California, formed a new group called the Black Panther Party.

The spirit to move from protest to resistance, as Greg had invoked in SDS the previous spring, was now bubbling up all over. We wanted to not only protest and expose university complicity, but also actually disrupt the cogs of the war machine—stop recruiters, interfere with the induction process—and generally gum up the works. There was little clarity whether that meant we were still committed to nonviolent tactics of the civil rights movement or if it meant a new kind of militancy in which demonstrators responded with violence to the consistent aggression and violence of the police.

The Oakland Stop the Draft Week, October 16–29, 1967, was among the first large demonstrations in which demonstrators planned ahead of time to respond to police assaults with mobile street-fighting tactics. Members of the Resistance, the radical pacifist group, initiated a coalition to plan the event, which quickly drew the full spectrum of movement activists in the Bay Area. These young people brought with them a wide variety of beliefs about the world, goals for change, and ideas and intuitions about strategies to achieve these goals.

On the first day, five hundred young men handed in their draft cards. In the days that followed, the slogan changed from "We won't go!" to "Nobody goes!" On Tuesday, over two thousand young people amassed before dawn to shut down the induction center. As demonstrators congregated around the entrances, hundreds of riot-clad police, apparently apprised of the plan by police informants who had attended the planning meetings, emerged from underground parking lots in formation to attack participants from several directions. They swung clubs, squirted mace, and charged at people with horses, injuring dozens.

After staggering initially, the marchers regrouped to surround their captured friends and prevent police from putting them in police cars. Others gave way to charging police and then vanished, only to reemerge around the block at the rear of the police offensive, throwing rocks and lighting cars on fire. Because the police were initially unprepared for this response, demonstrators were largely successful in regaining control of the streets and in shutting down the induction center for at least several hours, if not all day. There were, however, many arrests and some serious injuries. By Friday, the number of demonstrators had doubled and many had formed themselves into little *focos*, planning mobile street fighting instead of fixed lines of demonstrators presenting themselves to be assaulted by the police.

Many of those who were present were exhilarated by the sense of power that seemed to come from so many young people breaking down barriers of compliance, fighting back against the violence of the police with their own violence. One of the eager participants, Todd Gitlin, wrote a few weeks later,

> I hear that some SNCC guys were saying, after Washington [the Pentagon demonstration], OK boys, you've become men now,

we're ready to talk. They're right.... Of course the politics of the Oakland insurrection like those of the Mobilization are hazy. The point is that people have demonstrated their seriousness....[2]

In recent years I have reflected on the many forces and impulses that energized this new spirit of militancy. There's no question that young white men in the movement, like black men, were searching for new definitions of masculinity. They perhaps needed to prove that they were not refusing to fight in Vietnam because they were cowards, as they were so often called by taunting war supporters. As the civil rights movement spread north, young, politically active black men were emerging from a culture shaped by hundreds of years of forced humiliation at the hands of whites, and needed to celebrate their hard-fought, and still limited, new freedom to be confrontational. Both white and black men also were searching for a response to and a sense of commonality with the violence of dozens of urban riots the past summer. Besides, it *was* hard, as Greg said in his book, to face police violence without acting preemptively to try to protect oneself, without retaliating. I heard no one question the ethics of accepting an existing paradigm in which manhood and power were ultimately determined by physical force and aggression. The idea of fighting back was too new for most of us.

Although only a few women were moved to take up the front lines, many women also felt the exhilaration of fighting back, throwing the tear-gas canisters back, letting air out the tires of police cruisers, throwing rocks, and setting fires in trash cans. Women helped barricade the intersections and cheered as the canisters went flying back.

But as both Greg and Todd noted, beyond the moment, the point of all this militancy was unclear. There was certainly no consensus about goals. Was it an end to the draft? An end to the war? A voice of outrage at the government's moral choices? The building of a vast movement for vast change? A revolution? What was the strategy for reaching those goals, and how did the demonstrations fit in? One rationale, familiar to all young people, was that if you cannot be heard, create chaos. Many, I think, hoped that the rising chaos would move the government to withdraw from Vietnam. Mayhem is the weapon of the powerless, as the French learned in Algeria. Yippie Marvin Garson "described this new militancy as more 'street theater' than 'insurrection.' ...The moral of our play is that you cannot have imperialistic war abroad and social peace at home."[3]

A few weeks later, activist Jeff Jones noted that he "was torn between politics and mayhem" when his friend, artist Ben Morea, proposed breaking away from the Pentagon demonstration to trash downtown office buildings.[4] Morea, in fact, had previously challenged SDS to match the revolutionary fervor of a mostly black organization called the Revolutionary Action Movement (RAM), after its members had been arrested for attempting to bomb the Statute of Liberty. He then went on to form an anarchist band on the Lower East Side called the Motherfuckers, that did creative, absurdist agitprop theater around local issues.

Many believed that just shutting down the induction center for a few hours a day was one small step in impeding the war makers. Others took the swelling crowds to mean that urban guerrilla warfare could not be far behind. In the face of this focus on the movement's impact on the government, it was sometimes hard to also keep in mind whether these tactics positively or negatively affected our ability to convince more people about the illegality and immorality of the war and to become active participants against it. If these big ideas of strategy were discussed, however, it was among small groups of friends in living rooms or cafes and not in any coherent political forum.

It wasn't long before I encountered the issue of militancy very personally. The National Mobilization Against the War in Vietnam, a big coalition of peace groups led by pacifist Dave Dellinger, was busy planning a large antiwar demonstration in Washington on October 21, 1967. The Mobe, as it was known, formed in 1965 when leaders from several old-line peace groups like the Committee for a Sane Nuclear Policy (SANE) had come together to form a coalition that could lead large, national antiwar mobilizations.

Despite its long-standing commitment to local organizing, SDS had, of course, debated whether to support the National Mobilization's march. In the end, SDS did support it but did not pledge any resources to work on it. I agreed that national demonstrations didn't build organizations in which people could learn new ideas or new ways by participating in democratic forums. National demonstrations also seemed to favor a certain kind of self-promoting leadership style, and the Mobe was completely undemocratic in the way it functioned. In SDS the national leadership did see itself as accountable to the base of the organization and in service of that base.

The Mobe had wrested a permit to gather at the Lincoln Memorial and march to the parking lot at the Pentagon, where there would be a rally. At that time, some would engage in civil disobedience. Some of the Mobe leaders challenged Dellinger's plan to do civil disobedience at the Pentagon. They felt that it would set up a situation that was too dangerous with the large crowd expected. Dellinger, however, argued persuasively for the importance of including space for those who believed fervently in the power of nonviolent direct action.

As word spread about the mobile street tactics and the exhilaration they had produced in Oakland, many young people, including a great many SDS people in Washington already for the demonstration, began urging their friends to do the same there. Since leaving the national office, Greg Calvert had been working in New York, most recently as an informal SDS coordinator with the Mobe for the demonstration. He had become more and more committed to the philosophy of nonviolent direct action after long conversations with Dellinger and Barbara Deming, another lifelong leader of nonviolent confrontations who worked with the Mobe. He had decided to participate in the civil disobedience with Dellinger, Deming, and others, even though he knew this would run counter to the sentiments of most of his SDS friends.

Greg, Dave Dellinger, and other Mobe organizers listened uneasily to the growing enthusiasm for street confrontations and hurriedly called a meeting for the evening before the march for all SDS people in town and any other young people who wanted to come. Greg and Arthur Kinoy, a lawyer for the Mobe and an articulate and sometimes fiery orator with experience dating back to civil liberties struggles from the 40s and 50s, came to our house on Lanier Place. More than a hundred and fifty people stuffed themselves into our first floor. Greg argued passionately that we were facing one of the most violent institutions in the history of mankind, and we could not hope to defeat it by using violence. Like Gandhi, we had to mobilize the best moral instincts of people to our side, and we couldn't do that through violence.

The debate was fierce. Many in SDS argued that peaceful demonstrations had accomplished nothing but bashed heads and that those in power were laughing at us. As always, I was drawn to what I saw as the moral purity of the pacifist position, that one's life was one's argument, and one's willingness to sacrifice was the most powerful moral testimony. The Buddhist monks in Vietnam who had immolated themselves had moved me deeply. Nonetheless, I was also beginning to think that the government was showing they could tolerate this kind of dissent without changing policy, that they had contempt for us because they believed we didn't have the power to oppose them. Besides, I couldn't see how civil disobedience could allow me to express my anger, and if I didn't find a way to let it out, I felt like I would explode. Still lacking the vocabulary to articulate what I thought, I argued that we should try to shut things down but not attack or provoke the police. This was a completely unrealistic plan based on a vague idea of spontaneous civil disobedience, guaranteeing that the police would attack in full force and demonstrators could get hurt. Finally, the SDS people present, including the influential members from New York like Jeff Jones, grudgingly agreed to spread the word that people were supposed to follow the Mobe marshals and not break off into the streets of DC.

The next morning, the sun rose into a brilliant blue sky. Thousands of people gathered at the Lincoln Memorial and began the long walk to the Memorial Bridge, over the Potomac, where we were to proceed to the parking lot at the Pentagon. I was walking with friends from Washington SDS but also looking for other friends from New York and Chicago. Marches provided a chance to visit and catch up on personal and political news from around the country. In between the conversations we chanted "Hey, hey, LBJ, how many kids did you kill today?" or "Hell no, we won't go!" and the new slogan, "Hell no, nobody goes!"

As we came to the end of the bridge, a small band of marchers, led by someone carrying an NLF flag, broke away from the main crowd and started running up a grassy hill to the left. Some one yelled "Storm the Pentagon!" and many of the SDS people nearby started to run up the grassy slope. I looked at the people I was with, and we, too, ran at top speed, clambering over an orange snow fence trampled down by the leaders of the surge.

At the Pentagon, two opposite-facing sets of stone stairs led up to an intermediate platform, from which a wide set of stairs led up to the terrace. I was near the top of the second set of stairs when the people in front of me stopped abruptly, as the front line had come face to face with a line of helmeted, nervous MPs with drawn rifles with fixed bayonets. Behind me, hundreds of people still rushed up the stairs unaware of the soldiers at the top, pushing the front line right up against the bayonets. Greg Calvert and Jeff Shero, both of whom had been passed bullhorns, argued that everyone should sit down, as a way of holding our ground but de-escalating the confrontation. Slowly, over the next few minutes, individuals and small groups of people began to lower themselves in the tightly packed sea of people. Tension charged with the awareness of what could still happen crackled in the air. A few people started making short speeches to encourage the crowd and denounce MacNamara and the Pentagon for the actions in Vietnam. Someone had flowers and started putting them in the barrels of the soldiers' rifles. Other people set up first-aid stations lower down and organized a supply network, sending people for water, food, and cigarettes. The crowd chanted for the soldiers to "Join Us, Join Us." Skirmishes broke out between MPs and demonstrators on the edge of our terrace, and several people were dragged off and presumably arrested. An urgent debate broke out among the demonstrators about what to do. Meanwhile, the main part of the demonstration had continued around to the front of the Pentagon and was listening to speeches.

At one point, the bullhorn was passed to me by one of the male SDS leaders. I experienced this gesture as recognition of my stature in the organization; I was also aware that I would be one of the only women to speak. The previous speaker had spoken up against the war and tried to inspire people to stay and face whatever came. I wanted to rise to the occasion and give an inspiring speech, advising people of the best way to move at that point. With bullhorn in hand, however, I realized I didn't know what to say. While the moment seemed filled with drama and opportunity, I didn't know what we should do. I, like most people, had so far moved on instinct. I saw the potential for many people to get hurt, and while I wanted to stay, to express my anger, I wasn't comfortable urging others to stay and risk injury.

Unable to get past my own conflicted feelings, I said that we were staying to show the depth of our opposition to the war, but that everyone didn't need to stay if they wanted to express their opposition in other ways. Staying was not a measure of someone's commitment to stop the killing of Vietnamese people. I passed the bullhorn on, feeling inadequate. I wanted to learn how to speak in a dangerous situation like that, but I had no idea how to do it. I, like many of my peers, felt that doubt and uncertainty were signs of weakness and lack of resolve. I had to push through that doubt, I thought, to be the kind of decisive, charismatic leader I imagined I should be.

While I had been excited by Debray and Fanon, here in the heat of confrontation it was the model of the nonviolent confrontations of the civil rights movement that seemed most powerful. To the extent we had any power at the Pentagon, which didn't feel like much, it was the power of a moral witness. At the same time, our government and military were *so* violent, so ready to disrupt and sacrifice other people's lives. What good were we doing sitting out here, chanting against those impenetrable stone walls? We were hippies, students, and angry young people without a strategy.

As the evening progressed, the October air got very chilly. Some people started bonfires on the grass to stay warm, burning whatever wood had fallen to the ground from the many trees, parts of the snow fence, and posters and banners people had carried on the march. Some people talked about staying all night. Others started to drift away. The tension in our section eased somewhat, and a few of the soldiers talked quietly about the war and their futures. Young people returned with cookies and soda, which they passed around to everyone.

As it got dark, I began to think about leaving. Around 9:30, the crowd was sprayed with tear gas as the MPs were replaced by paratroopers, some veterans of Vietnam. It turned out that their mission was to form a wedge through the main body of demonstrators—still several hundred—that remained on the terrace. By 10:00 PM they had begun the operation, but rather than being a clean military procedure, it was characterized by prolonged beating of those demonstrators sitting in front. Soldiers purposefully kicked women in their breasts. One woman reported that she had been knocked over, and one soldier had stepped on her hair while another proceeded to drag her in the opposite direction.[5]

At some point the rumor went along the line that MacNamara had arrived at the Pentagon. Around the same time, the soldiers' assault stopped, although by then many dozens had been arrested, and the crowd had been pushed back to the top of the stairs. In the quiet period after the last skirmish, however, it became hard to articulate the goal of staying. Clearly, it was a war of attrition, and eventually everyone would be arrested. Most of us decided to leave. A small group of a couple of hundred people stayed, seeing their presence as an act of civil disobedience. There was value in that, I thought, but for me, not enough to merit being out of commission for a while and facing a string of court dates. I wanted to be working, keeping up an offensive. Along with a couple of friends, I left about 11:00 PM and walked back into Washington where we caught a bus home.

The next day, Dave Dellinger argued with me that the demonstration had been a successful show of opposition.[6] I wasn't convinced, still feeling that it had largely been a failure because we had done nothing concrete to stop the war. We had gained the steps of the Pentagon, but then had been unable to agree on what to do next. The disunity and lack of coherent strategy troubled me. I worried that eventually the physical cost of protest would become astronomical. Just as the Vietnamese were defending themselves against US military incursions, we needed a strategy to defend ourselves against the growing brutality of police incursions here.

Dave assumed that eventually political pressure would force Congress and the president to end the hostilities. In this he shared the views of Ho

Chi Minh and the Vietnamese leadership, which counted on the democratic nature of the United States, along with the Vietnamese military
strategy of self-defense, to end the war.

I, on the other hand, continued to feel that Congress was too compromised to act, and the president was too ideologically mired in the
Cold War and indebted to the campaign contributions from military contractors like Brown and Root. Instead, I thought that maybe we were
having the most impact by interfering with the war machine, regardless
of government response. I had a sense that the way we confronted power
was deeply connected to our success in convincing more people to join
us, but as of yet I was unable to articulate how this fit into a broader
vision for social change.

There were almost 500,000 US troops in Vietnam by October 1967; the
draft was reaching into every sector of society and US losses were
mounting. While demonstrators had been relatively self-contained at the
Pentagon, largely as a result of Greg, Dave and Arthur's arguments, the
aggressive assaults by the paratroopers convinced many young people
that the mobile street confrontations, including some amount of
inevitable property damage, were the way to go. Without a pacifist
vision, young people needed other ways to feel powerful in the face of
violence.

Three weeks after the Pentagon march, New York SDS joined a large
demonstration, organized in part by the Fifth Avenue Parade Committee,
to protest a speech being given by Secretary of State Dean Rusk. He had
been invited to speak at the Foreign Policy Association, a group that had
relentlessly supported the administration's Vietnam policy among academics, businessmen, and intellectuals. Columbia SDS students and others in
New York planned to block the entrance to the hotel where the event was
to be held.

Police responded to the provocative chants as the first demonstrators
stepped off the curb into the street, wading into the crowd on their horses
and slashing out indiscriminately with their nightsticks. Many demonstrators responded by pelting police with rocks (which they had brought with

them, rocks being scarce on Manhattan streets) and then swarming back into the spaces police had already cleared. While the police appeared to have been taken by surprise by the massive militancy, they also had come prepared with a new tactic. Undercover officers watched the crowd and identified anyone playing a leadership role or anyone previously known to the New York Red Squad as a citywide leader. Once these young people were identified, uniformed police officers aggressively went after them, wading deep into the crowd to arrest them. Among the arrested were Columbia SDS members Mark Rudd, chapter cochair Ted Gold, and Ron Carver, who, unbeknownst to me, had been dating my stepsister Haven. This demonstration introduced militant street fighting to the East Coast, much in the way that the Oakland Stop the Draft Week demonstrations had on the West Coast.

I wasn't at the demonstration, but when I heard the glowing reports over the next few days I found myself troubled this time by the personal nature of the confrontations. Throwing rocks at police and taunting them in response to police assaults was a whole new thing. I could feel an undercurrent of individual bravado getting stronger, although I couldn't have named it at that point. It was connected to the exhilaration I had felt tearing up the hill toward the Pentagon. I, too, wanted to find a way to show my commitment and courage. I couldn't figure out why, then, these engagements so bothered me. More to the point, I couldn't imagine attacking someone who was bigger and heavier and was armed to the teeth. What was the point?

Nonetheless, I wasn't ready to dismiss street fighting as an effective tactic. I remained equally dissatisfied with nonviolent resistance which, while playing an important role, clearly seemed insufficient. Germans who had disapproved of Hitler had generally done nothing while Hitler went after union leaders, communists and socialists, homosexuals, Gypsies, and then the Jews. At each stage, though many disagreed, they had had many understandable reasons for being silent. Above all else, we did not want to be silent. We were obliged to try to close the induction center and to block the entrance of the hotel. In the absence of anything better, maybe mayhem was the way to go. I desperately wanted to interfere with the smooth operation of war, to make some difference to the Vietnamese, however tiny, right then.

While the antiwar movement escalated its tactics, a SNCC delegation, including Stokely Carmichael and Ralph Featherstone, traveled to the Southwest to meet with Thomas Banyacya of the Hopi Nation, and Reies Tijerina, head of the Alianza Federal de los Pueblos Libres in New Mexico, a Chicano organization that had been founded several years before to address problems of civil rights and economic exploitation. They all signed a treaty seeking fair treatment of Chicanos and the return of land and water rights taken from the ancestors of the Spanish-speaking residents of the Southwest.

The coming together of these organizations provided me with a glimpse of what it was we were fighting for. Here were different peoples, coming together to address common problems and experiences. They were negotiating how to equitably divide up the resources and get along in a reasonable, nonbelligerent way. I understood that this treaty was largely symbolic, that developers, ranchers, and mining interests had long since gotten their government representatives to seize control of both land and water rights, but the symbolism nonetheless helped me imagine the way the future might unfold if we ever had a chance to be thoughtful about it.

Shortly after the Pentagon demonstration, Tom Hayden, who I knew only in passing from the early days of SDS, invited me to a meeting in New York City, at which he asked if I would be interested in joining three others, two men and a woman, on the first student trip to Vietnam. He had just returned from North Vietnam with three prisoners of war, amid a great deal of publicity. The Vietnamese had asked him to help set up the student trip.

Tom was only about six years older than I but he seemed of a different generation. He had been in Berkeley the summer of 1960 amid protests against the runaway anticommunism of the House Un-American Activities Committee (HUAC); he had been the *Voice* editor at the University of Michigan and had worked with SNCC; and he had drafted the Port

Huron Statement of SDS. Since then he had been national officer of SDS, and had helped found the Newark ERAP project and the Newark Community Union Project. Tom had traveled to Hanoi for the first time in 1965, with Staughton Lynd and Herbert Aptheker, head of the Communist Party USA. On his most recent trip he had accompanied POW fighter pilots released by the Vietnamese. I was awed by his knowledge about the movement in this country and in international affairs.

I was surprised to have been selected, and wondered why. I found out later the first two choices had been unable to go, and my name had come up as a woman who straddled both old and new SDS. I worried that I had neither the skills nor the knowledge to represent the movement on such an important mission, but at the same time, I was eager for the opportunity. I was aware that an experience like this, much like my election to the Christian Association at Abbot, would provide me with both a pulpit and a challenge to learn how to speak more eloquently. Tom seemed to think that my varied experience in SDS was sufficient for me to represent the organization, and that I would not do anything outrageous. I was aware that not very many women got selected for opportunities like this. I also wondered who had thought to make a point of selecting an equal number of men and women.

I accepted the invitation to go, along with Jeff Jones, a recent graduate from Antioch College and leader of New York regional SDS, Steve Halliwell from Columbia SDS, and Karen Koonan, a young Bay Area activist and journalist. I already knew and liked both Jeff and Steve, and looked forward to meeting Karen. We were to leave on November 16, so I had only a couple of weeks to raise or borrow the $1600 for the round-trip ticket and to find people to carry on the work I had been doing, while I was gone.

I didn't tell my parents about the trip and hoped they wouldn't find out, naive, given that the point of the trip was to publicize student support for the Vietnamese and to educate the public about what was really going on in their country. The press was at the airport when we left and a photo of the four of us boarding the plane was in the *New York Post* the next day. So much for anonymity. We flew first to Paris to pick up visas from the Vietnamese embassy. We boarded another plane, which stopped to refuel in Greece, and Ceylon.

Our final stop was Phnom Penh, Cambodia, where we were to meet again with Vietnamese officials and then take the daily international mail plane up to Hanoi, the only air transport the United States allowed into North Vietnam. Cambodia maintained friendly relations with the United States while insisting on its neutrality in the war. We were met at the airport by an official and taken to a hotel in town, passing water buffalo and oxcarts on the road. Phnom Penh was bustling with pedicabs, pedestrians, and small European cars. The street in front of our hotel had banana, pineapple, and mango trees. What a humane city, I thought: free fruit.

We had been told that as soon as we washed up and rested a bit we were to come to the Vietnamese mission. We found that in Phnom Penh we could occasionally find someone who spoke either a little English or a little French. Certainly, the hotel and shopkeepers were no strangers to international visitors. We presented ourselves at the mission late in the afternoon and were introduced to Ambassador Nguyen Van Hieu, who had been assigned to see to our needs. He greeted us warmly, and when we were all seated he proceeded to tell us that while we had been in the air, the United States had resumed saturation bombing of Hanoi, so there could be no flights into Hanoi for the foreseeable future. They had tried to reach us in Paris to stop us from coming, but we had already left. We were stunned. A wave of disappointment washed over all of us. Then, a wave of shame. Here this man was telling us apologetically that our government was trying to kill his family, friends, and colleagues. Karen started to cry quietly. She wanted to go home right away to get back to work.

Ambassador Hieu suggested that we think about what we wanted to do, and he would see us again tomorrow. Before we left, however, we asked more specifically about the bombing. So far, he said, it had been limited to Hanoi, although within hours Haiphong, the largest harbor city in the North, would also be hit again and again. He began to discuss recent US troop movements. It became clear that none of the four of us had much knowledge of Vietnamese geography or of the details of the war. Ambassador Hieu said that when we returned he or someone else from the embassy could give us some background on the war.

Finally, he said, it would be a shame for us to leave Cambodia without visiting its national treasure, Angkor Wat. What's that? we asked, once again showing our ignorance of the region. They were eight-hundred-year-old temples that had been partially excavated, he replied. They were very beautiful, and since we were only a couple of hours away by car, we really should see them.

We returned to our hotel, exhausted and devastated. We felt a tremendous urgency to go home and continue our antiwar work. At the same time, we had been invited to stay for several days to meet with the Vietnamese and to travel to Angkor Wat. Before we left each other for the night, the two men sleeping in one room and Karen and I in another, someone pointed out the low, uneven drone we could hear vaguely through the wide-open windows. It was the sound of US bombers on evening raids on the Vietnamese border with Cambodia. Later we would find out that these raids regularly strayed quite far into Cambodian territory.

The next morning we decided that we would all stay for several days more, and trundled expectantly to our meeting with the Vietnamese, represented this time by a professor working with the embassy who took on the task of educating us. We communicated in a mixture of French and English. I was the only one who spoke French, but I had not spoken at all since the summer of 1964 and had forgotten most of my vocabulary. I was able to understand the general outlines of what was being said, however, and translated them into English for the three others. We replied in English.

In a series of three more meetings, we learned a brief history of Vietnam and its continual struggle for independence and unity, against China; then the French, after World War II; and then the United States after 1954. We learned that the basic economic organization of the country relied heavily on agriculture because its lands were fertile and it had a great deal of available fresh water. Finally we were schooled in the US war effort in the South, and the stages of the war from the point of view of the Vietnamese. They stressed the ongoing difficulties of the United States, such as the heavy equipment mired in mud, the difficulties of distinguishing between Vietnamese patriot and US sympathizer, and especially the plummeting troop morale as the greatest weakness of US forces. They attributed the low morale to the already existing divisions in US society, the divisions of race, poverty, and education, which were carried over into the military. After our first session, we were invited to dinner at the Vietnamese mission and, on another day, a performance by the Vietnamese National Liberation Dance Troupe. That afternoon we explored Phnom Penh. Karen and I were both taken by the ubiquitous booths selling beautiful fabrics of all different designs. Both of us bought several yards of different patterns. Back in our hotel room we experimented with how to tie the fabric as skirts as Cambodian women did.

Earlier in the day someone had discovered that in the little bodega-like shops all over Phnom Penh one could buy packets of cigarettes containing marijuana. They had bought a pack of cigarettes and were eager to try them. I was wary, but also, as a rule, pushed myself to try new things. I was never an avid marijuana smoker, tending to get more disoriented or sleepy than I did pleasurably high, but this time, by the third pass of the cigarette I felt myself drifting somewhere very deep. Panicked, I realized that maybe there had been some opium mixed in. Everyone else seemed to be pretty out of it as well and yet we had a dinner date with the Vietnamese in a mere three hours. As I lay across the bed, I was overwhelmed by my own immediate paralysis, by the intensity of this trip to the other side of the world, and by my immense sense of inadequacy. I felt deeply accountable to the antiwar movement to make the most of this trip, and here I was passed out on the bed.

Fortunately a couple of hours and a lot of Coca-Cola rendered us sensible enough to get dressed and, giving the address of the mission to two pedicab drivers, we arrived only a few minutes late and mostly recovered. Four or five Vietnamese staff at the mission, and the ambassador and our professor welcomed us graciously. We were all seated and given tea and hors d'oeuvres. Of course, we ate heartily. By the third or fourth course I was full and could eat no more. To my horror, my hosts chastised me, saying that as a guest I should try the scrumptious dish now on the table and that the main course, still to come, was also to be delicious.

The next day we made arrangements, after some pointers from our professor, for a three-day trip to Angkor Wat. That evening we prepared to attend the performance of the Vietnamese dance troop. Karen and I decided that we would wear our new Cambodian skirts to the event. We arrived at the enormous outdoor stadium just before the performance and showed our tickets at the door. As soon as the ushers saw our tickets, we were given great deference. As we were led down an aisle, a hush fell over the stadium all around us. Many people turned to stare at us.

We couldn't figure out why. We certainly weren't the only white westerners in attendance, and there was no sign on us saying we were US citizens, which might have caused some extra curiosity. I felt extremely self-conscious, not knowing why we had become the center of attention for such a huge, disparate crowd. After we were seated in the third row, a western woman in the second row turned around and with a big smile introduced herself as Vessa Ossikovska, the wife of the well-known Australian journalist Wilfred Burchett, whose engrossing, fact-filled articles and books had been my primary source of information about Vietnam. She was there with her children while her husband was covering the International War Crimes Tribunal taking place in Stockholm that week. In French, she welcomed us and invited us to tea at her house the following day.

Then the performance began. The numbers were a mix of classical Vietnamese dance and contemporary dances based on themes of the war. In Vietnam, the young, talented dancers sometimes danced for both fighters and villagers, on simple stages in liberated areas and in fields, near the front lines. They were in Phnom Penh now, recovering from two months they had spent in underground tunnels during a particularly long and vicious pounding of an area called Chu Chi, north of Saigon. Despite the bombing, during which villages had been completely razed and the landscape was reduced to a moonscape, the US had been unable to safely send in ground troops. (After the war, the maze of tunnels below Cu Chi, with schools, hospitals, and living quarters, became a tourist attraction, for those who can handle the close quarters.)

When the dancers were clad in the everyday clothing of troops and villagers, women as well as men were depicted as fighters and clever rescuers. The grace and elegance of the dancers, an equal number of young men and women, moved me deeply. One of the contemporary dances featured villagers who were seeking to hide a wounded NLF soldier from US troops. Near the end of the dance, when the villagers were threatened with death by the US troops, the wounded soldier crawled out of hiding and threw a grenade at the US soldiers, killing or wounding them and allowing the villagers, in the momentary confusion that followed, to capture their enemy's weapons and chase the survivors away. While the whole stadium applauded enthusiastically, I felt conflicted. I was aware that my silence would cause tension in the audience around me and might well be misinterpreted, so I clapped politely and briefly. I *did* share the sentiments of those around me, glad that the villagers in the dance had defied death and protected their soldier, but I also saw and identified with the US troops who were victims of a different kind, so I was saddened by their pain and death. There was no easy emotional refuge here, and I was left hating the war even more.

The next day, we went to tea at the Burchetts' house, surrounded by lush tropical vegetation. The children were in their rooms and the sounds of the Beatles came wafting through. Their pet monkey perched judgmentally on a bookcase, watching our arrival. Our hostess explained to us why the audience had been so dumbfounded when we walked in. It seemed that the beautiful cotton fabrics that we had seen in the market place each represented a different ethnic and regional pattern. We had chosen patterns that were Chinese and Laotian. This caused a lot of puzzlement, because at that time, Cambodia, under Prince Sihanouk's leadership, was seriously at odds with the Chinese. The Chinese, through formal diplomatic channels, and also through the large student following they had in Cambodia in the Khmer Rouge organization, were pressuring Cambodia to break its neutrality and align itself with China. Right before we had arrived, Sihanouk had ordered the arrest and detention of many of the Khmer Rouge student leaders, including a young man called Pol Pot. We had known about this because it had been covered in both the English language and Khmer papers when we arrived. The audience must have wondered who these Westerners were wearing Chinese patterns to a Vietnamese performance in Cambodia.

The next day we had our final session with the professor, and the following morning we boarded a minibus for the trip to Siem Reap, a town on the northeast shore of the Tonle Sap, the huge lake in the middle of Cambodia, and the headwaters for the Mekong River. There, a couple of small hotels were within bicycling distance to the temples at Angkor Wat. The countryside was breathtakingly beautiful, with few signs of poverty as we sped on a two-lane road through lush farmland and cozy villages of houses built on stilts. We were told that this lake had the densest fish population of any body of water in the world. It was hard to be hungry in the Cambodia of those days.

As the Vietnamese had suggested, we rented bicycles to explore the temples, which went on for miles. We wandered in and out of three or four over the course of the next day, learning that they had originally been built as part of a massive thirteenth-century irrigation project, which also served to unify the country into a single monarchy for the first time. Some of the temples had been completely cleared and were well maintained, but most were in various stages of reclamation by the jungle. Thick vines hid whole sections, and trees still grew in courtyards. Monkeys were everywhere.

At one point a couple of us decided to bicycle off into the surrounding woodland-jungle to see what the villages looked like under their cover of tropical vegetation. As we approached one village we heard a large industrial clackety-clacking getting louder and louder. When we turned a corner on the packed dirt path we had been following, we saw a corrugated tin structure with the Coca-Cola logo on it. Sure enough, there in the jungle was a Coca-Cola bottling plant. It reminded me of my childhood, when in the Swiss railroad station bottles of Coca-Cola had been thrust through the train windows by vendors. I wondered, is this in part why we are bombing Vietnam?

Our final night we discovered a dance performance of traditional Khmer dancers on the vast steps and plaza of one of the temples, lit by a few dramatic floodlights and the moon, a dreamlike experience. We then headed back to Phnom Penh. We were anxious to return home and share what we had learned. Before we left, we agreed to write five articles for *New Left Notes* and divided up the different topics.

I returned to Washington to resume my work on campuses. During the month before my trip I had become involved in a casual relationship with a reporter from the *Free Press*. Shortly before I left on the trip he had to move out of his apartment so he moved in with me until he found something else. When I returned, I found that he had moved my belongings into the closet and had spread out in my room. I quickly took issue with this. What on earth was he thinking? Within five minutes I was packing up his belongings and enlisted a friend to drive them over to the *Free Press* office. That was the end of our relationship.

As soon as I got settled, I immediately got to work on my two articles. In the first one, I gave a brief report of the trip and then described our experience going to the NLF dance performance. "Our experience indicated that most of the Vietnamese do not have specific recommendations for activities for the peace movement in this country," I noted, "although they are all enthusiastic about large actions which receive a lot of international publicity… After [the dance] program was over, we were all excited about the possibilities for more guerrilla theater in the US."[7] In the second, I explained the governing structures of the liberated zones of South Vietnam, and then the military situation.[8]

I went on to explain that the dry season, from October to March, was the time when US forces and their heavy equipment could mount offensives, while the rainy season during the rest of the year was the time for the guerrilla forces. The Vietnamese had explained to us which territory the United States had secured during the first three dry seasons since regular troops had been introduced. Contact with US GIs often solidified peasant support for the NLF. I also wrote about the weapons the United States was deploying, such as napalm and cluster bombs, and the costs to the civilian population.

In late December, I went up to New York briefly to see my father and stepmother, and then went on to see the rest of my family in New Hampshire for Christmas. To not have done so would have constituted a complete break, but relations remained strained. My mother found it inconceivable that her daughter had tried to go to Hanoi. It was so upsetting to her she never mentioned it during the two days I was home.

I also was unable to look past my own experiences and engage with her about the new life she was creating for herself in New Hampshire. I never asked about her new job as a teacher in the local schools. We had so little familiar between us by now, only fears. She saw only dangers in the course I had chosen, while the only danger I saw was complicity with the status quo. Although the rapid changes in our lives made us wary of confidences, my sisters and I remained close. Christmas was the only time during the year when we could all be sure to see each other. Despite the cold, I found time to go for a long walk through the woods, which went on for miles behind our house. I missed my childhood access to the natural world.

I had decided that I should put together a couple of short speaking tours about my trip as a way of bringing the information from the Vietnamese beyond the readership of *New Left Notes*. My time with the Vietnamese had strengthened the part of me that wanted to believe that we could convince a majority of the people to actively oppose the war. The sense of powerlessness I had felt at the Pentagon receded for the time being. I absorbed the optimistic Vietnamese belief that most people deep down did not want to live by aggression and manipulation, and that with conversation, they could move past the misinformation and fears to reject leadership based on brutality. The Vietnamese were clearly not looking to US antiwar activists to help them fight. They wanted us to win the hearts and minds of US citizens, to oppose our predatory foreign policy.

I sat down and made a list of about forty colleges from Virginia to Maine, and wrote letters to the SDS chapters or, if there was none, to the student governments at each college. In response, I got offers to speak at about fifteen colleges. Some of the schools were small state colleges like Towson State in Maryland, and others were elite New England schools like Connecticut College and Wesleyan. I also spoke at chapter meetings at the local Washington campuses. Often there would be a crowd of over a hundred students, since SDS members had put up flyers around campus that someone who had just met with the National Liberation Front was speaking. At first, I read from a prepared text, sharing the history of the war and the way it was viewed by the Vietnamese liberation forces. After several presentations, I began to feel more confident, knowing that people would be moved and that they were generally very interested. I began to feel less self-conscious about my skills as a speaker when I remembered that the talk was about the Vietnamese, and I was just a vehicle. The more confident I became, the better I was able to engage the audience and the more I began to enjoy myself. After the talks there were good discussions and questions. If there was no SDS chapter on campus and someone wanted to start one, I gave them copies of *New Left Notes* and told them how to get in touch with the national office. If there was already a chapter on campus, the talk often helped the chapter bring in new people.

At the December national council meeting in Bloomington, Indiana, Greg Calvert and Carl Davidson submitted a proposal to encourage local chapters to research local collaboration with the war and to grapple with the questions about how to frame a local campaign. The proposal, which came to be known as Ten Days to Shake the Empire, or Ten Days of Resistance, urged local chapters to plan a series of events for the last ten days of April 1968 that would dramatize the presence of the military-industrial complex on campus. It suggested that students could expose Defense Department–funded research, institutes, or policy makers who held university positions or spoke there; they could protest ROTC, military recruiters, and campus cooperation with the Selective Service System through class ranking. Chapters at the smaller schools and those without a tradition of liberalism could draw from the experiences of the bigger, more elite schools like the universities of Wisconsin, Michigan, and California. The activities could consist of leafleting, teach-ins, impromptu speak-outs, speeches, picketing, or even more direct confrontations of government and corporate representatives. The proposal also suggested that those who were now working off-campus experiment with different ways to implement the proposal along with other constituencies.

Much to most people's surprise, the proposal ran into serious opposition. The acrimonious debate exposed more than ever how several big, unframed and unresolved questions about SDS's identity prevented us from agreeing on any course of action. What were the responsibilities of leadership? What structures promoted democracy *and* efficiency? What motivated people to change and to act?

The opposition to the Ten Days proposal was led by young people who, while members of SDS, were also members of a small, somewhat secret organization called the Progressive Labor Party (PL). On the floor of the debate, PL members opposed the proposal for two immediate reasons: They opposed all draft resistance, believing instead that those drafted should go into the service and organize against the war and for revolution from inside. Secondly, it seemed that PL believed that people only changed when they perceived it to be in their self-interest, and most people's primary concerns revolved around their jobs. They believed that SDS should stick to strictly campus-based organizing and leave the "more serious" organizing of working adults to them.

The main force of the PL assault—and that's what it felt like—did not focus on these particulars, however, but was a frontal, personal assault on the national leadership of SDS. PL accused them of being undemocratic, completely preempting the debate about the actual content of the resolution. It was an ad hominem attack as old as the hills.

Who was PL? In the early 60s, a few hundred political activists had split from the Communist Party USA (traditionally influenced by the Soviet Union) to form PL, which was more closely aligned with the ideas of Chinese communism in the then-developing Sino-Soviet conflict. They had been influenced by Marx's speculation that one class, the working class, would be the agent of change. They were unimpressed with the attempts to rethink this analysis by the writers of the "New Working Class" paper.

PL also subscribed to Russian Marxist Vladimir Lenin's belief that to succeed, any popular uprising of the working class had to form an organization or a party of their own, composed of the leaders and activists of the movement for change. The brutalities of Tsarist Russia had convinced

Lenin that victory would be impossible without it because police agents would sow rampant dissension in popular organizations and assassinate their leaders. A secret, disciplined party could coordinate the fight. At first, they would be a small, self-appointed minority, but they would lead in the name of the people. In all likelihood, the intellectuals, not the economic and political elite, would form the core of the leadership and representatives. If the intellectuals could be drawn from among the working people so much the better, but it was not essential.

As the leader of change, any Leninist party would make all the decisions about how to proceed, and only party members could contribute systematically to the process of making those decisions. Lenin wrote that a party should be both democratic and centralist. Within the party, theoretically, issues would be discussed democratically at the lowest levels of the organization, with the leadership of that level bringing the conclusions up to the next level, where it would again be discussed, and so on until it reached the highest level, the central committee, the collective leadership at the top. There, a final decision would be made along with plans to implement that decision, which then had to be followed with complete discipline by everyone in the party, regardless of whether or not they agreed. Members of a "democratic centralist" party, as these Marxist-Leninist organizations were called, were called cadre, hence the name cadre organization.

PL also accepted the Marxist axiom that the violence of capitalism could only be ended violently. Of course, they didn't see the final confrontation happening until they had organized a party that was strong enough to win. Consequently, building their party, a Leninist cadre organization, became the immediate task at hand. While their original mission focused on organizing adults, especially blue-collar workers, they had recently begun to see SDS as a place to recruit more young people. Many of them had recently joined local SDS chapters in targeted cities with the intent of recruiting young SDSers to their own organization. Some PL members were openly members of both organizations, while others kept their PL membership secret, speaking publicly as if they were regular SDS members.

The founders of SDS had explicitly rejected the elitist nature of both the Leninist model and the system in the United States in which candidates were often handpicked by corporate sponsors and other special interests. The Port Huron Statement had pointed out that the course of events in both the United States and the Soviet Union proved that *any* elite was doomed to succumb to pressure for favoritism and privilege. The only assurance of true democracy had to be governance by the people. Hence, participatory democracy.

The Bloomington national council was the first time I had really seen PL in action because they had chosen not to organize in the DC area. I reacted against several aspects of their presentation. First, their spokespersons were almost all men. Second, they were always confrontational, rarely had a sense of humor and seemed to dress the same—short hair, shirts tucked in, and definitely no bell-bottoms or beads. They opposed all drugs and communal living, and were deeply suspicious of all attempts to invent alternative lifestyles.

I didn't have any problem with their desire to organize GIs to become antiwar. In fact it seemed like a humane thing to do, since GIs were in the thick of things, they should at least find some comfort in understanding what was going on around them, and do their best to save their own lives and that of others. It seemed silly to me, however, to set this work in opposition to efforts to resist the draft.

PL's charges that the leadership was manipulating the membership, however, caught me, and most everyone else, completely by surprise. Suspicion of strong leadership had been a recurring phenomenon in SDS, as many members had experienced frustration with unaccountable leaders in other contexts. On the eve of 1968, however, any complex conversation about leadership was drowned out along with discussions about SDS's structure, by members' preoccupation with the escalating war in Vietnam, the draft, and the continuing upheavals in the northern US cities. The ideas in the Ten Days proposal were the same ones that we had written about and implemented in some places, including Washington, during the previous year, but many new members became suspicious of the intent, nonetheless.

The effect of PL's assault on the legitimacy of the national leadership of SDS, including my friends Bob Pardun, Mike Spiegel, and Greg Calvert, was confusion. Many new members, horrified at the charge, had no basis on which to judge the national officers or the charges. The debate lasted for several acrimonious hours, and in the end the proposal was voted down. PL could never have convinced a majority of SDS members to oppose a draft-resistance resolution in any other way. Without a thoughtful conversation about leadership, however, there was no way to resolve PL's charges. In the end, supporters of the resolution hurriedly put together a whittled-down version of the proposal that contained little analysis and that could not serve as a strategic guideline for future programs. This version ultimately passed. The fear that some cabal was trying to take over SDS, however, had been deeply planted.

While SDS struggled with its confusion about structure and leadership, the Marxist-Leninist blueprint would continue to bubble up everywhere because it was the main existing ideology that could claim some success, especially in China, Cuba, and Vietnam. It provided a script for how to proceed and definite ideas about the responsibilities of leadership. Leaders were those individuals or groups that could come up with the most sound analysis of the national and world situation, and an explanation for how this analysis mandated a particular course of action. Ironically, this view of leadership was little different than that of capitalism, except that Leninist leaders were theoretically concerned about the welfare of all the people, rather than just individual, political, or corporate competition. Over the coming months the allure of this coherence grew stronger, even while the assumptions about change embedded in it lay unexamined in the crush of events. SDS's inability to sort through all this was both a symptom of its spinning apart and a cause of further disintegration.

The other big issue before the Bloomington council meeting was a resolution on women's liberation. A group of women, including a few SDS members, had continued to meet weekly in Chicago since September. On November 13, 1967, while I was preparing to leave for Vietnam, these women wrote an open letter to women that argued for an independent "movement for women's liberation."

> Our political awareness of our oppression has developed thru the last couple years as we sought to apply the principles of justice, equality, mutual respect and dignity which we learned from the movement to the lives we lived as part of the movement; only to come up against the solid wall of male chauvinism.[9]

Women, they believed, needed to meet among themselves to explore, through reading and an examination of their personal lives, the many facets of sexism, and the way it affected them in every sphere of public and personal life. Most of these women had many years experience in a wide variety of movement organizations, from SNCC to SDS to the Resistance, and they brought with them common experiences of disrespect and exclusion. Although some of them continued to work in the movement, they did not want, and knew they couldn't get, approval from SDS or any other organization for their independent exploration of these issues. It had become clear to them that they couldn't embark on this journey while accountable to any or all movement groups, all of which were dominated by male leadership. As a result, these few women began to devote more and more of their time to working with other women exploring issues of importance to women, including women's identity, reproductive rights, access to childcare, and equal pay for equal work on the job. In the next couple of months the ideas coming from this group, along with other such groups in New York and Boston, increasingly challenged all women in the movement to consider whether they should do the same.

At the Bloomington national council, women met to develop a programmatic proposal to follow up on the women's resolution from the June national conventional. Again, some of the men challenged the right of women to develop an analysis of women's oppression by themselves. Some men, it appeared, were having trouble giving up control. I was more conflicted by the actual analysis and program piece than by the commotion caused by a few men.

I had just returned from Cambodia with an immediate commitment to focus on the war that I hoped most SDS members would share. Some of the women, however, were now arguing that women should work in separate structures, within or outside of SDS, and that anything else was selling out women's interest. They were seized with excitement about the power of the new analysis of women's oppression and could not understand the reluctance of other women to join their explorations. Their own experiences with SDS, in chapters, regions, at demonstrations, and in personal relationships, had unequivocally convinced them that women needed to act collectively if men were to listen to them. Some of these women had suffered through repeated personal encounters with political men that had been so hurtful they wanted to disengage immediately. Having struggled to construct and articulate this new analysis, they felt betrayed by women who didn't see its priority, and worried that they would once again be shuttled to the side and trivialized.

Like the majority of SDS women at the meeting, however, I was there because SDS had provided the opportunity for me to be an active, thoughtful woman in the midst of an exciting and powerful movement. I knew there were times SDS prevented access for women—I remembered many earlier experiences in SDS—and thought we needed to address that. I was taken by the analysis that I had read about women's restricted roles in society and found it true and exciting, but I didn't think women's programs should supplant the war as a focus. Women students and student organizers should primarily be modeling a different way of being, rather than becoming obsessed with the problems with the current society. Women like Marilyn Webb would change my mind about this over the next year, but I wasn't there yet.

Despite the passionate and sometimes angry pleas of a few of the women present, the December SDS resolution maintained a focus on antiwar work, urging SDS women to organize more women into the movement and into SDS to fight the war. Women would be free by becoming equal leaders in the movement and by fighting sexism in personal relationships. Despite language in the introductory paragraphs implying that the problems of sexism affected every aspect of women's lives, further inquiry was relegated to "research topics." The only concrete part of the proposal was a provision to offer child care at the next national meeting. The resolution addressed none of the issues that had appeared in the statement by the Chicago women's group: equal opportunity, equal pay, access for low-paid women workers to union resources, equity within family structures, or the commercialization and exploitation of women's identity by Madison Avenue. SDS women had not figured out how to move off campus anymore than the men had.

I remained more or less oblivious to issues of working women, especially issues like day care. My own mother had stayed home until my youngest sister was in grade school. I had no idea how the lack of quality day care in so many ways represented the low status of women and the even lower status of children. I had little current connection to any community beyond the campuses or to any particular jobs or professions. I remained focused on young people like myself and believed that when women came into the movement, they would have opportunities to grow by leaps and bounds. To me, that seemed the priority, especially given the urgency to stop the war.

The conversations did provoke me to consider the questions about women's identity that had been raised. What did "feminine" mean? What characteristics, if any, were gender-based? The women's developing critique of Madison Avenue was consistent with everything I had come to believe about the growing overemphasis on consumption, but I continued to be somewhat impatient that the women's response to these insights was to feel victimized rather than to just walk away from engagement with all that. Like most women of the time, I didn't understand that as more and more women began exploring and publicizing these issues, the conversation could introduce millions of women to questions of how society worked and of its underlying values.

CHAPTER SEVEN

1968

■ ■

In early January, Michael Ferber, Dr. Benjamin Spock, Reverend William Sloan Coffin (the Yale chaplain who had spoken at my Abbot graduation), and other draft-resistance activists were indicted for conspiracy to counsel, aid, and abet young men to resist the draft. Bob Pardun of national SDS issued a call for demonstrations Friday, January 12. In Washington, local SDS members from various chapters joined a mélange of about four hundred activists in front of the Justice Department to support those who had been indicted. A few others and I spoke briefly, and an impromptu group performed a lively theatrical skit. After the protest, over a hundred of us moved to Western High School to pass out leaflets urging resistance to the draft and the war.

I loved the energetic spirit of the demonstration and it validated my belief that, even though Washington was the staging area for repeated national gatherings, we could have our own local identity. There was a political heart and soul to the city and region independent of both the government and national demonstrations. I could see that the students were invigorated by this new way of coming together and feeling our strength. I felt proud, too, that my efforts to support the chapters and to further communication between them had contributed to the strength of the demonstration.

The following Monday was the opening day of Congress. An antiwar coalition of women from religious, civic, and peace groups calling themselves the Jeannette Rankin[1] Brigade arrived in Washington to lobby their representatives and present petitions calling for the immediate withdrawal of US troops from Vietnam. The debate about how women could be most powerful—and the confusion about determining models for change—reemerged in this forum. A number of the young women from women's groups in Chicago, New York, and Boston, including Marilyn Webb and Charlotte Bunch from Washington, met with coalition leaders and questioned the effectiveness of women petitioning Congress, arguing that it was demeaning because it reinforced the traditional stereotype of woman as supplicant without any real power.

The radical women believed that the time for petitioning Congress had passed. Instead, they argued, women should hold a militant and confrontational march rather than a traditional nonviolent rally. This would allow them to challenge traditional roles for women and to protest the war. The older women, however, specifically wanted to focus attention on the responsibility of their elected leaders to heed the wishes of their tax-paying constituents. They, like some of the women in SDS, feared that attention to women's issues might draw urgency away from the movement to stop the war.

Unlike the younger women, leaders of the Jeannette Rankin Brigade wanted to play up their identities as mainstream housewives, mothers, and taxpayers, as a way of making the point that it wasn't just a "radical fringe," as the administration was fond of saying, that opposed the war. Since they insisted on a peaceful demonstration with no confrontation of any kind, a number of younger women planned a secondary protest to happen at the same time.

Since I had lost interest in working with Congress in any form, I didn't attend any of the planning meetings. Besides, I was busy with the region's Justice Department demonstrations. While wary of the more traditional culture of a mainstream women's organization, I could see that they could play a valuable role by contributing to the breadth and variety of people speaking up urgently against the war.

In the end, Vice President Humphrey did not allow the petitioners access to Congress, and instead the women had to settle for sending a small delegation to the Speaker of the House and Senate majority leader. Signed by tens of thousands of women, the petitions were delivered by Coretta Scott King, eighty-seven-year-old Jeannette Rankin, and a few others.[2]

During the discussions among the younger women over the course of the weekend, the debates were sometimes fierce. Nonetheless, the women reaffirmed their desire to put the issue of discrimination against women onto the movement's agenda. The meetings spawned yet another new women's group, this one in Washington where Charlotte Bunch and Marilyn Webb gathered other interested women to begin meeting regularly.[3] Marilyn would soon invite me and any other women from SDS who might be interested. This would bring the challenges arising from women's issues right to my front door.

Over that winter, several activist groups had come together to rent a small three-story house at 3 Thomas Circle in Northwest Washington. The *Washington Free Press* moved to the first floor, and Dick Ochs and others set up a print shop in the basement. The Washington Draft Resistance Union (WDRU), the group I and other SDS members had recently initiated, moved into a room on the second floor. A new alternative news service, Liberation News Service (LNS), which sent out both print and graphics to the alternative media around the country, took the third floor, and a local chapter of the Resistance (the draft resistance group started by Ferber and Coffin) took another room on the second floor. Other groups occasionally used the space and received mail there, including the Washington Women's Liberation group.

I had begun to spend a few hours a days sitting in our new WDRU office. We publicized the existence of the WDRU and our counseling services by leafleting at various demonstrations, near the bus and train stations, and at cultural gathering places for young people. Most days one or two young people would call or stop by with questions about the draft or requests for assistance.

Late in January, a young man with an innocent face and curly blond hair walked in. Bill Willet had joined VISTA after graduating from Williams College and had been assigned to a project in Washington where he had been helping tenants work for improved housing conditions. He and his coworkers encouraged residents to define problems, bring them to landlords or management, and persist until changes were made. One group of frustrated public housing residents had decided to go on a rent strike until basic electrical, plumbing, and structural maintenance problems were addressed. When the strike was announced, Bill was called into his supervisor's office and told in no uncertain terms that he had to defuse the situation, that strikes against the federal government—the landlords of all public projects in the District of Columbia—were off limits because VISTA workers were federal employees, even though VISTA was strictly a volunteer program providing the most meager living stipend.

Angered by this hypocrisy and rather than betray the people he had been working with, Bill walked out of VISTA. This left him immediately eligible for the draft. Nonetheless, he had come to 3 Thomas Circle as much to find a new arena of work as he did to get draft counseling. We started talking about what had happened with VISTA and moved quickly to SDS, the war, and our campus work in DC. An hour into this free ranging conversation I told Bill that I had to leave to drive out to a Maryland suburb to speak with a group of high school antiwar activists and asked him if he wanted to come along. By the end of the afternoon I had come to really like him and asked if he wanted to work for SDS in the region. Within a couple of days, Bill moved into the house and became the second more-or-less full-time SDS staffer. He was a natural fit, with his own passion against the war and an intuitive empathy with anyone resisting cultural restrictions of any kind.

I continued to write. An article about my trip to Cambodia appeared in the University of Maryland student paper. In February, I wrote an article for the *Washington Free Press* about the SDS program for Ten Days to Shake the Empire, with the hopes of encouraging a variety of Washington organizations, including the Resistance, Women's Strike for Peace, and the Institute for Policy Studies to join with SDS for a week of all different kinds of activities. "While continuing to work on the original targets," like Dow Chemical and military recruiters on campus, "we must also expand ... to build coherent political organizations capable of exercising real pressure on university support and cooperation with ... America's foreign policy." Furthermore, I wrote, "students must encourage the development of and work (respectfully) with other groups resisting the illegitimate authority of the US.... We must foremost resist the efforts of the government to keep the movement divided against itself for so long."

Later that month I attended a rally called by the local SNCC group, to support one of their most active members, Jan Bailey, who had refused to sign any papers at his induction physical. He had been released temporarily from Fort Holabird Induction Center in Maryland, where SNCC members and supporters had demonstrated outside. I stayed in touch with Jan about his case and included information about it in our work. We also got together occasionally to talk about local strategies for organizing around the draft, and I kept him informed about the activities of the WDRU. Usually, rather than talking by phone, which we by now assumed was tapped (it was), I went to visit him at his job as a used-car salesman.

I saw Jan's case as the only opportunity I had to develop a relationship with Washington SNCC. While I had several friends who had friendships with black activists before the advent of black power, I felt constrained from initiating anything new. The current position of SNCC was explicitly that whites should organize other whites. Stokely Carmichael in particular was quite clear that he thought whites should not meddle in black struggles. In the summer of 1966, Carmichael had described black power by saying, "When the Negro community is able to control local offices, and negotiate with other groups from a position of organized strength, the possibility of meaningful political alliances on specific issues will be increased."[5] By 1967, Rap Brown, the new chairman of SNCC, spoke clearly about the need of the black community to be self-reliant, to develop their own movement for change.

Carmichael had recently moved to Washington after his term as chairman of SNCC, but instead of aligning himself primarily with SNCC, he set up a new organization called the Black United Front, with the hope of helping Washington's distrustful black organizations join together in an effective coalition. He also started the New School for Afro-American Thought, to teach black young people about African and African American history.

I wasn't sure what we could do about Jan's case other than publicize it and bring people to the occasional rallies organized mostly by SNCC members at Howard University. During the spring of 1967, Howard, supported by Washington SNCC, had been the campus in Washington with

the most militant wave of activism. In one final confrontation, five professors and forty students walked out of an address on Vietnam delivered by
Arthur Goldberg, US ambassador to the United Nations. Two weeks later,
thirty-five students disrupted and left an address by General Hershey of
the Selective Service System. Finally, activists called a one-day boycott of
classes to protest their administration's attempts to stifle these outbreaks of
dissent by suspending students. Some 80 to 90 percent of the students
stayed out of class for the day. That summer, five faculty members, including Dr. Nathan Hare, and sixteen students were dismissed from the
university, laying the basis for renewed activism the coming year.

The DC SNCC office had been staffed by Marion Barry, an early
chairman of SNCC, who had come to Washington in 1965 from the
South. He was intrigued by the possibilities of using traditional politics to
serve and mobilize the chronically powerless. Barry had been impressed
by the extensive community organizing carried out by Julian Bond's successful campaign to become a Democratic state representative from
Atlanta, and Barry looked around for ways to mobilize Washington's black
community, even if they included working in coalition with whites.

This focus led him, and others, to form the Free DC Movement
(FDCM), dedicated to gaining representation for Washington, DC. Washington had always been governed by a congressional committee rather
than a local government, its citizens able to vote only in federal elections.
Since the committee had traditionally been dominated by Southern
Democrats, the local administration which they appointed had paid little
heed to the voices of local citizens, especially those in the black majority.[6]

By the time I arrived in Washington, Lester McKinnie, also a Southern
SNCC veteran, had succeeded Barry as the leadership of the local SNCC
office. McKinnie, too, had come under attack by many in SNCC, accused
of still believing in the model of integration as a long-term strategy and of
not effectively mobilizing Washington blacks in separate local projects.[7]
While the Free DC Movement may well have offered a chance for white
students to work in coalition with black activists, my suspicion of electoral politics at that point blinded me to these possible opportunities.

On the Vietnamese New Year (Tet) on January 31, 1968, the National Liberation Front launched a month-long offensive, simultaneously attacking medium and large cities all over South Vietnam, including targets in Saigon. They penetrated the inner sanctums of the US military command centers. The success of the widespread coordinated attacks stunned Johnson and McNamara, who had been saying the NLF was almost defeated. In February, General Wheeler, the chairman of the Joint Chiefs of Staff, relayed a request from General Westmoreland for 206,000 additional US troops.

I talked to Jeff Jones on the phone after we heard about the first few days of the Tet offensive, and he pointed out that in many ways our Vietnamese hosts in Cambodia had as much as told us that this was about to happen. I reworked the talk I was giving on campuses to include the recent events, trying to spread information accessible from the European and anti-war press that had been denied by our country's leadership. Day after day government spokespeople told us that the war was near the end, that US and South Vietnamese troops had everything under control, just a few more mopping-up exercises to do. Meanwhile, a host of young photographers filled the papers and TV with images of a more embattled reality. Without any alternative, coherent explanation of what was going on, however, many still believed that US troops were victims of random, senseless killing by vicious guerillas out to destroy US attempts to build democracy.

My job, I thought, was to explain the perspective of the Vietnamese independence movement. While people could agree or disagree with that version, at least it provided a coherent analysis of what was happening that matched the reality far better than the official US version. If you were a potential draftee, or the parent of one, what you really wanted to hear was the most reliable projection of what was going to happen.

Even though I had grown cynical about the democratic process, even though I was deluged by examples of public officials bought off by private interests, I had no other model for change. Revolution was still just a word, albeit a hopeful one. While I knew the current popular definition involved an overthrow of the state, I couldn't imagine what that would look like in this country. Yes, I believed in revolution, and in socialism, equally blurry in my mind, but until those ideas came more into focus, I, like most of my contemporaries, continued to concentrate on convincing the electorate to take policy into their own hands by making it impossible for the government to fight the war.

A few days after Tet, we mobilized the region again in support of black students at South Carolina State, in Orangeburg. They had come together a year earlier to boycott classes in protest over paternalistic campus rules and the nonrenewal of contracts for three politically active white teaching fellows. In February 1968, campus groups had protested against a local bowling alley whose owner refused to admit blacks.

Student anger increased when city officials refused to respond to their various demands. On the night of February 7, frustrated students pelted cars with rocks and bottles and took part in other scattered acts of vandalism. The escalating strife in Orangeburg reached a climax the following day when police called for a fire truck to extinguish a bonfire started by the students for warmth during the chilly evening. Backed by National Guard troops, police began their reoccupation of the campus. When a policeman was struck by a banister post thrown by a retreating student, his fellow officers, thinking that he had been shot, began firing on the students, many of whom held up their hands or fell to the ground. Thirty-three black demonstrators were shot by police during the barrage of gunfire. Three died of their wounds.[8]

Unlike the coverage given to the great battles of the early civil rights movement, like those in Selma and Montgomery, the papers barely covered the event. I knew that more than a dozen civil rights workers had been shot and killed in the past few years, but this was the first time black students on a college campus had been shot outright.

It felt to me like another moment in which reality was dissolving and reforming in a new way. These students were doing nothing that wasn't already routine in Oakland, New York, and Washington. It was clear that black activists were suffering a response to protest that was different from whites. (While the Orangeburg black activists were initially charged with inciting to riot, and then, later, the soldiers faced federal civil rights charges, no one was ever convicted for the killings.) Maybe, I wondered, it was only a matter of time before they would be shooting at us as well.

No one I knew in Washington considered for a moment that the escalating government violence meant we should back down. I was horrified by what had happened in Orangeburg. We would have to be tough to withstand this kind of punishment, I thought, but surely, if we could reach enough people with information about what was truly going on—the awful price of privilege—the balance of pressure would change. We mobilized those we could on twenty-four hours notice. Marilyn McNabb and others hurriedly researched what kind of office the state of South Carolina might have in Washington, and the next day we picketed and leafleted at the DC office of the South Carolina Chamber of Commerce, telling passersby what had happened.

The following Monday, we mobilized outside Congress where their Subversive Activities Control Board, a holdover from the McCarthy era, was holding hearings about the DuBois Clubs, a small youth spin-off from the Communist Party. The heat was definitely on, and it was beginning to seem less and less like a coincidence that one government body after another was going after movement activists. Somewhere, it seemed, a group of officials had decided that the antiwar movement had to be stopped.

In these weeks after Tet, young people on Washington campuses continued to organize around the war. On Wednesday of the following week, American University students had a twelve-hour learn-in organized by a large coalition that included SDS. One of the sessions showed a film distributed by SDS on Vietnam by Felix Greene, a historian covering Vietnam and China. I spoke about my trip briefly after the film, which was attended by several hundred students. I continued to enjoy public speaking, realizing my skills were adequate to convey the information about the war and the broader web of collaboration. That Friday, the Justice Department indicted seven young men in Oakland, charging them with conspiracy in their capacity as organizers of the Stop the Draft Week demonstrations in Oakland the previous fall.

I was writing another article for *New Left Notes*, purportedly on how to set up a draft resistance union, modeled on the work we had done in DC, but really I was driven to try again to bring some coherence to the swirl of ideas in my brain and writing seemed to be the best way for me to try to sort out my thoughts. One stubborn question lodged in my head above all others: why was it that so many in the United States seemed blind to what was happening, and to the human cost? Why would people believe the obvious falsehoods being thrown at them, especially about the war, and go about leading their lives, giving tacit support to it all?

Racism, I thought, shielded many people from looking at the consequences of their actions, or inaction, in human terms. By diminishing the humanity of some people we could justify the inequalities that characterized society. Once people agreed to these terms and allied themselves with this point of view, they became vulnerable to the argument that whites in the United States really did have something to fear from the Vietnamese, or from black people. Fear of others made people accept improbable explanations from the government, and then they listened to no one else, especially not to those they feared. The hierarchies that divided us encouraged us to see the world as made up of groups of allies and enemies.

In the end, however, I wrote that even if self-interest were the *only* human motivation, people were not acting in their true self-interest to support these policies. The people to benefit from this fragmentation of society were the executives and major stockholders of big corporations who could move from one poor area to another lowering wages and raising dividends. Even Eisenhower had warned of the growing immorality of the military–industrial complex.

At that time, I didn't have the knowledge to understand how three factors in particular had deeply endowed my parents' generation with renewed trust in the government and the economic system: the opening up of economic opportunities for whites who had suffered through the deprivations and hardships of the Depression; the success of the CIO (Congress of Industrial Organizations) in raising wages for tens of thousands of workers; and the sense of international security that came after the war. Furthermore, the rhetoric of Johnson's War on Poverty reaffirmed the popular belief that those who were poor were so because of their own inadequacies, a view that allowed many to completely ignore the long-lasting consequences of slavery and Jim Crow, the servitude of Chinese and Mexican laborers, and the ongoing discrimination and violence against women and children.

The other issue I puzzled over in the article was the problem of how to improve the current system. The movement, I wrote, was an alternative culture that tried to work without competition and aggression. We needed to build programs that demonstrated that our values of cooperation, generosity, and hard work, in combination with a diverse, vibrant culture, could feed the planet and provide intellectual nourishment. Our values were superior to the mean-spirited, fearful, racist world of advanced capitalism.

I noted that we lacked a political-economic program other than a vague belief in socialism. While we could learn from struggles for socialism in Latin America, Vietnam, and China, I said, we must find a way to envision it in this country, based on the particular conditions we find here. I didn't know enough yet to speculate how to combine positive aspects of socialism—such as central planning for some sectors of the economy, especially those necessary for daily survival like food, utilities, insurance, education, and transportation—with the role competition played in increasing efficiency, initiative, and creativity.

This article was my most ambitious attempt yet to come to grips with why our country had seemed so mired in war and racism. I had little time or patience, however, to approach this task with rigor. I was an activist, not an armchair radical, I said to myself.

The pace of events didn't let up. On February 26, *New Left Notes* carried a short piece saying that SNCC and the Black Panther Party (BPP) had joined forces and merged. Not only did I find this news surprising, so did many members of SNCC and the Panthers.[9] I had only learned about the Panthers in January, when the *Guardian*, a radical newsweekly in New York, carried its first article on them. I had also seen a startling photo of a couple of dozen young black men and women, in black leather jackets and berets, holding shotguns while they stood in formation on the steps of the Alameda Court House. The BPP was started quietly by two young black activists, Huey Newton and Bobby Seale, who attended community college in Oakland, California. Frustrated with the two previous student-oriented organizations they had joined, they sat down in a local poverty program office and wrote a ten-point program for community development. They squarely addressed racism, but did so in the context of an activist agenda, heavily weighted toward self-reliance. The ten points read, in part:

1) We want freedom. We want power to determine the destiny of our black community.

2) We want full employment for our people.

3) We want an end to the robbery by the capitalists of our black community.

4) We want decent housing, fit for shelter of human beings.

5) We want education for our people that exposes the true nature of this decadent American society. We want education that teaches us our true history and our role in the present-day society.

6) We want all black men to be exempt from military service.

7) We want an immediate end to police brutality and murder of black people.

8) We want freedom for all black men held in federal, state, county, and city prisons and jails.

9) We want all black people when brought to trial to be tried in court by a jury of their peer group or people from their black communities, as defined by the constitution of the United States.

10) We want land, bread, housing, education, clothing, justice, and peace. And as our major political objective, a United Nations supervised plebiscite to be held throughout the black colony... for the purpose of determining the will of black people as to their national destiny.[10]

In early 1967, Newton and Seale recruited a few friends to help them implement the ten-point program by instituting community patrols to follow police and monitor all interventions and arrests. They carried legal weapons in their cars for the sole purpose of defending themselves or those being physically intimidated or assaulted by police. They also carried along law books so they could quote the law to police officers if need be. News of the patrols spread quickly in the poor black community of Oakland, which had a long, troubled history with its police force. More and more young black men volunteered to join, swelling the ranks of the organization and increasing the number of patrols.

In April 1967, in the wake of a police killing of a young man fleeing from a stolen car, they put out the first issue of *The Black Panther*, a four-page mimeographed newspaper. Also in April, the police department, furious that they were unable to take any legal action against the patrols, submitted a bill to the state legislature outlawing the carrying of weapons without a permit in the city. It was at the June hearing for the bill in Sacramento that the fourteen Panther men and ten Panther women had appeared on the steps of the State House. Pictures of these armed black young people would eventually be seen around the world. The pride and seriousness radiating from those young faces captured my attention even more than the shotguns.

Huey Newton was a creative strategist with a complex sense of the way the drama of events and human consciousness worked together. He and Seale combined self-reliance, self-respect, and armed self-defense with a broad intellectual vision, naming the problems of the black community in a way that was meaningful to many and posing solutions that were completely independent of white approval. While their vision fell far short of a full-fledged development plan, their concrete local focus led them to take many more steps in that direction than most of their contemporaries, including SDS. Significantly, the Panthers' dedication to the black community had not led them to be either antiwhite, as many young civil rights workers had become, or antipolitical, as many poor black youths were. The Panthers were willing and at times eager to form alliances with white organizations.

The final part of this fertile combination was Newton's abilities as a teacher and Seale's as both a teacher and orator. Newton brought the skills of economic and political analysis to everyone around him. In his memoir *This Side of Glory: The Autobiography of David Hilliard and the Story of the Black Panther Party*, David Hilliard recounts how several times a day Newton launched into "raps" about the way the US economy had always been organized around having blacks at the bottom, whether it was in the form of slavery, sharecropping, or the exclusion of blacks from unions. Many of the Panthers' inner core were young men in the throes of their first years of looking for work. They held a series of jobs in which they were yelled at, humiliated, and disrespected. The world of work held little promise of dignity or advancement. They were eager to understand their experience in a broader perspective. Newton also introduced an international perspective that allowed young people to understand the war and the antiwar movement in the context of their own experience.

Frequently, Newton made suggestions about what people should read. He challenged members to tackle difficult works like Fanon, and when they complained, he reassured them that their efforts would pay off.[11] In addition to required study, new recruits were enlisted to work in the Breakfast for Children Program, collecting food donations and setting up the breakfasts at multiple sites every morning, serving as one of the models for the free breakfast and lunch programs now institutionalized in public schools. They started local literacy classes using black history as their text, much as SNCC had done in the freedom schools in the South. They opened a free clinic with volunteer doctors. The Panthers generated a vision that ambitious young blacks did not have to leave the community to find fulfillment. They had a simple, coherent, and imaginative program to involve young people from poor communities in social change. It was stunning.

It was also incredibly ambitious, demanding organizational skills, resources, and a core of dedicated activists. Newton and Seale came with a deep sense of purpose and more than a passing awareness of history, while dozens of others brought expertise and creativity of their own. Their early success, however, inevitably plunged them quickly into a host of new challenges, as hundreds of young people flocked to join. Their problems became even more complex when, after the Sacramento demonstration, they became a target of federal as well as local law enforcement.[12]

Most of the Panthers' early activities were unknown on the East Coast.

The January 1968 article in the *National Guardian* presented a brief history of the BPP, and then focused on an incident in October 1967 in which Newton's car had been stopped by Oakland police, and, in the ensuing gunfire, one police officer had been killed. Newton, badly wounded, was arrested and taken to the hospital, where he was charged with murder. The Panthers were organizing efforts to support his claim of self-defense, although the article did not offer any explanation about what had happened, perhaps on the advice of his attorneys.

Even as the faces full of pride filled me with hope, the aggressiveness of their stance with rifles and shotguns unnerved me. I worried about how vulnerable these brave young people appeared, even though this strategy of self-defense seemed more likely to be effective than any other I had heard about. I was reminded of the way the rock throwing in New York made the conflicts seem so personal. I couldn't help feeling that a showdown with guns staked out a very male-defined turf. Yet, a number of black women had joined the BPP as well, and seemed to feel comfortable with the strategy, and the same men who carried shotguns were also pouring milk into cereal bowls for five-year-olds. Still, I wondered if they had the staying power of SNCC in the South, or if they would be overwhelmed by the police response.

On March 1, 1968, several dozen black students demonstrated at Howard University's Charter Day exercises commemorating the founding of the university in 1866. The students were members of a black awareness organization on campus called Ujamaa. While many of them had participated in SNCC's antiwar, antidraft initiatives of the previous year, they now focused on changing what they called "the plantation curriculum" of the university. Howard's classes, they argued, only prepared them to abandon their communities and become part of the tiny minority of blacks who were accepted into a small and powerless black middle class. They proposed reconstituting the university as the Sterling Brown University, with a curriculum that would allow them to learn about the history of blacks in Africa and in the United States, and prepare them to take on the problems of the black community. Students also demanded the reinstatement of faculty and students dismissed the previous spring.

The university responded by sending out thirty-nine hearing notices similar to those received before the expulsions the previous spring. Immediately, on Tuesday, March 19, Ujamaa and several other campus organizations, including the student government, mobilized over a thousand students to rally and then march to the administration building to demand a hearing with university president James M. Nabrit. Finding that he was gone, students moved in and took over the building, including all keys to the university and the incoming telephone switchboard. They insisted they would not leave until their demands were met: a more enlightened curriculum, assurance of democratic participation of students in all aspects of student life, and an end to reprisals against activists.

That night there was music, and speeches by student leaders. Stokely Carmichael's Black United Front sent donated food, and Carmichael came by to give a brief talk on "the revolutionary aspect of the students' actions."[13] Later, student leaders formed committees for sanitation, public relations, security, first aid, food, education, and entertainment. By the following day, demonstrators were back in the dorms, talking and organizing to increase their support. They devised a schedule in which the sit-inners could leave the building in shifts, to return to their dorms for showers and go to classes. All this was two months before the more famous takeover at prestigious Columbia University.

Support poured in from dozens of area campuses, local churches, and community groups. Students cheered when they learned that Morgan State, Cheyney, and Fisk universities, all black colleges, had all been shut down in similar struggles.[14] Carmichael and Courtland Cox from SNCC returned and spoke; Malcolm X's autobiography was passed around, as were the writings of other black leaders. Jacob Ngwa, a graduate student from Africa, spoke about the recent Sharpeville massacre in South Africa, and US involvement in the Congo. When the university trustees threatened a federal injunction, students voted to stay anyway.

Finally, on Friday night the trustees began negotiating with student leaders. Discussions continued until a compromise was reached for students to vote on. Before the final vote, one of the steering committee members, Judy Howe, reminded students that "if they voted to accept the proposals they must do so with the idea that this was just the start of things. The proposal(s) provided a base, a first step on the way to getting the reforms they wanted. She said that the students must be prepared to get into the committees proposed by the trustees and work hard not only there, but in every phase of student activity to make Howard a truly Black university."[15] At 10:00 PM students voted overwhelmingly to accept the proposals, and they returned the administration building to the university in more or less perfect order.

It was clear that Howard students were fueled both by the pride of black history and by the tremendous sense of possibility that lay ahead of them if they left behind "the plantation" relationship to whites. I did not know then how profoundly this approach differed from the kind of takeover that would sweep Columbia and other campuses within weeks. For black students, the university represented a tremendous potential resource, while whites would be increasingly paralyzed by the dilemma of the university system's complicity with national and international economic agendas.

On March 4, just four weeks after local police shot at students in Orangeburg, South Carolina, the state of Texas brought five students from Texas Southern University, another black school, to trial on murder charges. These students had participated in an earlier peaceful campus demonstration, during which police surrounded and then charged into the crowd of students. Once again, police had fired on demonstrators and one of the bullets had ricocheted, this time hitting and killing another officer. Alleging that they had been fired upon, the police then arrested students for rioting and indicted the five for murder. They were tried, convicted and sentenced to life in prison, despite the fact that no weapons were found. These young people served several years before their convictions were finally overturned by a higher court. A ballistics test finally showed that the officer was killed by a bullet shot from a police weapon.

Later that week I set off on the longest of my speaking tours, a seven-campus journey through New York and New England. Near the end of the tour I spoke at Amherst College, where my father was still active in alumni affairs, serving as chair of the alumni committee. He continued to feel very grateful to Amherst for "waking him up" to the larger world and for providing a place where he could become an intelligent, responsible adult. I knew that some of his friends and colleagues might attend the speech, and I looked forward to presenting the antiwar case to them. I thought that even though my father did not agree with me, he would still be proud that I conducted myself with intelligence and dignity. At the same time, I worried that the overlap of these two parts of my life that I had tried to keep separate might result in something unforeseen.

Halfway through the tour I was joined by SDS national secretary Mike Spiegel, with whom I was beginning a relationship, and Jeff Jones. We met with Amherst students before the talk, and they filled us in on their local struggle to do away with compulsory daily chapel. That seemed reasonable to me. Students should be able to choose their own religious activities. The problem was that I had been invited by the college to give my speech at the regular chapel. The students implored me to refuse to speak out of solidarity with their struggle and to speak later, when people could attend voluntarily.

At the chapel, I was given an enthusiastic introduction by a dean of the college, an acquaintance of my father. In the front row I saw several of my father's friends, whom I had known since childhood. I stepped up to the pulpit and asked for a show of hands for how many of the people in the hall were there voluntarily. Only the front rows and a small sprinkling of others raised their hands. In a somewhat rushed, embarrassed three or four sentences I explained that I would not speak and why, and told the audience when and where I had scheduled the talk for later in the day. We all then walked out of the chapel amid the cheers of many students.

That evening, I spoke before a tiny crowd of about thirty students and no community members. Only then did I realize the consequence of my choice. I had passed up an opportunity to provide a large body of people with concrete information about the war that was inaccessible in the mainstream press and to pose some challenging questions. Instead, I had given priority to a student-power struggle of young white men, among the most privileged in the whole world. The incident embarrassed me.

After returning briefly to Washington, I set off for Chicago, to attend a meeting of the national interim committee. While I was there I sat in on a meeting of the Mobilization Against the War, which was planning a protest at the upcoming Democratic National Convention in Chicago. I wasn't entirely sure I would go to the event since I still did not see electoral politics as a productive forum. I thought it was unlikely that either Bobby Kennedy or Eugene McCarthy, who were running on antiwar platforms, could unseat President Johnson or win the election.

Mike Spiegel gave a speech in which he argued that while McCarthy and Bobby Kennedy were using the war issue to win over young people, they did not stand for fundamental change, for a system of true participatory democracy. We should therefore oppose them. By then, not only did SDS desperately want to end the war, but the prevailing sentiment in the organization was a hope that the turmoil stirred up by the war would encourage young people to fight for more radical changes in the system. Attempts to channel antiwar sentiment into the Democratic Party seemed like a domestic form of pacification. Having fought so hard to distinguish ourselves from the great white American "we," our fear of being co-opted yet again made us wary of complexities. The clarity of total opposition seemed safer.

After the Mobe meeting, with a national council meeting scheduled for Lexington, Kentucky, the next weekend, I helped out around the national office and visited with Mike and others who were in Chicago. At the national council, I again worked for a resolution supporting antidraft organizing, which this time the delegates passed. The other major resolution at Lexington was inspired by Carl Oglesby, ex-SDS president and author of *Containment and Change*, who spoke passionately about our need to shift our focus from the war onto the problem of racial oppression, especially the attacks on those young black activists like the students at Orangeburg and Texas Southern.

Carl supported a resolution on racism which included several objectives: to give "visibility to the black struggle for liberation"; to "make the state pay as high a price as possible for genocide" (in black communities, in Vietnam, and in any country where people were resisting the control of the military-industrial complex); to institute internal education programs around racism;

and to "give physical and financial aid to those black people now the object of state repression."[16] I had come to the national council focused on antidraft organizing and the war, but when I left, I was mulling over the debate about racism, thinking we needed to do more in Washington.

The national council had a dramatic ending on Sunday evening, when several of us returned to the rambling old house where we were staying, and watched a major policy speech by President Johnson on Vietnam. Not only did he call for a partial bombing halt, but he also announced that he would not run for election again. We were jubilant. Clearly, all the trouble around the war had been having more of an impact than we knew. We knew we would have to think how this would affect the upcoming primary election, but for the moment, the main impact of Johnson's announcements was as a tremendous sense of power.

The euphoria was short-lived. On Thursday April 4, several days after we had we driven back to Washington, Martin Luther King was shot and killed in Memphis. Word spread like an electric shock throughout Washington, with people pouring out onto the sidewalks, seeking the solace of community in the face of an impossible affront. I was in the WDRU office when a member of Liberation News Service rushed through the building spreading the news. We gathered around a radio. The phones started ringing and the Washington activist community began to rally, trying to figure out how to respond.

By dusk, the anger and hurt sought an outlet. There was never any question what that would be; after four summers of urban rebellions, everyone had wondered when Washington would erupt. Activists from the SNCC office, in conjunction with Stokely Carmichael, decided to rally those who were already out on the streets to participate in a march of grief and protest, hoping to waylay any rioting. Carmichael and other black leaders intended the march to be peaceful, but angry young people began to spin off from the march, breaking windows of white-owned businesses as they passed through prominent commercial strips in black neighborhoods. Carmichael and Lester McKinnie tried to stop the break-ins, calling out to stone throwers that this was not the way to pay respect Dr.

King. At one intersection, Carmichael grabbed a gun from a man who had been shooting into the air. But it was to no avail. The march disintegrated as young and old alike followed behind the window-breakers to take advantage of the portable goods, food, furniture, and clothing. Frustrated, saddened, and angry, SNCC leaders gave up. Some stores were burned and the fire trucks that came to put out the fires were also pelted with bottles and debris, with the result that some of the fires spread to other buildings, including people's homes.

The city of Washington had originally been designed by Lafayette with its defense in mind. The White House and Congress were situated near the Potomac River. Half a dozen major streets emanated out from these two hubs on diagonals, like rays of the sun. All the other streets in the city ran between these diagonal streets like the supports in a spider web. The National Guard and army knew that to defend the downtown area only those major streets had to be blocked off.

Sure enough, that evening police began to define and defend perimeters of the downtown area, and moved to encircle the black community of Northwest Washington. Shortly after midnight, the DC police closed 14th Street from N Street north for over two miles, sealing the black community off from the rest of Washington. The SDS, LNS, and other movement offices at Thomas Circle stood at the intersection of 14th Street and M Street, one block south of the cutoff point, at a strategic intersection of three streets. The White House sat only four blocks down. That night the fires throughout Northwest Washington lit up the sky.

Many white activists felt it was our job to go to the black community to be witnesses to any large-scale brutality by the police or military. Peter Novick and Craig Spratt of Liberation News Service were standing outside the office talking with three black citizens when the police roared up in a squad car, leapt out, and threw the three black men up against the wall to search for weapons or stolen goods. Craig Spratt challenged the arrest and was told to move away. When he refused, he too was arrested. Peter asked why they were arresting Craig, and he too was arrested and thrown up against the wall.[17]

On Friday, twelve hundred students met at the chapel of the University of Maryland to attend a prayer service and teach-in, and later students demanded and won the closure of the university for one day. One thousand Georgetown students, along with priests and nuns, were given a police escort to the White House. Some of these demonstrators later joined with a couple hundred others of us at the nearby district building to demand that troops not be called into the city. Many from the *Washington Free Press*, regional SDS, and students from American, George Washington, Georgetown and Catholic universities, and various religious groups then joined a protest at the White House. With a bullhorn, we attempted to have an impromptu rally, at which I and several others spoke briefly. After just a few speakers, however, several dozen helmeted riot police attacked, pushing the group off the sidewalk that was directly in front of the White House to Lafayette Park, across the wide and busy Pennsylvania Avenue. [18]

Meanwhile, at Bowie State College, a black school in Maryland, King's murder coincided with ongoing student efforts to demand higher standards for faculty hiring, better course selections of black history and other subjects, and an end to dangerous physical plant conditions. After a student boycott of classes on Friday and an occupation of the campus administration building, students marched to the statehouse. There, Maryland Governor Spiro Agnew, later to become Nixon's vice president, had 290 students summarily arrested and the campus shut down. In response, the black student union at Johns Hopkins University held a "black unity rally," attended by black students from Morgan State, Goucher, and Bowie. SDS held a support rally outside the auditorium with a hundred and fifty white students.

At 4:00 PM on Friday evening, President Johnson sent all federal employees home early, declared a 5:30 PM to 6:30 AM curfew, and despite our lively protests called in over two thousand National Guard and over eleven thousand regular federal troops. Anyone on the streets after the curfew had to show identification and justify their reason for being out.

As the night progressed, the anger sparked more fires and looting. By morning, dozens of blocks had all their stores burned out. By Saturday, there was no source of food or medicine within walking distance of many black neighborhoods, and all buses had been rerouted or canceled; many people had lost their homes along with the commercial buildings; the threat of hunger became real. Volunteers from various churches and political groups began to carry food into those neighborhoods, where a scattered network of churches began to distribute supplies.

The city was essentially shut down over the weekend, with military checkpoints active on the perimeters of the black communities, but sporadic looting continued until Sunday. Police continued to focus on centers of movement activity, including 3 Thomas Circle. On Sunday, police rounded up several members of the Liberation News Service staff who were returning from a food distribution center at the nearby Luther Place Church. All had willingly showed ID, including press passes, but to no avail. One of them, Ray Mungo, also had a DC police press pass allowing him access to restricted areas. Still, all were arrested. One officer, badge 1627, remarked, "I see we got a bunch of them long-haired bastards. . . . if we can't draft them, let's kill them. . . ." He later vowed that "We're gonna get every nigger and long-haired sonofabitch!"[19] The reporters were held for twelve hours with dozens of other local victims of police sweeps, in a cell with a backed-up toilet. The police kept all their property, including keys, glasses, and press passes, and it was only after the Institute for Policy Studies enlisted legal help after their release that they were able to extricate some of the property.

Later we heard that Oakland police had stopped several carloads of Panthers the night of King's murder. In *This Side of Glory*, David Hilliard described how the incident had come about in part because some of the Panthers, enraged by King's death and filled with bravado, had actually set out to look for an undefined confrontation with police. Others had gone along to try to moderate, but the police found their car first and after they opened fire on the Panthers, the Panthers returned fire. Eldridge Cleaver, minister of information, and Bobby Hutton, a local teenager, escaped to a nearby shed while David Hilliard, Panther chief of staff, dove through the window of a neighboring home. After ninety minutes of shooting, during which Cleaver lay wounded, police bullets finally set fire to the shed. Hutton and Cleaver came out together, Cleaver hobbling as a result of his wounds and holding on to Bobby Hutton. Then, with the squad headlights shining directly on them, the police told Bobby Hutton to run to the car, killing him instantly as he did so. Only the shouts of community onlookers kept them from doing the same to Cleaver. Bobby Hutton was only eighteen when he died.[20]

By Monday, much of Washington's black community was smoldering. Over 5,000 Washington residents had been arrested and the bails were set high enough to keep almost everyone inside. Eight people had died. The devastation was sobering. The black community had made a powerful statement about the extent to which thousands of black citizens were angered by King's death and by the persistent lack of economic opportunity.

The War on Poverty didn't seem to be addressing urban needs, but it was also hard to see how the ghetto uprisings and the destruction of one's own neighborhoods without any plan or resources for rebuilding, would lead to positive change. Many reporters in the movement press, the free press, and even occasionally in the mainstream press commented that perhaps this was the beginning of urban guerrilla warfare at home. I tried to imagine how these rebellions would become part of a historical political account, "History of the Victorious Struggle for Socialism in the US," the way early uprisings were glorified in histories of Vietnam or Cuba or China.

The urban upheavals certainly were clear statements of anger and disappointment, but besides the movement, who cared, I wondered? Was the threat of future riots an effective threat? Why would the government of rich people care if young black people ran in the streets and were shot for their trouble? I wasn't sure it would make a difference. But I also felt relieved that this rage had been expressed, that such deep emotions had found a public expression, that black people were heard beyond the ghettos, even if that cry had yet to declare a vision of future equality.

The tension continued to build. Within days we heard that Rudi Dutschke, a popular leader of German SDS, had been shot by a right-wing fanatic earlier in the month. He was close to death. I knew almost nothing about German SDS, but, like many, I thought it was cool that there was another organization of young people opposed to the war and the military-industrial complex, that had the same name. In recent weeks Dutschke had repeatedly been attacked by a right-wing newspaper. It occurred to me then, that not only could we be the targets of government attacks but also those by private citizens. Organizations like the US's White Citizens' Councils and the Klan in the South, and paramilitary groups could point the finger while anonymous activists did the deed.

On April 18, we held a small demonstration in solidarity with Dutschke, in front of the West German embassy. It seemed important to speak out about these attacks at every opportunity to show that we were not to be disabled by paranoia the way communists in the United States had been crippled as a result of Senator McCarthy's witch hunts.

The day before, we had heard about a bombing of the Albuquerque offices of the Alianza Federal de Pueblos Libres, Reies Tijerina's land-rights organization in the Southwest, which at one point had staged an occupation of a section of federal land. Supporters of the Alianza chased a man they saw running from the scene, but, although they caught him and turned him over to police, he was never charged. Instead, Tijerina was arrested on kidnapping charges for holding onto the suspect before turning him over to police. Then on May 3, police in LA followed up the April attack on the Panther office with an assault on a house where several Panthers lived, breaking in and arresting seven young people.

In thinking about these events, I remembered that someone at the national council in Lexington had suggested that the movement would be increasingly defined by how we responded to government attacks on the black struggle as it grew more militant. Recent events, especially King's murder, lent strength to the argument that moderate action would become more and more difficult, even futile. Working within the system seemed increasingly unrealistic when movement leadership was under such constant attack.

Along with many in SDS, I wondered if some elite business and government leaders had finally decided to break away into a secret cabal and conduct an all-out assault on the popular forces of change, especially on activists of color. Perhaps we were reaching a critical turning point in American history. We knew that members of the overtly racist Citizens' Councils in the South were also business leaders, policemen, and political officeholders. To what extent was this true about Hoover and his federal apparatus of repression? I had no way of knowing then, but after Watergate, we would see that many of our fears had been based in reality.

FBI surveillance of dissent was as old as the FBI. J. Edgar Hoover, director of the FBI from 1924 to 1972, had been involved in active, offensive actions since early on in his FBI tenure, long before official counterintelligence programs were initiated. At least as early as 1918, while rising through the ranks of the FBI, Hoover had initiated plans to destroy the popular black leader Marcus Garvey "under the guise of 'criminal proceedings.'"[21] The FBI had gone on to play an active role in suppressing efforts by miners and other working people for better conditions and pay. By the 1930s, the FBI was immersed in efforts to ferret out and immobilize anyone calling themselves an anarchist, socialist, or communist. In other words, the FBI assumed the right to determine what was acceptable political opposition in the country and to criminalize anyone they didn't like.

This legacy of intelligence gathering combined with political meddling continued through the McCarthy era, the civil rights movement and into the 60s. Hoover institutionalized this dual purpose in 1956 in the first of what would be many counterintelligence programs (COINTELPRO). This one was directed at the Communist Party, but others followed. In 1967, the FBI established a COINTELPRO for "black nationalist hate groups," in order to target SCLC, SNCC, the Revolutionary Action Movement (RAM), and the Nation of Islam. It had targeted the Nation of Islam as early as 1957, and then, as the civil rights movement grew, the FBI became increasingly worried about King, instituting wire taps on SCLC offices in the North and the South, and infiltrating the organization with the goal of undermining King's stature. The FBI activities included the targeting of financial supporters for both SNCC and SCLC. According to an August 25, 1967, FBI memo, "[T]he purpose of this new counterintelligence endeavor is to expose, disrupt, misdirect, discredit, or otherwise neutralize the activities of black national, hate-type organizations and groupings, their leadership, spokesmen, membership, and supporters..."[22] To underscore the importance of preventing any sustained, strong leadership from developing, a March 4, 1968, memo, directed all field offices "to prevent the rise of a 'messiah' who could unify, and electrify, the militant black nationalist movement." It cited Malcolm X and King as examples.[23]

In the case of the new left, the FBI had had "mail covers" (interception, copying, and resealing of mail) on SDS at least since 1964.[24] After the 1965 SDS march on Washington the FBI intensified its scrutiny of the organization, adding wiretaps and infiltration to their surveillance, both of which were later found to be unconstitutional by the courts. In its initial attempts to gain information, the FBI interviewed various SDS members, seeking to entice supporters to infiltrate for the purpose of regularly sending information, to "[h]ave proper coverage similar to what we have [on] the Communist Party."[25] The FBI also contacted university administrations to reinforce cooperative agreements between it and campus authorities. In February 1966, FBI headquarters issued a directive that "agents investigate all 'free university' activities associated with student power advocates."[26] The bureau also exchanged information with other intelligence agencies. By October 1967, the FBI had initiated with several university presidents "get tough" agreements on the student left.

In January 1968, the FBI set up their "key agitator index," regularly sending reports to the White House. On May 9, 1968, after the Columbia uprising, the FBI's C.D. Brennan sent a memo to Mr. W. C. Sullivan: "Subject: Counterintelligence Program, Internal Security, Disruption of the New Left."

> . . . [I]t is our recommendation that a new Counterintelligence Program be designed to neutralize the New Left and the Key Activists. The Key Activists are those individuals who are the moving forces behind the New Left and on whom we have intensified our investigations. . . .
>
> The purpose of this program is to expose, disrupt, and otherwise neutralize the activities of this group and persons connected with it. . . . [T]hese instructions require all offices to submit an analysis of possible counterintelligence operations on the New Left and on the Key Activists on or before 6/1/68, including any specific recommendations for action.[27]

Using forged letters, documents, and phone calls, agents sought to exploit every small disagreement between activists, insinuating personal hostility and betrayal. They spread rumors about individuals for the purpose of provoking distrust and anger from their coworkers or those in coalition with them.

In the national office of SDS and then in Washington, I became accustomed to hums and beeping on the phones, to mail arriving with clear signs of tampering, or not arriving at all. Occasionally, trim-suited, short-haired white men were seen sitting in cars down the block from our building or lurking on the edges of demonstrations. When I inquired about my own FBI files in the early 1980s, under the Freedom of Information Act, I discovered that there were "tens of thousands" of pages. I began to request these files one at a time, for ten cents a page. When I received them, over 80 percent of the text was blacked out. The next step would have been to litigate each file, page by page. I had neither the time to do this myself nor the money to hire a lawyer to do it, so after the first few hundred pages I let the matter drop, and have not been able to pursue it since then. Many others, however, have received and litigated their files, and it is not hard to surmise what mine would have looked like.

I did discover that a local Washington field office file on me was opened within months of my arrival in 1967. Recently I learned that I even merited an individual FBI tail as I moved about in my work. My cousin, an art student at George Washington University living off campus in 1968, had put up a friend of a friend who was a young FBI agent in town for a training session. He had discovered, to his horror, that his hostess was related to the same Cathy Wilkerson he was learning about in his training sessions. I was under regular surveillance and, according to the agent, "in a lot of trouble." Fortunately, my cousin did not share this young agent's alarm. In fact, within a few months she designed and drew the cover for a pamphlet I was preparing on women's liberation.

Around this time, the national office printed up James Forman's article "Liberation will come from a Black Thing," in response to the call at the recent national council for literature on racism. It quickly became one of SDS's primary educational pamphlets on racism and the black movement. Forman argued that the history of black people in the US was a history of

At far right, with my mother and sisters at our piano in Stamford, 1952.

A family picnic with my father, sisters, grandmother, and friend, in our backyard on Mayapple Road, 1954.

With Ann and Robin
grocery shopping for our
boat trip in a port on
Long Island Sound, 1956.

At the Two Bar Seven Ranch in Wyoming, 1957.

Jeff Jones,
Steve Halliwell,
Karen Jo Koonnan,
and I departing for
Hanoi, 1967.

At a demonstration in support
of draft resistance outside the
Justice Department in Washington, D.C., 1968.

Black Panthers at the Alameda County
Courthouse in California, 1968.
UPI/BETTMAN

women: the
struggle
for
liberation

AN INTRODUCTION

Cover of Washington SDS Women's Liberation
pamphlet, drawn by Sarah Wilkerson, 1969.

At women's demonstration during days of rage.

Diana Oughton, 1968.

Terry Robbins, 1969.

Teddy Gold, 1970.

The wreckage of my family's townhouse on West 11th Street in which Diana
Oughton, Ted Gold, and Terry Robbins died. UPI-BETTMANN

FBI Wanted Poster issued April 1970.

resistance to oppression and a refusal to accommodate a colonized role in the US economy. As a result, he said, their movement could be seen as an anticolonial fight for liberation from oppression much like the wars in Vietnam or Mozambique. In the United States, he wrote, colonialism had taken the form of slavery, and then a very coercive, debt-based, sharecropping system. From these institutions, a system of racism had developed that kept black working people in the lowest economic ranks by denying them rights to unions, universities, and loans of all kinds.

These economic barriers were reinforced by a government that looked the other way, or actively colluded, when vigilantes and mobs attacked any individual, organization, or community that stepped out of place, and used lynching, mob violence, or even burning down whole black communities, like those in Wilmington, North Carolina, and Tulsa, Oklahoma. Because of this colonial relationship, Forman argued, the black movement needed to organize separately to fight for their own liberation.

Forman called his ideology "revolutionary nationalism" and distinguished it from what he called "reactionary nationalism." Advocates of this latter philosophy argued for unity based on skin color, but did not see themselves as part of a movement working for equality and fairness for all peoples. Forman argued that revolutionary nationalism was part of a worldwide movement of national liberation fighting against the injustices of capitalism and imperialism. For the present, Forman wrote, black activists should organize for independent political power based in the black sections of large urban areas, which in Washington, made up well over half of the city.

I responded to Forman's anger on an emotional level, for anger at the stupidity and inhumanity of so many people had been simmering in my own heart as well. The more I learned and the deeper my commitment to change, the closer my anger approached a full boil. The ongoing attacks against black activists especially the steady numbers of fatal ones fanned the flames.

I remembered that Fanon talked at length about the long uphill struggle to heal the wounds of colonialism, and the redemptive power of struggle. Debray also talked about how the process of disengaging from patterns of acceptance of exploitation and oppression in itself educated and trained people to take moral and political leadership. These realities augured a prolonged period of black and white people working separately. Despite the fact that I shunned electoral politics in other contexts, I could see that Forman's vision of electoral politics was part of broader strategy for gathering and deploying the forces of the black community.

I read the pamphlet carefully, and we distributed it to all the campuses where we worked in DC. It became the foundation of what I understood to be the analysis and the mood of the black power movement, not just for SNCC but also for young urban ghetto residents, other civil rights organizations, and the Black Panther Party.

Like many other white radicals, I embraced the exploration of African black identity and black nationalism in the context of the post–World War II push for national independence, and the rise of liberation movements battling colonial powers. I didn't think much about the history of nationalism as a broader idea, or its origins in Europe as a vehicle to argue for secular control over science and commerce. North American colonists had fought for independence but had excluded blacks one way or another, so it was only fair they should get to create their own nation. Having read little of earlier writers like Frederick Douglass, W. E. B. DuBois, or Ida B. Wells, and having never even heard of Marcus Garvey, I knew little of the history of black cultural self-definition independent of the idea of nationalism. I accepted Forman's argument that black people could never develop an independent economic base without political independence.

I didn't know what organizational backing stood behind Forman's call to action, since SNCC was in disarray by then and Forman's organizational allegiance unclear, but I assumed that the knowledge and the will to mobilize around his plan existed in at least some sectors of the black movement. If and when there was a way that we could support it, beyond popularizing the ideas among young whites, I would hear about it.

Forman's call for black liberation did not silence the black voices that continued to call for work on integrated projects. Bayard Rustin, a senior statesman of both the civil rights and peace movements, argued all through

this period that since blacks made up only ten percent of the US population they could never win anything separately. Reverend Galamison, a
leader of the New York City public school integration struggle, also held
out stubbornly for the importance of working with whites when whites
were truly working in the interests of blacks. Much of the original leadership of SNCC, including John Lewis and James Lawson, also continued
to hold this position, but I heard little of these voices.

I did not understand, then, that black activists did not differ about
whether the black community should have its own identity or shape its
destiny. Black communities already were separate and shaping their own
destiny. Clearly integrated organizations in which whites tried to call the
shots were unacceptable to all black activists. How black and white cultures would come together on the individual level remained to be seen,
but that wasn't the primary issue. The purpose of integration was never to
affirm the humanity of blacks or provide a loving community beyond
small circles of activists, but rather to provide equal political or economic
opportunities.

King and many other leaders attempted both to acknowledge the
widespread anger and to keep encouraging the spiritual work that allowed
people to join together across the divisions. This was what Greg wanted to
do, too. But King's spiritual energy was closely associated with religious
institutions, institutions whose legitimacy was often weak or nonexistent
for young people, many of whom, myself included, were thoroughly dis-
gusted by religion's past accommodations of and silence about racism. In
the absence of these institutions, however, we lacked a secular forum
among in which to explore and validate the possibility of change, redemp-
tion, and forgiveness.[28]

My major responsibility, it seemed, was to educate other whites to the
point that they could understand why Forman's analysis and plan made
sense. Since it was up to black people to determine their future, I had to
remain passive in any further deliberations about the question of race in
the United States. Given this line of reasoning, the problem of knowing
who to support, when there were divisions within the black community,
was troublesome, especially as COINTELPRO became more aggressive,

and the black movement became more fragmented. Furthermore, without any collaborative conversation between blacks and whites, the meaning of support remained obscure and often inaccessible.

Nearly forty years later, this conversation has progressed a great deal in some ways. The intellectual and political ferment of the late 60s has produced a rich literature, both fiction and nonfiction, that explores the black experience. We've seen a great variety of strategies for obtaining both political and economic power, although racially motivated barriers to loans and insurance and other advantages given to whites are still far too common. We've also been treated to many examples around the world of nationalism run amok, especially when it was rooted in racial, religious, or ethnic identity. As a caution to the collaborative approach, we have to admit that beneath the surface, as in the field of education, researchers and policy makers still pay scant attention to specific, diverse needs of different sectors of the black community. In other words, we have a long way to go and absolutely no reason to relax our vigilance.

At the time, I was humbled by the fact that I, like most other whites, had so innocently hoped for integration at first without realizing how much more complex the problem and the solution must be. It hadn't occurred to me that there might be a distinction between equal opportunity and integration. Furthermore, angry black separatists pointed out that integration as I had conceived of it had been entirely based on the assumption that white culture was the norm and everyone wanted to share in it. I had not, at first, even thought about what it might mean for a multitude of different but equal cultures to negotiate common ways to learn from each other and share, without one dominating another. I heard no one raise the question as to how to create a broader, more diverse consensus based on common national beliefs, ones that bind people together.

In Chicago, unbeknownst to me, my friend Greg argued vehemently against reprinting Forman's pamphlet because of Forman's oppositional approach to change. Greg felt strongly that it was counterproductive for people to organize themselves primarily around their separate experiences of oppression. We needed more shared experiences, not less, to learn how to work better together to tackle the big problems that affected us all. Perhaps Greg understood as well that the model of national liberation was a response, as Fanon had argued, to the belief that the differences were irreconcilable and could only be resolved through force of arms. Soon after, Greg left Chicago and returned to Austin, Texas, discouraged about SDS's future. He and I never discussed the Forman piece, but when we saw each other for the next and last time, we argued about his belief that liberation had to be rooted in one's own experience. By then I was impatient with this concern, having been drawn to the urgency of supporting black power. I made fun of him for believing that women's liberation or gay liberation, which was an issue of personal relevance to him, could rival black liberation in importance, or that one could only fight for all of them, not one alone. Greg was hurt by my challenge in a realm that he felt so immediately and personally, and he retreated. I walked away from this once-important friend and mentor, and dismissed him as someone who was not keeping up with the times. Black power, as I understood it, offered an absoluteness in its vision that was similar to some versions of Marxism. It assured me that there was a fix to the problems, if everyone just agreed to pull together.[29] Ironically, having rejected my parents' belief that "progress" would fix all, I was now tempted by a solution that was different in its particulars, but which shared a comforting veneer of certainty.

Later in April, I flew to Chicago to join Mike Spiegel for a short trip through Iowa, Kansas, and Wisconsin. As national secretary of SDS, he had been invited to a few campuses, and I was invited to others to talk about my trip to Vietnam. The time was also a chance for us to consider whether Mike would come to Washington after his term ended in June, both as an organizer and as my partner. In addition to hours spent speaking to campus groups about Vietnam and SDS, we hung out with friends and took a long acid trip at a beautiful lake in Manhattan, Kansas.

A couple of weeks later he came to Washington. Like with most of my relationships up to this point, I paired with Mike because we shared a common interest in politics and enjoyed a physical relationship. I had no expectations for lasting love or deep passion. We went together to Mike Klonsky and Sue Eanet's wedding. I still didn't understand why anyone would care about getting married, especially someone like Sue who had been an active participant at various women's meetings in SDS. Nonetheless, I admired their independence in bucking the trend.

While we continued to plug away at our work, events were taking a far more dramatic turn in New York City, especially at Columbia University. Over the previous year, antiwar and SDS activists on campus, including cochairs Ted Gold and Ted Kaptchuk, had built up a strong but minority antiwar following among students. They distributed materials, held rap sessions in the dorms, protested recruiters, and held referendums, first on student ranking and then on military recruiting.

By April, a number of students had become increasingly frustrated with SDS's inability to substantively change university policies that supported the war effort. SDS also began to work with black students who had recently been protesting yet another Columbia incursion into Harlem, this time to build a gym on precious park space. Led by future Weatherman leaders Mark Rudd and John Jacobs (known as J. J.), among others, these young people came to feel that anything but decisive moral action was fraudulent.

Soon after King's death, Columbia's president, Grayson Kirk, spoke at the college's memorial service for King. Mark Rudd, inspired by the outrage of young blacks around the country, stood up and disrupted the proceedings by accusing Kirk of hypocrisy for lauding Dr. King even while Columbia exploited its black workers and stole parkland from the surrounding black neighborhood.[30]

Over the next few days, this kind of moral charge mobilized thousands of young people. Confrontations over the war and the new gym escalated when hundreds of students occupied campus buildings and shut down the university. Rudd and the rest of the action faction, as they came to be called, believed that acting in itself transformed those who participated, much as Debray and Fanon had argued. Acting therefore satisfied the demands of morality as well as serving to educate and convince a majority. Indeed, at Columbia that spring, militant minority action appeared to mobilize far more young people than the previous debates and protest. The big strikes at Berkeley and Wisconsin had also drawn in thousands of young people who had never before stepped up to be counted. The camaraderie and spirit of the events opened them up to new experiences. Everyone's commitment was ratcheted up a notch. The Columbia student strike was taken as evidence that the time for action was here. Those like Ted Kaptchuk and Teddy Gold who had argued for more education before proceeding to risky action were decisively overruled and discredited.

If the method of confronting difference is to demand that your opponent change, however, how do you address difference *within* your ranks? Confrontational action aggressively imposed the will of the minority— theoretically, a majority— without power on those with the power. As the leadership of the Columbia strike spread out around the country afterward, many of them used this same aggressive confrontation to dominate their opponents in the movement, bullying them into silence or using humiliation to discredit them. It was a style that embraced certainty as a primary credential for leadership. None of these practices were new to SDS, which had inherited similar ones from some traditions of academic discourse, the so-called Talmudic left, and most recently from various parties like PL and sects that sought to dominate discourse within SDS. The growing intensity of the war and attacks on the black movement seemed to necessitate decisive moral action and, ironically, seemed to justify the top-down charismatic leadership emerging from Columbia. Perhaps it was no accident that events on an all-male campus, whose SDS chapter and leadership was all male, gave a particular boost to this style of leadership.

Like most SDS activists, I cheered the actions at Columbia when they happened. On May 6, the headline of *New Left Notes* read, " Two, Three, Many Columbias," a variation of "Two, Three, Many Vietnams," a slogan coined by Che Guevara, in which he argued that fights for self-determination in one third-world country after another would eventually weaken the economic stranglehold of big powers beyond the point of no repair.[31] It was a persuasive argument rooted in the reality we saw in every day's paper. Our job, then, was to be in a position to bring down the critically weakened center from the inside. With the quick adoption of this slogan, national SDS soon took sides with the action faction and all that it entailed.

The slogan tapped into a reservoir of energy and reinforced the outlook and sense of urgency in Forman's pamphlet. Soon, Rudd and Jacobs would become national figures, instrumental in the creation of Weatherman, and Teddy Gold, Robbie Roth, Peter Clapp, David Gilbert, and several other Columbia veterans would be won over and join enthusiastically.

Certainly on the two coasts these events continued the trend for black student activism to serve as a catalyst for white activism, in the tradition of the civil rights movement. The demands of black students, however, tended to be morally clear and often attainable, encouraging sustained efforts. They focused on equal opportunity and civil rights, although by then most black student groups were also openly antiwar. Increasingly, white students in SDS felt compelled to fight for big issues like ending the war; redefining the relationship between corporations, the military, and the government; and redefining the role of the university system.

One group with concrete goals that actively sought help from the SDS in Washington was the United Farm Workers (UFW), the union of migrant workers, led by César Chávez, that had been organizing in California. These laborers were not protected by minimum-wage laws, were continually exposed to toxic pesticides, forced to use dangerous tools, and suffered under abusive management practices. The farmworkers had chosen to focus on the huge California grape crop in their fight for the right to unionize. When the growers refused to negotiate, the UFW organized a nationwide boycott of California grapes and wines. The farmworkers' DC organizer, Felix,[32] actively sought our help to support the boycott in the Washington area.

Felix was one of dozens of experienced farmworkers working for the UFW at subsistence pay. Farmworker supporters, often members of churches or religious organizations, provided him with free room and board by inviting him into their homes for several weeks at a time. His only expenses were transportation around the city. When we started working with him in late 1967, he had been away from California for many months, and was unable to return to see his family, even for Christmas, for

over a year more. Because of his efforts, many, many organizations contributed people to walk picket lines in front of supermarkets all over the
city and suburbs. Tens of thousands of leaflets explaining the boycott, many
printed at 3 Thomas Circle, were distributed.

Felix's seriousness and commitment moved me deeply and inspired me to
work with the same dedication. To me, he was like a Vietnamese soldier, ded-
icating his life and sacrificing everything to work for equality. Felix never
had any down time, where he could party, or relax in his own world. Instead
he went home at night to someone else's home, someone else's culture.

While we also worked tirelessly, we saw our own rebellion from our
culture as a critical aspect of our identity. We were on a mission to establish new cultural practices and beliefs. Our celebration of rock and roll,
our exploration of drugs, and our house on Lanier Place all nourished our
work for peace and justice, which in turn provided us with the context of
personal and intellectual challenges that made every day exciting.

On May 17, a different kind of drama took the spotlight for a moment.
Nine members of the Catholic left concocted a batch of napalm from a
recipe they found in a Special Forces handbook. They then broke into a
Selective Service office in Catonsville, Maryland, removed a large batch
of draft files, poured their napalm all over the files, and burned them. Some
of these radical pacifists would later serve six years in prison for this act.

These activists, I thought, challenged the government's irresponsible
wielding of power, not with equal and like power but by arguing that
morality and sanity should trump raw power. They could have done a lot
of damage after breaking in, but they believed that by exercising a *restraint*
of power they would to demonstrate a more humane and intelligent way
to engage with and resolve conflict. It was this restraint that was perhaps
the most powerful element of the action, indicating that the perpetrators
were rising above their own, personal anger and dismay at the war, setting
an example of a kind of leadership that was far more creative and thoughtful than that of the current administration.

While I was moved by the action, I didn't see the power of this restraint
at the time. Instead, I thought these Catholic activists seemed to only be
appealing to the morality of the people in power, but they stopped short

of challenging the structures that supported the economy and government. By then, my thinking was that we had to raise the question of power at all times, finding ways to wrest concessions from those in power. I no longer thought that an appeal to reason or morality would convince anyone in the administration to replace the whole system with a more humane and egalitarian one.

In late May, New England Resistance, the organization of pacifist draft resisters, gathered at the Arlington Street Church in Boston to support one draft resister, and one young soldier who had gone AWOL rather than return to Vietnam after his first nine-month tour. The Church was providing them with sanctuary, ushering in yet a new forum for educating about and resisting the war.

Shortly thereafter, Bobby Kennedy was shot and killed just after winning the critical California primary. With Johnson, and now Kennedy, out of the race, the only one left to oppose cold warrior Vice President Hubert Humphrey was Gene McCarthy, a genuine antiwar candidate with little chance, I thought, of winning the nomination. While I had not had much hope that Bobby Kennedy would or could disentangle himself from his family and corporate ties, he had seemed to lend some genuine support to both civil rights and antiwar efforts. His murder was yet further evidence that progressive leadership would be gunned down if it got too close to power.

During that spring of intense activity, I began to recruit more people like Bill Willet to come to Washington to work with SDS full time. One of the first people interested was Jonathan Lerner, then called Jonny, who had been working with Jeff Jones and Phoebe Hirsch in New York. Jonny had grown up in the Washington suburbs and had attended Antioch College with Jeff where they had become close friends. By the spring of 1968, he wanted to leave New York and was intrigued by the possibility of returning to his hometown, especially if he could work with high school students. He came on July 1 and immediately went to work helping Sue Orrin and Jenny Stearns set up a "free school" for high school students in the Maryland suburb of Silver Spring, with summer classes in topics including radical Christianity, Marxism, graphics, drug awareness, and the

US in Asia. The school, a place where young people could congregate, was a joint effort of SDS and other members of the Washington activist community. I also talked with the current residents of the house, all of whom organized their lives around some form of work for the movement, about my aspirations to turn the house into an official SDS organizers' residence.

Later that summer, Tim McCarthy arrived. He had been working as the printer in the national office and all-around jack-of-all-trades and was ready for a change, especially after the new officers took over in June. Several people from other chapters also joined the regional team, including Hank Topper, Helen Selhorst, and John Fournelle from Georgetown University.

I was excited about the prospects for the next year, and proud of the role I was playing as regional organizer. So much was happening, so fast. I saw in Washington a wonderful opportunity to build our local community, to bring hundreds more young people into the movement and dozens into committed, full-time work.

In June I traveled to New Hampshire to attend my sister Ann's wedding. The previous fall she had started dating Frank Olson, a member of the Coast Guard who was serving in Washington. Frank came from Pasadena and looked the quintessential clean-cut, blond Scandinavian. Finding law school not what he wanted, and consequently faced with the choice of signing up or being drafted, he used his love of the sea to apply for the Coast Guard. Because of his classic good looks, generous social graces, and enthusiastic competence at pretty much everything, he was assigned to be in the president's honor guard.

I had met him the previous Thanksgiving when Ann cooked dinner at her tiny apartment, bringing together Frank, my father and stepmother, and myself. Our childhood closeness remained, but I continued to feel that she was part of an older generation with a more traditional lifestyle, compared to my experience of the cultural explosion of the 60s. While she liked folk music, she had not become a rock-and-roll fanatic like my friends and I had. She didn't smoke, drink very much, or experiment with drugs as far as I knew.

Our most significant difference now, though, was that I couldn't imagine committing myself to building a life with one man, putting everything else secondary to that promise. It wasn't that Ann was particularly deferential or dependent. Far from it. Nonetheless, getting married seemed to mean a choice to bind oneself to one's partner's work and family, and to make life's big decisions together. I wanted the freedom to explore everything and to make choices that I might not yet be able to justify or even articulate clearly to another person. I found so much joy in being a part of a broader community that being in that kind of a couple seemed limiting.

I knew Ann was against the war and supported civil rights; she too had rejected the path to a traditional middle-class life. She had been living happily since VISTA on the most meager of salaries from the Friends. But I wasn't sure she saw the revolution coming.

Ann and Frank chose a Quaker ceremony in the big old barn next to the farmhouse where my mother and stepfather lived in New Hampshire. My father and stepmother came from New York for the event, as did a number of cousins and various friends of Ann. Ann and Frank then returned to Washington for six months while Frank finished up his tour of duty with the honor guard. They then left for California on their way to Kodiak, Alaska, where Frank was to serve on board a ship.

I returned to Washington and helped paint walls and scrub floors at a small rented space we were preparing for the summer free school. Volunteers had stepped up to add new classes and workshops, including auto mechanics, taught by "Nick Lives." Nick was a young man I had met through the draft resistance union who later turned out to be AWOL from the Marines. He had moved in with me for a few months, until Mike came. The idea for the summer school was to provide a place where high school students could hang out and explore things they were interested in after spending the winter months in alienating high schools. It would be an opportunity to bring them into the community we were building in Washington and encourage them to learn more about their world. A number of college students had committed themselves to teach there during the summer, some of whom stayed at our house at Lanier Place.

At the end of June, Bill, Johnny, and I, and several other SDS members, took off for the five-day June national council meeting in East Lansing,

Michigan, in our old red VW van. The national council discussions were fractured and contentious, and while various proposals were put before the body, few got anywhere. An attempt to fix the structure of SDS failed yet again. The Columbia veterans argued hard for a confrontational approach to organizing antiwar protests. It was not a convention at which members could wonder about things, trade ideas, or tentatively formulate questions.

Those who came from chapters in which PL often dominated the agenda, arrived already frustrated and ready for a showdown. The real struggle took place over the election of officers, control of the resources of the national office, scant though they were, and editorial control of *New Left Notes*. During the questioning of candidates, someone asked Bernardine Dohrn, who was running for "interorganization secretary," whether she considered herself a socialist. "I consider myself a revolutionary communist," she said. Indeed, she had earlier presented a paper with Steve Halliwell and Tom Bell for the structure debate, in which they argued that SDS should be "using radical movement in the work of making revolution." The task of national leadership should be to transform SDS into a "revolutionary organization." They even had a rudimentary plan: focus on larger cities, working on campuses, but reaching outside to high schools, community colleges, welfare mothers, and young workers.[33] While not explicit, the focus was on young people.

As usual, "revolutionary" could mean anything you wanted it to mean. The previous December, the proposal for Ten Days had talked about resistance without spelling out any assumptions as to how the resistance would effect changes in policy. By April, SDS National Secretary Mike Spiegel, in his report to the membership, had talked about "state power." In Marxist ideology, "state power" meant the power that resided in the government, and it was necessarily something that had to be seized, presumably by force, if you wanted to bring about any significant change on behalf of most people. Now, in June, the Dohrn-Halliwell proposal focused on building a "revolutionary" organization.

In the chaos that was now standard in the big floor debates, no one from any perspective addressed the assumptions behind the idea of revolutionary organization: whether change could happen through some kind of transformation of our democracy, whether a seizure of state power was necessary, or whether they envisioned some other strategy for change.

When Bernardine declared SDS's mission to be the building of a "revolutionary movement," I thought she showed both courage and foresight; if she hadn't explained what she meant, she had, I thought, made a commitment to take on that challenge. I longed for some coherence to the swirl of movement beliefs and strategies—often at odds with each other—and thought that perhaps she and her supporters were prepared to take on the onerous responsibilities of creating that coherence. Like most members, I didn't sort through the full implications of this push to unite everyone in the creation of a revolutionary organization. For the moment, I was comfortable with my own sense that revolution meant tumultuous, rapid change in the location of power. I assumed the details would become clearer as we went along.

The question of how to achieve change, and the possibility that the answer did not lie within the democratic process was now squarely on the agenda. Bernardine and Mike Klonsky from Los Angeles were elected to office, as was Fred Gordon. I looked forward to seeing what this new leadership came up with in the coming months.

While I supported Dohrn and Klonsky, I found the arrogant contempt that Mark Rudd and some of the others from Columbia used in the debate to be obnoxious. Nonetheless, I had to admire the work at Columbia and couldn't help wondering if that style had helped contribute to their success. Perhaps it was justified by the intensity of factional divisions in New York, I thought.

After the convention we all returned to Washington, where I resumed work for WDRU. Revolution notwithstanding, life went on, and the regional work needed to get done. A week later, Mike Spiegel arrived with the news that his parents were passing their old Buick Special on to him. We decided to take a drive-away out West to see friends in San Francisco and then drive up the coast to his family in Portland, Oregon, to pick up the car. I was exhausted by the fast pace of the spring and looked forward to San Francisco and the entirely different culture out there.

I loved the three-day summertime trip across the country. When we drove into San Francisco we decided to go directly to Golden Gate Park, which had so enthralled me on my last visit. As we wended our way around, we came upon a huge crowd, with psychedically painted vans pulled off on the grass here and there. We pulled over and asked a stoned, bearded young man what was going on, and found out that Janis Joplin was giving a free concert. I thought I had died and gone to heaven. Dylan validated my alienation and anger; the Beatles, the absurdity of the public world; but Joplin forged together her power and vulnerability into something breathtakingly beautiful.

We spent a couple of days in San Francisco, visiting with SDS friends and exploring the city's hippie scene. I bought a pair of striped bell-bottoms, the first departure from my standard jeans, and I tried to let the laid-back hippie approach to life wash over me. Clearly, I was way too focused and driven for this to seriously alter my style, but the opportunity to slow down and reflect more on the bizarre and beautiful aspects of life nourished my soul. We then headed to Oregon, where we spent a few days visiting with Mike's parents.

By the time we headed back to Washington, the main event on the horizon was the Democratic convention scheduled for Chicago in late August. While national SDS refused to endorse the demonstrations, many older SDS members and veterans were recruited for different roles by the demonstration's leadership, which included both Tom Hayden and Rennie Davis. Many current SDS activists in the leadership of different regions and in the national office were also drawn to the event because they knew that tens of thousands of young people would be coming to Chicago. Many of these young supporters of Gene McCarthy would presumably be open to hearing a more radical analysis of the world.

A lot had happened in the national office in the past month. Bernardine Dohrn and Mike Klonsky had collected a new team and were trying to shape SDS into the revolutionary leadership of the movement. Bernardine wrote about SDS's relationship with the Panthers, in an article entitled "White Mother Country Radicals."[34] "Mother Country" referred to the United States as the hub of a global economic system. The Black Panther Party had decided to use the electoral forum as a way to bring its message to thousands of new people. It had invited Carl Oglesby to run as second to Eldridge Cleaver on the Peace and Freedom Party in the upcoming elections. Carl had brought the decision to SDS's leadership, who decided to reject the offer because of its emphasis on electoral politics. "The main point," Bernardine wrote, "is: The best thing that we can be doing for ourselves, as well as for the Panthers and the revolutionary black liberation struggle, is to build a fucking white revolutionary mass movement, not a national paper alliance."

It was becoming clear that a substantial number of SDS members were abandoning any hope of reforming representative democracy. The system was too compromised by the massive wealth and corruption of the small elite of the military-industrial complex that now seemed to be running the show. Quietly, in the midst of the change, many of us were giving up on the idea of democracy altogether, although I, like many others, was still trying to hold onto what I saw as the best of both ideas: the participatory nature of democracy along with the strong leadership and coherence promised by revolution.

I had long since abandoned any hope that Congress could initiate change or even support it, until a majority of people actively sought change. During this period, however, I began to consider the possibility that Congress couldn't even follow the majority because too many of its members had been bought off by major corporate interests. What other access to changing policy did we have then, other than revolution? I still believed in participatory democracy, but I continued to worry about the problem of why the majority seemed so content to ignore the costs of racism and to accept the distortion of truth about the war. I thought we needed a new model. My attention was drawn to the stories I heard and read about popular participation in literacy and in health and in local governance in Cuba, China, and North Vietnam. Cuba had eliminated illiteracy, something we had not done here. China had eliminated fly-born diseases in some parts of the country and was working on eliminating other dangers to the masses. In all of these countries clinics were being set up in the rural areas. In China, the poor were being trained as barefoot doctors. I imagined something like that in urban areas or in Appalachia in this country, where poor people would be empowered to address their own needs, and where people became involved in local government and participated in decision making instead of being treated as helpless dependents of the state. Still I had no idea how to get there.

Greg Calvert noted in his book *Democracy from the Heart* that over the previous year black power and nationalism, urban rebellions, the struggle with PL, the power of Debray and Fanon and other writers, the surge of third-world struggles, and the Red Guards in China had *all* contributed to the growing acceptance of the inevitability of some cataclysmic struggle. The assassination of King and then Robert Kennedy had given added weight to this view. No one ever voted explicitly against reform or for revolution. No one suggested that there might be other choices. It was just a shift, barely noticeable to most of us.

Two weeks before the Democratic convention, the front page of *New Left Notes* showed a photo of a helmeted police officer in leather jacket and sunglasses scowling at the camera with a headline that read, "HOT TOWN PIGS IN THE STREETS.... BUT THE STREETS BELONG TO THE PEOPLE! DIG IT?" If SDS's strategy was to reach young people coming to support McCarthy, I thought, this was an odd way to do it. It wasn't all that long ago that I myself had been a naive believer in the power of elected officials to make things better, and I was quite sure that the smugness of the graphic would have turned me off completely. It was true that Chicago's Mayor Richard Daley had been provocatively threatening, saying he would call out the National Guard, that he would issue a shoot-to-kill order, and that no demonstrators would be allowed near the convention. Daley's police had killed twelve people in the recent King riots in Chicago, and had moved tanks down the main streets of the West Side. Maybe SDS had an obligation to let these young people know what could happen.

I wasn't particularly driven to go to Chicago. In the end, however, Jeff Jones convinced me to come. He wanted to put out a large-format one-page wall newspaper each day of the four-day convention. Jeff had asked his friend Jonny Lerner, skilled in graphic arts, to help. He asked Mike and me to help too. I had loved working on *New Left Notes* and was impressed with the idea of a wall newspaper. Many popular movements had used them to get out information; most recently, one called *Barricades* had been used in Berkeley a month earlier.

When we arrived at the national office, the first edition of *Handwriting on the Wall*, as it was called, was just coming off the new Heidelberg press, which could print the huge poster-sized paper. It quickly became clear that my efforts were not wanted for writing, but for production and distribution. The first issue had the same mix of taunting, macho rhetoric. Again I was somewhat put off by it, but I was among friends, I decided that maybe it was all in good fun. I had been impressed by Jeff's creativity in the past, his ear for new cultural styles, and his willingness to embrace them in a political context. Within hours of arrival, we were setting up distribution teams much as we had organized the spray painting of buses during the Pentagon demonstration. Armed with a variety of pastes and tacks we set out to cover the downtown area site of the convention and the demonstrations, as well as campuses and neighborhoods where visiting young people were likely to be staying.

Despite our efforts to avoid detection by the Chicago police, however, halfway through the second day, our VW van with its out-of-state plates attracted the police, who pulled us over. They demanded we all get out and put our hands up on the van while two officers immediately started ransacking the van. In a heartbeat they found the posters and paste pails and started manhandling the two men who had been in the van. It looked like we were in big trouble.

At that moment, one of the men from our group collapsed on the ground showing signs of the beginnings of a seizure brought on, apparently, from tension. At first the two officers searching the van assumed the young man was faking it and started to kick him to stand up. When they saw me pull down his jaw to put my finger in to flatten his tongue, however, they hesitated. I knew that this friend had had a couple of seizures before, and it became obvious that he was not faking it. The police stopped manhandling the others and allowed us to try to gently restrain him until the seizure passed. At this point the police put us all under arrest, told us to get back in the van, and escorted us to the station where we all piled out. They confiscated everything in the van.

At the booking, one cop started asking me the usual questions about name, address, phone numbers, etc. Then he wanted to know where I had grown up. I was now twenty-two years old and no longer obliged to give my parents' names and addresses, I said. "Why do you want to know?" I asked. "Oh, we're just confirming that you went to the Hoyt School in Stamford, Connecticut and then to high school in Massachusetts." He went on to recount my moves for the next six years until I arrived in Washington, as well as my mother's name and address. I was obviously on some list that they had researched ahead of time (computers were few and far between then, and those that existed did not yet have the ability for rapid connections between databases). Clearly they were trying to intimidate me with the fact that they knew all about me. I was nonplussed.

We did not yet know about the COINTELPRO program of the FBI, but in hindsight it is obvious that they had pulled in my file from the Washington FBI field office. After processing all of us, they told us that they were only charging us with disorderly conduct, but if we were arrested again for anything that week they would charge us with felonies. Not wanting to get stuck in Chicago, I decided to keep a low profile. Later that night, under the glare of TV lights, police waded, batons swinging, into tens of thousands of peaceful protesters, in what would later be called a "police riot" by the Walker Report, *Rights in Conflict*.

This moment, in which Daley's rampant brutality was exposed for all the world to see, was interpreted differently by various segments of the movement. Many people in SDS took note of the fact that the largely unprovoked violence had dramatically revealed the violent nature of the system to thousands of young people. It was similar to the way that Columbia's President Kirk's decision to call in the NYC police department to remove students—and the police's choice to use excessive force—had exposed the university's willingness to use any means necessary to protect its growing relationship with the nation's military-indus-trial complex.

The leadership of SDS took this reasoning one step further, then, becoming convinced that SDS should plan future confrontations in ways that provoked this violent police response as a means of educating still more young people about the violence faced on a regular basis by the poor, people of color, and people of the third world. After their own experience with police violence, students and other young people could more easily believe the stories told by angry black victims of police brutality. It remained to be seen whether there was a difference between the political effect of unprovoked violence and that which had been provoked by throwing stones, verbal taunts, and fighting back in the streets.

After returning from the convention, we settled in to building the region. I was vaguely uneasy that we had not distinguished ourselves in the Wash-ington region with this new, heightened militancy, but I couldn't figure out any way that I should change our approach. I wanted to be part of a community and, in Washington, our house was a small unit in a much broader group of people that included many SDS chapters and other movement groups.

We all settled into our spaces and began to make a plan. Once a week, everyone on staff, both Lanier Place residents and those from campuses, sat on the floor around the wire spool and listed all the particular chores we needed to do for each project we were working on, dividing up incoming requests that didn't fall within regular work areas.

I still had no idea how to connect to the black movement in Washing-ton. On September 8, we heard that shots had been exchanged outside of the DC SNCC office on 14th Street, between members of SNCC and emissaries of the Black Panther Party. There was a similar incident the next day and then we heard nothing more. It made me feel that the black movement had moved to another level, and both of these organizations now had factions that had become extremely aggressive.

What had actually happened was that Lester McKinnie was working in the SNCC office one day when two young men came in claiming to be representatives of the Black Panther Party on the West Coast, and that they had been sent by Huey Newton to take over the daily operations of the office. When commanded to hand over the keys, McKinney refused, saying he'd heard nothing about this beforehand, and an argument ensued. In a phone call to the West Coast office he learned that they had sent no one, and in fact the brief alliance between the Panthers and SNCC had never materialized formally. The next day, the imposters called and again demanded the keys, saying they would shoot their way in. Again, McKinney refused, and shots had been fired.

Evidence uncovered in later cases (*Bin Wahad v. the FBI*) revealed that, indeed, COINTELPRO was actively and successfully trying to divide the two organizations. No arrests were ever made, despite the fact that the office was attacked on three successive days with guns and a molotov cocktail. Fortunately, there were no injuries. At the time, however, I, and most others, did not suspect the FBI, and the incident successfully contributed to marginalizing SNCC and Panther credibility in both black and white communities.

The big event for the SDS region in September was a mobilization of the whole Washington community to expose as both silly and sinister the House Un-American Activities Committee (HUAC) investigation of the leaders of the Democratic convention protests. At one of the support rallies we had lined up speakers from the area. Jerry Rubin, one of HUAC's prime targets, showed up at the last minute, just before I was to start the program, and demanded to be given the microphone. I was about to get up on the small outdoor platform and I felt utterly disregarded as he looked past me at the microphone even as he spoke, giving the impression that I was just an impediment he expected to brush out of the way. There's no doubt that the event would have benefited from a little levity. We were organizing on his behalf, so normally I would have been glad he was there. However, I had just heard Jerry give a speech in which he attacked the "straight-laced left." Given his decidedly disrespectful and uncollaborative approach, I didn't trust him not to take over this rally, *organized* by this so-called straight-laced part of the movement, and undermine my own ability to speak. The rally was also part of our local strategy to educate young people and bring them into the work of the region. I told him he couldn't speak until the end. He was furious and started to make his way to the stage anyway. I stood between him and the steps to the stage door. Calling me all sorts of names he realized he would have had to push me out of the way, which he didn't do, or leave, which is what he did.

In retrospect, the incident reveals the damage caused by the movement's unresolved position on women's leadership. Even before the incident I had been uncomfortable with the yippies' charismatic, aggressive, but unaccountable style of work. Neither Jerry nor I had any vision of how to bridge the gap at that moment.

Toward the end of September, Les Coleman came from the national office on a multicity tour to see what was happening. It was the first time someone from the national office had come to visit the Washington region, except when people dropped by during national demonstrations. I thought we deserved the attention. Les was somebody who presented himself as an important but understated figure. I had gotten to know him a little on visits to Chicago, when we discovered a mutual penchant for drinking straight bourbon. On a few occasions, I enjoyed hanging out in bars with Les for an hour or two, talking politics.

Nothing about Les was ever explicit. When asked where he came from he would say something oblique and philosophical. When I asked others in the national office, they said that he and his partner Kathy Archibald used to work with SNCC and were friends with James Forman. Those were intense credentials. (Although somewhat misleading, it turned out.) Les, however, never talked about himself. He spoke in the vernacular and accent of a poor Southerner. Only years later did I find out that he had been in PL and had left shortly before he showed up at SDS. In fact, like many SDS members, he came from a reasonably well-off middle-class family in Texas. I had seen some of the men in the Chicago ERAP project try to take on the cultural and personal characteristics of the young men they were trying to organize, and I sensed that maybe Les had done that in his own past somewhere. We were all busy reworking who we were. Since it wasn't so easy to figure out how to connect with different kinds of people, I understood why Les might be the way he was. I accepted Les. I liked him, but didn't quite trust him.

During the visit, Les suggested that he, Mike Spiegel, and I write an article on false privilege, a concept that had been kicking around in discussions both within SDS and among women. In retrospect, I suspect that Les recruited us to gain a broader legitimacy for his own efforts to fight PL, that it was a shrewd, calculated move. Even if I had been more aware of this aspect of Les's invitation, however, I would have jumped at the opportunity to develop my thinking about the role of the university.

Peter Henig had first introduced me to the university's growing importance to the military-industrial complex. Columbia students had taken it a step further when they demanded that the university end its complicity with the war effort, and that they stop helping themselves to the resources of the local black community. I was trying to understand the individual, political-psychological experience of buying into a liberal university education, so we could better explain to students what the issues were.

"False privileges," we said in the article, were "the values of individualism—being one-up, individual recognition for social accomplishments, being in a position to control other people's lives to one's own advantage. With them comes the attitude that not everyone can make it, but if a few do on the backs of the rest, if I do, I like the system."[35] Universities offered a liberal arts education, but in fact they enveloped students in the individualistic, amoral values of the system, and trained students to become functionaries in that system. Therefore, while a university education seemed like a privilege, it was in fact a false one, in that it was not what it said it was. Instead, it dehumanized its participants by allowing creativity and initiative only in service of a system that offered increased income for the few, at the expense of the many.

The other aspect of the idea concerned the privilege of democracy, that we had a supposedly free society here because others, slaves and contract labor, provided a major part of the economic underpinnings that allowed democracy for some. If everyone didn't have equal access to freedom, what did freedom mean?

We were grappling with important ideas, the pros and cons of individualism and the relationship between democracy and equality. An exploration of the complex and sometimes conflicting roles of universities was long overdue. Nonetheless, the article suffered acutely from a lack of gray area. Everything was all or nothing. Our oversimplifications led us to the absurd conclusion that we needed to shut down the universities, as had been done at Columbia and UC Berkeley, because they could no longer be reformed. I was aware that the strategy was lacking something, that unless we believed we were on the brink of a mass insurrection, we would just be endorsing a country without higher education.

Most of SDS's original leadership, frustrated with the inevitable chaos and dysfunctions of a rapidly expanding youth organization, had moved on to other work. This left the phenomenal workload of maintaining and leading the ungainly student organization to activists who believed, for a variety of different reasons, that young people were the most powerful social grouping in the country at the time, and that they were the most powerful engine of change. These activists, like Dohrn and Klonsky, took up the challenge of figuring out how to combine the exuberance of youth—and, sometimes, the willingness of alienated young people to completely let go of social restraint—with a strategy for fundamental social change.

By the fall of 1968, SDS's national leadership reported in *New Left Notes* that they had begun to meet as a "national collective" to thrash out their ideas about what to do. From late summer to the December national council, individuals in the national leadership, along with some of their allies, traveled the country and continued to write a steady stream of articles for *NLN*, articulating the major themes of their developing ideas, as well as revealing persistent areas of confusion.

One of these articles, about SDS activities in Ohio and Michigan, was written by Terry Robbins and Bill Ayers. Bill Ayers was a former University of Michigan student who had worked in an alternative preschool in Ann Arbor for the past three years. Terry Robbins had been working in various capacities with ERAP and SDS in Ohio, since dropping out of Kenyon College. Terry and Bill described their excitement about an influx of young people enthusiastically flocking to local SDS chapters, many inspired by the upheaval in Chicago.

At Case Western Reserve, several students, including Lisa Meisel, leafleted the campus and gathered about a hundred young people to meet in a revived SDS chapter. At the first meeting, the article reported, Terry and Bill, excited about Columbia and Chicago, talked about the possibility of revolution before the gathering broke up into workshops to discuss specific issues like the draft, university complicity, women's liberation, and protests for the upcoming elections. The next day Terry and Bill and about sixty exuberant students joined a "shout-down" demonstration in Cleveland, where presidential candidate Hubert Humphrey was speaking. Dozens of such protests had popped up whenever administration spokespersons tried to speak, using proven falsehoods to argue their case, such as the imminent victory of US and South Vietnamese forces.

At Kent State, a nucleus of young people, including Rick Erickson, Candy Erickson, and Howie Emmer, had started an SDS chapter the previous year, in conjunction with ongoing antiwar work. During the summer, Howie joined with members of the Cleveland ERAP project and other regional activists to begin the Cleveland Draft Resistance Union. Terry Robbins, who had been living with members of the ERAP project and working on an alternative newspaper, joined them for a while at the start of the summer. Bill Ayers also went to Cleveland to help them set up an alternative school modeled on the Children's Community School in Michigan where he and Diana Oughton worked. Bill and Terry, his roommate for the summer, wrote a lengthy paper about the Children's Community experience to serve as a model for others who wanted to set up similar schools.

By the end of the summer, Howie, Bill, Terry, and others were talking excitedly about a regional strategy for helping SDS grow in Michigan and

Ohio. Howie returned to Kent, where he was still a student. He, Rick, Candy, and others worked hard during registration to bring sixty people to the first SDS meeting and, after further work in dorms and around campus, two hundred to the second. They had tentatively planned to put together a guerrilla theater performance around the elections as part of SDS's national program to protest the elections.

Bill and Terry also traveled to the University of Michigan, eager to use the long history of SDS on campus to stir up activity. The SDS chapter at the University of Michigan in Ann Arbor had been one of SDS's first. During the 1967–68 school year, the SDS chapter had decided to hold a student referendum on whether the university should discontinue its policy of assisting the war effort. The University of Michigan had several major contracts with both the Department of Defense and the CIA that were directly related to the war, including the same Institute for Defense Analysis that had been an issue at Columbia. Ann Arbor SDS saw the referendum as a way to bring the facts to a broader circle of people.

As intended, the issue provoked extensive debate on campus. Many students from the engineering school, a recipient of many defense contracts, frequently challenged SDS, supporting both the war and the university contracts providing resources for it. When students voted in the spring, the majority voted against severing ties with government and private defense contractors, just as they had at Columbia, although a substantial minority supported the resolution.

That fall of 1968, in the wake of the referendum, Bill, Terry and others decided to challenge this established leadership, just as the action faction at Columbia had done the previous spring. The Jesse James Gang, the name adopted by Bill, Terry, Jim Mellon, and others, challenged the wisdom of the previous year's referendum. Here was the dilemma again of what to do when the will of the democratic majority seemed to demand that the whole acquiesce to behavior that the minority found morally reprehensible.

The James Gang's answer was clear. They felt that the introductory meeting was "boring": "If you think the only thing to do with war research is to burn it up; and the only thing to do with bad classes is to take them over, and the only thing to do about bullshit candidates is to run them out with your own lives, then let's talk."[36]

This response, they wrote, had both moral clarity and the ability to bring more young people into the movement. In the next meeting, they explained their position:

> The students know that their lives are on a one-way street to corrupt and hedonistic suburbia, that their personal problems and hang-ups are common to their peers—but they don't see politics as the answer to their problems. They've heard all the old radical arguments, but people don't accept arguments just because they sound correct. They accept them when they see that the arguments make sense OUT OF THEIR OWN LIVES. [The] politics of confrontation provides activity based on an élan and a community which shows young people that we CAN make a difference, we CAN hope to change the system, and also that life within the radical movement can be liberated, fulfilling and meaningful—rather than the plastic of suburbia or the tired intellectual arrogance of the old left. . . . [C]onfrontation, we argue, is a way of building a base.[37]

The James Gang pinpointed the fact that the old culture of the chapter, while productive and politically in tune with the majority, did not appeal to many of the younger students now in the university. These younger students were hungrily searching for validation and refuge from a world of family and school that frowned upon their lifestyle and their vision of their future. This infusion of alienated young people, drawn in more by culture than politics, was becoming the norm in many SDS chapters. They weren't looking for a complicated discussion about how to bring about change, but for validation, for a community, and for a way to express their anger about the war.

The James Gang offered a tight, validating community within which members could express their rage and frustration about the ways things were, and their empathy for others suffering on the planet. They asserted their youthful virility and fun-loving natures in contrast to the "boring," "stodgy," old guard of Michigan SDS. It was a contest of cool as much as a substantive difference about when and how to act. Not surprisingly, many young people responded. Characteristics of leadership traditionally associated with male aggression were woven into this veneer of coolness, although the toughness and aggressiveness had its appeal to women who were exploring their own independence and strength.[38] Most of the new recruits were young, freshmen and sophomores who indeed might well have drifted away from the abstract, intellectual discussions of the original chapter membership, much as I had at Swarthmore. The leaders of the James Gang provided them with mentoring and a sense of belonging.

The original chapter members, however, called the James Gang "crazies" and "brownshirts." They seemed to them more like bullies than organizers. Nonetheless, when, at the third meeting, the James Gang caucus proposed classroom disruptions, burning exams, publicly critiquing courses and professors, and a program to disrupt the elections in November, they were able to win a majority vote of the chapter on all issues. The "Radical Caucus," as the old elected leadershipand members who supported them called themselves, walked out and formed a second, separate SDS chapter.

Just as at Columbia, these disagreements raised issues that were complex. Only a sophisticated democratic structure and leadership could support a discussion that thoroughly explored them. Over the course of the next months, Chicago, Michigan, and Ohio became the hothouse of strategic thinking about how to build on the confrontational politics of Columbia and the Democratic Convention Demonstrations. In the pages of *NLN*, one national leader after another pointed to Michigan and urged other chapters to follow suit. The theme of all-or-nothing, of "join us, or be discarded on the refuse heap of history," emerged quickly and strongly in the pages of *NLN* as the fall progressed, with each of the national leadership weighing in with challenges to chapters to be more aggressive, more militant. If anyone noticed that the uprising of the previous spring seemed to have left the Columbia SDS chapter befuddled about its next steps, no such remark was heard.

While the James Gang was unable to organize a large uprising at the University of Michigan, there were several large campus eruptions that fall including ones at the University of Wisconsin, Kent State in Ohio, and, especially, San Francisco State in California. Once again, the events at SF State began with black student activism. In this case, black students went on strike after university officials fired a popular black professor who was also a member of the Black Panther Party. They were quickly joined by white students, including SDS and PL members, and then some faculty. At the start, the SDS chapter focused on reaching out to the majority of white students who had not yet struck. They went to classes and explained the ten demands of the black students and answered questions. By the end of the week so many students and faculty had joined the strike that the president was forced to close the school.

At Kent State, the activities initially planned at the beginning of the year were upstaged when black students, loosely organized into a group called Black United Students (BUS), noticed that on November 13, the Oakland Police Department was coming to recruit on campus, invited by the Kent law enforcement training program. Black students, familiar with the Black Panther Party and with Huey Newton's upcoming trial, could see the outlines of an intentional plan to bring more white policemen into a police department already plagued with a culture of racist beliefs and practices. New recruits from Ohio would have little choice but to buy into this culture, knowing little about Oakland itself or its residents. Black students planned a protest.

In support, SDS issued three demands to the university: (1) the Oakland Police Department be denied access to the campus, (2) the university agree not to spy on or intimidate campus protest organizations, and (3) the Kent State police disarm. SDS students rallied, and two hundred and fifty students marched across campus, through classroom buildings, to sit-in at the placement office, where they were joined by black students. After negotiations with a Kent State representative failed to yield results, the university called in the highway patrol to clear the area. When they arrived, however, the university stalled for several hours and eventually students left, with no arrests and the Oakland police department interviews prevented.

The next day the administration brought disciplinary charges against both black and white students, which caused a series of rallies and demonstrations demanding amnesty for everyone. Supporters swelled to over a thousand with fourteen hundred signing petitions saying they had been there too, so why single out eight people? Caught in an absurd situation, the administration backed down. After that, SDS meetings grew, and many more members fanned out into dorms to participate in educational rap sessions.

Significantly, chapter organizers and many of the younger students who came into the chapter at that point began to congregate at the "haunted house," a ramshackle house rented by Rick Erickson and his wife, Candy Erickson, who was an English graduate student and popular teacher on campus. Almost daily a crowd would gather to read and talk about US foreign policy, the causes of poverty and racism, and strategies for change. Rick, Candy, and Howie were inclusive and eager to share their sources and ideas with everyone. The culture was warm and no one was afraid to ask question or to voice a tentative idea.[39]

Terry Robbins, who was also reading and thinking intensively, came by frequently in his capacity as SDS regional traveler for the Ohio region, and was often a part of these conversations. He came to be known as someone who could break down complex ideas in a way that made them comprehensible, someone who could listen and answer questions. His passion was contagious, and people found him very compelling.

That fall, national SDS's previously confused and contradictory utterances about the upcoming elections were resolved in a resolution submitted by Jeff Jones, Bernardine Dohrn, and John Jacobs and passed in October at the Boulder national council. "The Elections Don't Mean Shit—Vote Where the Power Is—Our Power is in the Street," ran the full-page headline in *New Left Notes*. Students should go on strike for two days, voters should boycott the election, and demonstrations should support national GI week. The French students and workers had deposed a government that summer by voting in the street, why couldn't we? In the rush of events, I did not stop to think carefully about *why* or *how* the massive demonstrations in France had destabilized the government so successfully. I certainly agreed that since Humphrey and Nixon both supported the war effort a hundred percent, it didn't make any difference who won.

On October 2, 1968, Mexico City police shot directly into a crowd of tens of thousands of young people peacefully protesting the resources spent on the upcoming Olympics. Not only were almost a thousand young people killed; the government quickly cleaned up the mess and hid information about it from the press and the public. While the *Guardian* ran a story about the killings, they had no facts about the numbers. Only much later, long after the Olympics, were photographs published of bodies lined up in the city's morgue where parents came to look for their children. At the time we knew enough to be shocked.

For the election program, Washington SDS held a film festival the weekend before the elections, showing recently released newsreel film on the Columbia strike; *End of a Revolution*, a film about the murder of Che in Bolivia; *Last Summer Won't Happen*, on the summer of 1967 in the Lower East Side in New York; *Hanoi 13*, about North Vietnam; and *Nosse Terra*, about the liberation movement in Portugese Angola. On Tuesday, we had a big rally at the Washington Memorial, at which I was the MC, Carl Oglesby was the featured speaker about the war, and a local high school student spoke about student organizing. We marched to the White House, where we got into a tussle with the police who pushed us across the street to Lafayette Park.

Looming over this activity, however, was the growing sense coming from national SDS and friends in other regions that if you weren't preparing for confrontational building takeovers on campus, you weren't staying up with the times. Aggressive confrontation had become the standard against which to measure the success of campus work, and we in Washington didn't seem to measure up.

As a regional organizer, I still did not feel comfortable proposing or instigating the Columbia type of confrontation beyond the first steps, such as a verbal confrontation with recruiters on campus. While I took my own development as a leader very seriously, I tended to focus on the theoretical questions or on the very practical organizational challenges of setting up programs and structures to enhance those programs. I wasn't a charismatic leader, but I thought I was doing okay.

I was competitive enough, however, to be upset at the prospect of being left behind. I was impressed by the coordination of the national leaders and their formation of a national collective, as they called it. There seemed to be a firm hand on the leadership of the organization. They were passionate, articulate, worked hard, and had style. I didn't like their occasional contemptuous tone or all the hyperbole. Their inaccurate estimates of their following were unsettling. But they had pulled in Oglesby, Les, Jeff Jones, and several other very different SDS regulars. I should try harder, I concluded in the back of my mind, to be pushier in my organizing style.

Nonetheless, most of the local chapter leaders were also hardworking, earnest, and not particularly flashy, and we continued on. I became a bit more impatient with those who refused to abandon hope in electoral politics and those who asked nervously whether the Vietnamese were communists. It was tempting to dismiss reluctance of any kind because addressing it demanded more work. In my sense of urgency to respond to events, I was losing some of the wisdom I had garnered in Chester: the importance of listening to those you were organizing and valuing each and every person, the way we wished our society would.

The heart of organizing, I would say now, is helping people notice things that don't make sense, and helping them formulate their own questions and find ways to investigate these questions. Columbia militants and the James Gang helped many people to do that and so did the less confrontational work at San Francisco State and Kent State. Moral outrage could be expressed in many ways, and each of them spoke to and brought in many people. Then, however, many of us didn't have the insight or confidence to see that we needed to have enough depth and diversity to be able to provoke and support this questioning in many different ways.

Women from Chicago, New York, Boston, Washington, and Florida had met in Sandy Springs, Maryland, in early August. It was first such gathering since the Jeanette Rankin Brigade the previous January. The intense, sometimes acrimonious conversations about women's freedom explored how each woman experienced oppression, or didn't, and what to do about it. Questions abounded. What was the cause of the problem, men or capitalism? Should women abandon the antiwar movement and concentrate on women's issues, or bring more women into the antiwar movement? What *were* women's issues? How should women address race, should they work to integrate the group? Many women of color wanted to meet separately, or didn't see women's equality as their priority. What should the task of women's gatherings be, to explore women's experiences or mobilize women to fight against the larger system?[40] The women agreed to plan a conference at Thanksgiving for further discussion, and to continue to meet in their local groups.

During the fall, I occasionally attended the weekly consciousness-raising group that usually met at Marilyn Webb's apartment. Marilyn had been active in generating the women's resolutions at a national level in SDS, as well as been busy networking with the new women's groups. She managed to be completely passionate about tearing down the barriers to women's equality *and* stopping the war.

Many women in the group worked primarily at academic or professional jobs. Many, like Marilyn, were recently married. While all the big questions made an appearance in the group, the most intense discussions were those concerning women's self-image, our roles in relationships, and how our identities were being affected by the growing onslaught of Madison Avenue images.

I found the conversations in the group intriguing. I knew that few women were in positions of power or leadership, and that we were kept out of many professions and jobs altogether. I thought the fight for equal opportunity for women, for equal pay and so on, was important. People should fight for their own liberation and do the work. Black people were doing that, or at least trying to, even while under attack, and women should do the same. I also agreed with the developing analysis of how Madison Avenue targeted women, promoting trivial and passive definitions of femininity in order to encourage the consumption of a plethora of products.

At the same time, I agreed with other women in SDS that the main purpose of thinking about and meeting as women was to bring more women into the movement. Many of the concerns of women in the group seemed self-indulgent. I found it confusing to be in discussions about the ways in which business used women, manipulating ideas of beauty, to make a profit and yet it seemed to me that these women continued to use many of these products. In our house, women used few of these products, especially makeup, because we couldn't afford them. I, with my purist inclinations, had taken it further, rejecting almost all commercial products and insisting that women's natural state was more beautiful and strong than anything else. When Marilyn and others from the DC group joined about a hundred women to protest the Miss America Pageant, I thought it a bit trivial in the midst of the war's brutality, however satisfying it was to have women speak out against that symbol of 50s' womanhood.

Likewise, if they thought marriage was such a big problem, why were they still married? I rejected the idea of marriage, seeing it as a contract that required women to sign away their rights and independence, agreeing to clean up after a man or to argue with him about it. I had made the decision to not have children, at least until the war was over, although I had looked forward to having children since I was young. I knew that if I had children I would want to focus on them, at least during their early years. That was time I wasn't willing to give now. I believed every woman had to make these choices for herself. Although I never wavered in my willingness to make the sacrifice for the movement, I envied women with children.

Another issue discussed was the lack of recognition and opportunity for women in academic and professional schools and jobs. Again, I could imagine the day when middle-class white women would be fully integrated into the professions, while poor women would fare no better, still working at low-wage jobs, while doing the housework and raising their children. I worried that the focus mostly on the concerns for middle-class women did not bode well for the direction of the women's movement.

This issue of women's rights, more than any other so far, threw into relief the tension between Greg's conviction that liberation must start within oneself on the one hand, and, on the other, my worry about the tendency of people to fight for themselves at the expense of those with less power. There were many historical examples of this: working people who set up racist unions to exclude immigrants or blacks; men who fought to exclude women; educated white women who put their right to vote ahead of ending slavery or enfranchising black men. The situations were never easy, but as I listened to the arguments around me, I was increasingly persuaded that those who suffered most had a moral claim to have priority. Furthermore, I thought then, looking after the needs of the most oppressed would ensure that the movement advance to make a more equal and just society.

Besides, my stoic childhood training inclined me to believe that once a problem I encountered was identified, I should do my best to root it out, change my situation, and move on. The angst-filled discussions in the women's group bordered, it seemed to me, on self-pity. We Wilkerson girls did *not* complain! My father would have insisted that defining oneself as a victim just gave you an excuse to do nothing about the problem.

While my fears about the self-absorption of middle-class white women were well-founded, I missed the bigger picture. I didn't appreciate how recently the world had changed for women, with the widespread intro-duction of electric refrigeration, the electric washing machine, and other labor-saving devices. Naturally women on a massive scale were both ready and able to redefine their dreams and expectations of their lives. My own mother had been part of this awakening. The process was bound to be messy and fraught with conflicting interests.

I, however, was trying to live up to the more extreme models of courage and sacrifice of Vietnam, of the civil rights movement, of Forman,

King, Fannie Lou Hamer, Gloria Richardson, and Ho Chi Minh. I expected everyone around me to do this as well. Once when my friend Phoebe was visiting from New York, I served her oatmeal for breakfast, insisting that anyone who wanted to be a revolutionary should be able to subsist on oatmeal because it was cheap, filling, and reasonably nutritious. I was also my mother's child, infused with the ideology of her generation of middle-class white women who overcame one challenge after another to serve family and community. While they supported one another, they reached inside themselves to find the strength to endure pain and sacrifice. While I now saw service in an entirely different way, as service to revolution, I still instinctively reached for self-denial as a source of my power. The previous five years had nurtured and expanded my sense of who I could be, but I had not yet had time to significantly alter the rather formidable models of my upbringing. Nor did I fully understand the critical role played by community in supporting the Vietnamese women who sacrificed so much, or the women who walked to work for miles on painful feet during the Montgomery bus boycott. While I was consciously working to build a community at Lanier Place, my stoicism averted my attention away from the personal or emotional dimensions of this effort.

Since change involves a complex interaction between rejection of the old and imagining the new, it requires healing and entails false starts, dead ends, and temporary solutions. Large-scale social change can only be generated by the energy released by all these messy upheavals. Sometimes, perhaps, the change can be guided by those with a more global perspective, but more often it is driven by internal currents. The women's movement was increasingly propelled by a massive response to pent-up yearnings for self-expression and equality, to technological changes, and to structural changes in the economy. The resulting outpouring of women's thinking and emotional explorations raised profound and important questions that have framed much of the public debate for the past forty years.

On November 17, I spoke to a gathering of women students at George Washington University, organized by the SDS chapter. Marketing strategies were increasingly defining who and what women should be, I said, as I talked about the various ways in which women did not receive equal treatment in the United States. Women, I said, could reject the passivity and dependence of traditional roles of consumer and wife and become strong, active people as they fought for a better world.

I realized that we didn't have anything in writing to explain the analysis that was being developed in the various women's groups, or at least the part that I agreed with. I decided to put together a pamphlet on women for local distribution. I gathered the few materials I knew of, especially a pamphlet by Lynn Wells of the Southern Student Organizing Committee, containing photos and stories about working women and children in the United States, especially in the textile mills. The conditions that women had to contend with, such as six-day weeks at fourteen hours a day, sexual slavery, and separation from children, had been horrifying. My main writing partner and consultant for the pamphlet was Marilyn McNabb, who also found the history of women's struggle for equality to be inspiring. Marilyn Webb also read and critiqued the draft for me.

The resulting twenty-four–page pamphlet, "Women, the Struggle for Liberation," began with "Women are caught in a void between a fantasy world they can never achieve and a reality which is oppressive." Women are seen as sexual objects to "titillate and satisfy HIM. The man's ego must be catered to and bolstered at all cost." This was followed by sections on women as consumers, as lower-paid or unpaid workers, and on women's roles in the family.

I was proud of the pamphlet and distributed it to campus chapters to put on literature tables. While women active in the chapters were interested in reading the pamphlet, neither I nor any of them could tear our focus away from the war long enough to focus on discussions about the issues raised in the pamphlet or about specific projects we could undertake, as the pamphlet suggested.

Meanwhile, small independent groups of women were popping up: WITCH (Women's International Terrorist Conspiracy from Hell) formed to identify and act on anti-imperialist women's issues; Red Stockings formed around the belief that gender was the root form of social domination, and other forms of domination, racial, religious, class, stemmed from it. They also believed that this form of domination wasn't particular to capitalism; it predated it, and existed independently. Therefore, even if the movement defeated capitalism and established socialism, it wouldn't solve the problem of women's domination. Betty Friedan's NOW formed to fight for women's equality within the context of the existing system.

After the election, we began to prepare for a region-wide education conference to be held the third week of December. The Georgetown University chapter had been thinking a lot about how to educate themselves and new members. They had published a plan in *NLN* and provided much of the energy for the regional conference

In preparation for the December national council meeting in Ann Arbor, *NLN* carried a fierce debate between members of the national collective and PL. On the eve of the national council, *NLN* carried an article by Mike Klonsky, called the "Revolutionary Youth Movement," which summarized the direction of the national leadership over the past six months and charted its future. The people who would really change society, Klonsky said, were young people. They were the ones who were willing to rebel, take risks, and be creative. Klonsky added a new twist, however, when he specifically named "working-class youth" as the "agent" of change, using a traditional Marxist vision of change. "Our struggles," Klonsky wrote, "must be integrated into the struggles of working people." "Young workers are our link to the class struggle."

It was true that SDS's most dramatic growth in the past year had been on the campuses of state universities and community colleges rather than at the more elite schools where SDS had started. Many more of the newer members were the children of blue-collar workers. Most of these young people, however, had joined because they were against the war and the draft, the same as young people from middle-class backgrounds.

Klonsky argued that there were inherent limits on a student movement. Students would only be willing to go up to a point in challenging the system. Since changing the country meant committing to an oppositional showdown, students could not lead in the long run. This was certainly consistent with our experience in Washington, where we had never been able to organize even a local eruption like the one at Columbia.

If the idea of moving to a working-class base wasn't very well filled out yet (nowhere did Klonsky explain how we would "organize young workers") at least it was a bold, new shift for us, indicating that we were maturing and beginning to take our responsibilities more seriously. Reform, as it was traditionally understood in the United States, was not working. The self-perpetuating interests of the wealthy did not seem reconcilable with the long-range interests of ordinary people.

Again, I thought it was impressive that the leaders of SDS were stepping up to chart the course off campus.[41] It was mysterious to me how Klonsky proposed to shift the center of SDS off campus so that adults, even if they were young adults, would define the agenda, since SDS had little experience supporting change among young people who were already working.

I continued to be troubled by the hard edge of some of the confrontations, and by the contempt heaped on opponents during various debates. This style of internal debate and leadership got a boost from the then-unfolding Cultural Revolution in China. That fall, journalists Felix Greene and Anna Louise Strong wrote articles for the *Guardian* newspaper about young Chinese who were rising up to challenge the bureaucrats, to relight the enthusiasm and passion for equality and justice for all. They challenged those who were slow to try new ideas, and humiliated those who practiced corruption. Here was the dynamic, many of us thought, that would save China from the ossified, corrupt, and oppressive bureaucracy that had doomed socialism in the Soviet Union. At the pinnacle, Mao supported the young people rather than the entrenched administrators in his service. It was very exciting.

Quotes from Mao, many from his recently available *Little Red Book*, began to appear in *New Left Notes*. Many of us obtained copies of Mao's book. His short, inspirational aphorisms were drawn from his extensive writings about war, economics, philosophy, and social change. The total affect was similar to many of the self-help books popular today, especially for those of us interested in change.

I was particularly fascinated by a section titled "Criticism and Self-Crit-icism," in which Mao challenged all of those responsible for changing the old ways (in China that was feudalism) to the new (socialism) to look crit-ically at their work, and constantly reevaluate and learn from their mistakes. These few small passages reinforced my own sense of how to build organization; they validated my frustration with people who were so afraid of being wrong that they couldn't accurately assess the effective-ness of their efforts. I thought we needed to be much more rigorous in looking at what we did in the chapters and assessing what worked and what didn't. When Jeff and Phoebe came to visit, I excitedly told them about that section, encouraging them to read it. It didn't occur to any of us that the noble, youthful impulse to fight corruption would soon, for a variety of reasons, metamorphose into a degenerative zealotry.

By the end of 1968, SDS started to openly try to shed its role as an organ-ization of students and young people, and take on the task of providing leadership for the whole movement. Tens of thousands of young people now identified, at least partially, with the movement and with youth cul-ture, and were unaffiliated organizationally. SDS leaders sensed that if these people could be brought into an organization with a unified strategy, their energy could be directed more efficiently toward the goal of stopping the power of racism and ending the war, or, as many of us now thought, of bringing down the government.

The absurdity of glossing over all the questions about how to do any of this, and about how the current structure of SDS could assume that kind of leadership when it barely functioned at its current size, was lost on me. I, for one, wanted to believe that SDS could do this, because it might bring the end of the war closer. In fact, the organization that we loved was already far along in the process of spinning itself into hundreds of smaller units of energy. It had neither the mechanisms of democracy nor the theoretical coherence to process all that was happening. SDS, which had been unable to pass a consistent series of programs since its inception, now had trouble passing anything of substance at all. Instead, we clung to the powerful images of Che, Fidel, Ho, and Amilcar Cabral (the anti-colonial liberation leader of Portuguese Guinea and the Cape Verde Islands), all of whom, while in their twenties, had formed tiny organizations that blossomed into revolutionary movements. Maybe that would happen to us, despite all the confusion at the moment.

The one issue that kept me somewhat vigilant about the process for a while longer, however, was the issue of women. I was wary of yet another male cabal seizing control of the public space. If I were sincere about my desire to organize more women into the antiwar movement, then I had to have a program and work to show for it in the Washington region.

CHAPTER EIGHT

THE QUESTION OF POWER

■ ■

The first order of business in January 1969 was a huge demonstration at President Nixon's inauguration. Once again, the Mobilization had issued a call for a massive gathering, three days of conferences and marches. Mobe leaders tried to include the broadest possible collection of organizations, including pacifists, religious groups, and local community organizations of all kinds. By recruiting yippie leaders, they also tried to appeal to young people who identified primarily with cultural rebellion.

While national SDS refused to endorse a strategy they thought wouldn't work, many SDS activists expected another "happening" like that at the Chicago Democratic convention. In Washington, I had the usual mixed feelings about the demonstrations, but preparations for the demonstration began to affect many aspects of our work. I started attending the planning meetings late in the fall and was on a committee with Dave Dellinger, Paul Potter, Lee Webb (Marilyn's husband), and others, to draft a statement for the event. I was hopeful that the statement could serve as a unifying tool to join the badly fractured parts of the movement.

As the day approached, I joined with some other local activists to hatch another one of our *foco* group actions, this time aimed at wealthy Republicans who would be in town to cash in on their support for Nixon, and attend the inaugural balls. These wealthy Republicans, we believed, shouldn't dress up in their jewels and party all night without being reminded that their wealth came from corporations, backed by US military power, paid for by US taxpayers, and causing such unnecessary suffering.

On the day of the balls, several of us from the area set off in the afternoon, armed with cans of shaving cream and whipped cream. The attendees, dressed to the hilt, were required to arrive in late afternoon because of the logistical complexity of assembling so many VIPs. My group headed to a ball being held at one of the monumental museums on the mall. As we approached, we saw a long line of expensive cars and limousines waiting to be admitted to the underground parking lot. Starting with the last car in the line, we ran up from both sides, opened the back doors and squirted foam for a few seconds, then slammed the doors and ran forward to the next car. The element of surprise allowed us to continue our way up the line for more than a dozen cars, before some of the drivers began to chase after us. Gleeful, we continued down the mall, looking for the next gathering of partygoers. Eventually we returned home to celebrate our accomplishments.

In the meantime, the Mobe held its own counter-inaugural event with a rally and speakers. Later that night they scheduled a counter-inaugural ball. One of the speakers was Marilyn Webb, representing the new women's consciousness-raising groups. She had prepared a speech about the aspirations of women, demanding equality for women both in the movement and in the larger society. As Marilyn began her speech, dozens of men in the packed audience began to catcall and boo. When she continued, more men joined in and the din got louder. Some of them began to chant, "Take it off! Take it off!" "Fuck her down a dark alley!" Marilyn was stunned and hurt. Shulamith Firestone tried to continue with a second speech, but soon both women were forced to abandon the stage in the pandemonium.

A similar reaction had greeted the first attempt to present women's analysis in SDS, but in the ensuing months that kind of reaction had become defused, as more and more women challenged the individual men in their daily lives. By this time, public catcalling was unacceptable in SDS, despite the fact that in most other respects, the daily practice of most men was little changed. In the Mobe, however, hundreds of men had never been exposed to this conversation and there were no organizational sanctions against such behavior. Whether COINTELPRO was behind at least part of the catcalling has never been investigated, but given the FBI's mandate to sow dissension within and between groups by exacerbating existing tensions, it is likely. At the time, no one knew this kind of manipulation was even a possibility. While the Mobe leadership—all men—were also upset by the attacks, they didn't join Marilyn on the stage to back her up.

Badly shaken, Marilyn retreated to her apartment with several of the women, to process what had happened. As they shared their fury and astonishment, the phone rang. When Marilyn picked up, a female voice said, "If you or anyone else ever gives a speech like that again I'm going to beat the shit out of you." The voice of the unidentified caller, Marilyn said, sounded just like me and the speaker subtly inferred it was me. Marilyn assumed it was me, in part because of a conversation a few days earlier when I had visited Marilyn in her apartment. She had been full of enthusiasm for a set of four old wooden chairs she had bought, re-covered, and painted herself. As she showed them off, I reacted with my most spartan contempt for physical objects, disdainful of the time and effort she had spent creating creature comforts while people were suffering. I then proceeded to put my bare feet up on the new fabric, while continuing the conversation. Marilyn was angry and hurt, but said nothing.

The bitterness of this recent encounter led Marilyn to believe that the caller was me. But, of course, it was not me. Despite my abrasive asceticism, I recognized the difficult role that Marilyn played, along with other women in the DC group, and I wanted to support her thoroughly, up to a point. She had challenged my thinking about women, and when I wrote the draft for the women's pamphlet, she was one of the people who read it and made helpful comments. In the weeks before the counter-inaugural, I had written a long letter to Bernardine Dohrn in the national office, urging Bernardine to accept an invitation by the women's groups to speak at their gathering during the inauguration:

> I told Marilyn Webb to call you vis-à-vis the women's conference. She wants you to speak. It is important that you get filled in [on] the national faction fighting of women's lib, which is the cause of the blandness of the current agenda [for the conference]. It's the same sort of alignments as in other parts of the movement, but seems even more acrid. Ughhh. I am not going to the conference,

because I've got things to do here, but also because I can't handle
that scene right now. But a lot of people are coming from DC
who are by and large very very good! Marilyn is good, although
I think she has been a little cowed by the intensity with which
the N.Y. and Berkeley man-hating freaks have been attacking her
and the others who have been working on the conference....[1]

It is embarrassing to report on my use of language: "Man-hating freaks"
seems to me now clear evidence of the way I reduced the rich and important conflicts in this stage of the women's movement. I didn't understand
then why some women wanted and needed to work separately from men,
or how necessary this separation would be to exploring many of our own
assumptions about women. Nor did I understand why some women
activists were so angry at those of us who challenged both the wisdom of
separatism and their right to separate.

The idea of women separating, either temporarily or for long stretches,
wasn't even that new. For centuries, women had created separate spaces to
gather strength and to support each other. I, however, still associated the
idea with the women-only spaces of my childhood, in which women or
girls were excluded from the main intellectual or public activities and were
left to focus on relationships and domestic concerns. I could not yet imagine that women together could explore different ways of defining not only
womanhood but humanity as a whole.

If I didn't make the call to Marilyn, who did? There were some women
in the movement dead set against the women's movement, but it's unlikely
they would make such a threat. It's more likely, however, that this too was
part of COINTELPRO's dirty tricks, and it is probably not a coincidence
that the caller sounded like me. It was in 1968 that these activities were systematically initiated against the student and antiwar movement. As a leader
of Washington SDS, with an FBI file over a year old, it was inevitable that
I would be targeted. Just as COINTELPRO had perhaps reinforced the
catcalling to divide women from antiwar activities, it would certainly serve
their purposes to drive a wedge between Marilyn and me, and between
SDS and the flowering women's movement, which is exactly what hap-

pened. Neither Marilyn nor anyone else said anything about the phone call to me, too stunned to know what to say. I did not learn about this story until I read it in Todd Gitlin's *Days of Rage* during the 1980s, and then spoke with both Todd and Marilyn at an SDS reunion soon thereafter. I had wondered at the drastically cooled reception I got from various women in Washington, but I ascribed it to the increasing tensions between different segments of the women's movement and that movement and SDS.

Arriving later that evening at the counter-inauguration was my friend and DC staff person, Jonny Lerner. Jonny had remained close to national collective member Jeff Jones, his Antioch friend. In order to raise the confrontational level of the Mobe's demonstration, he, Jeff, and others had hatched a plan at the last minute to organize for Oakland-like street fighting during the inauguration. Arriving at a late stage of the counter-inaugural ball while a band was playing, the small group squeezed through the crowd to the stage area. Jonny leaped on the stage, seized the microphone from an unsuspecting singer between songs, and proceeded to urge the crowd of several thousand to form affinity groups for the march the next day. Affinity groups were small bands of close friends who moved together in a crowd. In this case, Jonny said, activists should throw things at the procession, take to the streets, and tie up downtown traffic.

Thinking he was part of the planned Mobe events, the youthful crowd cheered wildly. Mobe leaders, many of whom were angered by this slight of hand, reiterated the official program to set the record straight, but undoubtedly many young people, especially as it grew later in the evening, drew their inspiration from the excitement rather than from the words of official leaders.

At the march the next day, there were indeed bands of militants that threw rocks and pennies at the procession, and ran in the streets. There was a confrontation with Mobe people over an American flag, and there were a few opportunities for mud throwing at attendees to a reception for Vice President Agnew.[2] These skirmishes were the same type of action Ben Morea and others in SDS had wanted during the Pentagon demonstrations, but which Dellinger, Kinoy, and Calvert had staved off.

Despite my friendship with Jonny, I was not privy to the "invasion" of the Mobe rally. Nor did I realize the extent to which this core of people were coalescing nationally, to narrow in on these confrontations to the exclusion of reaching out in other ways to young people. While the pool of those ready to express their anger and frustration had grown, SDS's leadership was becoming increasingly detached from the broader movement. Nonetheless, I also was sympathetic to the frustrations of big demonstrations, wondering what else we could do to get those in the halls of power to listen.

Soon after the inauguration, Bill Willet left the staff in Washington to move to Chicago to become a support person for the national collective. In June, Jonny left to join them as well.

I continued to assume, not incorrectly, that this tightly knit group of friends and coworkers were talking about how to lead SDS. When Bernardine came to Washington later in the spring, I didn't sense anything else, or that she might have been testing out my willingness to commit myself to their leadership. There was little formal structure to this emerging national leadership group, and at its heart it remained a group of friends. It was this informality that would emerge as one of its most quixotic characteristics, leaving others to wonder how one joined it, or how to determine at any given time who was in and who was out.

Within weeks of Klonsky's article "The Revolutionary Youth Movement" and the anti-inaugural demonstrations, J. J. (John Jacobs), now one of the leadership group, was hard at work at a more comprehensive theoretical document that would set a course for SDS and articulate its claim to leadership of the whole movement. In the coming months, his draft circulated among a small number of people, in preparation for the upcoming June national council meeting.

On January 17, John Huggins and Bunchy Carter, leaders of the LA Panthers, were gunned down at a meeting of UCLA students, called to establish a black studies department. The Panthers had been invited by some students to provide a counterbalance to members of another black organization, Ron Karenga's US (United Slaves), because some students had felt intimidated by the armed men from US that had recently insisted on speaking on their behalf to the administration.[3] Several people at the time saw who had done the shooting, but those identified were not arrested. Instead, police jailed seventy-five members of the Panthers that night. One was the widow of slain John Huggins, even though she was the nursing mother of a three-week-old baby. John Huggins was a Vietnam vet who had left Lincoln University in Pennsylvania to work with the Panthers. Many suspected at the time that US had been infiltrated and was being used by the LAPD to get rid of the Panthers.[4]

When news of the shooting reached us, I was stunned. The police response, to do a sweep of Panthers and not arrest anyone from US, seemed strong evidence that informants or agents were somehow involved.

On the national level, SDS had embraced the Panthers wholeheartedly, despite SDS's earlier rejection of joint electoral work. In December, *NLN* had run a long article by Huey Newton, in which he argued for the importance of revolutionary organization and criticized the anarchists in France, blaming their inability to sustain the uprising of the previous summer on their lack of strong organization. In the face of repression, Newton argued, strong organization was essential. No one would be entirely free until the whole society was free, and that freedom had to be won in a protracted revolutionary struggle.[5]

By February, national SDS agreed to cosponsor celebrations of Huey Newton's birthday with Panthers around the country, and local SDS chapters were urged to build relationships with the Panthers or, if there were no Panthers, with local black student unions. While some chapter members in the DC area had personal relationships with black students union members, especially at Howard and Johns Hopkins in Baltimore, they did not extend to programmatic relationships. The celebration of black power was strong on the local campuses, and I had grown no wiser about what it meant for whites to be supportive when black students seemed committed to self-reliance.

In April 1969, the police rounded up almost twenty leading New York City Black Panther members and charged them with conspiracy to carry out an armed attack on a police station in the Bronx. Ultimately, twenty-one Panthers, including two women, were indicted. Bail was set prohibitively high, so no one could get out. Those charged in the case came to be known as the Panther 21 and included Afeni Shakur, pregnant at the time with Tupac. Many would remain in jail until the trial, a year later. After weeks of testimony and evidence, the jury, outraged by the shoddy evidence they concluded was fabricated by three police infiltrators, acquitted all defendants on all charges, in less than an hour. In the meantime, however, with most of its leadership out of commission, the New York Panther chapter had mostly disintegrated.

Militant demonstrations erupted on several campuses that April. In Berkeley, black students and white supporters went on strike, demanding an autonomous black studies department. Governor Ronald Reagan called in the National Guard. At Michigan State in East Lansing, nine hundred students briefly took over the administration building and then, rather than face arrests, dispersed to the dorms to continue organizing to get a popular professor and SDS member reinstated. At the University of Chicago, four hundred students occupied the administration building over the firing of a popular woman professor, Marlene Dixon, and sixty-one students were suspended. Nine hundred National Guard members were called in to a strike at the University of Wisconsin, where students were demanding an autonomous black studies department.

In Washington we had also been busy. I continued speaking about Vietnam and women. On February 25, five hundred American University students had occupied a building after university officials refused to allow students to invite Dick Gregory, a political black comedian, to the campus. When San Francisco Mayor Joseph Alioto came to DC, we disrupted his local speeches in support of the San Francisco State strike. We had a similar demonstration later when University of California, Berkeley president Hayakawa came to promote his vision of the new "multiversity," ever more completely integrated into corporate designs.

At George Washington University, where I visited most regularly, chapter activists at weekly SDS meetings led discussions about the war, the draft, local campus issues, and other regional movement activities. Many students came because the draft was pressing down with increasing urgency. There were then 540,000 troops in Vietnam, rotating on six-month tours of duty. The military needed constant replacement to compensate for deaths, injuries, and desertion. There were no easy choices. Nonetheless, it was hard to get students to sacrifice their time to contribute to the organizing effort. The chapter had a committed leadership, a core of twenty to thirty students who came regularly, and another couple of hundred who regularly attended events, but we still had not succeeded in building momentum like they had at Columbia the previous year.

By spring, several chapter activists and I were feeling frustrated about having nothing more dramatic to show for all our work. It seemed that there had been at least one major upheaval in every big city except Washington. George Washington University SDS students had unearthed a good deal of information about the Sino-Soviet Institute, a GW think tank dedicated to researching the Soviet Union and China for the purpose of bolstering the US cold-war strategy. Although we didn't unearth any specific connections to the war in Vietnam, we knew that US cold-war policy propelled US involvement in Vietnam.

We had an issue at GW, but there just didn't seem to be enough passion, beyond a small group of us. I began to think that if we too could stage a dramatic confrontation with just a few people, then maybe we would create enough drama to bring in hundreds more. After discussing the problem, we decided to try to occupy the Sino-Soviet Institute, which was housed in a rambling old house, go through the files, as they had at Columbia, and expose the university's complicity with the pro-war US policies. Since we didn't have a lot of momentum for this kind of action, we came up with the best plan we could think of. One night, we would show the newsreel film on the Columbia rebellion, and, using the enthusiasm generated by the film, lead those in attendance over to the Sino-Soviet Institute for a takeover.

We leafleted widely on campus about the film and the discussion afterward. At least one hundred and fifty students came and watched the film. Afterward, we talked briefly about the Sino-Soviet Institute and university collaboration with the Cold War and the war in Vietnam. We then declared that some of us were prepared right then and there to go seize the building and demand that the university sever ties. Leading chants, we formed a thin column that marched out the door and headed across campus to the Institute. More than half the audience followed us.

A nagging voice in the back of my mind wondered if this was legitimate leadership or manipulation. I hadn't ever clarified my thoughts on the distinction. We also hadn't talked much about the consequences of a takeover and certainly hadn't mentioned them in our inspirational talks. At Columbia some of the students had been expelled, but all the other students had rallied in their support. I wondered if that would happen here. But, what was the big deal, I then argued to myself, compared to what the Vietnamese were going through.

As we crossed the campus we attracted the attention of a large group of fraternity students, some of whom may have been the same ones who enjoyed regularly harassing and baiting SDS students. They supported the war and Nixon, and thought we were communist rabble-rousers. They asked where we were going and were told. They followed, and, as we reached our destination, they made a last-minute attempt to block our way. It was late, and the building normally would have been closed. Someone in the chapter, however, had left a door ajar earlier in the evening, and we were able to get in. We immediately plunged up the stairs and into a series of offices, announcing the building takeover in case anyone was working late.

I found myself in a large office containing several standing file cabinets. This is what I had been looking for. Before I could see who was around to help me go through them, however, two or three young men with long hair and bandanas came crashing into the room shouting that the revolution was here and started overturning the file cabinets and chairs, sweeping everything off the desk onto the floor and emptying desk drawers. I tried to stop them, demanding to know what they were doing and telling them we wanted to go through the files, but they didn't listen. I didn't recognize them as GW students, nor as regular members of the chapter. They announced that they were yippies, and this was their demonstration too.

Before I could get over my astonishment, the damage had been done.

They stomped on the file cabinets and bent them so that we couldn't get the drawers out. One or two of the drawers had started to open when they were overturned, and were crushed in a slightly open position. We were able to extract a few papers, later printed in the *Free Press*.

For the first half hour confusion reigned. We had to defend the building against students who were opposed to us while letting in those who supported us. The chapter leadership, other regional SDS members, and I attempted to bring some cohesion to the group, but in the face of the militant young men, whoever they were, we failed. Before long, both campus and DC police began to assemble outside. It was clear that we did not have the spontaneous support to hold the building. In hurried informal conversations among people in different parts of the building, we concluded that our point had been sufficiently made and we didn't need to stay to get arrested. Amid the confusion of demonstrators outside—some in opposition, some in support—and the multiple entrances to the building, we were all able to leave without being arrested.

I left feeling somewhat unraveled. What had happened? That wasn't what I had imagined. Of course, as a chapter, we *hadn't* imagined what was possible, and that was a problem. Without a plan, or without a group of individuals who *did* have a plan or the bravado and imagination to wing it regardless of the risks, the odds were high that we would end up in confusion.

While I will never know for sure, I again think it is highly likely that the two or three young men that prevented us from examining more of the institute's paper work were sent there by the FBI. It was unusual that people from off campus came to campus events, and our publicity for the film had focused on GW students. While Washington had its share of alienated hippies and angry militants, their absolute disregard of my pleas to stop would have been unusual. With so many young people facing drug charges, the FBI and local police were frequently able to get young people to do their bidding in exchange for leniency for themselves or their friends.

The few documents we did obtain included correspondence that discussed the placement of academic personnel from the institute in international positions, which would allow them to gain and relay intelligence to US government agencies. This behavior fit a pattern of CIA use of academics and journalists around the world that was beginning to be documented in *Ramparts*, *Viet-Report*, and the *Guardian*.

The damages to the office allowed university officials to belittle the political motives of the chapter and to charge several students with criminal offenses. Days later, as rumors had predicted, the Washington, DC, police arrived at my door at 5:30 AM with an arrest warrant. After dressing hurriedly in the presence of a female officer, I was taken to the station house and charged with breaking and entering. Later in the day, I was released on bail and given a court date. The government filed an injunction against my setting foot on any campus within a fifty-mile radius of Washington. Many of the organizers from the big chapters like Kent State faced similar injunctions.

Days before the end of the term, several of the chapter organizers from GW were expelled or suspended from school. I could no longer go on campus to help with a plan to fight the university's retaliation, as I wasn't prepared to pay the bail or violate the injunction until I made some larger decisions about what I was going to do next. These events left me confused about campus organizing and where to go with it. I didn't want to continue organizing without a clearer sense of what to do and of what my role should be. I worried that I had, in fact, abandoned the GW students who were expelled from school.

Besides, I was also feeling that I was ready to tackle the problem of change on a larger scale, and had already been wondering if it wasn't time for me to leave campus organizing and move on to something else. I was twenty-four years old. But if I didn't work in the SDS region, I wasn't sure there was anything else to hold me in Washington. Jonny and Bill had already left. Several others were considering a move as well. I wondered whether any regional staff would continue or if new ones would come, and whether that mattered or not. There were active chapters on most of the nearby campuses that would continue with the basic work, but we had built up a region with the capacity to support the local chapters through regional conferences, literature, and films, and by providing extra work and expertise on specific chapter projects. We helped support other local organizing by educating and mobilizing local chapter members. I loved SDS, and if there was a way to stay connected to SDS programs that would be my first choice, but I was willing to look elsewhere, as well.

In June, we piled into the red van once more and drove off for the June convention in Chicago. My main goal was to find a place to go next. As it turned out, various segments of SDS, most notably PL and the collective around the national office, had mobilized for an all-out battle, and there would be nothing typical about this convention.

Almost a thousand young people showed up, including PL members ferried in on specially hired buses and even by airplane from the West Coast. The national collective had printed its long theoretical paper, "You Don't Need a Weatherman to Know Which Way the Wind Blows," aimed at defending SDS from an expected PL move to take over the organization. The paper, quickly dubbed the "Weatherman paper," had received its name at Kent State. A few weeks earlier, Terry Robbins had been studying the draft at the kitchen table in the haunted house, while Candy Erickson was listening to Bob Dylan and writing down the lyrics, in preparation for her class on modern poetry. Terry loved both poetry and lyrics and he enjoyed playing with the meanings. When Candy repeated the "Weatherman" line from the song, Terry picked it up, delighting in the way it fit nicely with the draft in front of him.

The paper started with the question "What is the nature of the revolution that we talk about?... and what are its goals and strategy?" At last, I thought, someone was tackling the right questions. The analysis of world events drew on ideas that were widely held, similar to those in Carl Oglesby's book. The conflict between US imperialism and the struggles of people in the third world for liberation represented the central conflict in the world. In the United States, the paper stated, black people were part of their own nation in a conflict with the state, framed by the idea of national liberation. The goal of revolution was to defeat and dismantle US imperialism so that developing countries, including the black nation in the United States, could develop independent and self-reliant socialist economies, so that we could establish socialism here as well.

What quickly became known as the distinctive Weatherman analysis then followed: "The main struggle going on in the world today is between US imperialism and the national liberation struggles against it.... [T]he goal of the revolutionary struggle must be the control and use of [US] wealth in the interests of the oppressed people of the world... Black people within North America... are an internal colony..." White people's primary job was to support national liberation, especially black people in the United States, because, cumulatively, these upheavals would bring down the colossus of imperialism. Furthermore, the white people most likely to join the revolution were young, and, while SDS had thousands of members in college, we needed now to bring in young people who were working or out of work. Young people, they asserted, were ready to understand that reforms wouldn't work; the violence faced by the civil rights movement and the relentlessly aggressive foreign policy were proof. "The antiauthoritarianism which characterizes the youth rebellion," the paper said, "turns into rejection of the State, a refusal to be socialized into American society."[6] Young people were ready to fight, and whenever SDS initiated fights with "the system," young people would join us. It was in their self-interest to do so because they would end up on the winning side of the world revolution.

This theme had been developing for a year, from Columbia, Chicago, and People's Park in Berkeley. Finally, the paper argued, in order to survive the violent response of the state, we would need to build a Marxist-Leninist party and be prepared to fight to "smash the state." We were on the cusp of world revolution, led by black people in this country and by the third world. Our job was to build an "International Liberation Army" to prepare to join in and support the upheaval. The immediate strategy should be to build collectives of young people who were attracted by SDS's willingness to fight for revolution. In good capitalist spirit, the collectives had to compete with each other to prove themselves in practice.

Although I didn't notice it at the time, the authors never actually answered the question at the beginning of the paper. Their vision of revolution meant that people in other countries, and black people here, would fight for their independence, and whites were supposed to support that. But what would it actually look like here? There was talk about power, about raising awareness of power, and about protecting ourselves from the power of the government, but very little about how we should work to change that power. The paper referred to the goal of shutting down the universities as an example: Everything had to come to a halt before institutions could be rebuilt for the good of all people. Did the authors see change coming step-by-step, or were we working for a conflagration in which there was mass chaos, confusion, and loss of life as the government disintegrated? That's what had happened during the Russian revolution after World War I, but at that time, the vast majority of Russia's population lived on the land or in small villages, not densely packed into urban areas, as we were fifty years later in the United States, extensively dependent on public utilities. How was this chaos to affect the understanding and consciousness of the majority of the population that were still ignoring the long-term consequences of the government and corporate power? Would it help people understand better, or would the chaos push people to rely on their basest instincts, as fascism had?

I imagine now that these questions were half formed in the minds of most SDS people as they were in mine, but I never brought them into focus enough to ask. Our goal was to build a party and the party would "smash the state," and somehow all answers would flow from that. I was still wary of this leap and of the abrasive style of these new leaders. Was this the world we were working for? On the other hand, I knew I didn't want to hand SDS over to PL. As Carl Oglesby had said: "Who or what will replace landlord, owner, sheriff? Never mind, says the revolutionary, glancing over his shoulder. Something better." And later,

> To [the rebel], total change means only that those who now have all the power shall no longer have any, and that those who now have none—the people, the victimized—shall have all. Then what can it mean to speak of compromise?... [Their] repudiation being total, it leaves exactly no motive—again, not even the *motive*—for creating that fund of specific proposals, that *conversation*, without which a compromise is not even *technically* possible.[7]

From the moment the convention was called to order, charges and countercharges started flying. The most notable thing for me was that much of it was incomprehensible, and it was hard to keep up with the drama. There were bitter fights over procedure that really had to do with the fight with PL, but unless you were on the inside you had no idea *how* these issues were connected. By the third day, the battle with PL had reached a crescendo. Suddenly, Bernardine Dohrn called on everyone who wanted to be rid of PL to move into another room. That split SDS. Many chapter members were so confused by the whole debate that they wandered back and forth between what then became two plenary sessions. Later that evening, the anti-PL SDS moved to another building. Divisions within the ranks of this group quickly emerged when the authors of the Weatherman paper squared off with Klonsky and others opposed to Weatherman's more-or-less exclusive programmatic focus on supporting national liberation.

The group that coalesced around Klonsky, soon to be known as Revolutionary Youth Movement 2, or RYM 2 also focused on young people, but wanted to turn toward the workplace, rather than confrontation, as the forum within which to challenge pro-war and racist sentiment. They hoped that young people's common interests around their futures could help educate and mobilize them to oppose government/corporate policies.

I had friends in both groups, and was attracted by parts of both analyses. I was impressed by the scale and seriousness of the Weatherman paper. Over thirty pages, it was an enormous amount to digest all at once. They were setting forth a complete revolutionary theory of change in the United States, I thought. Was this what Ho Chi Minh had done in Vietnam in the 20s and 30s, and what Mao had done before the Long March in China? In both those instances, theory had led to consolidation of leadership and control of a communist party that led the movement for change. This might be the beginning of something historic, I thought. These folks had taken on the challenge of providing a theory and had committed themselves to the fight. I thought it was courageous.

Both factions believed in the necessity of forming a Leninist-type party and saw themselves as the core of that effort. The founders of SDS, many of whom were raised in the old left, had explicitly rejected this idea when they laid out a vision of reinvigorated democracy as an alternative strategy for change. In 1969, I heard few voices from the old left warning about the dangers of simplistically adapting the particulars of a Marxist vision of change that was almost a hundred years old. Too often, in any event, their words of caution, like the contributors to *The God that Failed*,[8] were accompanied by their flip-flopped new allegiance to corporate liberalism, which betrayed our most fundamental beliefs in equality and justice. As a result, their voices lacked legitimacy.

Much of the current SDS membership, myself included, had never explored or engaged with the full weight of the argument against a Leninist party. China, Vietnam, and Cuba, the three most successful liberation struggles, continued to shine as successful examples of this model of revolution. Especially in Vietnam, the party had led the successful defense against the aggressive military incursions of the French and now the US.

I, for one, didn't think about what we would have to give up to accept the necessity of a Leninist party. The paper never argued against participatory democracy as a strategy for change, it just insisted that a Leninist party was necessary, to withstand the brutal power of the existing corporate/government cabal. I was no longer thinking about the one-on-one work to help empower people to take control of their own lives, to define and redefine a popular vision over time. I was thinking only that participatory democracy had not addressed the irreconcilability of the interests of the wealthy and of the rest of us. The power of the elite was so strong that millions would lose their lives in the time it took for enough people to open their eyes to demand government to change course. Those changes might not even be possible in the midst of repression, war, and hunger. That price was too high. Popular democracy must be a luxury that we would have to forgo until the world was a more peaceful place. We didn't have it now, anyway.

While I was intrigued by the Weatherman paper, I still found the aggressiveness that characterized all the debates to be troublesome. There was a lot of yelling and very little discourse about the content. I still had a lot of questions, especially about the superficial inclusion of women's issues. Yet the fact that many of my closest friends, including Jeff Jones, Phoebe Hirsch, Bill Willet, and Jonny Lerner were closely aligned with Weatherman's national collective, drew me toward them.

To my dismay and astonishment, by the end of the convention, the ten or twelve people from Washington regional SDS staff split among the various factions, and the bitterness between the debates quickly seeped into our relationships. All of a sudden, people who were my housemates and friends were no longer speaking to me nor I to them. Our family was breaking up.

All of the factions were recruiting for projects that summer. My friends in the Weatherman group asked me to join one of their summer projects. But Sue Eanet and Mike Klonsky were thinking about working in the South, perhaps hooking up with Lynn Wells, the author of the Southern Student Organizing Committee paper on women that I had liked so much. So I declined the suggestion that I join one of Weatherman's several summer projects, wanting to think about what I would do next. I needed more time to process all the ideas in the paper. I decided that I would take some time away from SDS and travel, especially to the South, and look for a new place to live and work that way. Mike Spiegel, with whom I was still in a relationship, felt similarly, and decided that he would like to come along too. We hadn't taken time off for a long time, and a trip would be fun as well.

In conversations with women I knew about the underestimation of women's issues in the Weatherman paper, several of them encouraged me to write a critique of the paper for *NLN*. After the convention I set to work immediately, typing at my desk in Washington, while people moved their belongings out of the house and disappeared. As a starting point, I returned to the question of why it seemed so hard for people in mainstream US culture to identify with the suffering and unfair exploitation of others. People looked only at their own little square of turf and made decisions based on what would benefit them in the short run. The thing that still puzzled me was why people couldn't see that what would work in the short run might actually hurt them in the long run, like pollution or racism.

It must be that we all needed to belong to something, I reasoned, and once we decided to align ourselves with some particular identity, we looked at the world through that lens. Mainstream US culture promoted this sense of belonging to some of its citizens—those who were white, who had secure enough jobs to be consumers, and who felt entitled to the historical wealth of the country despite the horrible toll some of it had taken on others. Like my parents, people wanted to put the difficulties of the past behind them, ignoring the legacies of those difficulties.

They signed on to a future that was bright, and in which they were privileged. They were better-off because they were better people, the reasoning generally went, omitting the point that many such opportunities had often been purchased at other people's expense. Once people signed on to a worldview and its spokespersons, it was hard to shake their perception of the world as it was constantly reinforced by a selective input of information. They believed only what their leaders said, regardless of whether or not it was firmly grounded in fact. Remembering my earnest childhood patriotism, I called this phenomenon a sense of allegiance. I was aware that this dynamic continued to define for me as well, but thought my new community was rigorous about searching out the facts, and engaged in wide-opened debates and analysis.

If people looked at the long view, however, and saw that equality and justice for all was both moral and in their own interest, would they then be able to see past their need to feel superior? Since many white people did benefit enormously from economic and social racism, a much more personal way to penetrate this veneer of entitlement was to address women. It was harder for women to say everything was okay because despite the privileges accorded being white or middle class, we experienced incest, violence against us, and job discrimination. Women also had to run interference for kids in all the instances in which families and schools considered kids' interests last. Women could benefit greatly in the short run, as well as the long, by challenging the assumptions of the system. If we could get women to question the way things were, would men be far behind?

At the end of the article, I suggested that women fight against the way girls are tracked in schools, organize against low wages of women's jobs like nursing, teaching, and secretarial work, and educate women about the traps of consumerism. Building on stories I had heard about the early days of the Chinese, Vietnamese, and Cuban revolutions, I also included an idea of forming neighborhood women's militias, which could respond to men who were abusive or to parents who kept their daughters locked up at home. I didn't think of the militias as being armed, but as groups that publicized abuse with leaflets on telephone poles, to make men accountable within their own neighborhoods. Militia women should be available to offer protection to other women when they were under attack. The goal of the organizing was always to bring all kinds of women into the movement for revolutionary change.

The article appeared in the next issue of *New Left Notes* under the title "Revolutionary Women's Militias." Graphics of an Arab-looking woman with a gun surrounded two sides of the article, even though the article never mentioned armed struggle and instead talked of the militias as educational and agitational tools. Most curiously of all, the paragraph proposing the women's militia had been edited to remove the sentences on women's abuse by their husbands and boyfriends. This change, along with the graphics significantly distorted the actual content. It was hard to tell what the point of the militias might be. By the time the article was printed, however, I was on the road and didn't notice the changes until years later.

Casting a final glance back at the wonderful house on Lanier Place that had held such a diverse group of people together through so many good times and days of passionate work, Mike and I set off on a trip through the South. I had packed all of my belongings in a trunk, including my childhood teddy bear and my Cambodian fabric, and left it with an older woman who was a member of Women's Strike for Peace. I pawned my violin and packed a small suitcase and my autoharp to take with me on the journey. Everyone I knew was rethinking what they were doing and where they were going.

Our first stop was a visit with Mike Klonsky and Sue Eanet in Atlanta, and then with other SDS friends in Alabama and New Orleans. I had always been interested in taking up the challenge of organizing whites in the South, and I loved Southern food and the lush countryside I had seen traveling to campuses in Virginia and North Carolina. I was hopeful and excited to be on the road again. In Atlanta, Mike, Sue, and a few others were trying to set up a new organizing project that specifically focused on people in jobs, possibly starting with those who worked in the big plants around Atlanta.

We went out to a Burger King and while eating dripping hamburgers we talked about the options. I had never had fast food before, sensing that it was addictive and unhealthy, and more expensive than cooking at home. Part of me, however, felt that I needed to find a way to ease up on my puritanical tendencies, and so on this trip I let myself be open to everything. I liked Sue and Mike. She had a wonderful appreciation of the absurd; in the face of all the horrible things going on in the world, and our own increasingly serious passions, it was reassuring to be with someone who could still laugh.

I liked Atlanta but couldn't wrap my mind around the thought of settling down there, getting a job in a plant in order to organize, and giving up my ability to express my rage at the government. The sense of urgency seemed to be growing faint here. So, we moved on to Birmingham where we knew some SDS folks who worked on an underground paper. After a few days exploring Birmingham, visiting the church that had been bombed and other civil rights landmarks, we moved on to New Orleans.

We visited briefly with more SDS people there, and then went to Bourbon Street to see the legendary jazz bars and listen to music. We walked through the small old-fashioned neighborhood as dusk fell. It was wonderful. One of the styles of music we heard on Bourbon Street was Cajun. It was the first time I had heard it and I fell in love. We learned that this music was made south of New Orleans, in the bayous where French, African, Caribbean, and English traditions mixed in a unique way. So, we left the surging currents of the Mississippi River near New Orleans, setting out early in the morning to explore the land of tall delta grasses and narrow winding roads. An hour south of New Orleans I was reminded of the terrifying moment on the *African Queen* when Humphrey Bogart and Katherine Hepburn get lost in the Ulanga River Delta. I could see that only local folks would dare negotiate the interconnecting channels that wound hidden behind the tall grasses.

I was also stunned by the heat, which was similar to what I had experienced briefly in Ceylon. When we returned to New Orleans at dusk, I discovered that the glue on my autoharp had melted, allowing half the wood pulled by the tight metal strings to be curled back like a potato chip. The wood was split in several places. Sadly, I left this last artifact of my musical past in a roadside garbage can, and we headed north.

Having found no project in the South, we would head to Chicago to visit our friends there and see what we could learn from a stop at the hub. I was drawn back to Weatherman by their emphasis on race and by their anger. Away from the turmoil of a convention, I wanted to talk more. I was also eager to see if I could get some feedback from my article.

The next section of this book tells the story of Weatherman and of my own path as part of that organization. My story is only that, my own. I, like many participants, experienced a certain liftoff from reality as I pushed myself as hard as I could to respond world events.

The writers of the Weatherman paper had bravely stepped up to the task of "leading the movement." Weatherman's leaders had quickly mastered the language of certainty and discovered the power of images. It proved to be a dazzling combination. Several were close to the yippies and the Motherfuckers, both of whom conjured up images creatively and skillfully. Their goal was to rally as many people as quickly as possible, taking advantage of the vast numbers of alienated young people, despite the fact that these young people were hardly committed to fundamental change. The sense of winning seemed so urgent. At the same time, the Weatherman group occasionally spoke with such practicality and initiated such detailed plans that they seemed dedicated to the most serious long-term view of leadership.

A different segment of those attracted to Weatherman, including many of the women, were drawn to the impulse for self-sacrifice in the face of the government's overwhelming cruelty. I was of this group. We welcomed the language of certainty. Rather than rely on rallying images to gather the forces, however, we focused more on the day-to-day work, trying to fill out the dramatic scenarios of war with the details of our own risk taking and the unglamorous grunt work of organizations. We threw ourselves into the possibility of remaking ourselves as more effective tools for humanity's benefit to the point of sacrificing our own humanity and certainly losing, in the process, our individual voices. If the efforts to change the system required participation in an international liberation force, as described in the Weatherman paper, then we would do it, as hard as it was to bring it into focus emotionally or practically.

These two groups would talk past each other throughout the life of Weatherman, with no one, I think, ever figuring out the extent to which we were speaking two different languages, one of image and metaphor and one practical, however absurd. Ironically, these two strains of Weatherman—and there were others as well—also complemented each other once we were underground and ensured our survival, for better or for worse. All of us, of course, shared a bit of the others. I found the vision of quick and easy victories, of tens of thousands of people responding to the images of rebellion, to be reassuring and seductive at times, even if at other moments I could see that the predictions of mass insurrection were highly improbable at best, and an indication of serious flaws in judgment at worst.

In the end, we would lose sight of the potentially resilient qualities of people and of our own movement, qualities like flexibility, compromise, forgiveness, creativity, intellectual rigor, and the valuing of each life as much as possible, that are all essential to the long-term survival of the species. We forgot our mission to find the experiences and social dynamics that nurture these qualities, as earlier movements had done, most recently the civil rights movement of the 50s and 60s, and the uprisings of young people in support of peace and democracy in the early 60s.

In many respects, our efforts were doomed to crash and burn—which we certainly did in the townhouse nine months after the June 1969 national convention. During this time, and during the ensuing six years, we caused no small amount of damage to both ourselves and other organizations, even while tens of thousands felt heartened by our voice of outrage, our sacrifice, and our ability to elude capture.

CHAPTER NINE

WEATHERMAN

■ ■

We drove into the vast grid of Chicago streets, filled with children finding ways to pass the hot, steamy summer days, and I was anxious to find a place to land, to begin to work. We started at the SDS national office, where the massive Heidelberg press was running leaflets for the Black Panther Party up the street. The few staff people around seemed intent on their tasks, none of which seemed to involve casual talk. The familiar, dusty rooms no longer felt like a place for travelers to hang out and exchange stories. Instead, we arranged to meet with friends Jeff Jones and Phoebe Hirsch later that day at their apartment uptown.

Jeff and Phoebe had moved from New York to California the previous winter and had immediately immersed themselves in the active political life of the Bay Area. They leafleted to support the chemical and oil workers' strike, along with a mixed conglomerate of other movement activists. They got involved in the student-faculty strike at San Francisco State, which had continued for most of the year, even as they were immersed in the celebration of counterculture in Berkeley and the struggles to sustain it.

In June, however, Jeff had been enlisted by his friends, the coauthors of the Weatherman paper, to run for SDS national officer. When he reluctantly agreed, Phoebe resigned herself to going too. Phoebe became a member of the local Chicago Weatherman collective, while Jeff worked out of the national office as part of the national leadership collective, now dubbed the Weather Bureau. I imagined the Chicago collective to be like our Washington collective, although perhaps more disciplined and with less spontaneous side activities. Both Bill Willett and Jonny Lerner from the Washington staff were around, but I didn't know where exactly, or what they were doing. Both, it turned out, were working on specific tasks for members of the Weather Bureau as sort of aides de camp, and neither was formally in any collective.

When we got uptown, Jeff, Phoebe, Mike, and I sat around their tiny kitchen table. As always, I was glad to see them and wanted to catch up on the happenings since the convention. Immediately, Jeff got down to business, launching into his summation of Weatherman's current activities and thinking. In the five weeks since the national council, Weatherman had set up collectives in almost a dozen cities. The primary work of these groups of between ten and twenty young people was to establish themselves as the most militant, aggressive, outspoken voice in the area, on the theory that this would attract untold numbers of alienated young people. Many out-of-school youths didn't take movement people seriously, they believed, because local activists were all talk and no action. So people in the collectives would prove incontestably that they were the "baddest dudes in town."

Weathermen were also addressing another problem. The police had been harassing and threatening black activists with a relentlessness and brutality rarely used against white activists. If Weathermen constantly challenged the police, they argued, they could divert some police energy onto themselves, distracting them a little from the black activists. This strategy also enabled the organization to prove its resoluteness and to be taken seriously as allies of the black movement. In any event, to sit by quietly while the black movement was undergoing such a pummeling seemed yet another instance of hiding behind the cloak of privilege.

As I listened to Jeff and Phoebe make this argument, I wondered if this was what we had been doing in Washington. For the first time, I began to look at the aggressiveness displayed by many of the current Weather leaders in a new light. The strategic objective of their provocations, both to other activists and to the authorities, was to challenge whites in the most immediate way to step up and not be silent. I still wasn't convinced that physically aggressive, provocative confrontations would organize many more people, although events sometimes seemed to prove me wrong. But I had never before considered that our *failure* to "go berserk" meant that the police assaults on blacks went unchallenged. This was both a moral argument—to not be "good Germans"—and a tactical conjecture, that we could draw away some of the intensity of the heat. This direct challenge to complicity would compel others to actively confront police racism.

This strategy seemed to be working, at least in part. Already by late July, the national office staff was being followed, stopped, and charged with petty offenses by Chicago cops on a regular basis, just as the Chicago Panthers had been for months. Suffering from the same extralegal police sanctions as the Panthers did seemed to me then like a first step in equalizing the stakes. It also fit in with my long-held belief that until you walked in someone else's shoes, you could not really understand their feelings and thinking. Besides, while racism dehumanized black people, being complicit with it, either because one agreed with racism or because one chose to ignore it, dehumanized whites as well. The only way not to be entangled with it was to be loud and clear in support of the black movement. Since Weatherman believed that black efforts to gain equality were part of a worldwide phenomenon, this confrontational strategy to disassociate ourselves from the prevailing racism could only serve to strengthen this international upheaval as well.

Weatherman's leadership seemed to have developed a close working relationship with the Panthers. Since the advent of black power, I hadn't found a way to act on my commitment to racial equality the way I had during the civil rights movement. These people seemed to have found a way to do that, and I wanted to learn more. I found the thought that I had not been doing enough unsettling, especially if, as a result, I might have actually contributed to the suffering of black people.

Where this strategy was leading was still a mystery to me, but, having heard nothing else that summer that seemed better, I was willing to listen and was predisposed to make sense of it. Not only was I impressed by the boldness of it, but also by its purity. It was hard work to try to meet people halfway in their thinking, to present new information that engaged existing misconceptions so that people rethought their views on the war or poverty. This confrontational strategy seemed like it might move such aims much faster.

Jeff went on to explain that the various "Weather collectives" were made up of people who committed themselves to being cadre, full-time revolutionaries. No one was working with students since it was summer. Instead, collective members were preparing to reach out to young people who were out of school, either already working or on the street. Each collective was planning a series of confrontational actions to initiate their program locally. In the fall, the collectives would bring all of the people they had organized to Chicago for a confrontational national demonstration. Membership in the collectives was by invitation only, and, once approved, you had to agree to be disciplined to the collective decisions and to the leadership of the organization. Jeff proposed that Mike and I apply to join the Chicago collective with Phoebe.

I found the talk of collectives and cadre exciting because I was always interested in organizational efficiency. I accepted the necessity of hierarchy in this context because it allowed a more sophisticated division of labor and therefore greater productivity. This organizational structure would also enable Weatherman to protect itself from the increasing government infiltration.

I knew that the authors of the Weatherman paper saw these collectives as the first step to forming a Marxist-Leninist party, but I imagined that things were still quite informal. They were trying to create new revolutionary personalities, to remake themselves to be their very best to serve the revolution. Phoebe was proud of her progress in the martial arts training they were doing every day. It was very intense working with a collective, she added. She was unhappy that members of the Weather Bureau were arguing that she should stop living with Jeff because her relationship with Jeff, and the resulting potential access to the leadership collective, gave her special status and privileges over others in the Chicago collective. Phoebe could understand the argument, but she really cared about Jeff and thought there should be another way to deal with the bureau's concerns. She didn't agree with the antimonogamy philosophy, and she didn't, she said laughing, want to move out.

This was the first I heard of Weatherman actually acting on their new "antimonogamy" philosophy. At this stage, they argued, existing monogamous relationships between men and women held both people back from

new challenges, and from an open-minded approach to remaking themselves as "socialist men and women" unburdened by the individualism and
selfishness that characterized the society we came from. Some of the early
writing by the women's movement had argued that monogamous marriage was initially formalized to ensure male parentage so a man could
bequest his wealth to his own offspring. (I had not yet read or thought
about the fact that the social taboos arising from monogamy had served
women in many ways as well, offering them, in theory, some protection
from sexual assault as well as support for their children.) Monogamy,
according to Weatherman, was implicitly sexist, and relationships between
men and women needed to be rethought. In our conversations, no one
made note of the fact that, in this instance, it was the men of the Weather
Bureau dictating "women's liberation" to a woman against her wishes.

From the conversation with Phoebe I gleaned that you could be part of
the collectives and maintain a somewhat critical stance; it wasn't all or
nothing. The challenges outweighed the weirdness. If I was serious about
revolution, even if I had no idea what it might look like or entail, I needed
to join with other serious people to figure out how to create it. The only
group around that seemed to focus on the issues of both race and poverty
was Weatherman. If it seemed too heavy, well, my two of most light-
hearted friends, Bill and Jonny, were in it. Now Phoebe, a lover of theater
and music like me, was also giving it a try. Besides, if this was the cutting
edge, I didn't want to be left behind. I decided to join, and, Mike, too,
wanted to sign on.

The new ban on monogamy didn't really bother us as it was clear that
while we had enjoyed our relationship, it wasn't headed anywhere deep.
In fact, the antimonogamy provision seemed to provide a graceful way to
separate without the hard work of sorting it through. We never even talked
about it. I wasn't convinced that monogamy was bad, but since it worked
in my favor at the moment, it didn't seem like a big deal.

Having nowhere to live and little cash, we were to stay with one of the
members of the Chicago collective on the North Side. That evening, we
would formally meet with the group to be evaluated, one at a time. In the
meantime, after adding our sleeping bags and few belongings to a pile of

others in a corner of the apartment's living room, we went to join the members of the collective at martial arts instruction at the small storefront. I was eager to see what martial arts was all about.

At the storefront, about twenty people were standing in rows, practicing kicks and yells in response to a teacher in the front. Most of the faces were new to me. As I looked at them, absorbed in their physical tasks, I couldn't help wondering who we were going to be using this against. Certainly not the police armed with billy clubs, handguns, and mace. Perhaps these exercises were a symbolic way to toughen the spirit, to teach self-discipline. I was more than willing to take advantage of the opportunity.

I was told to do twenty push-ups, fifty jumping jacks, and some stretches to warm up. Twenty push-ups? I couldn't do one! Despite my active tomboy past, I had never been able to develop any upper body strength. I started with the jumping jacks, but being a heavy smoker, and never having exercised before, I was winded after twenty. All the other women, some of whom I knew to be smokers as well, seemed to be engaged. So much for my self-image as a member of the fighting forces. I felt pathetic. I pushed myself to do my best, and faked it as much as possible.

That evening, the collective assembled for a meeting, and I was summoned. Most members had known each other and worked together at the University of Chicago. The leader of the collective, Drew, was also a member of the Weather Bureau. I had never met him before, but knew he had a reputation for having read widely and being a theoretical heavy. That summer of 1969, Drew had dropped out of the University of Chicago graduate school, where he and a few other graduate students and faculty had tried to replicate the model of Columbia, with some limited success. In the process he had collected around him a large number of undergraduates, several of whom comprised the majority of the Chicago collective with him. The collective, about ten before Mike and I joined, included seven women.

That evening, I was queried about the main ideas in the Weatherman paper and asked to explain my politics, as we phrased it. Since I had written many articles for *New Left Notes* over the past two years, I thought most people there should know what I thought in general. Nonetheless, since I didn't know these people, I plunged ahead, explaining that I agreed with most of what had been in the Weatherman paper except what I had discussed in my recent *New Left Notes* article, which I summarized.

When I finished my short summary, Drew began to challenge my understanding of the Weatherman analysis. My thinking was incomplete and sloppy, he said. Occasionally one of the other collective members, especially a couple of the women, gave further examples of the points Drew was making or restated the critique in a different way.

They thought I had not given sufficient importance to the black struggle and to the Panthers in particular. Why had I not organized more support for the black movement in Washington? Why had I not mentioned the Panthers in my article and talked more about my own white-skin privilege and my unwillingness to let go of it? It was true that in my article I had concentrated on the issue of women and had not given priority to the fight for black economic and political equality. I had, however, stated that the overarching conflict between the US and the third world framed everything. I had focused on women, I said, because that issue had essentially been left out of the Weatherman paper. I was suggesting that working with women of all ages around issues of abuse at home and on the job should be a priority, at least for some of us.

When I tried to explain my thinking, however, I was told that in a "criticism session" I had to respond to what others said, and that by arguing with them, I was being defensive and evasive, fearful of looking at the truth, perhaps protecting myself in some way. This was not the way I had thought about criticism/self-criticism when I had studied Mao's "little red book" in Washington. I had imagined the whole process to be much more informal. In Chicago, the conversation seemed to be framed by Drew's analysis, the Weatherman analysis, which was the only way to look at the world. Any deviation from that indicated a personal weakness. The structure felt like that of judge and supplicant, rather than one of equal exchange.

I was taken aback by this close, somewhat hostile cross-examination. In my earlier conversation with Jeff and Phoebe, I had felt open to challenges to my thinking and my work, always concerned that I could be doing more.

Under Drew's scrutiny, however, these concerns were turned back at me as an accusation burdened with judgment. It was true, I had not focused on black organizations in the work we had done in Washington, and I thought that was interesting. Why was it that I never had a relationship with any of the leadership of any well-known black organizations, and certainly not with the Panthers? Perhaps, I began to think, if I had had a better analysis, I would have been more effective in understanding how to support SNCC and the Panthers in Washington. Instead, their separatist and sometimes anti-white stance had seemed reasonable and had also intimidated me, so I stayed away. I was afraid to state this explicitly, however, because it would leave me open to the charge of racism, which I didn't think was fair.

The session, Weatherman's version of a criticism session, became increasingly confrontational. It had already been a long day when we started, and as we continued late into the night, I grew tired. My questioners moved on to the role of women's issues in the broader struggle. By arguing for women's militia or women's organizations of any kind, they said, I was encouraging women to pursue their own selfish interests. My passion rose up inside me, strengthened by my previous arguments with Marilyn Webb and other feminists in Washington. While I had rejected the middle-class preoccupations of much of their conversations, I justified it with a commitment to organizing women around issues that really mattered to all women, like protection from abuse and poverty. Women needed to organize around their own needs, just as the black community did, and to have opportunities for self-reliance and leadership.

Even this, I was told by the women in the collective, was "selling out the most oppressed." Women's liberation meant that women should be active in the fight to end racism and colonial exploitation, and it was that process that would integrate women into leadership and would gain respect and equality for women. I had thought that this was another important aspect of a strategy for women's liberation and had always supported SDS's resolutions for women to join the movement. But over the past year I had become convinced that there were times when it was important for women to organize together to work for themselves, if for no other reason than that sometimes, men wouldn't help.

By then it was way past midnight. Maybe I did need to rethink some of my beliefs about women, I thought tiredly. Only by putting support for the third world first, perhaps, could women have any chance. Certainly it seemed that the few political black women I knew of identified first with the black struggle and only secondarily as women. The Vietnamese women certainly saw their liberation in the context of a free, decolonized Vietnam. Maybe it was true, as Drew and the others said, that despite my beliefs and work of the past several years, I had been influenced by selfishness.

It appeared that my ability to join the collective hinged on my agreement with all the criticisms of my past political thinking and work, and not just a willingness to consider them. I was now more curious than ever about this group, in which everyone took themselves and each other so seriously. Suddenly it seemed urgent that I get myself accepted, if I really wanted to make a contribution to revolution. The criticism indicated that I was inferior to the other members of the collective, and I wanted the opportunity to prove that I had a substantial history of work and ideas, and that I should be considered an equal. So I agreed with the criticisms in general, and said I would rethink things in light of the criticism. I thought to myself, I could always change my mind.

The fact that I had to fake it in both of my first encounters with Weatherman, in the martial arts training and now in the criticism, should have served as a warning that all was not right. Any life experience that might have caused me to heed this warning, however, was drowned out by my growing desperation to be part of the most effective effort to stop the killing in Vietnam and the unfair treatment of people at home.

The Weatherman criticism/self-criticism sessions of that summer became famous throughout the movement. The youthful Red Guards had been using this technique in their attempts to sweep out the old, stuffy, bureaucratic procedures, and to democratize the communist movement in China, we thought. I, like many in SDS, had identified with the Red Guards, seeing them as the hope that would keep China from decaying into a corrupt, Soviet-style bureaucracy. Mao did warn that it was the ideas that should be criticized, not the person. The metaphors of disease that Mao often used with "bad ideas," however, definitely made the thought of having such an idea distasteful. The safest path was to remake yourself in the image of those in leadership, in order to win respect and power and avoid criticism.

Like many dedicated activists, I was vulnerable to any argument that claimed I was not doing enough. Furthermore, like many Weathermen, I was still trying to disentangle myself from the cultural and political assumptions of my past. The Chicago collective seemed to be willing to engage in the kind of intense scrutiny of beliefs and goals that I wanted. As Phoebe had said earlier, we were "remaking ourselves" into "new men and women," following the lead of Cuban revolutionary Che Guevarra. In our case, we were trying to redefine what it meant to be members of the "mother-country," who did not root our behavior or identity in being "better," entitled to privileges. My first encounter with this effort had been completely disorienting, but I felt that I needed to quiet my reservations for the time being, to take a leap of faith so I could become part of this community and see what the process had to offer.

While I had been attracted by Weatherman's commitment to efficiency, I didn't think about the implications of Weatherman's view of organization and leadership. Rather than the diverse and chaotic reality that had always been SDS, they were developing an image of an efficient, hierarchical leadership of committed cadres. Even if a majority of people in this country didn't support change, we were obligated to side with the greater majority of people in the world. Much of the script for change had already been written by leaders like Lenin, Mao, Ho, Fidel, and Che. Embedded in this view was an assumption that it was now left to the experts to interpret the script and apply it, with a slight nod to local conditions. I needed to suspend my own judgments, it seemed, and trust the more knowledgeable leadership. Besides, as a person of European descent, I didn't even have the right to enter into much of the discussion about how many aspects of the future would be determined, and why those determinations were made.

The collapse of my own sense of judgment that quickly followed my embrace of this philosophy exacerbated my already existing sense of inadequacy, the feeling that I wasn't doing enough. The source of power for my own voice began to dry up, leaving a languid, anxious passivity in its wake. There wasn't time for me to figure things out, I rationalized. Besides, I wanted too badly to hear that somebody had a foolproof plan to bring equality and justice to the world.

While these components set up much that followed, Weatherman's clumsy misuse of religious-psychotherapeutic technique helped the process along, leading smart, well-intentioned people in leadership to inadvertently make the most insidious assaults on other participants' ability to construct their own meaning of the ideas and realities we confronted. Those of us who participated in this process quickly became part of it. The idea of belonging to a vanguard was seductive, whether it was religious, corporate, or ideological. It felt good to be part of the elite, reassuring in an unsettled world. The process of rigorous self-discipline appealed strongly to that part of me that wanted to be a good soldier.

The highest form of sacrifice, of commitment, I believed, was to dedicate oneself to the cause without asking for recognition, to be without ambition, other than to serve. As a woman, I had been raised to serve, of course, although expected to serve husband, children, and society by doing good works. In high school, I had been moved to tears by *Nun Story*, a film in which Audrey Hepburn is torn between service in an imperfect organization and her own passions and hunger for challenges of the world. Here, I thought, I had the opportunity to serve in a far better organization and I could still live my passions.

In joining Weatherman, I was, finally and ironically, succumbing to the desire to be one of the chosen, to have power indirectly through my association with powerful men. Bernardine's unique place at the top only made it more palpable. I could not yet imagine power in any other way. Conversations among women were only just beginning to reveal the ways in which society was still defined by ancient agreements and social arrangements. Surrounded by the trappings of modernity, we had the ability to imagine something different, but I thought we had already arrived there. It would take years of conversation to realize that we were only beginning to imagine, let alone bring to pass, a different way of thinking about power. Women can replace men in the existing paradigm, as many have, and that is a tentative first step, although in reality, such a stance by itself can easily reinforce the way things are, even as it leads to something new.

Young people make their way in the world during times of great upheaval and uncertainty (whether global in scope like in the 60s, or whether the upheaval is local, even within the family), while being buffeted by a myriad of influences. I have never thought that anyone in Weatherman consciously set out to use techniques that could manipulate others or stifle dissenting opinions. In fact, what is most interesting to me about this story, is the way in which young people, and we were only one of many groups of young people who fell prey to this in the 60s and 70s, fall into cultlike behaviors under pressure, especially when the ultimate arbitrator of conflict is violence.

Nor is this phenomenon limited only to young people. I now believe that any hierarchical organization led by a charismatic leader and imbued with a sense of superiority, whether it be religious, corporate, or political, is vulnerable to cultlike behaviors. Only in a few cases does a messianic leader move beyond this stage to make himself—rarely herself—the object of obedience and worship. In most cases, the magnetism of these behaviors spin within their own reality for a while and then eventually collapse, either because of their own incoherence or due to some outside intervention.

While brazen egos and intellectual arrogance were no harder to find in Weatherman than anywhere else, all of us contributed to Weatherman's illusions because we had a variety of needs to do so. A confluence of factors corroded individual identity and encouraged passivity. We were riding the energy of 60s—a vast opening up of ideas and possibilities—and the blurry line between reality and delusion was easily stepped across.

The balance between individual agency and passivity differed from person to person at any moment. Some refused to subject themselves to the humiliation and stress of the collectives and left. Many later felt isolated, however, spit out of the movement and unsure of the alternative. They were plagued even more acutely by the feeling that they were not doing enough. Others jockeyed for a special relationship with those in leadership outside of collective discipline, which was what Bill Willet and Jonny had done. Still others say that they did not experience a pressure to be passive, but instead felt fully engaged with the development of the political direction of the organization, even when they were not in the main leadership and were situated in peripheral cities.[1]

Interestingly, the highest level of the organization, the Weather Bureau, did not subject themselves to this kind of collective self-discipline. Despite the cultivated appearance of a unified leadership, the Weather Bureau was in limbo during the summer, wobbling between the flawed and paralyzed democracy of SDS and their vision of setting up a disciplined organization. The dozen or so original members had significant differences and no established mechanisms for making decisions. Instead, informal grouping of friends and allies formed among them and their friends and allies outside. It was in these groupings, which were unaccountable to anyone, that Weather Bureau members hashed out what they thought, and developed strategies to provide leadership among the collectives. The contention for influence and dominance was exercised through control of different segments of the organization, like *New Left Notes*, the planning for the national action, or the leadership of individual collectives. This informal, fluid structure continued to metamorphose over the next several months, and was responsible for the very different experiences of the various collectives. Its informality and de facto invisibility to most members, however, made it appear inaccessible to most, who assumed, like I did, that each member of the leadership collective represented the reasoned conclusions of the whole group. Never in my conversations with Jeff, Drew, or, later, Terry, was I given reason to believe otherwise.

After my troubled entry into the collective, I tried to get a sense of how to fit into the group. There was little time for individual discussion. Instead we went to the storefront to practice martial arts, we read the material in *New Left Notes* and a few short pieces by Lenin or Mao about building

cadre organizations, and we worked on preparations for organizing for the
upcoming national action. We had long collective discussions about the
correct way to word each leaflet.

New Left Notes was still coming out, but the editor now was a mysterious Morris Older. I suspected it might be a made-up name, but once again
I couldn't figure out if it was in jest or for security. It was clear that the
editor had abandoned any pretense of representing SDS's varied membership. The most recent issue, August 1, 1969, was four pages and contained
only two stories. The whole front page was a long article on recent riots,
or rebellions if seen from another perspective, in the black community in
Columbus, Ohio. The author of this article wrote in a tough street slang,
with lots of cursing. I couldn't imagine anyone in the Washington region
relating to this kind of language. I was willing to believe that there was
another constituency out there that would be drawn in by this language,
but I hadn't yet come across it.

The author, a young woman I had never heard of, first described the
Columbus summer program. Twenty-five SDS members, many recently
recruited from Ohio campuses, moved into three working-class neighborhoods throughout the city. People worked mostly with high school and
gang kids, on the beaches, in the streets, bars, and pool halls. Some were
working in factories. The aim of the program was to develop cadre—"16-
year-old communist guerillas"—for the building of a citywide
revolutionary youth movement.[2]

The article continued with a detailed account of the three days of rioting that had erupted in the black community over a police shooting. The
author reveled in the enormous damage done the first night when the
chaos had succeeded in making it difficult for police forces to enter the
neighborhood (and impossible for firefighters). The article asserted that 99
percent of the damage was done to white-owned businesses, resented by
local residents for price gouging. Silently, I wondered if it was a little early
to draw that conclusion, since in all previous rebellions, many local homes
had been destroyed in the process as well.

The article also noted cavalierly that a "friend of the mayor's" who was
assisting police had been killed, possibly by a sniper bullet. With the police

driven back, the mayor had called in the National Guard, who were themselves stymied by the persistent activity of snipers. These snipers, the article asserted, were black Vietnam veterans who "made the Guard look as inexperienced as they actually [were]." I could only conclude that the Weathermen in Columbus must have had an intense relationship with black activists in order for them to know that.

Meanwhile, the article continued, SDS collective members had been under attack themselves. At the onset of the disturbances, someone had grounded all the SDS cars by drilling holes in the radiators. Everyone assumed law enforcement personnel were behind it. Undaunted, collective members produced leaflets explaining the many causes of the riots from the perspective of black participants as they understood it, and were leafleting in their neighborhoods to young white people. That night, police came to one of the SDS houses with a warrant to search for guns. Finding none, they arrested the residents anyway for being "suspicious persons." Once in jail, the charge was changed to inciting to riot, a fairly serious felony. In the newspapers, the mayor and other city officials blamed SDS for the riots, claiming, as Nixon did, that we were controlled by communists. The absurdity, not to speak of the racism, of the claim that SDS members had the credibility to incite a riot in the black community, increased the aura of surrealism surrounding both the conflict and the message coming from the article.

The unspoken assumption of the article seemed to be that we were on our way to armed urban insurgencies, with black communities defending themselves against police brutality and against the exploitation of white businesses. The riots would help black militants gain military and therefore political power, and it was only through the acquisition of this power that life could be improved for them. The article ended with a quote from Lin Piao, a Chinese military theorist during China's war with Japan, "Long Live the Victory of People's War!!"

Was it really true that black Vietnam vets were starting to take up arms in the inner cities? It was a fear that had lain just beneath the surface of white society since the Civil War. Was a race war coming, and if so, where would I be situated? I certainly didn't want to be one of the people against black citizens, but if all black people believed that all white people were hopelessly racist, then despite what I might want, I would be in some kind of opposition. The only solution to the dilemma, it seemed to me, was to get busy now, to speak up and act against racism, to show how we were willing to sacrifice everything to fight against it. Only if white people truly put themselves in a position of being as vulnerable as blacks could we build trust. Without this kind of record, there could be no possibility of future cooperation. This was the argument in the Cleveland SDS leaflet, printed as part of the article.

The other article in the paper was SDS's call for a national action in October of that year. The main slogan for the demonstration was "Bring the War Home." The same powerful analysis of injustice in the world was repeated, but again, there was little to guide my imagination of what that "war at home" would look like. Did it mean protests like the huge demonstrations from the previous August around the Democratic National Convention or did it mean armed insurrection in the ghetto, and, if so, how were we to relate to that? Was "war" a metaphor, or did they mean a war with guns? It was hard to tell, and I felt stupid asking. Exactly why were more people going to come to a demonstration like that?

Shortly after I joined the Chicago collective, the group planned to make a large replica of the flag of the NLF (National Front for the Liberation of South Vietnam), attach it to a pole and run down one of the lakefront beaches that, until recently, had been kept segregated by angry white beach goers. The idea was to challenge the bad idea that the NLF was the enemy. We took the train up to the beach and assembled. On a signal, we started to run down the beach chanting "Ho, Ho, Ho Chi Minh, NLF is going to win!" I concentrated mainly on trying to keep upright and not get completely winded.

Without our usual verbosity we were challenging beach-goers with the fact that not only were we against US involvement in Vietnam, we supported the other side. We were intruding on what we perceived to be the determination of the majority of the population to ignore or accept the war and its horrible costs. This was a meaning of "bringing the war home" that made sense to me. Nonetheless, out of habit, I wondered how this action would change anyone's mind.

After a few minutes of running, a small group of young men started to taunt us angrily, calling us "commie lovers" and other epithets. They overtook us as we left the beach and headed for the trains. The commotion quickly brought the local cops, who arrested us "for our own protection." They didn't give us a particularly hard time, and we were soon released with a disorderly conduct charge.

Sitting in the station house waiting to be released, the collective was jubilant. The action was considered a big success. We had presented ourselves as young people who were tough and "in your face." If we could gain the respect of the young men who attacked us today, they might join us tomorrow. The time for organizing around specific issues, from neighborhood stoplights to women's rights, was over, and now we were saying out loud that "the only solution is revolution," a slogan popular far beyond Weatherman at the time. To organize around any detail without recognizing that nothing substantive was possible without revolution was deceptive and would never bring in those people, especially young people, who already had a sense that it was time for all or nothing. While I saw no evidence yet that we had successfully reached anyone, I felt like there must be more to learn here.

I was still reluctant to discuss my thoughts in the collective for fear of revealing "bad ideas" or ignorance, further lowering my status. I was also reluctant to turn to Mike, as we had just ended out relationship. A week after I had arrived, Phoebe, the only other friend I had in the group, mysteriously disappeared. It was said that she had to return to New York to deal with some family matters. In fact, I learned later, she had become overwhelmed by the pressures of the collective and had left precipitously to go stay with her sister and try to make sense of what was happening. I only knew she was gone, and it never occurred to me that all was not well with her.

Over the next few weeks, the collective prepared for and carried out a few more similar actions, all equally odd and inconclusive, and none of which convinced anyone new to oppose the war as far as I could see. Part of me, however, enjoyed the macho posturing. As a young woman, I wanted to be proud of my fearlessness, of my willingness to try new things and endure discomfort and hardship. I liked wearing the leather jacket, jeans, and boots that were fashionable. The toughness was an ultimate rejection of the image of feminine helplessness that had saturated the literature and manners of my childhood. Because I was smoking a lot during the endless meetings, and eating little but cereal and coffee, I weighed little more than 100 pounds, the least I had weighed since sixth grade. I felt lithe and limber.

During this time the collective met daily, often for six or seven hours. We planned the actions, but more often we spent hours analyzing the smallest details of our work, things people said, the ways we each carried out our assigned tasks. No detail was too small for analysis, which continued to be saturated with the jargon. The most damaging motives, racism, selfishness, fear, were ferreted out in each of us with great regularity. Lack of participation in the criticisms would have elicited new criticisms, so everyone was sure to find some way to add on to what the two or three leaders were going after. There were, however, some unspoken alliances, in which people watched each other's backs and tried to deflect criticism from each other. I often found myself resentful at high-handed tactics, in which those who criticized acted as if they themselves were perfect or ascribed motives to others that I didn't see. Occasionally I would speak up when someone was under a particularly severe attack that seemed unfounded to me. This was the one kind of situation that could still arouse me to think somewhat independently.

I felt in my gut that this environment was brutal, but the idea of creating a party of cadre who would work as one, who were absolutely selfless, and who could maximize our effectiveness, remained an intriguing challenge. Perhaps all this pain would create something positive. We were "mother-country radicals," children of the central imperial power, so it was inevitable that we would be riddled with corrupt assumptions and expectations. We had never experienced the famine, war, disease, and servitude that were the lot of most of the world's peoples, so we knew little of real suffering. In our sacrifice, in our willingness to subject ourselves even to our excesses, I thought we were taking our beliefs seriously in a way few white progressives had before.

During the last weeks of August, articles in *New Left Notes* repeated over and over the litany of crimes committed in our name against the poor, both here and around the world. They celebrated the outrage of our response. The analysis of inequality and of who benefited from it was always crystal clear and eloquent, if oversimplified. The description of the people fighting injustice, however, tended to be idealized. Huey Newton, for instance, was involved in an incident in which a cop was killed. What really happened? What happened, too, with Los Siete, seven young Latinos arrested in another incident of police shootings that resulted in a police death. There was little discussion of the details: Was the thin line between offense and defense so obvious?

Near the end of August, the national action staff summed up Weatherman thinking:

> What became clear to [us]—through the struggles at Columbia and Chicago, at San Francisco State, and at Kent State—was that putting forward our politics in an aggressive way was the ONLY way to organize the masses of people in this country. That only by dealing with the issues of white supremacy, the black liberation struggle, Third World struggles, and the fight against imperialism, only by challenging the consciousness of the people could we ever develop a movement capable of helping topple the imperialist state.... *People change by being challenged, and it is in situations of sharp conflict that people are forced to act.*[3]

Many activists, including some within Weatherman, understood that Weatherman, for all its eloquent economic and political analysis, didn't have much of a strategy for moving beyond the immediate actions. Nonetheless, Weatherman did have its finger on something powerful, and it was that sense that allowed me, and many others, to overlook the dubious nature of their organizing strategy. When Weatherman portrayed defiant young men or women in graphics with guns in hand; when scowling, leather-clad Weathermen and Weatherwomen showed up at demonstrations ready to "kick ass" or strode into meetings with contempt for those preoccupied with the minutie of organizing, all this gave voice to the frustration, anger, and growing abandon that so many young activists felt. The images of guns and slogans of war were not unique to Weatherman and appeared in underground papers and leaflets of all kinds. They were ubiquitous in Panther literature. They seemed to electrify the imagination of a new constituency of young people, especially teenagers. Guns were the symbol of power. These were desperate measures for desperate times. Weatherman helped bring this voice to the white public forum.

Some of the leaders of Weatherman, however, mistook these youthful expressions of alienation for political consciousness. They confused the seduction of their own images with their ability to nurture a productive organization. So many people were desperate to provoke some human, honest response from the country's leadership that it seemed like they were also eager to undertake the hard work of sustained effort. While most wouldn't join, many cheered from the sidelines, adding more illusion into the mix. Many wanted to be convinced that if a few threw up the barricades, hundreds of thousands would follow.

Throughout its seven years of existence, Weatherman continued to be characterized by this confusion between the power of images to attract attention, and the capability to support the slow construction of the new understandings necessary for a sustainable commitment to change. The fact that this confusion was emblematic of the times contributed to Weatherman's tremendous influence and iconic status, despite its small size and enormous, even absurd, failings.

The last pretense that SDS was anything broader than the Weatherman subgroup disappeared when Mike Klonsky resigned from his work on the upcoming national action. In a letter to *New Left Notes* titled "Why I Quit," Klonsky said he too wanted to build a democratic centralist party, and believed that issues of racism should be raised to the fore at every opportunity. His strategy of reaching out through the workplace was, however, clearly at odds with Weatherman's strategy of mobilizing young people through confrontations. Furthermore, when Klonsky noted that many blue-collar workers in defense industries were in a strategic position to exert pressure on politicians, he implied that it was still worthwhile to try to bring change through the existing quasi-democratic procedures in place in the United States.

Mark Rudd and Terry Robbins responded to the letter in the same issue, challenging Mike's approach of reaching working people through their jobs and place of work. The first, and most urgent, obligation of whites, they said, was to fight in support of the peoples of the world who were "rising up against imperialism":

> The history of revolutionary struggle in this country has been a history of white people fighting their 'just struggle' at the expense of solidarity and material support to black and brown people and to the oppressed people of the world.

We needed instead, they said,

> . . . a fighting, anti-imperialist youth movement, which ... also shows people how to fight back ... and by fighting back provides material support to the vanguard struggles of Third World peoples for national liberation.[4]

We needed to be, Rudd and Robbins asserted,

> . . . a movement that fights, not just talks about fighting. The aggressiveness, seriousness, and toughness of militant struggle will attract vast numbers of working class youth, as did the Chicago demonstration last year—and it is the concrete way that white people reject white-skin privilege. By taking risks. By actually siding with the people of the world.[5]

That was the emotional heart of the Weatherman position. The only legitimate support for third world struggles was "material support," and only aggressive fighting was proof of the rejection of the privileges given us because of the color of our skin.

Mark and Terry also responded to a recent statement by the Black Panther Party, which had criticized the plans for the upcoming national action, saying it was irresponsibly confrontational and would turn people away rather than helping them understand the problems faced by poor black communities. Here was the group we said we were supporting saying that we were doing quite the opposite. This should have been more than a little disturbing, but Mark and Terry dispensed with the criticism by saying in a response:

> Because of the separate nature of the black liberation struggle, as well as the different levels of struggle, it is appropriate for the Panthers and Lords (the Latino Young Lords Party) not to engage in the National Action—but to build the struggle for liberation in the colony, while we engage in the strategy for revolution in the mother country.[6]

The Panthers not only said that they would not participate, but that the action itself shouldn't happen at all the way it was planned. Well, I thought, the leadership on the Weather Bureau must be talking with the Panthers about this, and it is just not time yet for the general membership to know about it. In the next few weeks, *New Left Notes* reported on further strained communications between the Panthers and SDS leaders, but each time concluded that the conflict had been satisfactorily resolved at high-level meetings.

In actual fact, relations with the Panthers were troubled, inconsistent, and characterized by growing distrust. In Chicago, Fred Hampton had recently been released from jail, and was busy with the many Panther programs and with figuring out how to respond to the repeated harassment and arrests of its members.[7] Conversations with Weatherman leaders about the intent of the national action had been difficult and angry. No one in the Weatherman leadership, however, publicly wrote about these mounting disagreements. I, like most regular members of Weatherman, had no idea that there were substantive conflicts between the two organizations, or that angry words had been spoken. To the Panthers, Weatherman's leaders must have seemed to be outrageously unaccountable for their words and actions.

The same issue of *NLN* that contained Klonsky's letter also sported a cover with a smiling young boy in overalls with the caption, "With a defiant smile, five-year-old Marion Delgado shows how he placed a 25-pound concrete slab on the tracks and wrecked a passenger train." I was mystified by the meaning of the cover, but since everyone around seemed to think it was so cool, I once again thought I was missing something obvious. Was it supposed to be funny? People might die in an attack like that. I was coming to accept that the slogans "Off the Pig," or "Smash the State" were meant to challenge people to think creatively, but I assumed they were not meant literally. Our goal was the public display of outrage, to interfere with the government's ability to define the terms of dissent. I certainly saw no one concretely advocating killing police or taking any steps in that direction, despite the popularity of the phrase. The immediate point was still to symbolize the depth of our opposition, even while, in the long run, we might prepare to actually fight.

I finally decided that under the guise of light-heartedness, the leadership of Weatherman was celebrating the absurdity of the war, responding to the administration's doublespeak with doublespeak of our own. President Johnson had said he was seeking peace by devastating the countryside of Vietnam, so we said "Bring the War Home," when really we sought to disrupt his war, in order to allow peace. Still, the picture and its caption remained unsettling to me.

In an environment in which honest, rigorous conversation was risky, the ambiguity of all of this language allowed and encouraged everyone's imagination to run wild. I had friends in Washington, as well as my sisters, all of whom were active in peace work or education, with whom I might have processed some of this, but I had turned away from them, sensing their reluctance to enter these uncharted territories. My outrage and fear that unbridled violence would rule the world had led me to shed cautions that they were not ready to shed. These Weathermen were the only ones who seemed to be grappling with the question of power; all other counsel would hold me back from the brink of a breakthrough.

Nonetheless, within the organization, as we were starting to refer to it, I didn't seem to be able to be part of the collective voice and still have a voice of my own, one with which I could articulate my questions coherently. So I tried to answer my own questions, and largely remained silent.

Because Terry Robbins was one of the people responsible for planning the national action, and was therefore based in Chicago, he occasionally came to our local collective meetings. In one meeting, he responded to one of the women with a tone of voice that many women, including myself, found offensive. We immediately challenged him, angrily accusing him of sexism, of disrespecting a woman's opinion. While Weatherwomen were committed to fighting for those who suffered most, we could fight sexism within our own ranks along the way. Ganging up on individual men had become the only forum in which it was acceptable for women to act together as women, and so vigilance within the collective was becoming part of the culture. On occasion, these confrontations turned physical. In this instance, when Terry at first defended himself angrily, standing up to aggressively make a point, two or three of us stood up to challenge his stance and tried to push him back into the chair. As we all wrestled, a small lamp was knocked over. The shattering glass bulb brought a quick and rather foolish end to our dramatic posturing.

Later, Terry, a few other women and I sat in the kitchen trying to resolve the conflict. The conversation evolved into an interesting discourse on what we really thought about the meaning of equality. We didn't agree, but I was conscious of the fact that this was one of the first times since joining the collective in which there had actually been a give and take of ideas, and not just people pontificating. I felt a kinship with the other woman who had stood up with me, sensing the same passion in her, and also a kinship with Terry, for holding his ground and following through, even if I thought he had been wrong. The moment, however absurd, had seemed more grounded in reality than most of our interactions.

After that day, I began to see more of the humanity of my collective mates; they were emerging as human beings with whom I could perhaps have real interactions. These tentative new friendships, however, had little opportunity to flourish over the coming months.

In the next few days after the scuffle in the collective, Terry, who had much more mobility and choice than I did since he was a leader, sought me out a few other times, after karate practice, or at other moments when I was not engaged in some daily activity prescribed by the collective. I increasingly began to look forward to our talks about music or world events, about things beyond the specific agenda of the organization and my collective. I found myself responding to Terry on every level. I knew that Terry had been in a relationship with Lisa Meisel, the Case Western Reserve student and SDS member he had met hitchhiking; I had also heard that the relationship was on the rocks.

Because Jeff had become so distant and aloof since my return to Chicago, Terry was the first person in the leadership collective that I began to be friends with. Already there was an aura of secrecy about many things. In the collective discussions, I had been introduced to the "need to know" principle used to maintain security by all kinds of organizations, including parts of the US government. This principle stated that if you didn't need to know a piece of information for your work, you didn't ask about it. I assumed, therefore, that I was not supposed to take advantage of Terry's position on the leadership collective to ask for any information or explanations that were not generally accessible to my collective. I also continued to incorrectly assume that the leadership collective functioned much like my own, and that the leadership held themselves to the same standards of discipline and austerity.

Meanwhile, *New Left Notes* reprinted James Forman's "Black Manifesto," a document that had been signed by an impressive list of black activists. Only two women were among the signers, but one was Fannie Lou Hamer, giving the document considerable legitimacy. The manifesto called for $500,000,000 in reparations to be paid to the black community by "white churches and synagogues" because they were wealthy institutions that had both benefited from and promoted racism during the slave trade and the development of this country.

The money was to be paid into a fund to support black access to and ownership of communications and technology resources, labor and welfare rights organizing, educational facilities for blacks, and support for liberations struggles in Africa. Members of the conference had been appearing in churches and synagogues around the country demanding that congregations pay up. *NLN* also ran further stories on the Panthers, reminding us that Panthers were continuing to be arrested and attacked, and fiery articles and posters promoting the upcoming national action.

In late August, the leadership announced an upcoming conference in Cleveland, which was to be the first coming together of cadre from all the cities.[8] I was curious to see who had joined, and what everyone was now like.

On August 29, after a few hours sleep, members of our collective piled into cars to drive to the three-day conference in Cleveland. In a big, empty room, the ranks of a couple of hundred people who were members of various collectives were joined by about fifty others who had recently been recruited, and a few people who were just curious.

Leadership collective member Bill Ayers gave the opening speech entitled, "Strategy to Win," a long pep talk for the national action:

> We have to deal with the fact that in a lot of ways all of us have elements of defeatism in us, and don't believe really that we can win, don't really believe that the United States can be beaten. But we have to believe it, because defeatism is based on individualism.[9]

Individualism was a high crime among young people who were striving to act in unselfish ways, to see the future as one of cooperation and shared responsibility. We were good at standing up to our personal, individual weaknesses. Were my lurking political doubts motivated by a sense of defeatism, I wondered.

Bill continued:

> We have to fight and show people through struggle our commitment, our willingness to die in the struggle to defeat US imperialism. . . . We're going to make them pay a price, and the price ultimately is going to be total defeat for them.[10]

We were not political activists just out of a sense of charity, we were fighting to determine the meaning of our own lives as human beings as well. This was *our* meaning of Greg's dictum that liberation had to begin from within oneself, I thought. Yes, I agreed, that unless we were proactive, the military-industrial complex would continue to define us, to claim our souls. Benefiting from the wealth of the United States meant that we had blood on our hands.

Speaking of those who argued against Weatherman's aggressive tactics, Bill said:

> A lot of these so-called movement groups are just going to have to get out of the way. We don't have to listen to them and get defeatist. . . . [T]hose tendencies, those notions have to be totally discredited, smashed, and destroyed. And, in the process of doing that, some of those individuals will come over. They won't understand if we sit and talk about it, they'll only understand if we smash their ideas.[11]

In other words, rather than engage in conversation with our friends who questioned aspects of Weatherman's analysis or tactics, we should shout them down or ignore them. Columbia, as always, was touted as the origin of this idea and the best example, along with Michigan and Ohio, of struggles in which these tactics brought in a massive influx of young people, tired of talk and wanting action.

I was inspired by Bill's talk, even up through his challenge to other movement activists. I could not, however, follow the next step in his reasoning:

> We're not urging anybody to bring guns to Chicago, we're not
> urging anybody to shoot from a crowd, but we're also going to
> make it clear that when a pig gets iced that's a good thing, and
> that everyone who considers himself a revolutionary should be
> armed, should own a gun, should have a gun in his home.[12]

This was totally out of my realm. It was true that *New Left Notes* had been
full of gun graphics for the past year, but I considered them as symbols of
our rage and of our solidarity with those engaged in armed struggle
around the world. If we were talking about ending imperialist power, then
ultimately, we would have to talk about war, about forming an army. But
the idea of shooting from a crowd or bringing guns to a demonstration
was absurd.

The Panthers had developed their image around the use of weapons,
but they had always used or displayed them in the interest of self-defense,
primarily against urban police forces that regularly shot young people in
suspicious circumstances. I wasn't sure how "defense" fit into the picture
of white revolutionaries.

I finally rationalized Bill's words, as I had those of others in the past,
with the thought that this talk is mainly intended to get us all thinking
about where we're all headed, to begin today to build the psychological
and organizational strength that might well be needed down the road.
Besides, I thought, if we do have to take up guns somewhere down the
road, however distant, then I, as a woman should be there; I needed to start
adapting myself to this idea. I needed to start thinking about this possibility very seriously.

I was also curious about guns, how they worked, how to use them, just
as I had been curious about the technology of how to print. As with all
technology, I was also intimidated; I had no idea how to learn about
weapons, other than to wait for someone to teach me. Nonetheless, since
the international language of politics seemed to ultimately boil down to
guns, I needed to understand how they worked.

The final part of Bill's speech reiterated Weatherman's response to the
women's movement. Weatherman was better at fighting sexism than the

women's movement, he said, because we, in our collective lifestyles, would do away with monogamy, just another form of individualism. If we were fighting for humanity, we needed to root our most personal lives in that collective sense of humanity. Monogamy would undermine collective strength and especially the ability of women to participate fully in the collectives. "... [W]e have to destroy ... the notion that people can lean on one person and not be responsible to the whole collective."

Despite the parts that seemed disconnected to me, Bill's speech appealed to and reinforced my desire to sacrifice myself wholly for the cause. The purity of total dedication scraped away many of the complexities of life and promised ultimate gratification. Besides, the competitive part of me wanted to be on the best team, the most passionate, the most sacrificing, the most uncompromising, and the most willing to follow each position to its extreme.

In order to strengthen the resolve of our collectives and root out any lingering vestiges of individualism, the remainder of the evening and most of Sunday were spent in a marathon of collective meetings, and various citywide meetings to bring in the new people who were there. Anyone who hadn't been subjected to criticism before was grilled by their group about their past opposition to racism, how much they had supported people of color and had challenged the racism of other whites. Had they confronted their parents, their teachers, their friends, their lovers? No one was without fault. I continued to speak up every now and then when I thought someone was being unfairly attacked, but I also contributed a couple of times to make sure that I myself didn't come under attack for hanging back. A few women remember being encouraged by my words of support, believing that if I could question some of the unreasonable criticisms, the organization might have more integrity than it appeared, and so they should not leave, much as Phoebe had unwittingly encouraged my participation even while she hid her distress.

The leaders of this frenzied gathering insisted that we keep going. By the middle of the night my eyes had become unfocused, and I could no longer follow the conversation. I was resentful that we were being pushed beyond the limit, yet dared not speak up. Finally we were allowed to collapse on the floor in our sleeping bags for a couple of hours. Early the next morning we were roused to participate in karate practice in the local park. Doughnuts and orange juice were passed around. Then more speeches and self-criticism sessions. Then, the women met.

In his opening speech, Bill had held up the Michigan women as the best and most exemplary. While a few of these women, Diana Oughton for one, had been activists for several years, most seemed very young to me, many recently recruited from colleges in Michigan and Ohio. All, however, seemed to have a spirit of toughness and militancy that was unmatched by any other grouping of women. I had read in *New Left Notes* that some women had charged into a community college class in order to challenge the students about their complicity with war and racism. When some of the male students in the class had objected to their takeover, the women from Weatherman pushed them back in their seats. When a couple of the men tried to leave, the women used their newly acquired karate skills to bar the door.

The Motor City 9, so named after their subsequent arrest, became the paragon of liberated women. In Cleveland, it seemed, Weatherwomen had an obligation to show women in the women's liberation movement what *real* sisterhood and solidarity with women meant, by immediately planning and carrying out a similar action. This would also allow all the women there to experience the kind of confrontation practiced by the Michigan women.

Someone proposed that all the women go to a high school in Pittsburgh, a city where black construction workers had recently been demonstrating to gain more access to construction jobs. Hundreds of people had marched to protest the fact that only 2 percent of the city's construction workers were black, while qualified black applicants were routinely turned away, especially on the entry level. One hundred and seventy five people had been arrested in support demonstrations. We would talk with high school students about rejecting their repressive schools, and challenge them to support the protesting construction workers. With little discussion of what our action would look like, but a lot of enthusiasm, the women told the men we needed all the cars. Late in the afternoon, almost all the women at the meeting set off for Pittsburgh, about an hour and a half away.

It *was* an amazing image, I thought, seventy-five fighting women. When we arrived in Pittsburgh, we descended on the offices of the American Friends Service Committee, demanding that they allow us to use their mimeograph machine for a leaflet that one carload of women had written on the way there. We also told them that we wanted to spend the night in the meetinghouse. They were not happy with this, but, under pressure, scrambled to find us another place.

That night we heard about the death of seventy-nine-year-old Ho Chi Minh, leader of the Vietnamese independence struggle for the past forty years. I felt Ho's loss personally, as did millions of other people around the world. Ho had been one of the most remarkable leaders of the twentieth century. Enduring for most of the century, the successful Vietnamese fight for independence had inspired similar struggles throughout Africa, the Americas, and all of Asia. His impact and influence were doubtless underrated by many in the West, in part perhaps because he often spoke gently and wrote poetry. Not only did he prepare the Vietnamese people to defend the country, but he also worked hard to ensure that they would resist the corrosive powers of hatred and revenge. While his fighters committed the occasional brutality, his troops never degenerated into wholesale bloodletting. Ho also fought against the cult of personality and worked closely with others in leadership in the country. His persistence, his iron determination in the face of sustained and, one might think, insurmountable odds, along with his flexibility in response to changing conditions, were breathtaking. The US government had underestimated Ho and the quality of the Vietnamese leadership for the duration of the war, at great cost to all.

Late that night, some of the group went out spray painting, and others found the parts of town where young people hung out, and marched down the block chanting "Ho Lives" and "Free Huey." On Thursday, we converged on the 3,000-student South Hills High School during their lunch break. The night before, the walls had been covered with slogans such as "Vietnamese Women Carry Guns," "Ho Lives," and "Jailbreak." We marched around the school chanting slogans and handing out leaflets about the national action. Some women ran through the school yelling "jailbreak." At that point the leadership attempted to start a rally, but several squad cars filled with police arrived. As they scrambled out of the cars, we ran in all directions with the police in hot pursuit.

I was headed toward a car about six blocks away, up one of the steep hills common in Pittsburgh. After four days with virtually no sleep, little food, and hours spent smoking Marlboros, I was only good for about three blocks. I saw no hope of blending into the neighborhood, so I turned a corner and considered ducking under the bushes in front of someone's home to wait for it all to pass. However, with all the commotion, including loudspeakers at the school beckoning the students back in the building, and the police sirens and bullhorns, I figured that any residents at home were by then looking out their windows. Someone was bound to see me, and then I might be charged with trespassing or unlawful entry as well as the inevitable disorderly conduct. So I kept trudging up the hill. Moments later a police cruiser sped up, an officer grabbed me, handcuffed me, and put me in the back of the car, where I joined two other women. Altogether, twenty-six women were arrested.

Most of us were booked and released but told to stay in the city. A long-time labor activist, a brave soul who worked in a bakery, imagining us to be traditional antiwar protesters, volunteered to let us camp out on the floors of his big old Victorian house. We tried to maintain the atmosphere of heightened struggle, with small groups going out at night to spray paint, leafleting about the upcoming demonstration in Chicago, and holding regular meetings to scrutinize our work.

The tone of our meetings, however, was less harsh than those in Chicago or Cleveland. Most importantly, we allowed each other to sleep, and to have downtime, cooking or watching TV, which I had not seen for months, and even to have some conversations of a more personal nature, not subject to collective scrutiny.

The high school action had been touted as a great success by the Weather Bureau. As the observer voice within me began to awaken again in the calmer environment, however, I didn't believe that we had convinced a single person to come to Chicago. Furthermore, I had no basis for knowing if we had made any contribution to the ongoing efforts to integrate the construction worker union. As far as I knew, no one in our group had ever spoken to anyone who was actually a member.

During this period I occasionally woke up in the morning to find out that another woman was gone, presumably, I thought, to return to important work for the leadership. Following the "need to know" principle, I didn't ask who was deciding who should leave and who should stay or why. It did feel, however, a little like middle school days, when classmates picked team members for a game. I tried to put a positive spin on the fact I was still there, by thinking that I provided a certain amount of support to the group; I was a good team player. I was not unhappy to stay.

Finally, in early October, we received word from one of the leadership people in Chicago that the half dozen of us remaining were all to return quietly to Chicago. Someone came with a car to pick us up. What about our upcoming court date? The upcoming national action was more important.

Chicago pulsed with tense preparations for the four days of demonstrations and marches. It was becoming clear that thousands of people were *not* coming, a fact that didn't surprise me in the least, and I still couldn't understand why it surprised anyone else. Moreover, having upped the ante with weeks of confrontational and violent rhetoric, everyone was increasingly fearful of the reaction of the police to our small numbers. Some were on the phones making last-minute, and not very successful, pleas for bail money in advance. Others were trying to secure protective gear for the demonstrations.

I tried to take all this in. The collective that had existed before I left for Pittsburgh seemed to have been reconstructed into different formations. No one was paying attention to the internal dynamics anymore, only to the upcoming demonstrations. The day after I returned, Terry came by where I was staying and asked me if I wanted to go out with him that evening to a predemonstration gathering with some of the leadership folks. I figured that the meeting was less about work and more recreational. I had seen Terry only once since leaving Chicago for Cleveland almost a month before. He had come through Pittsburgh once to pass on the latest upbeat reports on the national action, but he had only been there a few hours, and we had barely said hello. I did know, however, that his relationship with Lisa was over, and that she was possibly at the beginning of a relationship with someone else. I knew little of why or of what had passed between them. I hadn't dared to ask Lisa, still wary of her as potential competition for Terry.

As always, when Terry and I spoke personally, we had a deep connection, with the kind of chemistry I had felt only once before, with Mark. I quickly agreed to go, although I was somewhat puzzled by the nature of the outing. Later in the evening Terry picked me up. We drove out to the suburbs, where we entered a luxurious home. The owners, however, were not there. Instead, in the living room of pristine printed sofas, plush, light carpets, and huge picture windows were seven or eight others, all from one of the national leadership groupings, lounging on the furniture and on the rugs. Levity filled the air, as plates of food, including delicacies like caviar, obviously gleaned from the house pantry, constituted an evening meal.

Coming from two months of austerity in the collectives I was stunned. I had seen some of these same people earlier in the day when they seemed to be very tense about the demonstration. What was going on? Did they live like this regularly, or was this a special occasion? I was an outsider, there only because of Terry, and I hung back, unsure how to engage.

Things only got more confusing when the topic of a bombing the night before came up and several people joined in cheering. A full-sized bronze statue of a policeman had long sat in Haymarket Square in Chicago to memorialize the day in May 1, 1886, when someone, very possibly a company-paid provocateur, had thrown a bomb at police advancing on a peaceful demonstration of workers campaigning for the eight-hour day. Eight policemen had died and many demonstrators were hurt. While no definitive explanation or proof of guilt was ever established, four anarchist labor organizers had been hung for the bombing, despite proclaiming their innocence. The previous night, the statue had been blown off its high perch and damaged. I had heard the tail end of a story about it on the radio that afternoon, but a lot was going on, and I hadn't really paid attention. By then, I had heard of a few fire bombings of recruitment offices, campus war research centers, and Bank of Americas (a target because of their support of the apartheid government in South Africa). For his book *SDS*, Kirkpatrick Sale actually found reports of eighty-four bombings and attempts just on college campuses in the first half of 1969, although most were reported only locally, if at all.[13]

I listened carefully to the conversation that night to see if someone actually claimed responsibility for the bombing or acknowledged some direct personal involvement. Could it be possible that someone in Weatherman had done it? Responsibility for it seemed to be implicit in the conversation, although I didn't hear any specific reference. Once again, I felt like I had been blindsided. We were organizing for the national action. How could this bombing be anything other than provocative to the Chicago police department? Wouldn't it ensure their most brutal response to the demonstrators? I knew that all the rhetoric about revolution would be meaningless unless we addressed the question of how, in the end, we would be able to overthrow the government. Still, I had seen no indication that we were anywhere near that point yet, rhetoric notwithstanding. Since I couldn't imagine what it might look like, it was hard to connect it to the present. The trashing and firebombings of campus buildings had seemed exhilarating, but fairly harmless in the context of mass protests. In combination with the intense cadre formation of Weatherman, this bombing seemed to be sending an additional message. Or was it? The eve of a public demonstration seemed an odd time to introduce a campaign for armed attacks.

I spent the evening swimming around in the innuendos that could be interpreted in many ways, smiling at the inside jokes I did not understand, with marijuana and alcohol soothing the way. I wanted to be alone with Terry, but knew that our new relationship could not compete with what he had with his friends. I sensed that he needed and trusted them far more than he trusted me. The evening seemed to be an almost ritualistic bonding among this band of friends whose loyalty to each other, as well as to the cause, was affirmed by their willingness to break their own rules together, to set themselves slightly apart. I wanted too badly to pursue this relationship to do more than note the goings-on and my own status as an outsider, not even sure if I wanted to gain entry here. We spent the night sprawled out on sofas and thick carpets, with no opportunities for private moments.

The next day I returned to final preparations for the national action, which was to start that evening with a rush-hour demonstration in the Loop, the business district of Chicago. As twilight fell, I congregated in the park with a hodgepodge of others, and it became unavoidably clear that the only people coming were those who had been at the Cleveland conference, and maybe a few dozen others who had been brought in by the collectives. No one had been brought by the Chicago collective, as far as I knew. At first we stood around silent and wary, until, after dark had fallen, the Weather Bureau arrived. These few helmeted, leather-jacketed spirit-raisers stood shouting words of encouragement, while the rather forlorn crowd of a few hundred encircled them.

As soon as someone started talking about the Vietnamese, however, everyone focused in. Just that day the United States had dropped tons of bombs even as it stalled and obstructed the peace talks then going on in Paris. Clearly, there was no good-faith effort on the part of the US government to end the war. They were toying with the Vietnamese, who were negotiating for their very survival. So, of course, we must up the ante, and make the cost of this war at home unacceptably high. We had to not only protest, but also disrupt.

I had been told to bring a stick. I picked up one from the gutter. It was about an inch thick and had maybe once been part of a piece of furniture. Unlike the hot days of August, when every gesture had been analyzed for meaning, no one now was really paying any attention to me or, thankfully, to the seriousness of my stick.

Finally, the speakers announced the heretofore-secret destination of the march: the hotel where Judge Hoffman was staying. For weeks, Judge Hoffman had been presiding over the tumultuous trial of the Chicago 8, seven Mobilization leaders and one Black Panther, who had been charged with conspiracy to riot for their role in helping to organize the Democratic convention demonstrations a year earlier. Hoffman's freehanded approach to the law in silencing the defendants had angered many, and would later be overruled by a higher court.

We left the park immediately and hit the streets, marching down the sidewalk through the well-heeled downtown residential area called the Gold Coast, with large, elegant apartment buildings that edged the northern rim of the Loop. "Ho! Ho! Ho Chi Minh! NLF is going to win!" we chanted. Immediately, the edgy contest between demonstrators and police began, as had happened so often in the past year, as we overflowed sidewalks and spilled into the streets, obstructing traffic. All of a sudden, several dozen marchers in the front broke ranks, startling the dozens of police flanking our sides. Within seconds I heard the unmistakable sound of breaking glass. Before I could get oriented as to where the sound came from, everyone started running, myself included, and I heard shouting and more broken glass. To my astonishment, the march leaders and many others were smashing windows of stores and cars as they ran full speed down the street.

Immediately the police took off after the ones they had seen breaking the windows. I turned the corner at the first intersection, along with many other running demonstrators, none of us sure where the front lines had headed. Clearly we were not going to try to make it all the way to the hotel, because with the police angry now, we would all be arrested if we tried. Within half a block, our ranks broke up into small groups running in every direction. Without time to process these events, I relied on my anger to guide me. I tried whacking a window as I ran down the second half of the block, but my thin little stick bounced off. Realizing it was useless, I dropped it.

I had no further impulse to break windows and wasn't quite sure what else to do. The sound of breaking glass continued, although I couldn't tell what direction it was coming from. As I turned another corner with two or three others, I heard police shouting as they took up the pursuit of our little band. My recent experience in Pittsburgh was on my mind, and this time I chose to make myself scarce to avoid arrest, managing to squeeze under a van from the sidewalk side when a pursuing cop made it across the street just two cars down.

I held my breath as he paused and took off down the street. I had been saved by the dark. In five more minutes I heard the commotion fade and saw the night's stunned passersby begin to emerge from doorways. I crawled out from under the van, ignoring a few stares. Seeing no one else from the demonstration around, I headed quickly out of the neighborhood back to the movement center where I was staying.

The center was in the basement of a Methodist church that had routinely allowed its space to be used for community activities. I wondered if they had any idea what kind of demonstration this was intended to be and worried briefly that they might have been deceived. My moral code on even this point, however, felt less absolute than before, so I didn't question for long.[14]

When I arrived at the center, many small clusters of people were exchanging news, trying to find out who had been arrested. We checked and double-checked stories about unaccounted-for people. In the end, sixty-eight people were arrested. We also heard that someone had been shot by the police. The wounded person was apparently in the hospital, and no one knew how serious it was. I was stunned. Had this been part of the plan? Were we going to continue if in fact the police were now starting to shoot demonstrators? Under what circumstances had the shooting happened? Why was no one making a big deal about it, and, instead, it was being treated in a hush-hush kind of way? Even if our goal was to draw police attention away from the black community, that still didn't negate the outrage of police shooting at demonstrators, even if they were breaking windows. Had anyone thought ahead of time about the wisdom of planning a demonstration in which the tension was so high, but the power so unequally distributed?

I was not the only one who didn't quite understand how events had shaped up this way. Someone from leadership arrived and attempted to set a congratulatory tone, saying that we had in fact presented the city of Chicago with its first militant, street-fighting white demonstration. Many of the demonstrators, however, were, like me, huddled in silence, too much in shock to react. Still, there was a sense that we couldn't turn back now, not without looking like fools. Someone organized a few martial arts stretching exercises; first-aid instruction was given yet again on how to handle various kinds of wounds, and then we spread out our sleeping bags to sleep, too exhausted to try to sort through the incoherence of it all. It was long past midnight.

The next day was the women's march to the draft board in downtown Chicago. This time, expecting the police to be more prepared and hostile, we were given helmets to wear. Once again I was about to walk into a situation for which I had no sense of how it could possibly turn out. I assumed we would try to last long enough to demonstrate our rage and willingness to do anything to make the government rethink its policies. That seemed like a reasonable objective, and a brave one. I was glad there was no talk of breaking windows. The random vandalism still seemed like a tactic without the dignity to match the justice of our objective. The action had certainly disrupted the Loop for one evening. We were depriving certain wealthy Chicagoans of the ability to completely ignore the consequences of the US war, but would that momentary interruption make any difference in the outcome of the war or anything else? Would our actions organize others to oppose the war and racism? Did it really hurt the government or any of the others who profited from the war or from racism?

Had we looked at recent history, we might have realized that the idea of "exacting consequences" was yet another one of those slippery slopes. While deterrence can and has prevented aggression on occasion, it more often mixes with the desire for revenge, and has fueled ethnic and religious warfare for centuries at terrible cost. It was also not a strategy for change, and that was what we needed. Certainly civil-rights activists had every reason to want revenge for past and current transgressions. They also could easily have made an argument for self-defense. Instead, civil-rights leaders focused on the goal of changing society to make equal opportunity a reality, albeit at the cost of unfathomable sacrifice by many, mostly poor people. Self-preservation was definitely one aspect of planning, but always discreet. The strategies of legal action and massive, persistent civil disobedience in the face of racist laws and practices accomplished more than anyone had dreamed. Not complete success, but significant progress. At the time, however, it looked like the backlash would prevent further progress, or reverse what had been won.

One thing I was sure of: If anyone were going to fight, women had to join in. My childhood daydreams about the soldiers in World War II merged with newer images of selfless Vietnamese women fighters. Together these images reinforced my sense that the highest form of service was being at the forefront of the physical struggle, where one took the greatest risks. While I didn't think that fighting was necessary for all women anymore than for all men, like many young soldiers, I wanted to understand what it was like. I did not want to be a woman at home, waiting for her man. How could I ask someone else to make a sacrifice greater than that which I made myself?

As I took the El down to Grant Park for the start of the women's demonstration, I wasn't really afraid. I was in a daze. I was willing to die or be hurt, but I wished it all made more sense. Only about fifty women collected. Others had been arrested the previous night. Hundreds of police were waiting. Bernardine spoke briefly about the strength and courage of women and we marched off. Before we had gone thirty feet the wall of police stepped forward to grab us. They pulled up a paddy wagon and, announcing we were under arrest, herded us on. There was some attempt to keep everyone's spirits up by yelling obscenities and chants, but mostly I felt incredibly silly and embarrassed by the discrepancy between our tough talk and our lack of a realistic strategy to bring our anger to effective fruition.

Only four days after I had returned from exile in Pittsburgh, I was in jail again. After we were booked and signed into the women's cell block in Cook County Jail, we were released into the general population. The locked entrance to the cell block led past a unit guard station and into the day room with long tables and benches like picnic tables. Beyond that, a corridor continued through another gate into a cell block with individual cells with barred doors on both sides. A few leadership women were bailed out immediately, but most of us were processed and assigned cells. As we entered the day room, we were greeted by women still there from the night before, and we gathered around one of the long institutional tables that ran along the side of the common room. We filled them in, and traded stories about what we knew.

Back at the demonstration centers, the Friday actions at area high schools, modeled on the Pittsburgh action, were canceled while the leadership regrouped. Those who were left were sent instead to participate in an unrelated demonstration to support the Chicago 8, planned by a coalition of antiwar forces and the Black Panther Party. At that rally, Illinois Black Panther chairman Fred Hampton denounced the Weatherman actions of the previous days as being "anarchistic" and "Custeristic," and went on to argue that the "primary task for radicals was education." [15] In jail, however, we heard nothing of this.

On Saturday, police moved in on the Weatherman demonstration as people were gathering for the final march at Haymarket Square. The ensuing fighting continued off and on into the Loop, where a hundred were arrested. During the melee, the city's assistant corporation counsel Richard Elrod broke his neck as he tried to tackle one of the demonstrators, missed, and hit a concrete wall. Several demonstrators received less severe injuries.

Late Saturday night, yet more women were brought up to the cell block. The next day, we eagerly pumped them for stories of the past two days, how the leadership was thinking about it, how long they expected us to be in jail, what was next. Once again, a few women were bailed out almost immediately. After that, one or two women were bailed out each day. I realized that once again, I would be left in. We heard that on the outside they were having trouble raising bail money. I was perfectly comfortable with that for the first ten days.

The days took on a routine that, compared with my life during the previous two and a half months, seemed normal. I spent time hanging out with some of the regular inmates, many jailed there for longer periods. Some were curious about who we were and why we were so crazy. Some kept their distance. Generally speaking the women were respectful. I enjoyed having conversations again with people who were not in Weatherman. They showed us how to talk with the men by shouting through the hot-air vents to floors below. During the times we were locked down, there were often many such conversations. A number of the nonpolitical women carried on dramatic sexual conversations on a regular basis, sometimes with men they knew from the street and sometimes with men they had never met, who were therefore excellent objects of fantasy. The attempt to build intimacy in a situation with no privacy seemed strange to me. I tried to imagine what it would be like to be driven to that space. Was it need, theater, just fun, or self-abuse? When a man called up to my cell to see what the possibilities were, I commenced a conversation, although by telling him that I'd been arrested in the recent demonstrations, I forestalled any sexual overtures. Our conversations remained casual until he was moved to another floor.

As the size of our group shrank from several dozen to less than a dozen over the next couple of weeks, our conversations grew more informal, a respite from the intensity and confusion of the world of a Weatherwoman. There were three meals a day, conversation with a range of different kinds of people, and a bed of my own. After sharing floors on the outside, this seemed like a luxury.

Then, however, I began to get restless and wondered exactly how long they were going to leave me inside. Somehow, I had assumed that the people who had conceived of the national action had factored bail money into the plan. Certainly the leadership was quick to set up situations where we would get arrested. In the early summer, these arrests had not involved a lot of bail, but inevitably, once people started fighting with police and breaking windows, the bail shot up.

A few days later, one of the leadership collective came to visit, to fill us in on what we were supposed to do for upcoming court dates, and to see if everyone was okay. She asked me if I wanted to get out, and I was somewhat confused by the question. Of course, I said. I hadn't been back with my collective for over a month. Besides, I said silently to myself, I wanted to see Terry.

It turned out that my bail of $500 had been contributed several times over by friends and family, who had called in to inquire about me when they read about the demonstrations and hadn't been able to find me. The money had been put in one pot, which they used to get people out according to their own criteria. No one kept records of who donated, or thought to tell those of us who had been the designees.

I was finally bailed out after two and a half weeks. When I returned to the national office, I was told that new collectives were being organized; it was suggested that I work on the legal team. The decision had been made that those arrested during demonstrations would represent themselves. This would save us legal expenses and would also clog up the courts, as each person, no matter how minor the charge, demanded a trial by jury. Now in another way, we would make the government deflect some of their repressive resources from communities of color. I knew nothing about the way the courts worked, but agreed to do whatever was needed.

Once out of jail, I had expected to find a conversation about the effectiveness of the national action, now known as the Days of Rage, and discussions about why the estimates of attendance had been so overinflated. What strategy for change was embedded in this rage? Instead of a discussion of goals and strategy, however, I was presented with a new interpretation of recent events, a new line. We had been on a "death-trip," the reasoning went, and now we needed to reject that and affirm life, to celebrate our culture and each other, to lighten up and enjoy life. This was an abrupt turnaround—to now embrace a "life trip"—of the kind that came to characterize life within Weatherman. I had no sense of the process or of any individual's role within it that had brought about this turnaround.

I was more than willing to let go of my questions about the bombing of the statue, about the insinuations that we should arm ourselves, about the vandalism at the demonstration. Clearly, I assumed, all that had been part of the excesses. I was not alone in feeling somewhat dizzied by the abrupt change, but people around me seemed to breathe a sigh of relief. No more self-defense sessions or even criticisms. In fact, the legal team worked much as any work team would, each of us taking on one part of the job and collaborating when needed.

Soon after I emerged from jail, Terry and I started spending more and more time together. Mostly we took time out from work at the national office to go out for coffee, which seemed like a wonderful luxury at that point. We took long walks through the cold, desolate streets of the west side, talking about our feelings about the state of the world, about how we saw our obligations as young people during this time. We wondered what we would have done had we lived in Germany during the 1930s.

Terry was traveling in Ohio again, but when he was in town he started staying with me in the living room at the apartment of Don and Laura Stang. Don was a lawyer with the People's Law office and worked in the legal collective with me. He and Laura had recently moved to Chicago after Don finished law school at Harvard. Laura had been a graduate student there in English literature when they married. That summer she had been a member of the Chicago collective with me.

By now, for the second time in my life, I was head over heels for a guy. Around that time, someone told me that when Terry and Lisa had been together, Terry had hit or shoved Lisa a couple of times during arguments. I never dared ask him for details. I could not imagine this sweet, deeply moral person, with such a great sense of humor, being abusive. I knew Terry could *sound* abusive because I remembered our first meeting, when he had yelled at one of the women in our collective, and we had gone after him. I knew that he, like many Weathermen, had been quick to engage in a kind of theatrical fighting. I was sure, however, that underneath his tough exterior, he was trying to figure stuff out and be a moral person, the same as all of us. I imagined I would find out what had happened at some point. Because we rarely talked about our own personal histories, only about the future, the only thing I knew for sure about him was that his mother had died when he was young. In fact, I learned much later that Terry *had* hit Lisa on two occasions, and in one instance he had to be pulled away by another Weatherman who was there.

By the fall of 1969, Nixon's approach to Vietnam had become distressingly clear. The political flash point had become the death of US soldiers, not to speak of the enormous cost of maintaining a force of over 300,000 troops halfway around the world. Nixon would continue the war with renewed passion, but he would do so by withdrawing troops even while pouring money and weapons into the South Vietnamese army. Secretary of Defense Melvin Laird, a major architect of this policy, coined the phrase "Vietnamization." Over the summer we had heard shocking stories about the Phoenix Program, in which thousands of Vietnamese were rounded up, tortured for information by US-trained Vietnamese soldiers, and then killed or imprisoned. Thousands died immediately or rotted in three-foot-high belowground cages with grating only at the top, known as tiger cages. The tonnage of bombs and heavy artillery almost doubled that year.

What was the advantage of this policy for Nixon, I wondered? The Vietnamese were in danger of having their entire country, including their rich farmland, destroyed for generations, ensuring complete dependence on other countries for survival. Was Nixon going to force them to submit by beating the people and their economy into submission? From this perspective, it appeared that the greatest accomplishment of the antiwar movement had been to substitute US financed and trained Vietnamese soldiers for GIs. That was truly depressing. Once US soldiers were no longer dying on a large scale, it would be far easier to take the war off the evening news and out of that urgent space in people's minds.

In response to Nixon's renewed energy for the war, albeit a Vietnamized war, a number of antiwar activists organized a broad coalition of groups called the Moratorium Against the War to hold regular demonstrations, not only in Washington but in other cities around the country. The first series of demonstrations in October garnered two hundred and fifty thousand in Washington and tens of thousands in other cities. These marches and rallies, endorsed by a few members of congress and many celebrities, had been peaceful, mainstream, and well covered by the press. On November 3, President Nixon gave a speech in which he talked for the first time of a "silent majority." No matter how large the antiwar movement grew, Nixon was determined to marginalize us, to represent us as a small, crazed minority. I felt like a player in the theater of the absurd. If a march was big and broad he dismissed it; if it was big and militant he tried to criminalize it.

The second demonstration, to be held in Washington, was organized by a different coalition, the New Mobilization, which included the Moratorium. Various events were scheduled from November 13–15. The new Mobe, as it came to be called, made it clear they also wanted a "peaceful and solemn protest," [16] and did not want street fighting to be part of the activities.

Shortly before the November demonstration, however, the Weather Bureau assigned some people to go to Washington, seeing yet another opportunity to display Weatherman's readiness to fight and still believing that this would recruit large numbers of people to join us. I was assigned to remain in the national office to answer the phones and continue to work on legal business.

The Weatherman crew in Washington did their best to organize participants to take to the streets, to have hit-and-run confrontations with the police. Furthermore, when they failed to convince the Moratorium staff to front them bail money, the small group of Weatherman threatened to turn the place upside-down. Despite the Moratorium staff's refusal to respond, the Weather forces left without following through on the threat. That night, Weathermen did run in the streets and were joined by a few thousand others who were angry and discouraged at the seeming impotence of the antiwar movement. Nonetheless, they were just a brief eddy that spun amidst the half-million people who marched and chanted all through the course of the day.

That weekend, Seymour Hersch wrote an article picked up by the *New York Times* that revealed the details of the My Lai massacre, during which women, children and babies were executed by US troops. Instead of being pleased that some of the truth was beginning to emerge, I despaired. It was so little, so late, and presented as an outrage and an exception. It seemed hypocritical to get excited about this one little revelation. We had known about the systematic torture and killing for years. We had talked with vets who had told us about their training and experiences on "search and destroy" missions, and we knew that inflicting terror—random and overwhelming—was part of the strategy. Many GIs, themselves terrorized by a strategy that pitted them against an "enemy" who was everywhere, felt they had to participate to survive. What restraints could there be on the occasional sadist in these conditions?

By this time, relations between the Chicago Panthers and Weatherman leadership were very strained. While no one in Weatherman publicly criticized the Panthers, some of the leadership had begun to believe that the Panthers were devoting too much energy to their "Serve the People" programs like the free breakfasts for children.[17] Chicago BPP chairman Fred Hampton, on the other hand, thought that Weatherman was provoking confrontations with law enforcement in a way that was dangerous both to themselves and to the whole community around them.

The two organizations had a long way to go to figure out how to engage in any kind of sustained discussion. The FBI was well aware of these tensions and kept busy doing what they could to exacerbate them, much as they had encouraged tensions between the Panthers in LA and the group United Slaves (US). As early as May 1969, an FBI memo stated:

> Authority is granted to instruct selected BPP informants for use in creating a rift between the BPP and the Students for a Democratic Society. . . . [SDS] and the BPP are cooperating in several ways to exploit their common revolutionary aims. Together these organizations pose a formidable threat. Chicago has proposed that BPP informants be instructed to plant the idea that the SDS is exploiting the BPP.[18]

Six months later, the FBI was even harder at work trying to drive this wedge, busy sending notes and making phony phone calls between the two groups. One result of these activities came in late November, when Panther activist Jake Winters was shot and killed by Chicago police in a warehouse. Panther leaders wanted SDS to print the memorial poster, but SDS, being broke and out of paper said they couldn't. Possibly, some Weather leaders *were* slow in providing support because of their disagreements with Panther strategy. In any event, in the existing atmosphere of tension and political disagreement, no one had successfully tried to figure out an equitable distribution of resources. Hours later Panthers came storming into the SDS national office. In the ensuing conflict, several of the Weathermen were assaulted with fists and two-by-fours.[19] The membership of the organization, however, heard nothing of these encounters, or of the tensions between the two groups. Even I, who was occasionally working out of the national office during this period, heard only vague rumors. Weatherman's leaders kept the conflict quiet.

As November progressed, so did the Chicago court appearances. My legal support work had introduced me to the lawyers at the People's Law Office, including Dennis Cunningham and his wife Mona. Dennis and Mona had both been active in the Second City Theater Project in Chicago before Dennis went to law school. They had three small children. Their house was completely child-centered, providing an intense injection of sanity whenever I had the opportunity to go there. Mona later talked about how hard she had tried to be part of the rapidly developing politics within Weatherman, while providing physically and emotionally for her children. She was glad to be able to listen in on the many meetings that took place in her living room, but would later be faced with an empty refrigerator. The milk, dinner, and cereal for the next forty-eight hours had disappeared, gobbled down by hungry activists oblivious to any one else's reality. At bedtime, she sometimes found exhausted Weathermen asleep in one of the children's beds. She always found a way to make do.

By the end of November, Terry and I were on our way to a deeper intimacy, the antimonogamy policy notwithstanding. It was then that he told me that he would soon have to return to Cleveland to serve six weeks of a three-month sentence he had received for one of the Kent State demonstrations. He was extremely anxious because events were moving very fast, and he didn't want to be out of commission for so long. I had a sense that he was also worried about his status on the leadership collective, which seemed now to be in constant flux.

On December 4, I returned to Don and Laura's apartment after a day of work at the national office. Terry had been elsewhere for the day but returned that evening to stay with me on the pullout couch in the living room. We stayed up late, listening to music and talking with a small group of people, until everyone else drifted off to bed. Only a few hours later, around 5:00 AM, the phone rang. Terry, still half-asleep, reached over to answer it. The Chicago police, he heard, had run up the stairs to Panther leader Fred Hampton's apartment, sent a barrage of unanswered shots through the door, and then barged in. They stormed into Fred's bedroom where they shot him several times while he was lying in the bed, killing him instantly, just after his girlfriend, six months pregnant, scrambled out of bed. They also shot and killed Mark Clark, another Panther leader asleep in the apartment. It was unclear whether two or three others were wounded. Everyone left alive had then been arrested.

Still groggy, I wondered if the cops were about to come in our door too. Was this our Kristallnacht? The murders represented a level of brutality that was new and terrifying. Black activists had long faced lynchings, police brutality, and harassment, but a brazen, unprovoked attack on a well-known and loved community leader in his bed was certainly an escalation. It was the first time this had happened so close by to me. I hadn't known Hampton personally, but he was often in the national office, and I heard many times what a charismatic and passionate leader he was.

Everyone in the apartment was up immediately and we gathered in the living room. I tried to process this new reality. This is it, I felt, more than thought, to myself. This really is war. I would do anything, I vowed, anything to not let his murder be in vain.

Thousands attended Hampton's funeral. Terry, who knew Hampton personally, was devastated as well. The murder also increased his fears about jail. Was it going to be open season, now, on radicals? What would happen to those in prison? Once inside, would the authorities find a pretense to keep him there forever? Who would be killed next?

Over the next forty-eight hours, while the newspapers ran screaming headlines saying that the police had been shot at and attacked by the Panthers, more details filtered in. It appeared that someone had drugged Fred ahead of time by dropping something in his food or drink. While everyone else was running for cover when the police barged in, Fred never stirred. Contrary to the police story, no bullets had gone *out* through the front door, only in.

The Panthers opened up the apartment for the whole neighborhood to see. Thousands of people filed up the steps, past the bullet-ridden door and through the blood-soaked rooms. The community demanded an investigation. The police said there was no need. After a day of community viewing, however, the police realized they had a problem, especially after some of the press started to arrive. Police then came to take some of the physical evidence away. The most critical piece of evidence was the front door, which police said would show that they had been shot at. Lawyers for the Panthers, however, anticipating police tampering with the evidence, had already removed and hidden the door, already witnessed by hundreds of people. When the police demanded the door, lawyers went to court to protect it until there could be a public investigation. Eventually the door appeared in court. While the police were not able to show that a single shot had been fired at them, in a trial before a judge, all police were exonerated. No one was ever convicted of the murders. In a civil court more than ten years later, however, a jury found the police guilty of violating all department procedures, including the practice of shooting except in self-defense, and awarded sizable damages to the families of Fred Hampton and Mark Clark.

In the days after Hampton's death, we joined in the public mourning and demonstrations, at a loss for what more to do. The murders seemed to call for yet a greater escalation, so that at least this kind of police behavior would not silently become the accepted norm. I would do anything now. The rules had changed, and whatever Weatherman was planning, I wanted to be part of it.

Suddenly, it was time for Terry to go to jail. He was flying to a meeting in Washington first, and then he would go on to Cleveland. He asked me if I wanted to go on the first leg of the trip, and I agreed immediately. We flew to Washington the next day to stay with Andy Kopkind, a writer for several progressive periodicals. Andy and Terry had become friends when Terry worked at the Cleveland ERAP project. Andy later noted that the Terry he had gotten to know in Cleveland was "sweet and earnest. He was a little full of himself, but he was very sweet."[20] In Washington, we spent a last day together, and then Terry walked out the door of Andy's apartment, stepped into a cab, and drove off to Washington's National Airport. After he left, I stood at the window in Andy's living room, playing the Beatles *Abbey Road* album, so frequently in the background during our time together, trying to fix his presence deep in my soul. I then returned to Chicago.

Soon after, I met with two people on the leadership collective, who told me they had decided to revive the mass work of SDS. Teddy Gold and I had been assigned to take on the task. We were to go through incoming mail and visit some of the chapters that still wrote in with requests for a speaker from the national office of SDS.

This was an unnerving assignment. First, all indications were that Weatherman was moving in quite another direction, turning itself into a cadre organization in which membership was by approval only. Fred Hampton had been killed, and I had just said good-bye to Terry, who was afraid that, in six weeks, we could be under a state of siege.

Besides, there was no more *New Left Notes*. The police had raided the office a short time after the national action and taken all the addressograph files. The national office staff instead put out a few issues of a new publication called the *Fire Next Time*, named after the James Baldwin novel. This paper, distributed only by the Weather collectives, was filled with the provocative, militant language favored by Weatherman's most outspoken leaders. It would be difficult to use it to draw naive young students into conversation, I thought. It provided little information about the world or about the internal life of the organization. In today's parlance we would say it was mostly full of attitude, with headlines like "Kick the Ass" (from the popular slogan "Kick the Ass of the Ruling Class") and "Violent Revolution—Vietnam Did It," or "I Hear the Sound of Wargasm."

As an organizer in Washington, I had had a sense of regional strategy, of educational conferences, programs for high school students, for college students, for suburban activism, power structure research, and so on. After Fred Hampton's murder, however, I had finally made a commitment to abandon this kind of slow, transformative educational work, committed instead to being part of a group of young people willing to learn how to fight against the tide of death. I had made peace, of sorts, with what I perceived to be Weatherman's trajectory. In that context, I had no idea how to develop a strategy for campus SDS chapters on a national level.

Yet again, I could only think that there must be a hidden agenda in this plan because I couldn't make sense of the explicit one. I wondered if this was an attempt to distract the FBI and police. Or, did the leadership think that Teddy and I somehow didn't make the grade as fighters, and so we were being shunted off to do trivial work, while those with the more advanced politics were setting up something complex and important? I knew I was not alone in believing that some momentous change was in the air. If Terry had been there I could have talked to him, but he wasn't. I was still too insecure about my standing with anyone else in leadership to reveal my bewilderment or to explicitly ask my questions, especially having received earlier reprimands about not observing the need-to-know principle. The leaders that had spoken to me led me to believe that the Weather Bureau must have a whole strategy mapped out. In actuality, the leadership collective had further disintegrated by then, I had made a leap in surmising that these two or three of the leaders represented the whole. In fact, the disagreements had led several members to leave. Despite appearances, no one was really thinking clearly about the time and money consumed by the mounting arrests. There was no consensus on any strategy except upping the ante, and by late 1969, divisions began to open up about how much to escalate the militant tactics. Instead, smaller leadership groups within cities, composed of local members of the Weather Bureau and their confidants, argued for their own interpretation of policy within their own "fiefdoms."

Teddy Gold had been summoned to Chicago from New York and seemed equally nonplused by the assignment. He had been active in SDS for years, as vice-chairman of the Columbia chapter, where he had been criticized as being part of the "go slow" faction at Columbia, along with chapter chairman Ted Kaptchuk. During the strike, however, he had been won over to the "action faction." He had then played a leading role as negotiator during the strike. Later, he had worked with teachers to support black and Latino parents during the New York City school strike. I knew him from earlier national meetings, demonstrations and social gatherings. Like most people, I was drawn to his irrepressible energy and sense of fun. His passion for ending the war and for fairness and equality at home was so strong, it seemed to precede him into a room, affecting everyone. His dedication to the Vietnamese garnered my deepest trust. Of all the Columbia people I had seen in action, he had seemed one of the most approachable.

Teddy also stood out as the author of several songs, clever, exaggerated caricatures of Weatherman's most outrageous and violent pronouncements. Each time I heard or sang the songs, all to the tunes of current popular hits, I had wondered whether they were parodies of our excesses, meant to spur us on in this direction. I enjoyed the bravado.

Like me, Teddy seemed somewhat anxious about the possible implications of being cut out of the more prestigious work of the organization. Our mutual sense of duty, however, precluded any discussion of this. Instead, we took a stack of letters and phone messages from the national office and began to call chapter contacts, setting up a series of visits for the next couple of weeks in nearby Midwestern states. Sometimes together and sometimes separately we visited various campus chapters, mostly listening and encouraging chapter members in their work. A couple of times I spoke to larger groupings about the war and about Fred Hampton's murder.

In those few weeks in December, Teddy and I became friends. When we were in Chicago, we often stayed up in the attic at Mona and Dennis's house, sleeping in sleeping bags on the bare floor. We talked about the small band of propaganda workers that had worked with Ho to start the organization that later became the Vietnamese Communist Party, and the small band of fighters that had crossed the mountains with Fidel to triumphantly enter Havana. Weatherman, we imagined, might also be an early formation like that, with the potential to grow and someday take power. We were the most important organization for white people, I thought, with the most thoughtful analysis of the world. We didn't hide behind liberal niceties, where people could be revolutionary in some ways, but continue to benefit from imperialism in others. We were committed to giving up all of our privileges, to learning from the revolutionary leadership of the people of the world.

The insistence on vulnerability was what set Weatherman apart. We were determined to burn our bridges so we couldn't go back. Or at least that was the only way I was coming to understand the strategy of street fighting, with its many serious arrests and injuries. We had found a place of moral purity that was not dependent on pacifism. If the people of the world, in Algeria, Vietnam, and Cuba had to fight to win freedom, why should we white people be exempt? How could we alone have the privilege of winning freedom, an end to our complicity with US war crimes for instance, without fighting?

During this period, the leadership in Chicago continued to put a lot of emphasis on turning ourselves into new men and new women. In addition to our revolutionary goals we should celebrate our music, drugs, and each other. In mid-December, there was a revival of the campaign to end monogamous relationships and to establish a completely open social and sexual playing field. The leadership collective and many others seemed to think that this was terrific, and that one's enthusiasm for these changes became a measure by which one's commitment was judged. Since Terry was gone for the time being, I was curious about how this would work and what it was like. After I attended one party with everyone in town, however, which included public sexual encounters with virtual strangers, I was quickly convinced that this was no fun at all. For me, the pleasure of sex required intimacy, honesty, and vulnerability. I also knew that at least one of my sexual encounters that night violated the distance and respect of a friendship I had valued. I found the encounters uninteresting, and in the end felt I had been used and had used others. It left me waiting more urgently for Terry to get out of jail, knowing for certain that I was not interested in being intimate with anyone else. I didn't care then about the antimonogamy policy, and thought that he wouldn't either.

I knew that Teddy was not comfortable with all of the sexual experimentation either. He was looking for something more with someone, but the chaotic environment did not yield anyone. Our friendship served as a safe, albeit constricted, haven for both of us.

.

I had already told my mother that I would be unable to come home for Christmas. It would be the first time that I missed Christmas, but my absence was made easier by the fact that my sister Ann and her husband were in Alaska, and couldn't come either. I promised to visit in January after the national council meeting. Since I had attended these end-of-the-year national council meetings since 1966, they had a ring of familiarity to her.

Going home for special occasions was getting harder. Having been without a regular home for months, I no longer had the right clothes, and if I appeared only in jeans my mother assumed I did so just to annoy her. Besides, buying small gifts for my family seemed obscene in the face of the poverty and warfare that saturated my reality. I certainly could no longer afford to do so. Going home after the holidays was easier all around. By this time, I was looking forward to an opportunity to rest.

The day after Christmas, I was on the road from Chicago to Flint, Michigan. When I entered the cavernous rented hall there for the first time, it was hard not to feel the barrenness, although we would never have called it that then. It was cold and bleak outside; it was cold and bleak inside. On the concrete in front of the door a noticeable bloodstain remained from a gang shooting just the day before. Inside, undaunted, some people had put giant cutouts of rifles and guns around the sides, interspersed with posters of fallen heroes. Rather than liven the place up, if that was their purpose, the images added to the grimness. Clearly, the strategy of reviving SDS chapters on campus was out of place here.

The next few days seemed to unfold with a relentless, monotonous glorification of violence. The convention packet given out to all who attended stated, "Our strategy has to be geared toward forcing the disintegration of society, attacking at every level, from all directions and creating strategic 'armed chaos' where there is now pig order."[21] I could see the logic behind the idea that our strongest weapon was our ability to create chaos. Chaos might weaken and eventually bring down the government from the inside, while third world countries extricated themselves from US control. If we couldn't weaken the government, very likely we would have race war, sooner or later, I thought, so chaos now was better than the race-based chaos later on. Even then, however, I knew that chaos left a terrifying vacuum of leadership, in which the behavior of human beings under pressure could quickly degenerate into the most random violence. Surely we didn't want that. I assumed that the leadership at Flint had thought about this and had a plan to introduce us to weapons and fighting in a way that would avoid this disintegration. They must be making provisions to wage war responsibly.

Speakers denounced those who did not join us, saying that "if you are not with us, you are against us." Because a lot of people were unwilling to give up their privileges of security, comfort and consumption, despite the price of other people's slavery or oppression, we would "go it alone" if necessary. We were, then, the elite force, and there was some comfort in that. Furthermore, it was announced, many in Weatherman would be going underground to carry on the fight. I had no idea what that meant, but if they wanted to be hidden, I wondered, why were they announcing it in public? At the same time, I wondered if I would be picked.

Bernardine Dohrn had come to the Flint convention after walking through the Loop in downtown Chicago days before Christmas. There, she had been infuriated that people could lose themselves in a frenzy of Christmas shopping, while people were dying in their own city as well as in Vietnam. Even worse, while the public seemed disinterested in the gruesome human consequences of these events, they were voyeuristically hungry for grisly details of the recent Manson murders in Los Angeles.[22] In her speech, Bernardine astutely observed that rather than dealing with the real carnage, the press and population were obsessing on Charlie Manson and his tiny cult following. It was her outrage at this that provoked her famous comment, late in the first day at Flint, which seemed to glorify the gruesome sadism of the Charlie Manson gang murders: "Dig it; first they killed those pigs, then they ate dinner in the room with them, then they even shoved a fork into pig Tate's stomach. Wild!"[23] Perhaps, she was satirizing the public's prurient interest in the murders, or, perhaps, she was responding to the challenge incipient in the public's obsession with Manson: If only bizarre violence captured the public's interest, then those who wanted the public's eye would be forced to provide violence to get their attention.

At the time, the speech was seen by many, myself included, to reinforce the overall glorification of violence, presumably, I thought, in the spirit of Fanon. Violence was cleansing and resurrecting. Violence was the only act that could absolutely separate us from complicity with what the United States was doing to injure others. I couldn't see how *that* kind of violence was cleansing, but I guessed that we had to come so far to make sense of Fanon's idea that we were inevitably a little messy in our process. J. J. concluded the gathering by saying that we were "against everything that's good and decent in Honky America. We will loot and burn and destroy. We are the incubation of your mother's nightmare." [24] I found nothing appealing in the carnage of war, but maybe this frenzy was necessary to build up everyone's courage.

A few of the people who attended the Flint convention saw the whole spectacle as theater. For me, and I believe for most of those there, however, the implications were deadly serious. Now it seems fantastic that I responded to the clear signs of political idiocy by making a series of assumptions that rational, responsible planning lay behind the wild proclamations. It seems more believable, however, when I look around me today and see so many people assuming that George W. Bush's invasion of Iraq included a plan to avoid the sectarian violence that so many scholars predicted as the inevitable by-product of any intervention. Bush, we now know, had no such plan at all. It seems that when any of us cede authority to others we use these kinds of assumptions to cover over logical problems and inconsistencies. Our ignorance of information that is essential to reasoned judgment is accepted; our passivity is justified.

After Flint, I returned briefly to the national office and then flew to New Hampshire. I was exhausted. I slept and took long walks in the snowy woods. It was one visit during which my mother was not feeling particularly confrontational. I tried to find a few details of normalcy to string together to give a minimum explanation for my work. Mostly, I tried to avoid the subject. I was so wrapped up in my own reality, I mustered only superficial interest in the lives of anyone else in my family, accepting whatever news my mother cared to pass on to me. I knew that my sister Haven had been working in a GI coffee shop while studying to become a teacher, but she didn't share much of her political work with my parents either. My sister Robin, who had left the University of Wisconsin, was now working in the Harvard Co-op and working as a photographer. She drove around with a "No DDT" license plate on her car. My mother was teaching in the local schools at the time. After four days, I left and flew back to Chicago.

By the time I returned, there was no more talk of Teddy and I reviving work with the chapters. The police maintained constant vigilance; the phones crackled with several different taps. It was unnerving, although not surprising. Quietly, members of the leadership collective had let it be known that the national office would be shut down, that the printing press would be given to the Panthers if they could come and get it. Even though I could see no other direction, the end of the national office symbolized the end of SDS. I tried to frame this moment in some grand historical context, but mostly I thought about how I had loved the organization and many of the people in it, and was sad to see it end. Still, I couldn't argue with the fact that it was no longer possible to maintain it the way it was. We had moved on to a different time, I supposed, and this was yet another sacrifice. To linger would have been perhaps clinging to privilege.

Members of the leadership collective had been having individual meetings with each person to tell them where their next assignment would be. We knew that we had been infiltrated by police agents and needed to operate under strict security procedures. Anyone who was not trusted was simply not given an assignment. No one was to tell where they were going and no one was to ask.

One day, I found out that Teddy had left. I had no idea where he had gone. I continued to work at the national office catching up on legal work, answering the phones. I didn't have my meeting until the third week in January, at which time I was told to go to Seattle, and I was given the name of the one other national person who would be assigned there also. Seattle? Why was I being sent to Seattle? I didn't know anything about Seattle or the Northwest and had read little about their local work in *New Left Notes*. How was I to have any sense of what kind of militant actions would be effective or who we could trust? I was completely taken aback. Would I ever see Terry again when he got out of jail? He had written to me twice but I had not replied because I couldn't bear the thought of the FBI and the police reading my letters.

I expressed my disappointment without seeming to be disloyal to the leadership. I was told to give it a try and we would reevaluate after a while. At least I had been picked for something, I thought pathetically. The only alternative was to walk away from the organization, from the only people who shared the same deep fury that I felt toward the US government. If Seattle was where I had to go, then I would go. The next day, on January 21, after saying good-by to a few friends still left in Chicago, restrained because none of us could really say what was on our minds or in our hearts, I left. I had just turned twenty-five. The past year was already a blur.

In Seattle, I joined with an existing group. I had no idea what to do, but we had a few meetings to get to know each other, and I found out about some ongoing ideas the members of the group already had been considering. I was trying to learn names and faces and where each person had been working. Although I had come from Chicago, I couldn't report to the group on whether there was still a national organization or whether we were supposed to be working publicly or creating some hidden structure. There wasn't even a phone number in Chicago to call anymore.

Someone took me on a tour of the hippie parts of town. We went to a shooting range outside of town to do target practice, my first time shooting a gun since childhood. In the end it didn't matter that I was so completely rudderless. Within days of arriving I got sick with a serious case of the flu. I was forced to retreat to a small upstairs bedroom in the collective house; my fever rose and hung on for several dreamlike days. I drank gallons of water, the only liquid around, and occasionally someone appeared with a bowl of soup or bread.

After five days, still with a hacking cough, I wobbled downstairs to sit in on a meeting, trying to reengage myself in what was going on. A few days later, as my strength began to return, I received a phone call. It was Terry. He was out of jail and working in New York. Did I want to come? "Yes," I said instantly. "Meet me tomorrow afternoon at 5:00 at Nathan's in Times Square," he told me. "I'll be there," I responded and hung up. In less than a minute, my life had changed radically. Early the next morning I was on the first flight out of Seattle with space for youth fare.

It was a raw February day. When I walked into Nathan's, the most famous of New York hot dog stands, I scanned the dozen or so dark-coated New Yorkers standing along the cafeteria-style line waiting for food. Seeing no familiar faces, I looked up to a balcony surrounding the dining area. There, leaning slightly over the railing, his dark glasses still on in the bright lights, was Terry. With his leather boots covered by jeans and his pea coat, he hadn't changed since I saw him last in Washington. The current ran full force between us.

Terry was accompanied by J. J. The previous fall, just before Terry went to jail, J. J. and Terry had begun to get close, and clearly the two of them had resumed their friendship upon Terry's release.

As we left Nathan's, I slipped my arm through Terry's, our winter coats pressed tightly, a second conversation flowing beneath the more audible one among the three of us. Terry explained that a small, semiclandestine collective had formed. The existence of the collective and membership in it were to be shared with no one. For the moment, the core of the group was crashing in an apartment someone had lent them for two weeks, but when the occupants returned in about a week, Terry and the others would need a new place to stay.

The group, Terry explained briefly, had done an action already, a fire-bomb that had been thrown at the home of Judge Murtagh, then presiding over the trial of the Panther 21. Judge Murtagh seemed to be following in the belligerent steps of Chicago's Judge Hoffman, who had physically gagged defendant and Panther member Bobby Seale during the Chicago 8 trial in October. In the New York Panther 21 case, Murtagh seemed to take pleasure in summarily dismissing the normal rules of evidence to allow the police to introduce anything they wanted, while repeatedly denying defense motions. He had set up the courtroom with armed police, implying to the jury that he expected an armed attack at any moment. It was, Terry said, a way to prejudice jurors and make them frightened of the defendants, none of whom had ever engaged in armed political action.

I assumed the group's firebombing had been done after consultation with and approval by those Panthers that remained out of jail, although I now wonder. The Panthers themselves never did comment on the action publicly. The firebombing had been dangerous because Judge Murtagh's house was guarded by several New York City policemen twenty-four hours a day. The bottle filled with gasoline had broken against the front steps, burned, and gone out. At least the throwers had gotten away.

By then, of course, I was hardly shocked at this action. I had assumed for weeks that many small groups were being set up to do this kind of action. While firebombings still glowed with a somewhat surreal aura, I was at the point where I could imagine learning and participating in one. Certainly, everyone seemed to be doing it. Bombings were being reported roughly at the rate of one a day. A Senate investigations subcommittee later estimated that there had been 862 bombings from January 1969 to April 1970, and that was the conservative estimate. The Alcohol, Tobacco, and Firearms division of the US Treasury showed at least 5,000 bombings and attempts during this same period.[25]

There wasn't a state that wasn't affected by the rash of bombings. Many of the devices were simply bottles filled with gasoline, and with a rag stuck in the neck, which was lit on fire. When the bottle was thrown, theoretically, the glass broke, spraying gasoline, which was ignited by the burning rag that, presumably, had fallen within the radius of the gasoline. The reality was, they often didn't ignite.

Terry continued to update me: The New York collective was now planning to follow their first action with several simultaneous ones. The plan was to demonstrate not just the willingness to take up arms, but the existence of an organization extensive enough to carry out several coordinated attacks at the same time. The collective was in the process of picking the targets and assigning work. There would be another meeting tomorrow, where I would get to meet the whole group. In the meantime, if I were sure that I was ready to join the group, we would proceed downtown to the temporary apartment, where I would meet the other people in the collective's leadership group, which I would join.

Was I sure I wanted to join? Two things I was sure about. Uppermost, I was sure that I wanted to be with Terry. It never occurred to me that I could be outside of the organization and still have a relationship with him. True commitment to the fight for equality and justice was so interwoven into our passion that it was unthinkable to separate the two. I was also sure that I wanted access to the inner workings of the organization. The intensity of the New York collective confirmed my suspicions that Seattle must have been seen as a nonimportant arena of action.[26]

I was ready to embrace the illegal aspects of the collective's work. I had been ready since Fred Hampton was murdered. Democracy was failing to bring about change; a decisive moment in history, defined by wars of national liberation, was upon us. We, too, had to look to a more Leninist version of change, a change that would be led by those who were willing to take the risk. Even if we were in the minority, we were leading in the "interests of the majority." "We would do it alone if necessary," Terry and many others had said. I didn't question the moral absolutism of the sentiment. The final threads holding me to the idea of participatory democracy had frayed and broken.

I had come to agree with Fanon: nonviolence was a luxury of the middle class, of whites, in the contention for power. All around the world, people were fighting to gain control of their lives; we would have to, as well. There was no way to stop the destructive system except meeting its violence with violence, as the Vietnamese had been forced to do. I had come to accept that, as Mao said in his little red book of quotations, political power did ultimately, grow from the barrel of a gun.

I had been uncomfortable with street fighting because it seemed so easily reduced to a macho contest of egos rather than a political engagement with specific goals. Violent clashes in public protests would not lead to insurrection here, I thought, because the country was too large, with too few willing to join the barricades. Instead, it just led to arrests, bashed heads, and the burdens of bail and time spent in court. Likewise, the flinging around of violent rhetoric for its own sake seemed irresponsible and purposeless, if not repulsive. If, however, we were building a clandestine fighting force that could learn over the long run how to fight, then that made sense to me and I wanted to be a warrior in that force.

The US government had attacked popular governments in Guatemala, Iran, and Indonesia. The CIA had attempted to assassinate Fidel Castro in Cuba, and was suspected (and later proven) to have been behind the assassinations of Patrice Lumumba in the Congo and Samora Machel in Mozambique a few years later. Whether they used violence or covert actions, "the system" would stop at nothing to defend itself. Weren't the deaths of Malcolm X, the Kennedys, King, and Fred Hampton, and the attempted murder of Reies Tijerina evidence that they were possibly already using clandestine violence at home, whether carried out directly or through the encouragement of others? Likewise, the backlash against civil rights seemed to be increasing every month. Attacks on busing had brought many attempts at school integration to a standstill in the North. We needed to learn how to defend ourselves and others, how to operate in secret, how to protect people and, eventually, how to strike out to rid ourselves of such a violent system.

Finally, my fascination with technology pulled me toward the opportunity to finally learn how all the military stuff worked. How and why did Molotov cocktails ignite? It seemed like those with the scientific and technical knowledge were calling the shots. If we had to take up arms, I wanted to learn about them. Men should not have exclusive possession of this knowledge.

Yes, I wanted to stay. Still, I wondered, why couldn't we have developed a secret, armed capacity and at the same time preserved the public SDS? Wouldn't that have been safer than broadcasting our intentions? How did Terry feel about the end of SDS? What had been the point of the national action? What did he think when he heard stories about Flint? What was the strategy behind setting up all these small collectives like the one in Seattle? How did he envisage the next stage unfolding? Finally, I had someone I could talk to about all this, and I was beginning to find a voice with which to do it. I hoped we would have some time alone, soon.

Terry, J. J., and I took the train downtown and then walked through the biting cold to a classic Lower East Side tenement building, just off Houston Street. There we climbed up three flights of dingy stairs and knocked on a heavy metal door, standard for the embattled neighborhood. Much to my astonishment, who should greet us but Teddy. As we walked through the door, I saw someone else from the leadership and a woman who I only knew slightly from national meetings, seated in a cramped living room. I was glad to see Teddy and to find out where he had landed.

No joyous, quirky music rambled on in the background at this gathering, however; no one shared any hilarious stories. Instead, voices were muted and faces tense. Each of us had pursued our desire to bring change until it had led us here, to the question of power. Weatherman attracted people who had an intuitive sense of power, aware of who held it in any circle, intrigued by its dangers and possibilities.

Terry and J. J. wanted me to spend the first day getting integrated into the New York collective's leadership group. After a brief time with the whole group, Terry informed us that I and the other woman, Martine, needed to get to know each other, and they would leave us alone for a couple of hours. Everyone else trouped out into the cold. I began to realize that we were expected to have sex as a way of forging our ultimate loyalty to each other and to the group.

I responded to this latest twist with my usual openness to new experiences. As a physical act it seemed less threatening than the group sex, although I had never made love with a woman before. I knew that combat groups that depended on each other for their survival regularly ritualized their intimacy to recognize and seal their mutual dependence. Gangs did it with violence. Sex seemed a better way. Months before, I had sensed that the late-night party before the national action served that function for the leadership group, although I had been an outsider then, immune to the effects of the ritual. Nonetheless, since I had been absolutely focused on Terry for the past twenty-four hours, this latest development was, at best, disorienting.

I had no idea what role, if any, Martine had played in designing this plan. We first tried to talk about our mandate, but neither of us knew how to negotiate around the need-to-know rules or the awkwardness of my inclusion in this group at Terry's behest, which I sensed was an issue. Then we blundered through the physical act itself, confused that the stimulation of risk-taking did not genuinely transfer to sex. Inevitably, there was no sense of discovery, or power. Quite the opposite. It felt like a distraction from our much more important project. When the others returned we both put on those protective masks that we had learned to use so well in previous months, insisting that we were now the closest of comrades.

Had either of us been at all centered, something good might have come out of our encounter. We might have discovered some basic commonalities, which might have made the obligatory sexual contact impossible for us both. We might have bonded over the fact that we had both been leaders, and we had an intuitive if unarticulated awareness of issues of women and power in the organization. Ultimately, we might have understood together that the question of women and power rested on another. Were we seeking equality with men, or did women's experience have something unique and different that had been lacking in previous male paradigms of leadership? While I had been on the verge of articulating that question a year ago, I had since lost touch with it, embracing Weatherman's simplistic hierarchy of oppressions. Instead, our collaboration in this artifice injected a kind of wariness into the relationship. Each of us was struggling for secure footing in the larger whole. The experience left me feeling vaguely derailed, my intention to figure things out with Terry deflected by the need to make sense out of the previous hours. The fact that I have only a vague memory of the encounter is testament to its emotionally numbing impact.

Late the next day, the leadership collective joined several other young people. I had never met any of them before with the exception of one young woman who had been in an SDS chapter at one of the colleges in Washington DC, I was surprised to see her there, as I hadn't remembered that she had joined Weatherman back in July. Several others had recently dropped out of school and were still in their teens. The youngest two were sixteen and seventeen years old. I didn't know how they had been selected to be in a unit that was clearly on the front lines, given that they were so young. What qualities did they have, that apparently I was missing when I was banished to Seattle, I wondered?

The first order of business was that we, like other clandestine collectives, needed to secure different IDs that we could use to do illegal work, so that our real identities would not be implicated. The way to secure these IDs, apparently, was to steal them. Then, if something happened when we were using these IDs, the trail would lead back to a completely innocent person, presumably with a protective alibi. We decided that college campuses would be the easiest place for us to steal them since we knew the territory. We divided ourselves up, heading to campuses spread out along the East Coast.

This evolution of my values seemed perfectly natural. I had already accepted the morality of shoplifting to support the movement. In Washington, I had continued my occasional shoplifting, mostly for food to feed the staff. I never stole anything for personal pleasure (except maybe for the occasional pack of cigarettes along with the groceries). That would be immoral. I had read Lenin, who convinced me that we had to use whatever advantages we could in the fight for a better world. I knew that this reasoning had led to, or at least had not prevented, the hideous abuses of power carried out by Stalin. But, we knew better now, I thought. We would never do that.

My moral code now rested on the belief that standing up to the system was the most important action, and the more passionately one fought against the system the better. In this sphere of warfare, we would play by the rules of our enemy: power was everything, even to the point of sacrificing honesty, accountability, and, ultimately, human life. We were on the advanced edge of fighting an entrenched and violent elite that was riddled with corruption and greed, so whatever worked was moral.

I thought less, however, about the morality of how we had been treating each other, the all-too-frequent use of humiliation, dishonesty, sexual pressure. Was our Weatherman culture a harbinger of the world we would create after the revolution? The old moral code was corrupt, and we were constructing a new one, I told myself. We were creating new men and women, and if it was a little rough around the edges, well, we had a lot of sorting through of customs and values to do, and of course we couldn't get it right on the first try every time. We needed to forgive ourselves our mistakes, the inconsistencies in our ideas and the small cruelties in our behavior. We would do better, I thought. Little did I know that forgiveness without reflection often leads to a repetition of errors.

Stealing IDs was stressful, far more so than the shoplifting. Nonetheless, I was good at it. All my years of having to present a persona to the world came in handy. I could flirt, cajole, intimidate, or be invisible, depending on what the situation required. I projected a sense of entitlement mixed with a bit of female superiority. Any challenger must necessarily be quite uncool.

During my first week in New York, Terry and I saw each other little, as I worked primarily with a small group from the larger collective. Still, we found time late at night to renew our intimacy and try to find a way to nurture the trust that had begun between us before he went to jail. There was little time for talk, however, about the burning questions I had had on that walk to Houston Street.

One evening I told Terry I needed a presentable, warm coat if I was to move about unnoticed. We were on 14th Street, and I saw some fake fur jackets in the window of a shop that looked like the perfect start to a new persona. Just a minute, I said to Terry, and went into the store. Within ten minutes I was back on the street with the coat on, the store employees none the wiser. As I walked over to Terry, he beamed with pride. It occurred to me that this must be what it felt like to have a pimp. Curious, I thought, but basking in the warmth of his affection and pride, I didn't think about the complexity and dangers, of this terrain, about how the rush of passion generates such an invincible sense of possibility that all signs of danger are overwhelmed. I didn't think about how much power I had given to the organization, how much more I was now giving to this man, and why I was doing this, especially giving up the power to set the terms of my political imagination. I needed to believe in Terry, in the simplicity of his determination. At the same time, I could sense that he needed to believe in me. His need in turn gave me power, power that was beginning to awaken me from the stupor of the previous months. Soon, I thought, we will find the time to talk through my questions. The evidence indicated that Terry and I were on to something powerful, but I also knew I needed to address the parts that didn't make sense.

Within days we had amassed more IDs than we knew what to do with. Moderation was not a Weatherman trait. As the small groups filtered back to New York with their acquisitions, Terry turned his attention to the problem of finding a place for the leadership collective to stay. Furthermore, if we wanted to do a series of actions, we needed a place to work. He pressed me to think if I knew of any place. I explained again that since I had never lived in New York the only people I really knew in the city were my father and stepmother. We couldn't stay with them, and I knew from my sister that they were going away on vacation for a couple of weeks anyway. Unlike my sisters, I didn't have a key nor did I want one, because of the separation I kept between my family and my political life. When Terry heard they were going away, however, he wondered out loud if there was any way I could get a key.

The suggestion hit me like a ton of bricks. Although I was angry at my father for refusing to look at the way his chosen profession fed into damaging behaviors of both individuals and the economic system, I didn't want to wage the fight about values and economics with him on the turf of personal resources. On the other hand, clearly this was a resource I had, and I was, by the code I was following, obligated to take advantage of it as long as my parents never knew. I told Terry I would try.

That night I called my father and told him I had just come to New York and had come down with the flu. I asked him if I could stay at the house for a few days to recover before I went back to my work. He questioned me closely, but I stuck to my story. Reluctantly, he agreed that I could come by in the morning. He would give me keys, but I was to leave as soon as I felt better. He had already arranged for my cousin Steve to come by to water the plants and check the house. Steve, he said, would still be coming by.

The next morning I arrived and visited with them briefly as they prepared to leave for the Caribbean. I thanked my father and stepmother profusely, and they left. I called Terry, and two hours later he and Teddy arrived with our few belongings. We now had a place for the leadership to stay and a place to meet as well, so we could carry out the final preparations for the upcoming actions. Knowing that my cousin Steve's wife was pregnant, I put a note on the door for Steve telling him I was staying there, and that it turned out my flu was really the German measles. I promised him I would water the plants and look after things. I knew that he would not come in after reading that. If he had any questions, he would call, and I could reassure him.

My father had bought the small townhouse at 18 West 11th Street a few years earlier, when Young & Rubicam summoned him and Potter back to New York after more than ten years in London. The townhouse had four floors, with a kitchen, bath, and little den on the ground floor, a formal living room and dining room on the first floor, a master bedroom and my father's study on the second, and on the top floor, three very small bedrooms.

When everyone arrived at the house, I made it clear that we needed to be as respectful as possible of the space, so we could leave it exactly as we found it. The others readily agreed. Other than actually sleeping in the beds, we stayed in the kitchen area, which had a table big enough for six, a couple of overstuffed chairs, and a TV in one corner.

The following morning the whole group met to begin to talk about the next action. Terry proposed, as he had told us before, that we do at least three simultaneous firebombings for our next undertaking. We didn't discuss how this would fit into an overall plan for change, for building the movement, or even how it was part of a plan for developing Weatherman. It was enough that we had begun to define ourselves as a "fifth column." This was a reference to Spanish fighters during their civil war who worked secretly in Madrid to undermine the pro-Nazi loyalist government from within, while four columns of regular fighters attempted to move on the capital. We would work within the United States while "two, three, many Vietnams" chipped away at US power around the world.

I didn't know how all these coordinated actions fit into the work of the other secret collectives. From some small comment made by J. J. or Terry when I first came to town, I gathered that there were other fighting units as well, and that there might be something of a friendly competition to see how quickly we could each learn and act. I assumed once again that any discussion of other groups was too secret for general discussion. Now that I had work that I could sink my teeth into, I felt less urgent about understanding the broader plan. Our efforts to develop a small armed capacity seemed so much more grounded, so modest in comparison with the sweeping pronouncements of war and mayhem at Flint. I was satisfied to concentrate on the specifics of learning how to fight. Always the practical one, I began to focus on how to implement the given plan.

We agreed on a few possible kinds of targets, a university involved in war research, a corporation manufacturing arms, a government office, and broke into smaller groups to scout out each one and make a plan. No one mentioned anything about the future, about where all this was leading, about the broader political context, and certainly not about how anyone was feeling. While there was some open discussion about the pros and cons of different targets, the comments stayed on the level of tactical issues: possibilities, dangers, and the potential for the target to be covered in the press and understood for what it was. For the most part, participation by the younger members of the group was especially muted, silenced by their fear of our unknown trajectory, combined with their fear of criticism.

This passivity was reinforced by the occasional humiliation handed out by Terry and other members of the leadership. In one of the meetings during this period, Terry suggested that we each pick a pseudonym, a nom de guerre, that we would start using among ourselves, and that he and Martine, who, as I understood it, occasionally joined him, would use when they met with the national leadership collective. As we went around the circle and each person said the name they had picked, Terry singled me out as the only person who had picked a strong, self-affirming name. What on earth did that mean, I wondered? I couldn't tell any difference in the names, and I knew that those who had been derided couldn't either, but that they couldn't help but feel diminished somehow by his comment. I knew the episode reeked of the same kind of cultlike behavior I had experienced myself in Chicago, negative insinuations painted with ambivalent and inaccessible language. To question these conclusions risked accusations of insubordination or inadequate political understanding.

Not only was I aware of the rank favoritism I was receiving from Terry, but even while I disapproved of it I was comforted by it. Finally, he was openly validating his respect for me. I vowed to say something to Terry in private, but I kept silent during the meeting. Humor would have helped to dispel the power of these kinds of remarks, but by then our sense of humor, even Teddy's, was long gone.

Even though Terry and Teddy were only twenty-two years old, and Martine and I only a few years older, we four were intimidating under the circumstances. We had all been in or around SDS for many years and held enormous sway over the less experienced members of the collective. We had inherited a leadership culture lacking in accountability and fraught with favoritism. The informal and usually invisible ways that people in leadership considered new ideas and made decisions placed a premium on gaining personal favor with those in power. It was the only way to get enough information to construct a coherent picture of what was going on. Distrust of and competition for access to this group and its power were the inevitable by-products.

No doubt many initiatives for change start with an informal gathering of friends or coworkers, but Weatherman's leadership wore the mantle of a democratic election by SDS the previous June. This gave them added authority and the appearance of coherency, which they did nothing to dispel. Now I was in leadership and one of the older people in the group. I too was suddenly vested with some of that authority. Others couldn't have known of my internal collapse, anymore than I knew how or why each member of the Weather Bureau had constructed their personal vision of leadership. I was only beginning to stumble into such discussions about it with Terry. I was only beginning to search for words to name my confusion and to begin to think critically about the situation. I had not yet learned to trust my intuition and let it guide me. With my own sense of coherence in pieces, I clung to the practices of the prevailing leadership culture, noting that it was flawed, and hoping to be able to find time to sort it out later.

When the whole group reassembled several days later, we agreed on three possible targets. Two of them required a delayed ignition for the firebombs to allow us a few minutes to get away. We also wanted an ignition that was more reliable than the rag placed in the firebomb that had failed at Judge Murtagh's house. The new idea was to insert a commercial fuse so that we could place the bottle, light the fuse, and disappear in the minute or two before the gasoline fumes trapped inside exploded. I couldn't quite understand how it would work, how the fire, in any material, wasn't likely to go out as it passed through the neck of the bottle. Terry, who had gotten advice from someone outside the collective, assured us that it would work, though he didn't know how it would work either.

Late that night, we assembled around a can of gasoline behind a large supermarket. Each group had a bottle and a fuse. We filled up, placed our firebombs in shopping bags, and set off for our destinations. The next day, we eagerly checked the papers. At least two of the devices did actually go off, although the smell of the burning fuse had already alerted people who were able to douse the fires before any real damage was done.

Later, as we sat around the kitchen talking about it, I was again left wondering what the point was. The actions had received a small mention in one of the papers, but no one knew what they were about. It didn't feel like we had accomplished anything. Firebombing had become routine. We could do them until we were blue in the face, and the government wouldn't really care, and we wouldn't convince the US public to think about what the government was doing.

Shortly thereafter, Terry presented us with the idea of working with dynamite instead of firebombs. It was a lot safer to work with, he argued, and it had more predictable results. It was possible to buy dynamite from rural construction supply stores. Lots of people used dynamite to blow stumps out of fields or to root out burrowing animals. Using a small amount of dynamite, we could do more destruction, get the attention of the powers that be, and actually exact a price—which was our overall goal—from the military-industrial elite. He said that someone would train him how to do it.

I didn't understand how dynamite could be safe. I remembered stories I had heard from my stepfather, who had worked his way through college in the South driving a nitroglycerine truck in the summers. One out of every three drivers died. Now, however, I was assured that the nitroglycerin was mixed with other materials that stabilized it to the point that you could drop it off a roof and it wouldn't go off. The only way to set it off now was to have a little explosion inside. This could be supplied by an M-80 firecracker or by an electric blasting cap.

With an M-80, you had to light the fuse and run, which would indeed be a risky proposition both in terms of our own safety and also in terms of getting caught. So, without a lot of discussion, it was agreed that we would use electric fuses. Once again, we would try to do more than one action at a time.

We wanted to pick targets that were directly related to the war, to encourage the United States to get serious about the negotiations. We wanted targets that would speak for themselves more clearly than the previous ones. As the group brainstormed, a number of government, diplomatic, and corporate institutions were suggested. The one that most satisfied our requirements was the proposal that we do something at a military base. The pacifists had done a number of symbolic actions. In one, they had hammered at B-52s. While their goal had been to discredit war of any kind, these actions testified to the ability of vulnerable, unarmed individuals to stand up to the mighty US war machine. In most instances, however, they had been caught and were serving long sentences in prison.

We also talked about targets that were symbols of US imperialism—in general terms—where we could put a small device outside at night without it being noticed. I worried for a moment about passersby, but then decided that the chances of someone passing close enough at that exact moment to get seriously hurt were slim. Besides, getting lots of people to think about the consequences of US policy was the whole point, and if there wasn't a dramatic immediacy to the actions, would anyone pay attention? I had an image from the *Battle of Algiers*, of the revolutionary forces making life unbearable for the colonial interlopers, striking at the every-day routines of pleasure so that the colonial invaders could never forget that they were on someone else's territory. Of course we weren't trying to chase out colonial intruders; we were trying to undermine the colo-nial powers from within. We agreed to meet again the next day to identify specific possibilities within these categories.

That night, Terry and I had a rare moment to talk alone. Terry admit-ted his many fears about these latest undertakings, but any emotion could be overcome, he believed, by will. No one else seemed to be stepping up to the plate. Most people, even those in the movement, seemed willing to stand by while the United States rode roughshod over its victims. This infuriated Terry. We owed it to the Vietnamese to take some of the heat away from them. We owed the black movement to do the same.

Terry had never met directly with the Vietnamese, had never heard them express their hopes that we would contribute to a mass movement against the war. The Vietnamese liberation movement was not looking to us to assume the task of self-defense, a burden they considered their own. I had heard them explain this position in Phnom Penh. For Terry, how-ever, what the Vietnamese were doing spoke far louder than what they said: They were standing up to the mightiest war machine the world had ever assembled, and they were holding their own. The antiwar movement had failed to stop the war or even to make a dent in US policy, or so it seemed.

My own meetings with the Vietnamese in Phnom Penh now seemed like they had taken place in a different era. In the face of My Lai, of the bombing of North Vietnam, and of the napalming, I had lost sight of the broader goals we had had in mind earlier in the 60s when SDS began: for more people in the United States to have access to and take responsibil-ity for participating in the decisions that affect their lives. In the face of an uncertain future, I could see no success in the fact that hundreds of thou-sands of people in the United States were now awakening to political activism, to participating in public discourse. I could only see that those with power still seemed sanctioned by the public to pursue their wars.

Our sense of urgency was also propelled by our need to be heard. Who were we, this fast moving tide of young people propelled initially by the elders of the civil rights movement? Not only did we want peace in Vietnam, we wanted a seat at the table of power. Our voices were part of a great, diverse chorus that had been pouring out its hopes and dreams since this country's beginnings. As long as monolithic faces of middle-aged white men and their few chosen exceptions were the only ones to speak for the United States, we could not rest.

Young people in the black movement were standing up and being killed. It was time that we too stood up, not just to support everyone else, but also to draw our own battle lines. If we were too small to win, Terry thought, like Butch Cassidy and the Sundance Kid we would go out in a blaze of glory. We would be symbols; we would have at least spoken truth. Terry was ready to die in service to his vision of a loving world.

I mostly agreed with this until it came to the Butch Cassidy image. I wasn't sure if what we needed was an iron will or rather to take the time to learn what we needed to know, to build slowly. I assumed that Terry's fascination with the defeatism inherent in Butch Cassidy reflected his delight in pop culture. He and Bill Ayers had loved the film, two inseparable friends bound together, going into an uncertain future. I was drawn to Terry's existential belief in the power of will, but I also thought he was a bit obsessive.

He had been an English major during his brief stint in college, and a poet. Science was a foreign language, and he hated it for being undecipherable. Because this left him feeling powerless, it terrified him. He understood no more about what electricity or dynamite were made of than I did, and he was considerably less interested. Nonetheless, he believed that it was his job to learn how to do it and to bring the information back to the group, and he would do that. The tasks required to learn how to fight could be broken down into manageable units, I argued to him. We had already learned how to obtain IDs that would not leave a trail back to us. Terry's fear and dislike of anything technical could be overcome, I insisted. I tried to get him to see that it would be interesting to learn how all this worked.

We would risk our lives out of love and anger, I thought, not from a fear that had to be overcome by will. I was afraid of what we were doing, I was terrified of dynamite, but knew I could trust my determination and courage to help me learn what I needed to learn. I could trust my fury to keep me in it for the long haul. Terry was interested in what I had to say, but not yet convinced. His fear, his courage, and his rage against injustice were feeding each other into a white heat. He was in a hurry and didn't want to mull it over too much.

Everyone in the leadership collective seemed committed to the necessity of creating a new front on home soil. Each of us was fierce about it in our own, quite different ways, based on the threads of our own history and character. At a continuation meeting the next day, things got very serious very fast. The suggestion was made to investigate nearby Fort Dix, a major training facility. There was to be a social evening in the officers club on Friday evening, March 6, which would allow us easy access to the base and an entrée into the building. Regular soldiers, we reasoned, joined the military because they were drafted or needed a job or the educational benefits, but to train to be an officer meant that you were playing a leadership role in the US military strategy. These young men had an education; they had a responsibility to acknowledge the human consequences of their work. As such, we thought, they were fair game.

The goal, as I saw it, was not all-out warfare on the army at this point, but to dramatically challenge any complacency that officers, especially stateside officers, might have about their mandate to kill Vietnamese. If they were not moved by the immorality of what they were doing, then perhaps they would be discouraged if the glamour and privilege of being an officer was neutralized by insecurity and fear on the home front. Even here they were not safe from the anger of the people of the world, many of whom looked just like them. Perhaps fewer would then choose to be officers, thereby weakening the military forces.

While my sister Haven worked in GI coffee houses, and I had counseled GIs who were AWOL, I had had little exposure to the complex and conflicting forces that worked to keep troops aloof and shielded from the moral and political implications of their actions. The only individuals to emerge from the abstractions of the uniform were the ones who were in pain, who risked leaving, who were alienated. None were officers, though several were the sons of officers. I thought about how ineffectual we had felt with our previous actions, and that it was now time to get down to the real business.

When the proposal was floated about Fort Dix, no one argued against it, but the tension in the air seemed to crystallize into a fine mist. No one said anything out loud about the possibility of people getting hurt or killed. We all played out the imaginary scenarios we had in our own minds. As yet, however, we knew nothing concrete about the base, or exactly what we were talking about or whether it would be possible. We agreed to investigate other targets as well. We divided up again into small groups, made a list of all the things that needed to be done and set off to do them over the next few days. One team went to the each of the possible sites to do reconnaissance, one went to procure the dynamite, and another to obtain a car that could not be traced. Someone from the leadership team worked with each group. I arranged to meet my group the following morning at a restaurant, and we all dispersed.

The next few days were a flurry of activity. We reconvened after each group had carried out its assignment, happy that no one had any major mishaps. Our preparations had once again been excessive, and we had far more dynamite and blasting caps than we needed. The conversation focused on which of the targets we had investigated were feasible. Then we discussed the logistical details required for each action. We still didn't talk about the physical impact of the actions, either on buildings or people. Nor did we consider the political repercussions beyond the hope that a dramatic story would make a small dent in public consciousness. "You cannot act with such greed and recklessness without consequences!" I wanted our message to be, and I wanted to say it as loud as we could.

We were taking the first preparatory steps to going to war with the United States, as unbelievable as it seemed. How would it all play out? How could I expect it to feel like anything but a dream, I told myself.

We decided to proceed with the Fort Dix action and two smaller ones, to be done late at night, with a device concealed outside. In those two, we only hoped to break windows. As we proceeded with our final preparations, the national leadership arranged yet another shuffle of people around the collectives. Martine left and Diana Oughton arrived, joining the leadership team. She was coming from another collective, which I suspected was every bit as intense as ours. Nothing was said about why the changes were being made, or whether it made sense for her to come in while were we in the final stages of our actions. Diana had obviously agreed to come, even after being told what we were doing.

I had never had a conversation with Diana, but I knew that she had worked with the Children's Community School in Ann Arbor with Bill Ayers, her longtime boyfriend. I had seen her at Cleveland and at Flint, where she had been part of the militant group of women from Michigan held up to be our models. She had seemed engaged and fully supportive of what they were doing, so I imagined the work in New York would come as no surprise to her. Nonetheless, she was noticeably somber, as we all were, and I had no idea what she was thinking.

Teddy was intent on his assignments, as tense as the rest of us, determined to push himself to take any risk necessary. He measured himself against the guerrilla fighter in the jungle, with little to eat, far from his family, risking his life because he believed that anything less would doom him and his family to a life of subservience and oppression. Teddy was fighting against all the evil in the world, and he would fight however he needed to.

My friendship with Teddy felt suspended in the midst of all the intensity. Because we had never discussed our deeper feelings about things before, we didn't begin then. Teddy retreated into himself, into his rage. During this last week, when another member of the collective, recruited by Teddy, confessed to him that he was terrified and wanted out, Teddy responded by saying that he couldn't leave because he already knew too much.

My own attention was focused on nurturing my conversation with Terry, in which I was groping for a more coherent way to imagine this shift to warfare. I was focused on working things out with Terry first, because he held the position of power accessible to me. Of course my personal relationship with Terry reinforced this single-mindedness.

On March 5, our group met one last time, to go over everyone's responsibilities. Once again the feeling of powerlessness dominated. Could our plan shake up the power structure? Would it just be ignored? Although Terry had learned a basic circuit design, we didn't know whether it took one stick of dynamite or ten to blow a door down. We had been told that dynamite was stronger if it was encased in a pipe because it had to work harder for the explosion to get out.

Not very much dynamite can fit into a one-foot length of water pipe, however. Well, to make it do more damage, we thought, we could put nails in the pipe. With little discussion we agreed. I was thinking that even if the dynamite didn't cause much damage, at least the nails would go into the lights and walls and curtain and make a mess. The nails would wound people, too, and, in their suffering, perhaps they would develop more empathy for how the Vietnamese felt when the United States dropped daisy bombs, the antipersonnel bombs that had been dropped in huge swaths across Vietnam. Maybe this experience would set some limits on the willingness of GIs to violently interfere in other people's lives.

I didn't think about the fact that the nails might actually kill people. Of course it took quite of bit of denial to not think about it, but denial is essential for warfare. Like soldiers in most armies, I focused on the theoretical goals of the war, on defeating the enemy. The individual lives of those who were part of the enemy effort were an abstraction. If one empathized with the enemy it would be impossible to kill or maim. The US military did its best to nip empathy in the bud by calling the Vietnamese gooks and other epithets, to make the Vietnamese seem less than human, not worthy of empathy.

Terry gave a brief explanation of the simple circuit he had been taught for the timing device. One of the members of the collective raised an objection about its primitive design, which entailed only a clock, a battery, and the electrical blasting cap. There should be a safety switch, he said. I didn't know what they meant by a circuit or how a safety switch would work. Neither did Terry. Neither of us knew anything about atoms, or had ever heard of an electron or charge. As a result, Terry trusted the step-by-step procedure he had just learned, having no idea why or when a switch might make the circuit safer. To the young person who raised it, the argument was undoubtedly so obvious that he didn't realize others might not understand him.

Terry had been told to do it a certain way, and he was too insecure about his knowledge to debate it. He cut off the discussion. He was the leader and he would take responsibility for how it was done. He would build the circuits, taking the risk himself. No one else spoke up.

After the meeting, we dispersed. The leadership group stayed in my father's house that night. No one else was to be involved from this point on. The next morning, I rose early. Every one stripped their bed and I took all the sheets downstairs to wash and dry them. My parents were returning around 5:00 PM that night, and we had to be gone, all supplies removed and the house shipshape before then. It was going to be very tight. My main worry was getting all the sheets washed and ironed and back on the beds and the kitchen floor vacuumed. This contended with my anxiety about preparations for the action, which seemed so unreal that I took it on faith that all would proceed as planned, as our work had done up to this point.

By late morning we were still on schedule, barely. I had washed and dried all the sheets. Disguises and the packaging were ready. The devices were being armed, one by one. We had a car nearby to pick up the leftover supplies from the basement and transport them to a safe place. I had set up the ironing board in the kitchen with my back to the window above the kitchen sink. Gray light shined in over my shoulder from the backyard. Standing in my bare feet on the carpeted floor, I was ironing the sheets as fast as I could, so I would have time to make all the beds as well as fulfill my other responsibilities.

CHAPTER TEN

THE EXPLOSION

■ ■

Teddy Gold came up from the unfinished subbasement, which held only the furnace, other house vitals, and a primitive workbench. Terry had decided that that was the safest place to work on the devices. Teddy said he needed to go to the drugstore to buy some cotton balls and he'd be right back. I nodded and kept ironing.

A few minutes later, I was bearing down on the wrinkles on the white sheet covering the ironing board when a shock wave shot through the house. A loud rumble followed, growing in intensity. Under the thin burnt orange carpeting, my bare feet felt the old, wood floor vibrating with escalating intensity. The ironing board, too, started to tremble and then tilt as the integrity of the house was compromised somewhere deep below. I began to sink down, my feet still planted on the thin carpet as it stretched and slid across widening, disjointed gaps. I was still standing, still holding the hot iron in my right hand, my arm still obeying the signal my mind had sent fractions of a second before to press down on the crisp, white cotton. A blast reverberated through the house and in place of the ironing board, a mountain of splintered wood and brick rose up all around me. Plaster dust and little bits of debris blew out from everywhere, instantly filling the air. Even as I tried desperately to process what was happening, I noted with resignation that this was one mess I was not going to be able to clean up.

A sharper, louder explosion then shot out from the subbasement, and as I dropped two or three feet more, I wondered if I would continue to fall down into the subbasement. I needed to put the iron down to free up my hand, but there were no surfaces anymore, just a noisy, moving, three-dimensional swirl of disintegrating house giving way to the shuddering blast waves of force that had passed through it. For a fraction of a second I worried that, with all the splinters of woods and debris flying around, the hot iron might start a fire. As the muffled noise from the second explosion persisted, I knew it didn't matter. Besides, I couldn't see anything; the light was gone, unable to penetrate the thick cloud of dust that now filled every space and crevice and which crowded into my eyes, forcing them shut. From then on I could only open my eyes by blinking off and on, so that the tears could momentarily clear off the dust that grated like sandpaper beneath my lids and allow me to glimpse strobelike images of the changing terrain. I flung the iron away toward where the fireplace used to be.

In the same moment, the idea that Terry and Diana were both in the subbasement overwhelmed everything else. As I forced my attention there and to them, my lungs expanded instantaneously to draw in air and dust so I could call out. As I blinked in their direction to see if maybe—I saw the glow, like an engorged sun rising up from a huge gaping hole between me and the front of the house. That lungful of dust emerged as an anguished cry, as if that was the only way to connect in that last second with the spirits as they drifted upward into some limbo that hangs around after the body is gone but before absolute death. I cried out "Adam," Terry's nom de guerre, and scrambled to the edge of the crater, only to be blinded now by the brightness. Then, I heard the flames take up the silence left by the blast.

By then I was in the middle of the house, and Kathy Boudin, who had been taking a shower, heard my voice and cried out for help. She had to be nearby, I thought, because the bathroom where she was showering was also in the middle of the house. I called to her. "Are you okay?" I knew that in ten or fifteen seconds we would no longer be able to get out. "I can't see," she said, and I knew it was because of the dust. I moved left along the edge of the crater through the gritty haze toward her voice until I could grab her hand. For a fraction of a second I thought to turn toward the front door, until I realized the absurdity of looking for a door when there was no longer any distinction between floor and ceiling or space in between. Instead, we headed toward an opening where, dimly, it looked like daylight was trying to fight its way into the dust. I groped blindly, with each bare foot seeking something solid enough to hold my weight for at least a second or two.

The sound of the fire sucking air in from all directions grew louder behind us, reaching out to us. As we stumbled out of the opening in the front, it was only feet behind us. I was barely able to notice another explosion as I concentrated on climbing, still holding on to Kathy and both of us barefoot, out through the hole and over more debris onto the sidewalk. Helping hands reached out to us. Kathy was in shock. Someone wrapped a coat around her, even as she protested, as she was still wet and naked from the shower. Someone else directed us down the street. "Is there anyone else in there that we should go in for?" "No" I said, "there is no one now." Teddy had left the house, I thought, and I knew that Terry and Diana were gone. I was overwhelmed with grief, not surprise, nor questions about how this could have happened, only grief. But I knew that I was not prepared to answer anyone's questions about what had happened, not then. "Was it a gas explosion?" someone asked. "Yes," I said, "It must have been." I could not think about anything but getting away to let the grief take over.

Susan Wagner, a longtime resident of the block, offered us her home, and we followed her to another set of brownstone stairs leading up to her front door. We were covered with dust and must have tracked the dirt in with us onto the light-colored carpet as we climbed another set of stairs to a second floor bedroom with an attached bath. She showed us the shower and hurriedly pulled out some of her own clothes, which she left on the bed for us. She left us in the care of a middle-aged black woman working as her maid, while she returned to the burning house to watch in fascinated horror.

I knew that in only a few minutes, when the police arrived and ascertained that we were down the block, they would come to question us. They would know fairly quickly that this was not a freak gas explosion. We showered as quickly as possible to get the worst of the grime off, before diving, still only half-dry, into our hostess's clothes. My only thought was to get away, to grieve, to avoid the lengthy questioning and incarceration that were sure to follow if I stayed, and which would prevent me from abandoning myself to the sorrow.

I couldn't pretend that I didn't know what had been going on or weave any more stories in the face of what had happened. I knew I couldn't think straight at the moment. I needed to get away. There was nothing that could be done for either Terry or Diana, I was sure of that. It never occurred to me that Teddy had still been in the house. He must have lingered for a few minutes to look over the headlines in the paper, or maybe the sports scores. Maybe some artifact on a wall had captured his incessant inquisitiveness. When they found his body, it became apparent he had been crushed under the stone stairs that led up to the main front door as he was opening the ground-floor door underneath.

Although I was fully clothed, except for shoes, when I got outside, I had no money in my pockets. My first thought was to get money for a subway token so we could get out of the neighborhood as fast as possible. Quickly, I searched through an assortment of clothes that were in the closet of the guest bedroom. Finding nothing, I entered the master bedroom next door and tried again with the clothes hanging in the closet there. This netted one token immediately. I knew we didn't have another moment to spare.

At the front door, we ran into the maid who challenged the wisdom of our leaving so soon. We were only going to the drugstore to get some medicine for our scrapes, I said, and hurried out without waiting for an answer. We walked as fast as we could without attracting attention, despite the pink patent-leather boots now on my feet, but by then, all eyes looked past us as people rushed toward the fire streaming out of the front of the building behind us. The fire trucks, already arriving, were beginning to pour water into the flames. A block away, we scrambled down the stairs into the subway, and, hoping that our gender and the color of our skin would deflect the notice of the subway clerk, the two of us went through the turnstile together on our one token. A minute later the train came and we were truly underground.

CHAPTER ELEVEN

THE UNDERGROUND YEARS

■ ■

After a couple of stops for different clothes and a little cash, we managed to get in touch with someone from the leadership collective, who arranged to meet us the next day. In a small park, we were met by two people, who talked with us separately, and then sent us each in different directions. I didn't see Kathy again for a long while. I was so disoriented I couldn't fathom the scale of what had happened. At first I could only focus on the conversation I had been having with Terry about growing into the role of being warriors. If we had just taken a little more time, I thought, if we had just slowed down.

Then, everything was like a dream. Someone met with me and helped me change the way I looked, thereby beginning a long-standing and contentious relationship with hair dye. I was sent out of New York, where my photo was on the front page of every paper. In another East Coast city, I stayed with an old friend.

There, over twenty-four hours later, I heard about Teddy. I had begun to wonder why he hadn't found a way to get in touch, but I couldn't dispel my belief that he was okay, that seeing the fire on his return from the drugstore he had simply disappeared. It hadn't occurred to me that the unidentified, crushed body they had found was his. I had assumed it was Terry's. I was still reeling from losing Terry and Diana. I couldn't even take in that I had lost this friend, as well.

When the newspaper reports confirmed Teddy's identification, and I had to begin the process of accepting this death too, I was angry at first, angry that he hadn't left the house when he said he was. The grieving for Teddy came on more slowly, as I recognized that the anger I felt was a distraction, a stage of grief; as the weeks went by it settled in with its own relentlessness.

Several members of the national leadership came and crowded into my friend's small apartment, and for a couple of days there were more discussions about the past few weeks in New York, the story of the townhouse collective. I began to get a sense that it wasn't just a matter of going too fast. We had been a bright light burning itself out in its own intensity. We had become a voice of outrage whose single-mindedness had cut us off from the movement, from reality. We had created a bubble of our own reality, and the bubble had burst.

I began to see how much we had not thought through. How could we have taken these steps based on so little knowledge? I felt completely and utterly responsible. It was all I could do to absorb the depth and breadth of my own culpability. I knew others too, many others, were also responsible, but I didn't care about that then. I let go of everything but the fact that had I thought through what was going on with more complexity, Terry, Teddy, and Diana might still be alive.

Ironically, I knew too that even though our actions had been a failure, the intensity of our anger had at last been heard throughout the country. The voice lacked grace, even coherence, but the anger was clear, along with the despair. We were in way over our heads in most respects. But on this one thing, being a voice of outrage, we would be united until the war ended.

Only years later did I realize that it was only because our actions failed, because we had sacrificed some of our own, that our anger could be heard. Had our original plans been successful, any acknowledgment of our outrage against the war would have been overshadowed by others' outrage at us, for we, too, would have inflicted chaos and hurt without a realistic plan—if one would even have been possible—to move constructively beyond our anger and the damage.

It was clear that I had been accepted now into the hallowed underground, that ultimate elite chosen by the leadership, although I was not exactly an insider. In fact, much of what I had imagined about the underground was an illusion, one of many being spun by participants at all levels as we scrambled to keep up with events, to rationalize the bizarreness of our lives.

It turned out that while some degree of planning had obviously been going on—plans to build an underground had been announced at Flint—the central leadership collective had shed many members, leaving a core of six to eight people, and was still in the midst of redefining itself. They hadn't actually worked through any comprehensive plan about anything. Each of them had processed the events of the previous six months differently, and alliances among them were still shifting. Most of the Midwest and East Coast leadership were still careening forward on the trajectory characterized by Flint. Others, led by Bernardine and Jeff, had just started to rethink the self-denial, extreme self-righteousness, and violence of the course they had set during the previous few months, culminating in Flint and then in the explosion.

A few weeks after the explosion, the remaining leadership gathered on the West Coast. As I heard the story much later, one or two in the group maintained the view that the error of the townhouse had primarily been one of technical ignorance and incompetence. Bernardine, however, had begun to imagine a different kind of underground, reasoning that clandestinity would give us the protection to be less driven, to have more space to think without the daily interactions with police, the press, and others in the movement. These conditions would allow us to develop a more measured, coherent strategy. No attention was given yet to the thinking that had gotten us into such a frenzy in the first place.

By the time of the meeting, all but two of the remaining leadership had chosen this more measured path, and even one of the two holdouts was soon convinced. The one remaining hold out, J. J., oddly given the pseudonym CW in Bill Ayers' book, *Fugitive Days*, then left the organization, where there was no longer a place for his way of thinking. At the end of the meeting, the old leadership group was dead, and while the exact composition of the new leadership would not be clear for a while, it was apparent there was no significant contention from anyone else seeking to stay the course of the townhouse group.

Meanwhile, with the sudden vulnerability created by the townhouse explosion, every collective had to secure itself away from public scrutiny or disband. Otherwise they would run the risk of interrogations, some of which would likely be violent. Only a couple of months earlier, for instance, the Chicago police had hung Weatherman Robbie Roth upside-down out a window during an apartment search. Much worse had happened to civil rights and Black Panther activists.

Probably a couple of hundred people disappeared from sight over the next weeks, failing to show up for court dates in Pittsburgh, Chicago, and New York. Some would never be contacted by the leadership and would drift for weeks and months, trying to define their own underground existence. Most, however, found their way to the leadership over the next few months.

A few days after leaving New York, I was told that I should go to the West Coast, where there was less publicity about the explosion. I knew no one out there, and was vaguely aware that if I went, I would be completely dependent on this small group of people now assuming leadership. I didn't try to participate in this decision about my future, however, because for the moment I was completely dependent on them. I couldn't seem to pull myself together to make a plan on my own. There was no longer basis for trusting any of my judgments, I thought. I flew out without incident and was driven to a safe house.

The atmosphere in the safe house was as culturally distant from the townhouse as you could get. A couple of other people lived there, and two or three more came and went regularly. It didn't appear to be a collective in the old style, but a group that came together primarily for daily routines. I had met one or two of the people during the previous summer, but the others were completely new to me. No one was particularly in a hurry to do anything.

I had no money, but food was obtained by someone, somehow, and I had no other needs. There was a stereo with headphones and lots of records—the Stones, Dylan, the Beatles, the Band, Janis Joplin, Miles Davis, Jimi Hendrix, Otis Redding, and Ike and Tina Turner. The music, at least, was familiar. Outside, the neighborhood was quiet, beautiful, and unassuming. Nearby were beautiful parks and places to walk. Nothing seemed to be expected of me. So, I let go. I finally gave in to the grief, the ache of missing those I loved, half-expecting them to walk through the door with a quart of milk at any moment. Over and over, I played the songs that were, for me, infused with Terry's nuances, closing my eyes and trying to fix the feel of his body, the texture of his hands, the wry smirk he liked to keep planted on his face. I tried to understand that they were gone. Because I had hardly known Diana, my sadness was less emotional, while I felt the absence of Teddy and Terry with every fiber of my body. Conversation swirled around me from time to time, but I would drift off to a window that looked down on the street from far away.

I had landed, it seemed, in a different world. Instead of the cold, gray asceticism of New York in March, everyone here was celebrating the life of counterculture. All of a sudden, beauty, contemplation, and pleasure were the order of the day. What about the struggle, I wondered? What about the Vietnamese? What about the embattled Panthers? What was the point of being underground?

My colleagues seemed to now think that SDS and Weatherman had, in fact, come out of youth culture, and we should acknowledge our roots and anchor ourselves within this culture. We could be underground and still have fun, still circulate among free-living young people everywhere. The hippie/youth culture movement was here to proclaim that the future was filled with hope and pleasure.

I did not feel like I had come from youth culture at all, but rather from the antinuclear and civil rights movements. It was true that my first awakenings had been in poetry, but that was the poetry of Emerson, Sandberg, Lindsay, and Whitman, gritty American poets. These were people who had explored the emerging identities of those who came to US soil looking for land and work and who were intrigued by the possibilities of democracy. I had recognized the Beat poets as part of this tradition. Of course music had infused all of my experiences, but much of its power came from its role in building our communities, from its ability to draw us from our isolation by voicing common feelings of hope and anger. Even in Washington, where we had identified with the new music and explored psychedelic drugs, we had always considered ourselves quite distinct from the hippies, who often eschewed political activism, considering it a downer. We struggled to get the hippies to attend antiwar demonstrations, especially demonstrations on racism. Some *Free Press* staffers would say to me that we needed to make politics more fun, and I would disagree, refusing to believe that all of life could or should be reduced to entertainment. I, as much as anyone, enjoyed the irreverence and creativity of SDS, but I didn't feel it was the organizers' responsibility to entertain at every event.

I remained silent, however. Because I could no longer trust my intuition or my judgment, I could not speak. As a result, this redefinition of my history in ways that didn't make sense only further disoriented me.

I kept wondering if we might have prevented the explosion if we had taken more time. Then again, I was beginning to realize, with growing discomfort, what a disaster it would have been if we had been successful. I was aware that a critique was being developed of our collective, although I was not yet aware of the particulars beyond what had already begun to emerge: We had gone off the deep end of sacrifice, armed struggle, and war. We had been into a death trip. We had given up. I couldn't argue with that.

This silence and passivity became my way of coping with the world around me for the time being. I had landed in what I thought were the elite ranks of the underground, but found it an alien world. I listened, I reflected, but I did not try to take responsibility for the coherence of the conversation or ideas around me. I took only the tiniest of initiatives, even regarding my own survival. I waited for something, someone to pull me out of it.

After a few weeks in the safe house, I roused myself enough to realize that, since I felt incapable of contributing anything, I would rather leave this unfamiliar organization for the time being and strike out on my own. The day-to-day struggles for survival would help me regain my balance. I proposed that I get a job—some menial anonymous job—and work for a while to try to collect myself. The idea was rejected. I was told that my face was too well-known, and that I would endanger the organization if I were recognized. As much as I wanted to leave the confusions of the past many months behind for a while, I did not want to jeopardize these people in any way. Nor did I want to get arrested. My picture was on a wanted poster, posted in post offices around the country; I was wanted for murder. The FBI was busy, contacting everyone in my family, I had heard, and putting pressure on those they considered to be weak links. They had my address book from raids in Chicago, and presumably had phone taps on many of those they found in there. After weeks, my photo still occasionally appeared in newspapers.

Once again I felt like my instincts were out of step with reality, that I had again almost put others at risk. Any remaining trust I had in my judgment slipped further away. As a result, I decided that I should suspend my reservations and try to get into this youth culture exploration going on all around me. I lay on the floor in the apartment and listened to music, joined small groups going to the occasional movie or free concert, and spent hours exploring the neighborhoods near the apartment on foot. Now and then I dropped acid with different groups of people, a few times with positive results, but mostly managing only to heighten my sense of disorientation and anxiety.

I also began to read and study simple manuals that explained electricity—the difference between voltage and current, what a circuit was. This was my only move out of the profound passivity that now enveloped me. I had been easily convinced that the problems in the townhouse were not primarily caused by our technical ignorance. Nonetheless, I was still driven to understand electricity, what it was and how it worked. I was helped in this endeavor by a couple of the people around who had taken physics and had played around with radios. They also wanted to understand this technology, should we use it again. They bought simple trade manuals and gave them to me, and occasionally we got together and I could ask questions. We talked about relationships between voltage, current, and resistance. We played around with simple parallel and series circuits, like those used in schools. I began to get some idea of how it all worked. I began to understand the stupidity of the simple circuit we had used in New York.

About six weeks after my arrival, Nixon announced the US bombing of Cambodia. Those of us who had been following the war closely knew that US troops and war planes had in fact been in and out of Cambodia for some time, trying to find and stop the flow of supplies and weapons down the Ho Chi Minh trail, some branches of which strayed into Cambodia. The bombing seemed to signal Nixon's intention to widen the war to involve all of Southeast Asia. The response by hundreds of thousands of students on hundreds of campuses around the country is now legendary.

The government reaction to these uprisings is also legendary. Ohio Governor James Rhodes derided Kent State student activists, already in the midst of antiwar demonstrations, saying, "They're worse than the brownshirts and the communist element and also the nightriders and the vigilantes. They're the worst type of people we harbor in America. I think we are up against the strongest, well-trained, militant, revolutionary group in America." Days later, the nervous young National Guard troops under his leadership shot and killed four young students, shocking the country.[1]

I thought of Terry, of the days and weeks he had spent at Kent, part of the gradual organizing and support of the student movement there. I wondered what he would have thought, whether he too would have been stunned and then proud of the demonstrations and of the courage and humanity of the Kent State students in the aftermath of the shootings. It was inevitable, I thought, with all the police spying, intimidation, and threats that eventually not only blacks, but whites would be killed. We had even predicted it, but it was shocking nonetheless. Shocking and profoundly sad. For the first time, students everywhere had to contend with the fact that death and injury might be the price of protest within the US. Was the movement prepared to continue in the face of these kinds of assaults on public demonstrations?

Students on campuses all over the country responded to the invasion and to the shootings at Kent State. Thirty ROTC buildings were bombed in the first week of May. Scores of other bombings hit government and corporate targets. A week after Kent, 100,000 people amassed in Washington for a peaceful demonstration, which erupted that night, with hundreds rampaging in the streets. The next day, a student at San Diego State, following the example of Buddhist priests in Vietnam, burned himself to death in protest over the war. Then on May 14, police fired into a gathering of students at Jackson State, an all-black college in Mississippi, killing two students outright and wounding twelve. Another, albeit far less massive, round of demonstrations responded.[2]

It was as if the angry frenzy that had possessed the most active campuses and Weatherman was now visible all around the country, the voice of rage coming from hundreds of thousands of young people. Oddly, I felt like I was following these events from a great distance, denied access by my fugitive status. I tried to imagine my future without the movement that had sustained me for the past several years. I could see nothing, unless there was indeed a role for an armed group, one that was careful, reasoned, and restrained.

On May 21, 1970, Bernardine Dohrn released a tape, the first communiqué of the Weather Underground, in the form of a "Declaration of a State of War," a first attempt to articulate the political outlook of the new underground. Bernardine also officially acknowledged that Terry Robbins, whose body had never been identified, was the third person killed in the townhouse explosion. "America's youth," it said, should "use our strategic position behind enemy lines to join forces in the destruction of empire.... Black people have been fighting almost alone for years. We've known that our job is to lead white kids to armed revolution." It continued, "If you want to find us, [look] in every tribe, commune, dormitory, farmhouse, barracks and townhouse where kids are making love, smoking dope and loading guns." Finally, it taunted, "[w]ithin the next fourteen days we will attack a symbol or institution of American injustice." That action was the bombing of the New York police headquarters, which followed about three weeks later. This bombing set the tone for all that would follow: the device was secured in a safe hiding place, with a timer that was set to detonate the blast during the late hours of the night. A warning call preceded the detonation, with ample time for evacuation of night security personnel. No one was seriously hurt. [3]

"A declaration of war"? What did they mean by that, I wondered. Wasn't that exactly what we had rejected in the aftermath of the townhouse? I had agreed that in the townhouse we had recklessly endangered people's safety and lives, not only our own, but even more importantly, those who might have been victims. In my own mind, that criticism applied to the Days of Rage and Flint as well. I thought we were now committed explicitly to not hurting people. But then why use the same language? Why say "[w]e've known that our job is to lead white kids to armed revolution" or "[g]uns and grass are our weapons?" If people weren't going to be hurt, then how was it war? Why guns? Were we using the word "war" like Johnson used it in his "War on Poverty?" Besides, what were we fighting for in the short run, or the long run? How can you declare war without a plan for how to conduct that war?

Here it was again, that confusion between image and reality. As theater, Weatherman's antics and images in 1969 had flashes of brilliance, geared to stimulate our imaginations. The rhetoric, however, that frequently accompanied the public actions insinuated a more serious intent. Slogans like "Bring the War Home," could be interpreted politically or militarily, but "Off the Pig," and "Pick Up the Gun" did, after all, evoke images of absolute, dualistic confrontation to the death. The Days of Rage and the Flint convention had been the quintessential manifestations of this ill-conceived mixture of seriousness and theater.

As Weatherman transformed into the Weather Underground, this confusion only intensified. All of us had become convinced that moral honesty somehow demanded greater militancy, but what did that mean, and how would it increase our ability to change policy? Some continued to identify with the idea that we were something like the French resistance or a military unit whittling away at US armed strength from the inside. Others imagined the Weather Underground as a glamorous and sexy band of outlaws, more believable than the official pundits, and even lovable, as a source of information and analysis. By winning the battle of credibility, and coolness, they hoped to win the masses to the idea of revolution, however vague the concept remained.

I remained inclined to the first group, and the Declaration of War encouraged me to imagine scenarios drawn from the pages of Lin Piao and General Giap. I could see, however, that those who wrote the statement didn't seem to be actually preparing for war. In fact, I had seen a lot more grass than guns in my first few months underground. I now see that neither of these two visions—Weatherman as the leading military cadre or Weatherman as iconic band of rebels—could quite separate itself from the other enough to allow us to even realize that we were coming from such drastically different places. Each vision was attracted to and needed the other to justify the illogic of its path. As a result, both inclinations continued to coexist albeit in increasing tension with each other. I was primarily attracted to Weatherman's promise to take up militancy and then arms to support a black movement then under attack. Had I really looked at the prognosis of this strategy, I might have joined those who felt powerless to stem the ongoing attacks. The romantic rendition of the "war," however, was distracting. Likewise, those who were driven by the vision of a countercultural upheaval used the language of armed struggle to convince themselves they had credentials to lead.

My life continued in the same amorphous state of suspension for the next couple of months. I spent enormous amounts of time alone. Others in the underground helped Timothy Leary escape from prison, an action that made perfect sense in the context of spinning the image of cool. The bravado was appealing, even though Leary did much of the heavy lifting for the actual escape by himself.

In late summer, it was suggested that I move to a small apartment that someone else was vacating and that was completely empty except for a piece of foam on the floor and an old kitchen table and chair. The kitchen had a few dishes and old pots and pans. I moved there alone, but was soon joined by another member who was in transition for a few weeks, and then a different one for another few weeks with a stretch in between. The ensuing friendships were suffused with a kind of dreaminess caused by our complete ignorance of where each came from or what relationship each had to the organization; we provided a kind of tender comfort to one another in the midst of our confusion. We did not, however, talk substantively about the political life of the organization, fearing to violate the need-to-know rule.

As limited as they were, however, these were among the only contacts I had with people who knew who I was. While some in the Weather

Underground found ways to establish contact with some members of their family, I had no desire to put my family in further jeopardy. My sisters, I'd heard, were already being harassed by the FBI. Besides, I had no idea how I could establish a relationship with my parents again, even without security restraints. For the time being, I was relieved to be free of the tensions.

I was not the only one who responded to the organization with this kind of creeping passivity. As a result of the need-to-know principle, only the leadership moved from one collective to another. They knew the size and scope of the organization, who did the actions, what others were thinking. The central leadership digested all this information from a variety of sources and divulged what they thought was politically important. As a result, only they could facilitate discussions about the organization's program and direction.

Those in leadership were confused and frustrated by this epidemic of passivity. They were trying to devise ways of structuring the organization to maximize local initiative while maintaining control of information, public declarations and actions. They wanted people to find their own ways of living and supporting themselves, as well as ways of working together in small collectives. They seemed puzzled by little resentments that soon began to surface, especially after the first six months of stabilization.

It appears now that they didn't understand how that kind of organization encouraged passivity by punishing speculation and initiative. It also placed a premium on having a special, privileged relationship with those in power. By working or hanging out with the leadership, you began to have access to additional information. Without a sense of the bigger picture, it was hard to get oriented or be self-activated. It was hard to have an opinion about things when there was so little access to information about what we were doing, who was involved, or what else was going on in the movement.

Throwing members onto their own financial reserves acerbated existing social divisions and gave a subtle power to those able and willing to pursue people with money. With little clarity about what the organization's purpose or future was at this point, I could not find the legitimacy to go to anyone outside the organization to ask for money. Besides, in my case, my movements were strictly limited by the leadership for the first couple of years. With more access to money, one had more mobility, and access to private and public conversations. Those of us without resources were dependent on the political taste of members who had money, to keep up with the broad strokes of what was happening in the movement. Some, myself included, gave in to the sustained isolation, and focused exclusively on the leadership for access to information.

Occasionally, I tried to engage myself more with the people I had met from the other apartment. On those days, we prowled the coast in old cars, took acid trips in beautiful state parks, and listened to music. I enjoyed these outings, as I had loved my brief explorations of the Midwest and the South, although I continued to be mystified by what they had to do with making revolution. Occasionally someone from the leadership came by, bearing new enthusiasms about some music or a book of poems. At that time they had discovered the poets of Broadside Press, like Sonia Sanchez and Don Lee, and I, like many Weathermen, was introduced to a wonderful, rich world of contemporary black poetry.

Every so often, my study of electricity continued, as I tried to follow the reasoning of those who knew more than me and who were trying to devise a safer circuit, one that would protect as much as possible against stray current during the making and transport of devices. While I never heard any official sanction of this activity, I never heard any disapproval either. When a safer circuit was devised, I applied myself to learn how it worked and how to make it. I was determined that if, indeed, we needed to form an armed group, women would be represented. Also, I suspected that in the aftermath of the townhouse explosion, I was seen as incompetent by some in the leadership. I didn't think that was either accurate or fair. I had been politically wrong and personally irresponsible, like a great many others in Weatherman, but I did not accept being considered incompetent. I wanted the chance to prove otherwise.

US prisons began to be a major focus of activity in the movement as a whole because so many people were being sentenced to long terms, both for petty crimes and for political offenses, including draft and military resistance. Young people in prison, many without an education, serving years on relatively minor convictions, had begun to read, talk, and become political. This trend had started initially with members of the Nation of Islam that, inside the prisons, had for years been encouraging prisoners to learn to read, to study history, and to develop an internal code of behavior. More prisoners had begun to stand up for their rights. Just as on the outside, these activists started to face harassment, but inside, they were much more isolated and vulnerable to all kinds of attacks.

In California, young black men were becoming the majority of prisoners, and one, W. L. Nolan, was introducing other black prisoners, including George Jackson, to books on history, politics, and revolution. These young men had begun to agitate within prisons for minimal rights, especially the right to self-defense against racist white gangs, and the right to communicate freely with people on the outside. In 1968, Nolan, Jackson, and others had set up a self-defense organization inside, through which they became acquainted with Black Panther activists doing the same on the outside.

In January 1969, the prison transferred Jackson and Nolan, in retaliation for their political work, to Soledad Prison, a haven of racist violence. Within days, guards sent Jackson and Nolan into the exercise yard with a mixed group of prisoners where they were attacked by white prisoners almost immediately. During the ensuing fight, a guard shot and killed Nolan. Weeks later, soon after the local grand jury ruled the killing a justifiable homicide, a guard was thrown off a high tier of the prison and killed. With no physical evidence, Jackson and two others were charged with the killing. Soon thereafter, supporters on the outside, especially attorney Faye Stender, helped release a book of Jackson's eloquent prison writings, catapulting him and the case, known as the Soledad Brothers, to national attention.

In August 1970, Jonathan Jackson, George Jackson's younger brother, charged into a courtroom appearance of one of the Soledad prisoners. Convinced that the courts would never let his brother George out of prison, Jackson put a shotgun to the head of the presiding judge. He demanded his brother's freedom in exchange for the judge's freedom. In the fusillade of police gunfire that followed, he and the judge were killed along with two of the three inmates on trial.

Weatherman retaliated against this police assault by placing a bomb in the bathroom of the Marin County Courthouse, a beautiful building designed by Frank Lloyd Wright, where the shoot-out had occurred. Timed to go off at night and prefaced with a warning call, the bomb blew out the bathroom and damaged several surrounding rooms. I had argued to be allowed to participate in the action. Despite some misgivings from those who would have preferred to exclude me because of my association with the townhouse explosion, I joined the team. The success of the action—no one was hurt and the issue of prisons was put squarely in the public's eye for another moment—went a long way to assuring me and others that indeed I was as competent as the next person, under reasonable circumstances. In October, the organization issued a statement titled "Fall Offensive" and carried out two actions on the East Coast, one of which was a bombing of a courthouse in New York, in support of local prison uprisings.

In November, the leadership circulated a document that would be made public a few weeks later under the title "New Morning—Changing Weather." At the beginning, the statement put out the official analysis of what had gone wrong in the townhouse explosion, describing the "military error," the "tendency to consider only bombings or picking up the gun as revolutionary, with the glorification of the heavier the better."[4] I agreed that this was a good way to describe our mistake, and I agreed that I and everyone else in the townhouse leadership collective had made it.

I was taken aback, however, that the statement laid the blame for this way of thinking solely or primarily on the townhouse collective. What about the frenzy of confrontation and chaos that had been building throughout 1968 and 1969, clearly delineated at Columbia and amplified by some at the Chicago democratic convention demonstrations? What about the Days of Rage promoted by most of those on the Weather Bureau? What about the Cleveland conference, where members of the Weather Bureau had played such a pivotal role? What about the arrests of another leading member for possession of a gun in Chicago? Most importantly, what about Flint, dubbed "the war council," and the relentless rhetoric about going to war, about "offing the pig"? It seemed to me that all of these events helped pave the way to the elevation of armed struggle as the only kind of struggle. There was still no reckoning, no accountability for any of this, either internally or in the public eye.

I knew that I had been borne along, however willingly, in the center of a swiftly moving current generated by many people and factors. Having been in the townhouse collective, I bore particular responsibility. Nonetheless, those of us in the townhouse only shaped that one particular escalation, however dramatic it was. It wasn't that I thought the national leadership deserved the blame, but that we all did. An analysis of what had gone wrong required so much more than a simple pointing of fingers. Everyone in Weatherman had been drawn to it in some way, and certainly everyone in leadership had contributed heavily to the development of those politics.

I was willing to accept more blame than anyone else alive for the particulars because I had been there, I was part of it and I didn't stop it, but the story of my personal responsibility in no way did justice to the larger, far more important questions. Nor did I think that Terry, despite his intensity and despair, was any more responsible than anyone else, even though he might have played a focusing role at the end.

Despite my dismay, and resentment, however, I still felt in no condition to speak up or contribute to the discussion. I was glad that the criticism of militarism had been articulated clearly. The townhouse explosion had narrowly prevented a great number of other losses, not just by our organization but by the hundreds of other young people, many of whom had preceded us into the use of dynamite and who were just as angry and desperate to voice that outrage. We needed to be clear about the mistake.

The ongoing use of inflammatory language, however, continued to muddy the water. Were we renouncing armed attacks on people or not? Would we only do symbolic bombings of buildings from now on? "New Morning" asserted that "white youth of Babylon will resort to force to bring down imperialism." We were sorely in need of a model to bring down imperialism. We still believed that the future of global politics would revolve around "two, three, many Vietnams," but what would that look like here? Spontaneous insurrection had failed in 1969, and, while popular discontent had erupted on its own in 1970, it was not sustained. Like the 1968 uprisings in France, the moment had passed, and everyone had returned to concentrate on specific issues. If not popular insurrection, then what?

To fully reconsider that early thinking we would have had to examine our beliefs about the way change happens, look at the match between the structure and culture of the organization and its goals, and agree on the role of leadership. In fact, "New Morning" was silent on the questions of democracy, organization, and leadership as they pertained to choices already made by Weatherman so far. "New Morning" only asserted that the Weather Underground Organization (WUO), as we now called ourselves, had organized itself into collectives and families, deeply rooted in youth culture, and that "leaders who respect their tribe are followed freely and with love." This inspirational description did not match the reality I knew, nor did it wrestle with any of the problems we were grappling with, like the stultifying effects of the need-to-know principle. It did, however, indicate a change of organizational culture from the obsessive collectives of 1969 and early 1970. Clearly, a critical look at what had happened required a sense of organizational and personal accountability that was way beyond us and most other organizations of the times.

Most of the rest of "New Morning" reaffirmed the value of the kinds of education and organizing work that SDS had done in the 60s. Without noting the irony, "New Morning" championed the work of those who had rejected Weatherman and other political-party–building organizations to work on new kinds of alternative institutions such as, schools, farms, and health and research centers. The statement did not explain what relationship the underground might have to this work or why it was the province of the underground to take on the encouragement of the mass movement. A serious envisioning of how society could be organized differently was not yet on the agenda.

After "New Morning," I continued in my small apartment. The winter was long, cold, and wet. Without any cash, I was tied to the outer reaches of my walks, and the cold and wet restricted those. I spent days in silence, reading and living on Bisquick biscuits. Political conversations happened only informally, when leadership folks came by. They continued to bring recent books or articles they had read, then mostly histories. I devoured these books on the history of Africa, China, and South America, and the repeated popular uprisings as the poor strove to gain control over their lives. I read about the long and complex history of the fight for the eight-hour day, and for safety laws for mines and factories, and about the exploitation of the vast natural resources of North America beneath the ground, in the trees and the prairies. I read DuBois on black reconstruction and other books on the history of black suffering and resistance in North America. I read all of Mari Sandoz, who wrote about the Great Plains and the Native Americans, and that led me to other reading about Native American history. A year later, I briefly had access to a large university library, and I ferreted out the journals of Mayflower voyagers, shocked to discover their open advocacy of using alcohol to subdue the Indians. I regularly read the output of Detroit's Blackside Press.

This was the first time as an adult I had actually had time to read with this kind of sustained coherence. I was fascinated but humbled by how little I knew about the history of the United States, despite the fact that I had minored in American Studies in college. While I learned about history, however, my isolation from the movement was growing. With only limited access to the ongoing news, I missed out on many major developments, especially those concerning women. I had little idea what groups were evolving or what major topics were under discussion.

I harbored some resentment against those in leadership for my isolation and poverty, especially when I picked up the odd clue here and there that they were facing no such deprivations. Nonetheless, almost a year after the townhouse, I had not yet put together a way to approach my new reality. I had survived adolescence by elevating suffering to a quasispiritual level, *Jane Eyre* being a favorite book. By 1971 I had again elevated suffering as an experience that built character and that could possibly cleanse and purify me from the mistakes of the past. Endurance became a manifestation of that strength, strength that I badly needed. This experience was similar to what others have gone through after joining religious cults of all kinds.

The yearning for the comfort of easy solutions leaves one utterly dependent on the intellectual and/or spiritual constructs of the authors of those solutions. Besides, I was still profoundly moved by the arguments in the statements that accompanied our actions, that white revolutionaries had to support and live up to the level of outrage and militancy evidenced by some black activists, even if we didn't agree on particular tactics. This focus on the level of militancy deflected attention from the particulars of the political purposes of militancy, details I was willing to shunt to the side, lacking a broader, rigorous conversation about social change. Given the toll on black leadership, our continued militancy seemed the least that we could do.

I now see that I might have framed more useful questions. Was the escalating militancy of both black groups and white groups the most effective response to the all-out attack on black leadership? Given the assaults on black initiative and leadership for the past three hundred years, was matching their risks and suffering, which was how I saw it, the most principled way to expose or deflect or end those assaults? How were the issues of urban poverty being addressed by any of us? Was there really no solution, even in the short run, other than revolution, even if we knew what that meant? Finally, what kinds of contributions could and should women make to change, and how was my experience helping me figure that out? Was it all-important that women learn to become armed fighters, or were we just gaining access to another political model cooked up by men?

The next spring I was again invited to move into an apartment with several others from the earlier group. We worked together on some projects to obtain or make identification, and to obtain a couple of vehicles and other supplies. I and a couple of others attempted to create a substitute for butyric acid, a compound that smells like rotten eggs, experimenting in unused woodlands nearby. I was trying to figure out how to make an efficient stink bomb from household chemicals or ones you could buy in the normal course of things from a chemical distributor. I thought these kinds of devices offered the opportunity for political clarity without the threat of physical violence. I did not, however, know enough chemistry to be even minimally successful.

My tenure with the collective was short-lived, however, because one breach in security at the top compromised a car, and a paper trail led to the apartment we were living in. Within hours the organization scattered. Once again I was off on my own for almost half a year in an entirely new city, this time joined by four and sometimes five others, one of whom I had actually known in years past in SDS. These stints away from the organization were defined by waiting, waiting to be contacted, waiting to help out again with another action. I wanted more chances to hone the skills and confidence required not only to build the devices but to deliver them. With both the political and personal stakes seemingly so high, I had an urgent need to explore all the dimensions demanded of a fighter. In the meantime, most everyone in my group except me had jobs and a life that was fairly ordinary, except for our isolation. I still was not allowed to work, and, by now, those with me were understandably somewhat resentful that I could not chip in to our minimal budget.

In the late summer of 1971, a series of guard attacks on prison inmates who were protesting for basic, humane conditions within the prisons caused the organization to remobilize. First, in California, George Jackson was shot and killed by a high-powered rifle while he was in the yard at San Quentin, allegedly trying to escape. This killing closely fit the pattern of the killings of other black leaders who had exercised broad and effective leadership, including Malcolm X, Dr. King, and Fred Hampton. Today, it is hard to look at this pattern without recalling the COINTELPRO mandate to "prevent the rise of a messiah" in the black community.

Around the country, word of Jackson's death spread quickly among inmates, many of whom organized restrained protests as a way to memorialize him. At Attica Correctional Facility, a massive medieval-looking fortress near Buffalo, New York, hundreds of inmates more or less spontaneously refused to either eat or talk during breakfast, so that instead of the normal din, the huge mess hall was completely silent. The inmates' ability to organize this level of unity and to maintain such discipline terrified the guards. A few days later, during a routine incident in one of the exercise yards, the guards overreacted, placing some inmates in solitary confinement. The next morning, in reaction to that incident, hundreds of prisoners refused to go in their cells. Soon after, inmates spontaneously seized control of major intersections within the prison, and hundreds of others took over one of the four large yards, taking a number of guards hostage. One guard died from wounds received during the takeover.

The protesters drew up a list of demands on prison conditions, such as the right to have toilet paper, and demanded negotiations. After five days of talks, the governor of New York ordered New York state troopers to storm the prison in the predawn hours. In the process, they shot and killed ten of the hostages and twenty-nine inmates, including the best-known spokesperson, L. D. Barkley, and activist, Sam Melville, who were intentionally targeted.

In response to Jackson's death, the WUO set off two small devices, one in a Department of Corrections facility in Sacramento and another outside the Bay Area branch office. In response to the massacre of inmates at Attica, the organization set off a device in a New York State Department of Corrections facility in Albany. As with many of the WUO actions, the targeting of the departments of corrections gave a moment of satisfaction to thousands of people who were outraged by more assassinations of young, articulate black men. At the same time, thousands gathered in legal demonstrations across the country. The Harlem funeral of many of the Attica victims was attended by tens of thousands, as marchers carried the coffins through the streets.

While my life in the organization was fraught with tension and confusion, these attacks on inmates who were trying to protest in any way they could against medieval prison conditions erased any doubts I had about whether I should or could continue to find a place for myself in the organization. I had to. I felt like our small actions gave a wider voice to the anger felt by tens of thousands of people at this callous, wasteful, and inhumane trashing of human lives.

I continued the pattern of periods of time connected to the organization interspersed with weeks or months on my own, until 1974. I had finally been given permission to work, and quickly found a waitressing job at a small family-run ethnic restaurant. This allowed me to finally gain some independence. During those first four years underground, the leadership and collectives had focused on two main tasks. First, we carried out the series of symbolic bombings, pointing the finger at those responsible for major problems faced by the public.[5] Second, we learned how to survive, to elude the police and to support ourselves (although there were always considerable differences among members in the comfort level of that survival—some had the cash to eat out, go to concerts, travel, and buy nice furnishings for their apartments, while others made due with furniture found on the streets and kept the spaghetti pot simmering at home).

By the end of 1973, the movement was undergoing a vast transformation. The energy that had finally gained momentum in the 50s and had been building since the civil rights movement crescendoed in 1970-71. Millions were at least vaguely aware of the critical problems with the prevailing model of development in the United States. Watergate and its aftermath had publicly confirmed much of what we had suspected about the government's attempts to crush the opposition, about their attempts to undermine the electoral process that the United States boasted about to the world. As young people dispersed, sobered by the excesses of Altamont and the growing sectarian divisions within the movement, the superficial clarity of the 60s evaporated quickly. The battles around discrimination still had to be fought industry by industry, school by school. Internal stresses in the movement that had always been there demanded attention, everything from drug use, exhaustion, and organizational incoherence to the desire of maturing movement participants for families and regular income. We, as much as anyone else in society, had to explore the meanings and impact of changing views on identity, especially around race, ethnicity, and gender.

While activists sobered, the profound shift in values and aspirations continued to take root in thousands of ways. Soon there were young people working on women's issues; civil rights; human rights; the environment; support for labor organizing; gay and lesbian rights; several different national liberation struggles; integration struggles; black nationalist struggles; Puerto Rican independence; Native American rights; support for GIs, veterans, deserters, and draft resistors; criminal justice and prison issues; rights for disabled people; education and health care; alternative businesses; organic agriculture; and on and on. Becoming a knowledgeable participant and innovator in any field of work takes years, and tens of thousands of 60s activists dug in to do the work.

Weatherman, however, found it hard to switch gears. The lure of easy, Leninist solutions was still strong; the lack of clarity about what the future might hold as the movement diversified and changed forms was too unsettling. Still, WUO members and supporters had to wonder how symbolic bombings fit into the multitude of organizations continuing to work for progressive social change. While the leadership began to think about this, their lack of an honest assessment of the past hobbled their imagination and led to a solution that reflected their isolation from the breadth of the movement. Encouraged by the positive response to the many conversations they had had about the books and articles they had circulated, Weatherman's leadership hatched the idea of writing a book summarizing their analysis of the world and of US history. From this analysis, they would map out a strategy for future activism, implicitly setting themselves up as leaders of that movement.

By late 1973, drafts of the book were circulating among the membership. In *Prairie Fire*, as the book was titled, the WUO held on to the model of change that seemed so promising in the late 60s: "two, three, many Vietnams." Leadership for this change in the United States, they asserted, would be provided by a Marxist-Leninist party. Weatherman, it was implied, might be the embryonic form of this party.

I found *Prairie Fire* to be dazzling. The scope of the analysis was broad, and I cheered the international framing of US history and the continued emphasis on the issue of race. I, too, held out hope for a remobilized movement that looked like the one we had known, inspired if not led by some new kind of organization, much in the way SDS had influenced activists. I didn't know of any other organization that was trying to pull the movement back together. (In fact, all of the Marxist-Leninist formations of the time saw this as their task.)

I didn't question the purpose of pulling it back together or wonder whether the vast spread and diversification of work was in fact the best thing that could be happening. The Marxist-Leninist vision of WUO leadership seemed bold and grandiose, making it easy to let go of my nascent questions. They had answered the biggest question about the role of the underground by implying that our role was to lead the movement; our credentials: a comprehensive analysis, *Prairie Fire*, and our track record of armed actions. I spent hours and days in meetings in which the leadership talked about how they imagined the book could lead the movement. I drank endless cups of coffee and smoked packs of cigarettes as I tried to make sense of these plans. I could understand the bid for legitimacy, but exactly what form was our leadership to take? What did we have to contribute?

I made a renewed commitment to accept the view of reality put forward by the leadership, my years of isolation and intellectual passivity leaving me ignorant of any other reality. I began again to try to have some input into the development of a strategy. Organizing was something I knew about. I wanted in to the circles of power in the organization and to secure my position. I really wanted to believe that they, we, had it all figured out.

WUO members designed and printed the book in an underground print shop. It came out in July 1974. Clandestine deliveries were made to selected bookshops and organizations. The book was then reprinted in public editions. In 1975, WUO also published a book of poems written by women members and supporters. I contributed one poem , "Women's Lament," that ends:

> Let us wail at the gates of the White House
> night and day
> Let us wail at air force and navy bases
> to give solace to young men who are resisting
> and to send in the echoes of the ages
> to arrogant men who think
> they are the torch bearers of "civilization."

And let us wail at the homes of the strategists
who masquerade
as ordinary citizens, determining the values
by which we live.

These men
must not conduct war in peace.
Our grieving
will become a cancer within ourselves
if we do not turn it into
vengeance.[6]

It was followed by a quarterly magazine called *Osawatomie*, named after the site in Kansas where John Brown's army had fought its first open battle against supporters of slavery. It was published and distributed in the same way as the book. The quarterly, however, took up issues more directly related to work that was being done in public organizations without explicitly revealing that aboveground members of the WUO participated in those organizations and shared information with WUO leaders. The magazine became one way the WUO argued for its views regarding the correct agenda for these public organizations.

During this period I was told that Weatherman was making a movie with Emile de Antonio, Haskell Wexler, and Mary Lampson, and that the leadership wanted me to participate. Since I was hardly in a leadership role in the WUO, I knew I was only being asked to be in a cameo appearance so that my history, my many years with SDS, ERAP, and *New Left Notes*, contributed to the historical depth of the Weather Underground, as many of the organization's known figures had only joined SDS late in the 60s. I was especially well-known as a survivor of the townhouse explosion. By this point, I was glad that at last I was getting some recognition from WUO leadership for my past role in the movement, and I thought the film presented an opportunity for me to again assert myself as a player in the direction of things.

On the way to the film shoot, we heard on the car radio that troops from the Provisional Revolutionary Government of South Vietnam had overrun Saigon, and that the last remaining US troops were scrambling aboard helicopters from the roof of the US embassy. The war was over. The National Liberation Front had won. The Vietnamese independence forces had not won a decisive military victory against the US as they had at Dien Bien Phu against the French. Instead, they outlasted the US. Like George Washington in the war against King George, they merely had to survive, and to retain the support and involvement of a sizable majority of the people until the will and/or resources of the invaders faltered. The rapid growth of the GI movement, along with the extensive use of drugs to numb the horrors that GIs faced, had finally and decisively eroded the US's ability to fight. It was astonishing. While some of my worst fears had come true—the deaths of millions of Vietnamese and the saturation of their environment with unexploded bombs and millions of tons of cancer-causing chemical pollutants—some of the other fears had not come to pass. Most notably, Nixon had not used nuclear weapons as he had threatened. Despite the fact that we had been saying since 1968 that the Vietnamese would win, I couldn't believe that it had actually happened. I was jubilant.

The film shoot lasted only a few days. I said my piece about the townhouse but otherwise remained unable to connect to the conversation. (In viewing the film recently, I was struck by how evident my intellectual paralysis was.) I did, however, listen, and in the course of conversations it became clearer to me that the leadership saw the film as one part of their strategy to introduce themselves to a larger public as prospective leaders of the movement. Soon thereafter, they led discussions in the collectives about taking the organization public. As the only member with serious charges, I wondered what that would mean for me, but I assumed that whatever happened, there would be a need for a clandestine organization to be part of it.

In the coming months, we thrashed through the analysis in *Prairie Fire* during more endless meetings. I learned more about the way the WUO was working with its secret aboveground members to encourage specific agendas in public organizations. I thought it ironic that it was just this kind of manipulation from afar that so distressed us about the Progressive Labor Party (PL) in 1969. Perhaps we had been wrong to object to that aspect of PL, I concluded, and instead should have understood that the fight was about PL's analysis of the world, not their view of leadership. Others confirmed this observation, though without any broader sense of irony.

By mid-1975, I had entered the mainstream of the organization. I worked on an article about prisons for the magazine. I spent hours in the library, learning about the history of prisons, trying to find out about the ebb and flow of the prison population over the years, in different parts of the country. I was stunned at how many people were incarcerated—at that time over a million. It was hard to get statistics on the racial composition of the jail/prison population, but it was clear that black citizens were disproportionately represented. That had always been the case, especially where prison labor was important to the local economy.

My article noted that prison conditions ate away at the humanity of those imprisoned, assuming that once in the system, men (it was mostly men, then) would stay for life, either continuously, or through repeat offenses, despite the fact that most black youth were initially imprisoned for minor offenses that many whites, especially those with education or money could avoid. The article appeared in an issue that emphasized a traditional Marxist-Leninist analysis of society and revolution, framing every article within the context of a struggle between the working class and ruling class. As a result, my article too used undigested Marxist rhetoric and an oversimplified framework that distorted many of the realities of the exploding prison population, neglecting especially the centrality of race.

The fact that our society is structured in a way that we now maintain millions of men and women in painful, degrading circumstances that are geared to wound if not deform the human spirit, should raise real questions for all of us. We all need to take responsibility for the fact that there are ways our society malfunctions—families, schools, economic system, spiritual life—generating thousands of angry, dispirited youth in both the smallest hamlets and the largest cities of the country, who are then scarred by this criminal justice system. We must especially look at the particular role that prisons have played in the eras of slavery, lynching, and legalized discrimination, and continue to play in our own era, when racist habits of mind persist and the legacy of past damages still wreaks havoc in some communities. While the article gave a lot of facts and figures, it did little to focus these big issues.

Over the next year, I was also assigned to meet with people who participated in public organizations of one kind or another and who were supporters of the WUO. I was to convey to them the opinion of the WUO. Sometimes I was assigned to raise money, and the leadership introduced me to people who had volunteered to donate. These meetings always seemed awkward and difficult, as I was not seeking to learn from what others were doing, about which I knew very little, but rather to impose a direction on them. Since the WUO's intentions were not always clear to me, despite long hours of discussion, I often felt insecure in implementing my tasks. I was intent on doing my best, however, so I could maintain my newfound position as a central player in the WUO.

By 1976, a variety of people associated with the WUO, especially those with close ties to public organizations, began to challenge the underground leadership and question both our strategy and our legitimacy as leaders. Too many times, the WUO had tried to bully people into agreement without listening carefully to all sides. By then, WUO members and supporters embraced a wide range of beliefs about what it meant to work for a more just and peaceful world. The primitive and hierarchical structure of the organization left it unable to manage any kind of accountable, democratic discussion about these differences, either within its ranks or with allies in other organizations. Instead, members were expected to go along with the leadership decisions on policy. With the end of the war, the old consensus that there was a necessity for unity, even at a high cost, quickly wore thin. Without this kind of unity, however, no clandestine organization can survive for long.

In early 1976, like a house of cards, the organization disintegrated rapidly, amid sometimes acrimonious discussions about sorting out recent events. Individuals without criminal charges drifted off, others attempted to form new organizations, both public and secret. It was time for us, too, to join the long-term work of rethinking the complexities of social change in the context of concrete work. Everyone, then, was on their own. What endured among all of Weatherman's members was a continued commitment to work for peace, justice, and change, and a commitment to one another. Despite the mistakes and the rancor, we had all tried the best we could to realize our fullest humanity during times of terror and great upheaval.

CHAPTER TWELVE

REENTRY

■ ■

When I had acquiesced to the WUO's pretentious plans to lead the movement, I had once again gone along with things that had not sat right with me. Once again, I knew something was fundamentally flawed about the way I was making decisions about my life and beliefs. I needed time to rethink. I wanted to go off by myself, get a job, and try to figure it all out. It was clear to me that I was in no shape to do any political movement any good until I found myself on more solid ground. This time around, at least I knew something about how to function as a fugitive and felt confident I could survive on my own. I was eager to do so.

I was thirty-three years old, and another concern was weighing on me. I had sacrificed my desire to have children to work for the movement. Now, I realized, was my chance. I had been half-heartedly trying to build a relationship with someone in the organization for the past year, and was at the time living with him. With the organization's disintegration, however, I realized quickly that only the constraints of the underground had made either one of us want to be together. With those constraints lifted, I was eager to move on. I hoped that my partner and I would be able to remain friends, however, and I had no desire to get into another relationship until I had sorted myself out. I decided that I wanted to get pregnant before I went off on my own, even though I knew that the prospect of having and raising a child on my own was daunting under the circumstances.

I also knew that my body was in no shape to harbor a healthy child. For fifteen years I had been subsisting on oatmeal, candy, doughnuts, coffee, the occasional egg or grilled cheese sandwich, and red wine and bourbon. And through it all I smoked. So I decided to take three months to eat right, take prenatal vitamins, and try to cut down on the cigarettes to prepare my body. I still had little money, but now I paid attention to maximizing the nutritional value for my dollar. Someone had a copy of Adele Davis's *Eat Right to Keep Fit* and Frances Moore Lappé's *Diet for a Small Planet*, and I read them avidly. They completely changed my attitude and understanding of food. At the end of the three months of preparation, with the reluctant consent of my partner, who also assumed the relationship would soon end, I was pregnant.

Meanwhile, the organization dissolved, in a haze of accusations and recriminations. I was unable to discern any truths or falsehoods by that point. I didn't even try. I agreed to every criticism, and thought only about how to extricate myself. It took me over a year before I was able to set myself up apart from both organization and relationship, until I was independent of everything from the past. Then I could begin to reconstruct my psychological center and independence. After more than six years with WUO, I finally stepped out of a life fraught with confusing crosscurrents. I felt an immeasurable sense of relief, even though I was afraid. I was also the sole support for a four-month old baby, named after blues singer Bessie Smith. Our lives lay ahead of us. In some ways, the situation looked bleak, but I was ready to survive.

I had considered what kind of community would be supportive to a single mother with few resources. I remembered the warmth and supportiveness of the Southern black culture in Cambridge and Chester, and what I had heard about in SNCC and other Southern groups. I remembered too the rich sense of humor that infused so many interactions. I knew I needed to live in a community with a sense of neighborliness, where neither my poverty nor single parenting would be judged or held against me. I moved to an urban neighborhood dominated by first-generation immigrants from the South. Rents were inexpensive, and I found a part-time job. Just a few blocks from my small but comfortable two-room apartment, I found a wonderful day-care provider, Mrs. Korn. There, my daughter was the youngest and the only white child.

After Bess had a few weeks to adjust, I found a full-time job, earning minimum wage. Half of my weekly paycheck went to the day care while most of the rest went to rent, electricity, and bus fare. I was left with $20.00

or so for everything else for the week. I spent most of that on food, saving only enough for the laundromat on Saturdays. Disposable diapers were out of the question, and I rejected their environmental cost in any case. When I didn't have enough money to wash the cloth diapers on Saturdays, I washed them in the tub. Since I was nursing, my other expenses for Bessie were minimal. I ground up the food I cooked for myself and sent a little along to day care with her each day. I found out later that Mrs. Korn and I did not see eye to eye on the food question, and she was liberally supplementing my vegetarian fare with grits, sausage, and ice cream.

I let our differences over food slide, however, because in every other respect this was an ideal setting. Mrs. Korn's whole family helped with the children, including Mr. Korn and their high-school–age daughter. The house was filled with warmth and laughter. Bess was in a playpen in the living room, surrounded by five or six other children who spent the day playing, or learning letters and colors and having bible lessons. They had a big backyard and often spent time outside. During the winter, Mrs. Korn's daughter started bringing Bess to the afternoon basketball games at her high school, filling my daughter's days with love, stimulation, and a sense of being part of a community.

The daily routine of my job was steadying. I was intrigued by learning how to parse the personal dynamics on the job. Was my boss a friend or foe? Who were my coworkers, and what were their own stories? I became friends with a young woman who had lost custody of her daughter because of her drinking. Although she had been sober for a year, she had still not won back visitation rights. She went out of her way to cover my work for me on the rare occasion when I was late because of some mishap with Bess. On another job, my coworker, who was white, had married into a Mexican family and introduced me to a mixed cultural community that was new to me.

Race often played a role in defining these relationships. There were always expectations that came with my skin color. Once, when I was working at a restaurant-supply company for several months, I was asked to work with a woman who selected the suppliers for each order. She had been feuding with a young black woman in the accounting department, with whom she was required to engage in regular transactions. I could tell that she assumed I would side with her and back her up in these feuds. When I figured out a simple extra step that would resolve the conflicts, she surprised me by being resentful, as if my validation of *both* sides of the issue was a betrayal of some sort of racial loyalty.

I became good friends with Bernice, a young woman in accounting. I was developing an interest in the problem of foster children, and she often shared stories about her mom, who was an unofficial foster mother. Most of her kids came from single moms, who paid a small amount to leave the children there six days a week. Occasionally, she kept small children for months without pay if the mom disappeared, because she knew if she turned the child over to social services the mother might never get another chance to raise her kids. One day in January, Bernice took me aside at lunch and told me that the company had gotten a notice from the IRS that there was something wrong with my social security number. Bernice said she could fix it until the following January, if I wanted her to do that. I said I'd be grateful. She never asked anything further.

I shared little about myself, even with the friends I made. One advantage of making up my résumé was that I could invent any history and persona I wanted. I could meet my coworkers as if we had relatively similar backgrounds. I was a single mom, recently arrived in the city, and without family nearby. Some of my coworkers concluded certain things from my evasiveness. I had possibly come from an abusive relationship I didn't want to talk about, or, perhaps, I had gotten myself tangled up in bad debt and was trying to start over with creditors on my heels. They had known people in these situations, and tended to be sympathetic, respecting my privacy. I was clearly trying to get my life together and they respected that.

It was hard to set up and maintain the different identities that separated the parts of my life. I lived with the anxiety that I would be recognized. Most terrifying was the thought that I would be discovered, and the police would come storming in in the middle of the night and take Bess away. I used a different name and address at work than the one where I lived, so my neighbors in the building didn't know exactly where I worked. Even

Mrs. Korn, while she knew my work number, didn't know exactly where I lived. On the rare occasion that I visited my coworkers off the job, it was always on their turf. As Bess got older, it seemed perfectly natural to her that I was called by different names in different situations.

Over the next three and a half years, life continued in much the same way. I had to move to different cities precipitously three or four times, bringing with me only what I could carry. Once, I tried to connect with friends of friends in a nearby political organization, but they had apparently been followed to the meeting by an undercover agent, who then followed me. Only a combination of quick thinking and luck had allowed me to lose the tail. Another time, teenagers broke into my apartment and stole my ID, making it unsafe for me to remain.

As always, starting over was hard. I arrived in another city with only enough cash for a week's worth of food, after paying the first month's rent on an apartment. We usually slept together on a piece of foam on the floor, and I managed to scrounge up a table, a couple of chairs and a few pots, pans, and dishes wherever we landed. Forced to find a job as fast as possible, I had to leave Bess in whatever day care I could find. On occasion, the providers were abusive or neglectful. When Bess reported these incidents to me, I had to explain that I had to leave her there until I could find somewhere new for her. If I had just started a job, I would have been fired if I took time off to search for another place. I moved her as fast as I could. She seemed to understand, and to survive.

The different jobs continued to be both steadying and interesting. I enjoyed learning how to be a good waitress, to learn what it was like to work on the line in a factory, and how to work in a parts-supply store. When I was still nursing, I worried about the danger from pesticides while doing agricultural day labor. In a pinch, I could always type, becoming the demure secretary, preparing coffee for her boss.

I was recovering. I would never have survived, though, if people around me hadn't continued to help out. When Bessie had her first ear infection and fever of 104 degrees one night during a terrible storm, I could not get her to a hospital. I had no pediatrician or doctor or phone. The woman in the apartment next door, herself a single parent, called her pediatrician on the phone at 10:00 PM, and the two of them helped me through the night, as I held Bess in a bathtub of cool water.

Often I had to dress Bessie while she slept, before dawn, and drop her off the minute the day care was open to dash off to buses or trains to work. Despite the frequent moves and other hardships of poverty, Bess grew to be a robust, endlessly talkative, and joyful child.

By the time Bess was three, I was coming to terms with the fact that I had made some huge mistakes in my past. I had always been conscious of my own weaknesses, but I had prided myself on the purity of my selfless motivation. Now, I had to accept that I, too, had also been motivated by some of what I considered to be baser instincts. I had compromised my personal integrity in a number of situations. Rather than listening closely to what people had said, I had tried to manipulate them into adopting the organization's current perspective, into carrying out the organization's wishes in order to protect my own standing. Rather than facing the complexity of problems, I had settled for simplistic solutions and for the fiction that we, the authors of those solutions, were somehow superior to those we sought to guide.

Like most people, I was corruptible, able to be seduced by power and everything that went with it. I was ashamed to admit that I now shared qualities with those who I had considered implacable, myopic, and selfish, with violent human beings, Nixon and Kissinger among others. My comrades and I had chosen to ignore whole chunks of reality so that the rest would fit nicely into our theory of change. We had allowed personal motives to distort judgment. We had ignored the voices of the opposition. The more I realized just how pompous and arrogant our behavior had been during past the few years, the more ashamed I became. How could I live with who I had been? I would need to reconstruct the basis of my self-esteem from the ground up.

Eventually I came to see that there was no quick and easy way to creating a more just and sustainable world. Human nature and the process of change are complex. There was no single, predictable solution to injustice, only sustained effort. There was no "after the revolution." No one could participate in the process of change without making mistakes. What mattered was our accountability, not in the rigid way the WUO and many others had interpreted Mao, but by focusing on collaboration. No individual could embrace the wisdom required for such a complex and unending task. After all, wasn't this the big idea behind democracy?

I also discovered that much of my understanding of race and gender, as incomplete as it was, did stand the test of time. On the job and in my neighborhood, my awareness of the many layers of social dynamics allowed me to participate in a wide variety of relationships. My willingness to listen to and learn about multiple perspectives allowed me to be trusted by people who might otherwise have dismissed me.

Working again in integrated environments, I also began to wonder about my belief in nationalism, and black nationalism in particular. How adequately did it speak to the rich, complex reality of our lives and our dreams? True, I came to see even more clearly the need for independent cultural, political, and personal spaces, and to understand why whites were reluctant to give up control over when and how those spaces could be nurtured. At the same time, I couldn't imagine a future without spaces in which we also tried to weave some common fabrics from our different histories and experiences. Without conversations and relationships between cultures, how were empathy and cultural intelligence to develop?

At a certain point, I realized I needed to be part of a broader discussion if I was to continue to reconstruct new ideas about change, especially with other women grappling with these issues. Besides, as long as I was isolated and on my own, I would never be able to even afford the newspaper, let alone have time to read it or do anything about what I read there.

It was 1979. The crescendo of popular struggles had receded to embattled corners, both here and around the world. It was clear that the system of global financial autocracy was more resilient than we had thought. Even more important, the problem of what to replace it with mattered a good deal. An idealized solution for the future was considerably less useful than immediate efforts to improve global and local environmental practices, and to provide more equal access to jobs, housing, education, and health care.

With no violent contest for power shaping up, I certainly couldn't see any role for symbolic bombings. Nor could I see any foreseeable need to sustain an underground capacity to protect people from a variety of threats. I had experienced one tiny aspect of warfare. I was proud that I had stepped up to do what I thought was the right thing, even though I could now see that I had been misguided. I knew that I was fortunate to have survived the experience, both of the townhouse explosion and of the difficult process of coming to terms with my culpability. I still felt connected to Terry, Teddy, and Diana, whose deaths had become for me a tree of wisdom which had taken root deep within. Perhaps I would not have wrestled so hard with sorting out the past if I had not felt bound to them to learn as much as we could from their deaths. They had made a sacrifice and we, all of those who had rushed off so precipitously to fight the revolution, were bound to be accountable on a daily basis to those three and the many others who died during the 60s and early 70s. I was grateful for all that I had learned.

I had been helped through the worst of the pain and disorientation during this period by my sense of wonder at the new, joyful person coming into her own at my side. I don't know if I would have been able to trudge through it all so resolutely if this tangible sense of renewal had not constantly infused me with hope.

When I focused my thoughts on rejoining the work once again, I knew that first I had to turn myself in and, I assumed, go to jail. While I thought it unlikely that the government could convict me of murder, I was certainly guilty of something. I had no desire to go to trial. I didn't mind the thought of jail, but I worried about what it would do to Bess.

In June 1980, Jimmy Carter was president, and there was not the national atmosphere of fear and hysteria that there is today, but rather a collective desire to heal and move on. I turned myself in, and, later, pled guilty to the charge of possession of illegal explosives. I was fortunate to be supported by attorneys Margaret Ratner and Elizabeth Fink. In November, I was sentenced to zero to three years in prison. The sentence was fairly standard for the charge.

My family was notified of my return the night before my sentencing. They were joyful about the addition of Bessie to our ranks. Over the following weeks we carefully began to reconstruct relationships, trying to be respectful of differences. In January 1981, I reported to begin serving my prison sentence at Bedford Hills Correctional Association, while Bessie was securely cared for by her father. I was fortunate that he and other members of my family were able to bring her to visit almost every week.

My time with the women inside was compelling. My sense of the absurdity of putting humans in cages, subject to an absolute authority, remained as strong as it had been during my first arrest in Chester. Bedford was filled with intelligent, interesting women, most of whom came from poverty and had succumbed to using or selling small amounts of drugs. Others had reacted to abusive or battering relationships by striking back in one way or another. There were a few exceptions, women whose psyches had been so damaged during childhood that there was little humanity left, but they were only a few.

We spent hours a day in lines: lines to meals, to job assignments, for fire drills, for showers, for the clinic, or waiting to be locked in our cells for count, with no talking or reading or knitting permitted. The prevailing culture, in which both guards and inmates were expected to act like morons, was the most stressful aspect of prison. I watched as it battered away at the humanity of all involved, inevitably eliciting the most defensive, despairing behavior from a few. I was lucky that Bedford still put women in single cells, before overcrowding necessitated the doubles, triples, and dorms that now characterize most prisons. During the periods when we were locked in our cells, I had the time and the privacy to read again for the first time in years.

After leaving prison, I entered a two-year program in electrical engineering technology because I had come to believe that math and science literacy were essential if I were to understand the critical political and economic decisions of the day. After graduating, I worked installing and repairing computerized telex equipment. After each installation, I trained those who would be responsible for running the equipment. Often I faced women and men almost paralyzed by their fear of technology. They were astonished when I was able to explain the basic principles of the machine in a way they could understand and master.

Two years later, I began working as an office assistant to my friend and attorney, Elizabeth Fink, who was working at the time on the "Attica Brothers" civil suit. Together we began the process of computerizing her practice. I was also asked to teach an evening math class to women in adult education who needed math to advance in their jobs at the phone company, post office, and other jobs involving more and more work with new technologies. After several years of part-time teaching, I left the law office and began teaching full time in a school for young people who had left high school without a diploma for one reason or another. I went on to get a masters degree in mathematics education and have been teaching ever since, including several years at the high school level. Most recently, I have been working with New York City teachers and principals to bring about more effective mathematics education.

This work has taught me to look closely at the complex interplay between experience and reflection, seeing that it is this process that drives learning. I began to see learning itself as a kind of change. Individuals or institutions change when they experience something new, reflect on it, and in response reorganize existing ways of thinking to incorporate the new information. This scrutiny of the smallest units of change has led me to look differently at problems of large-scale change, such as political and economic development, and movements striving to increase human equality and justice. The challenges of sustainable development and human rights has never ceased to be a focus of my life.

AFTERWORD

■ ■

When I look back over the years, I am grateful that the experiences of my youth allowed me to develop a political consciousness. This lens has required me to confront the burdens of our world, but it has also revealed many of its wonders and possibilities. I have been able to join in the public space where decisions are being made about our collective future. Unlike so many people in this country, I have not, as a result, been blindsided by global warming, sectarian or resource wars, or religious-based terrorism. The practice of wrestling with solutions allows me perhaps to look at the problems with a clearer eye.

Like many in SDS, the experience that most shaped my political awareness was being able to witness and be a small part of the civil rights movement. The strength and vision of hundreds of thousands of people rising up from fields, shacks, tenements, schools, and churches to affect such a profound change in our social fabric shaped the core of my beliefs.

Since the passions of the 60s and early 70s crescendoed, I have had time to think a great deal about the strengths and dangers of both capitalism and socialism and to learn from contemporary thinkers like Vandana Shiva, who focuses on decentralized forms of sustainable economic and political organization in *Earth Democracy*. I have continued to explore ideas about leadership in light of my experiences as both participant and occasional leader in SDS and Weatherman, and in the process I have become much more aware of how much I was influenced by women's earlier struggles to expand their horizons. It does indeed take confidence and assertiveness to lead, to offer ideas, service, and skills to a social effort. How quickly assertiveness can turn to arrogance, however, inevitably closing off the communication without which good ideas dry up and corruption moves in.

Some have argued that because of the secret nature of the WUO, discussion of its internal dynamics and their consequences amounts to a betrayal of our beliefs and the goals of peace and justice. Back then, however, many in the WUO used secrecy to secure their own leadership and manipulate the beliefs and actions of its members—both under- and aboveground—however innocently or in the name of good intentions. I was not immune. Secrecy, I now believe, allowed those of us who knew what went on to perpetuate illusions about what worked and what didn't and why, depriving those interested in change the opportunity to draw their own conclusions. Individual culpability for mistakes, however, is relevant only to the participants. The WUO was a product of the times, and the ideas that drove us were mostly not original with us. Many of those ideas, like Leninism, arise again and again because democratically led radical change is exceedingly difficult and slow moving.

Despite its serious shortcomings, Weatherman managed, for its moment in time, to serve as a powerful voice of outrage that spoke for thousands of angry young people. Especially during the early underground years, this voice helped to keep the spotlight on the cynicism and hypocrisy with which US leaders acted on the mandate of democracy.

Furthermore, Weatherman eluded capture at a moment when the full weight of the US justice system was focused on stamping out legitimate dissent, from the Democratic Party to the Black Panther Party. By surviving, we helped to show that there were limits to the government's runaway power to do this, regardless of how many threats they issued. The organization's perseverance and continued existence provided encouragement to tens of thousands of 60s veterans, who were digging in for the long, slow work of change in local arenas, many of whom feared the government's apparent intention to demonize and delegitimize dissent.

Finally, Weathermen made a commitment to address racism and its many manifestations, both past and present. We vowed to never look the other way and to listen to voices of color as we tried to figure out how to be better people. That we largely failed in that mission was regretful, but not surprising. The challenges of figuring out how issues of gender, race, ethnicity, class, and sexual identity can be resolved more equitably and creatively in our rapidly globalizing culture will continue to occupy us for generations to come.

To the broader conversation about change, however, Weatherman added only a chaotic mix of rebellion and rage. The Weather Underground's strategy of symbolic bombings grew from our acceptance that violence was the ultimate arbiter of power. It was not unreasonable to believe that only violence could confront violence, when the tide of national liberation seemed to be successful. If violence had a track record of working to promote the interests of the world's majority, it still could not be easily dismissed. However, while Vietnam won the war and political independence, the physical, economic, and emotional costs of the war were astronomical and will endure for generations. Now that the United States has shown its willingness to use depleted uranium and other weapons that are even more dangerous and long lasting, even wars of self-defense must be rethought. Individuals, however, must continue to rely on physical self-defense when all social and political efforts to achieve equality fail. Likewise, for women, gays, labor leaders in developing nations, urban youth and many others, attention to collective self-defense unfortunately remains an urgent necessity.

By accepting the existing assumptions about change, Weatherman missed an opportunity to help expand the range of our thinking about ways of fighting for equality and sustainability, even in the face of extensive violence committed against movements for change, especially in the assassination of its leaders. We were hardly alone. Weatherman's biggest mistake was to consider ourselves immune to the angst that gripped many of the other sectors of the movement by 1970. No one in the movement knew the way for the next segment of the journey, and it was clear that our inexperience and mistakes were proving increasingly costly.

Although technology has vastly increased women's ability to participate in warfare, I now wonder if the current access to and increase in women's power to kill and destroy makes a more just and sustainable world more likely. Recent examples at Abu Ghraib illustrate how easily women can be included even in the inevitable sexualized aspects of warfare. Warfare is and must be ruthless, and ultimately it cannot ever be cleansed of its more hideous aspects. In the end, it is always children and the women who care for them, and the elderly who bear the brunt of war, devastation, and displacement. Yes, women need to know that we too, given the access, can carry the weight equally with men in defending humanity when need be, but then we must also consider what the best way is to do that. There is no end to examples of women facing dangerous physical tasks and of confronting the possibility of death for themselves or those around them, if we look at pioneer women, immigrant women, Native American and black women fighting to help their families do whatever necessary to survive. More recently, we can look directly at women in warfare in the liberation struggles since the 60s, and in our own military service. At the moment this book is being written, women in Iraq risk their lives on a daily basis, and some have lost theirs. The willingness to kill and be killed cannot be the measure of courage.

The monumental changes of the 50s and 60s have now settled into the psyche of the country, despite the sustained efforts of a few to have us return to an earlier day. Attitudes about race, women's rights and roles, and the environment are immeasurably different from those we confronted in the late 50s. The challenge remains to generate concrete visions that will mobilize people for long-term participation in continued efforts for a just and sustainable future, even in the face of growing violence and the onslaught of emotionally manipulative information.

In forming a Leninist party, Weatherman sought to rescue society from itself. Even though the temptation to do this is even greater today, I no longer think there is any minority that can rescue the majority, even though the very life of the planet and its ability to sustain us is at stake. The great lumbering people will survive, or not, to the extent that we can mobilize our full intelligence and power in diverse ways.

At our best in SDS, we believed in the collective wisdom of all the people, a belief that separated those of us who called ourselves radicals from liberals and conservatives, both of which tend to place their faith in elites. I continue to believe that in the effort to strengthen equality and democracy, there can be no elites that hover in judgment above the fray, taking fewer risks, protected from the stresses and the mistakes. Besides, to be above it all is to be clueless about where and how people will generate the sustained effort, intelligence, and sacrifice needed to pull the world back from global self-destruction. While I have not shied away from exploring the weaknesses of SDS and the Weather Underground, then, like now, the gravest mistake is inaction.

Violence continues to escalate alarmingly. Around the world, hundreds of thousands die every year from epidemics, starvation, poisons in our food, air, and water, and human violence of all kinds, including state-sanctioned, tribal, or ethnic wars, nuclear and chemical accidents, terrorism, and government repression. Many men, uncertain of their place in a world of uncertain values, find comfort in returning to traditions of rigid order in which women serve, sexually and domestically, and men rule, enforcing that rule with widespread violence. Finally, like Icarus, our uncritical infatuation with technology coupled with an economic system that disregards humanity's future have led us to fly dangerously close to the sun.

In the midst of all this, I continue to learn how to construct a new kind of hope, one that doesn't depend on certain success, on "after the revolution." Instead it is a hope rooted in children's passionate belief in fairness, in their willingness to discipline themselves to create just solutions to problems. This hope draws strength from the most generous and courageous impulses of the human heart, which compel us to continue the fight even though so many successes happen in the context of tragedy. I am learning to hope even while grieving for those who suffer the most from the messes we have made around the planet. I am discovering a hope that can accept that we might fail, and already we can see the face of that failure if we look.

When I look back on the early years of my life, the tremendous accomplishments, the ignorant and arrogant mistakes, and the losses, I ask, "For the sake of what?"

For the sake of a future, I hope.

APPENDIX

■ ■

A. CHRONOLOGY OF WEATHERMAN BOMBINGS

From *Weather Eye: Communiques from the Weather Underground, May 1970–May 1974*, edited by Jonah Raskin (New York: Union Square Press, 1974).

DATE	LOCATION
June 9, 1970	New York City Police headquarters
July 26, 1970	Presidio Army Base MP station, San Francisco [in opposition to Vietnam]
October 8, 1970	Hall of Justice, Marin County [after the death Jonathan Jackson]
October 8, 1970	Criminal Courthouse, New York City
October 8, 1970	Harvard Center for International Affairs
February 28, 1971	US Capitol [US invasion of Laos]
August 30, 1971	Department of Corrections, Sacramento and San Francisco [after the death of George Jackson]
September 17, 1971	Department of Corrections, Albany, New York [Attica]
May 19, 1972	Pentagon [bombing of Hanoi]
May 18, 1973	103rd Precinct, New York City [police killing of ten-year-old black boy]
September 28, 1973	ITT offices in New York [US-supported coup in Chile]
March 6, 1974	Federal Offices of Health, Education and Welfare, San Francisco
May 1974	Los Angeles office of California Attorney General Evelle Younger [death of members of the SLA]
June 1974	Gulf Oil headquarters in Pittsburgh [Gulf's support of Portuguese colonial policies in Angola]
September 1974	Anaconda Copper [anniversary of the coup in Chile]

B. TED GOLD, DIANA OUGHTON, TERRY ROBBINS

TEDDY GOLD

From the first, Teddy Gold had a deep sensitivity to injustice. This was encouraged and deepened by the stories his parents, Hy Gold, a doctor, and Ruth, a teacher, told about the treatment of their families as Jews in Eastern Europe and Russia and as garment workers in New York City. He was inspired by their experiences treating and teaching poor and working people.

When Teddy was a child he played endless games of stickball with his father in the school yard just up the block from their apartment on the upper West Side of Manhattan. He loved following the Knicks and the Yankees with his father. As he grew older he became fiercely competitive in both sports and school, and won a place at the prestigious Stuyvesant High School. There, while his father volunteered his medical services to the civil rights movement in Mississippi, Teddy started a chapter of Friends of SNCC at school.

When he graduated, he enrolled at Columbia University, twenty blocks north of his family's apartment. There, he eagerly entered the varied social and political life of the campus, switching from pre-med to sociology so he would have more time to be politically active. He did well in all his classes in both fields.

At the start of his sophomore year, Teddy went to his first day of classes wearing an NLF button, which was commonly understood as a sign of support for the National Front for the Liberation of South Vietnam, the popular coalition then opposing the US/Diem regime. There he met a senior, David Gilbert, who had founded the Columbia Vietnam Committee and was a well-known and respected leader on campus. Gilbert approached this student with the NLF button after class to ask him what he knew of the professor. Teddy was flattered that David asked his opinion and gave a concise report of what he knew, impressing David with his earnest thoroughness. Thereafter they became good friends and Teddy worked with David educating other students about the war.

Teddy and David remained close friends even after David graduated. Along with Ted Kaptchuk, a high school friend, they rented an apartment off-campus. Teddy became involved with the Columbia SDS chapter and began to assume more and more leadership responsibilities until he became vice-chairman of the chapter when Kapchuck became chairman their senior year.

During these years, Teddy also volunteered with the Harlem Tutorial Project, an after-school and summer program for the young people of Harlem. The time Teddy spent with these young people convinced him that he wanted to become a teacher, and it also put him in touch with one of the more significant upheavals of the sixties: the challenge brought by parents and community activists to end New York's own separate and unequal school system.

The summer after the Columbia strike, when SDS and other radical students at Columbia organized a Liberation School, Teddy helped pull together a class on public education and teacher organizing. Almost seventy young people attended, eager to tackle the problem of under-achieving poor children. After several weeks of reading and discussion, a core of about thirty of these young people, now finished with school and some of whom were already working in education, decided to constitute themselves a chapter of Teachers for a Democratic Society. Teddy wrote several articles for the TDS newsletter as well as a pamphlet, "Education and Teacher Organizing" for TDS. In one, Teddy reported on TDS activities and goals:

> "TDS members have been active in Ocean-Hill-Brownsville, Two Bridges (Lower East Side) and District 4, 5, and 6 in Harlem and East Harlem, the South Bronx and Bedford Stuyvesant in Brooklyn, fighting along with parents and students to open schools in those communities. We have set up or helped set up eight 'education workshops' around the city, composed of teachers, parents and (not enough) students. . . . (to) discuss . . . What is radical education? How can we exploit the benefits and avoid the dangers of community control? How should a radical teacher relate to a community that wants only to improve its children's reading scores? How can we show teachers that since the struggle for community control can provide an atmosphere in which students need not view themselves solely as colonial subjects and thus may want to learn, it is in *their* interest as well as the community's? How can we combat the class-training implicit in devices such as the 'track system'? Should radicals aim for an eventual parliamentary takeover of the UFT, or should we wait until we are stronger and then split to form a community oriented union?

That fall, Teddy worked in a private school because his Columbia diploma had been "suspended" for one year. Nonetheless, in his free time, he joined with others in TDS to organize public-school teachers to oppose the strike and support the demands of the local community boards. Teddy also attended national SDS meetings, and continued to read and disseminate SDS materials amongst other politicized young people he worked with, trying to organize teachers against the war and in support of the Black Panther Party. He never stopped following the Knicks and the Yankees with undiminished passion.

In the summer of 1969, Teddy was caught up in the whirlwind of work defending Black Panthers, fighting against the war and the draft. In August, he signed up for a trip to Cuba, which offered young people the chance to visit the island and learn about the economic and social programs in force there. They were also able to meet with a visiting delegation from Vietnam. After the trip, Teddy returned to New York where he joined one of several "Weather collectives" for a short time, before moving to Chicago in December.

DIANA OUGHTON

Diana Oughton was born in January 1942, secure within a family that had been central to the life of Dwight, Illinois, for centuries. She grew up a thoughtful and intelligent child, learning to "do" school without undue studying—riding, and later, learning languages. But she also noticed contradictions about wealth, about the official histories and reality.

Diana went to Bryn Mawr and majored in German, spending her junior year in Germany. By senior year, she began to participate in a tutoring program in nearby Philadelphia and went on one of the trips to Cambridge, Maryland, to help with voter registration. After graduating in 1963, she signed up to go to Guatemala with the American Friends Service Committee's VISA Program (Voluntary International Service Assignments). Here, Diana grappled head-on with the reality and consequences of poverty. She eventually settled in the mountains and taught literacy in a country with 70 percent illiteracy. She also gravitated to other young people working in Guatemala who offered a broader view of the world, political explanations for why the poverty was so stubborn and various strategies for radical change to address the problems.

After her two years in Guatemala, she returned, eventually settling in Philadelphia where she got a job as a teacher for the Office of Economic Opportunity (OEO), a product of Johnson's War on Poverty. Her deepening interest in education led her finally to the University of Michigan where she enrolled in a Masters of Arts program to study teaching. There she met members of the University's Voice-SDS chapter. The following fall, she began teaching three mornings a week at the Children's Community, then a year old, while she continued her degree.

Within a short time of meeting Bill Ayers at the school, the two had fallen in love. Together they rented an attic apartment in the home of Nancy Frappier whose daughter was a student at the school. While their lives revolved around the school, Diana became increasingly integrated into the social life and work of SDS, as well. She too joined Weatherman in the summer of 1969 and became a leading member of the Detroit Collective with Bill. She traveled around that state, talking with students at other campuses and mentoring some of the younger members of the Detroit collective, many still in their teens.

One of these members, Lyndon Comstock, has noted how focused and present Diana always seemed. She listened closely to those who looked up to her leadership and responded thoughtfully. She was as passionate as most SDS members about the injustice of the war and an economic system that stacked the cards against less aggressive human beings, but in individual conversations she also remained sensitive to the personal particularities. Also full of fun, she managed to convince a would-be suitor she had met at some demonstration to ferry her and fellow organizers to meetings in his little two-seater sports car.

Diana remained in the Midwest in a semi-clandestine collective until she came to New York, days before the townhouse exploded.

TERRY ROBBINS

Terry Robbins was born on October 4, 1947 in Queens, New York. His mother Olga, the daughter of Austrian Jews, graduated from Hunter College during the Depression and soon after married Sam Robbins. The son of Russian Jewish immigrants, Sam worked in a coat factory in Manhattan after graduating from high school, rising up to become a manager. Olga had planned on becoming a teacher, but it was still in the heart of the Depression and New York City was not offering the licensing exam. With jobs scarce, she decided to open a dress shop with a friend. By the time they began to establish an economic foothold, however, the war was imminent and Sam enlisted in the service. Only after he returned from the war did they start a family.

When Terry was six and a half, Olga was stricken with breast cancer. She struggled with the disease for three more years, dying when Terry was nine. Sam Robbins, left alone with two children still in elementary school, relied on a nanny, hired years before, who the children knew as Auntie Annie. She provided the love and support that Olga had been unable to consistently give during the last two years of her illness. Both children, but especially Terry's sister Barbara, had quickly grown close to her.

As he got older, Terry began to write poetry, and, with Barbara and his cousins, discovered Bob Dylan and other folk artists. The music became his refuge when, two years after his mother's death, Sam Robbins remarried. When his new wife, Dorothy, moved into the house with her own daughter, seven years older than Terry, their lives began to change dramatically. When faced with the challenges of molding a blended family, both father and stepmother made fateful choices that led to constant tension and conflict—sometimes physical—at home.

While Barbara's response to adolescence and the trouble at home was to act out in school, Terry turned to his intellect for solace and for a home in the outside world. In high school, he found an outlet for his enormous curiosity about the world and a place to pursue his love of language. He remained in the honors track, and his friends were the others in his class who challenged themselves above and beyond the curriculum. He became an early fan of Barbra Streisand, a lover of Dylan and the Beatles. It was the lyrics especially that he savored. To many of his friends, he was witty and smart and questioned everything. Others perceived an edge there, perhaps sensing his struggle to contain his intense emotional life. To them, he had a controlling side, a part that was fearful of his own passion and of things unraveling in a way in which he would get hurt.

When it came time to apply to college, in 1964, he wanted to go to Antioch in Ohio, but Dorothy refused to allow him to apply. In the end, he went to Kenyon, a small liberal arts college in Ohio with little political or intellectual ferment at the time.

In college, Terry heard about SDS from Dickie Magidoff, an SDS traveler working in the Cleveland area. Magidoff was also involved in the Cleveland ERAP project. The summer after his first year in college, in 1965, Terry moved into the Cleveland ERAP house where he absorbed the talk of politics and basked in the warmth of the community that was being established amongst the older, politically and socially more experienced SDS members. He helped out on various projects, including some work with John and Kathy Roberts who had moved to Cleveland to start Inner Cities Ministries, recruiting resources from the suburbs to support community organizing efforts in the inner cities.

Terry returned to Kenyon for the following year and began to work in earnest to build an SDS chapter on the complacent campus. Weeks after he turned eighteen, Terry described the isolation and apathy at the campus in a letter to Jeff Shero in the SDS National Office.

> question#1 then becomes: is there a need to reach the students and faculty of such a (by choice) apathetic and secluded community? is there a valid chance to make head-way in such an environment? Assuming that the answer to both questions is 'yes,' then, how can one go about organizing? The point here is that radical tactics - presently, the anti-draft movement as a method of clogging up draft boards and hindering the war effort, draft-card burnings, etc. - when put before the eyes of a

not-so-liberal campus, is like running before you can walk. I guess that
one of our goals is education [but] how do we reach them (potential
supporters)?

In the kind of rigorous analysis that Terry was known for later at Kent, he tried
to distill the lessons learned from SDS's experience so far and then go farther:

> it seems to me from all the reports i've seen and heard, that the fantastic
> growth of sds since April, has been caused by people agreeing with our
> vietnam stand, and finding sds a good way to express themselves. but, how
> many people have we convinced, who were opposed to begin with? does
> anyone become a radical, or does it just happen, by the fact that you are
> you? it seems the latter is implied in the tactic of the adamant stand regard-
> less of campus opinion; that by your very presence as a radical or as an sds
> chapter people will 'see the light' and join up ... if this is true, it seems to
> me that we gain a few, but that the majority just doesn't join the band-
> wagon. is there, then some way to convince a large part of the population
> of the applicability and relevance of our position, say, as expressed in the
> Port Huron statement? (December 3, 1965)

He signed the letter: "for peace, freedom, and love, terry robbins, president, kenyon
sds." He also cc'd a copy to Dickie Magidoff, who remained his friend and mentor, and his personal file. Of course, Terry was also the *only* official member of
Kenyon SDS at the time.

In a far more informal letter to Dickie, Terry wondered what to do about the
fact that any attempt to put forth a radical analysis brought a charge of "communist" which effectively scared away potential listeners.

> it seems we are overlooking hostile campuses - ok - but what about
> places like toledo, bowling green, and now arizona state? [Where SDS
> chapters were banned by school administrations.] Is the only alternative
> "secret societies" or should a fight be made initially for the relevance of
> sds and the demand for the right to form on campus?

> It seems to me, dickie, that there are so many problems with university
> organizing - and we refuse to cope with them beyond the creation of a
> committed few. when and where can we seek a broader base? I know
> the erap people have little or no hope/contact for or with campuses -

but, shit, we are trying to establish a <u>movement</u> - not just an echo in a hollow chamber - and a movement is gonna require people - and <u>converts</u>: on the campus as well as in the community. (Dec. 9, 1965)

He concludes the letter, as he often did, with an exuberant discovery:

> i discovered, yes, i discovered that simon and garfunkel are for real ... their names are paul simon and art garfunkel; they go to queens college and are frat brothers of a good friend of mine, who proceeded to whip out a simon and garfunkel album which is real folky non-commercial and great ... i even heard the sound of silence without echo chambers, and understood the words 'the words of the prophet are written on the subway walls and tenements.'

By the spring semester, Terry reported to Dickie that he had devised a strategy for Kenyon, teaming up with the chaplain to start the Student-Faculty Committee on the War in Vietnam,

> devoted to gathering the facts and making a case for a critical approach to american foreign policy. There are five faculty members, and – catch this – tonight 18 kids showed up ... my shock was only overcome by exuberance and joy; we'll be getting off the ground soon, gathering and printing material, staging discussions, etc. the point is first to clarify the facts about involvement in vietnam, and then to intelligently (leftly, i guess, is a synonym) draw conclusions.

Terry was on his way as an organizer. He also began to travel to other nearby campuses trying to help people who had contacted the national office to start their own chapters. He wrote a long article for *New Left Notes* on his work at Kenyon. By now, he had talked with Dickie about his desire to leave Kenyon after his sophomore year to come join the staff in Cleveland. The isolation at Kenyon was getting to him, and when communication broke down, he could go weeks without hearing from anyone. As it turned out, the Cleveland staff urged him to come, so in July he moved into a project house on the West Side of Cleveland, determined to make himself useful. Cleveland ERAP participants—among them Dickie Magadoff, Carol McKeldowney, Kathy Boudin, Sharon Jeffreys, and David Palmer—had been attempting to build a community union to help poor residents mobilize campaigns around voter registration, tenant issues, welfare, job discrimination, and so on.

During that summer, the Cleveland Project decided that another desperate need in the community was a school where children could escape from the monotony and racism in the local public schools. To get help, they turned to Bill Ayers and Diana Oughton, of the Children's Community in Ann Arbor, Michigan, a school started a year earlier by parents frustrated with the limitations of the local public schools in 1965. That spring Bill came to Cleveland and roomed with Terry. They explored the works of educators like A.S. Neill, Paul Goodman, Sylvia Ashton-Warner, and John Holt. Like A.S. Neill, in Summerhill, they said that children should be encouraged to pursue their own interests. They also stressed the importance of valuing the home cultures of the children. Both schools had a mix of black and white, of middle class and poor, and were committed to democracy, both among the staff and the children.

After the summer, Terry's friendship with Bill and Diana became increasingly important. Terry was attracted to Bill's warmth and his sense of profound irreverence to all authority. Bill was impressed by Terry's wit, his love of wordplay, and his bizarre sense of humor and of the absurd. Terry visited in Ann Arbor and got to know a number of people in and around the Children's Community along with several other SDS members. He relished the long hours spent discussing what to do about the war and about poverty. The Michigan group included younger activists than Cleveland and they shared Terry's passion for music and for the sardonic. At Kenyon and Cleveland ERAP, organizers worked hard to find common ground with those in the community. In Ann Arbor, Terry could openly vent his rage and fantasize about emotionally satisfying responses to General McArthur's deadly strategy in Vietnam.

In Cleveland, Terry began to work with Carol McEldowny and David Palmer who had obtained a small press and set up a print shop for the local movement. Terry wanted to start a newsletter called *Common Sense*. He began to see writing as one way he could contribute to the work of "convincing" people that the anti-war analysis made sense, getting them to open up to the broader critique of society contained in the Port Huron Statement. Writing was another interest he shared with Bill. That winter, Terry and Bill wrote a long, carefully footnoted paper called "Turn Toward Children," reporting on the educational and political philosophies of the Children's Communities in Ann Arbor and Cleveland. Terry also continued to visit campuses in the Ohio region, including Kent State, staying with graduate students Candy and Rick Erickson.

The following summer of '68, Howie Emmer, a student leader at Kent State, Kathy Boudin from Cleveland ERAP, and others formed the Cleveland Draft Resistance Union, an attempt to bring together the community organizing of

ERAP with the SDS focus on young people and the war. Terry helped out for the early part of the summer. Then, in August, he moved to Ann Arbor to stay with Bill and Diana, and join them in preparations for the Chicago demonstration.

In the atmosphere of pumped-up rhetoric coming from Mayor Richard Daley that summer, Terry, Bill, Tom Hayden and a host of others began to imagine different scenarios of how the protests might unfold and what their responses could be. There was frequent talk of street fighting combined with speculations about escalating tactics. Terry's imagination started to heat up.

Bill loved a good fight and on more than one occasion had already sustained broken fingers and nose in fistfights with counterdemonstrators and police. Terry, however, had little experience nor, at first, inclination for personal combat. He was small, wiry, chain-smoking, and he carried himself a bit stiffly. At Kenyon and his first summer in Cleveland, physical confrontation wasn't part of any effective organizing strategy he considered. But Terry *was* angry—both about issues in his personal past and about the injustice he saw around him.

In the context of increasingly frequent militant street fighting and all the dramatic—if loose—talk about revolution, Terry, like many others, began to let go of his old taboos, both in his politics and his personal life. As his vision of what was possible grew, so too did his sense of himself. In Chicago at the demonstrations Terry picked up a tear-gas canister and threw it back at the police. He ran in the streets shouting angrily with thousands of others and was exhilarated by the experience.

After the demonstrations, Terry settled in Michigan although he continued to travel to campuses in Ohio, especially Kent State. Both in Ann Arbor and in Kent, Terry and others increasingly turned to the same questions that were arising everywhere about how to move beyond protest. They examined and argued about tactics of disruption—whether on campus, in the streets, or in the workplace—of the high price that might be paid and other alternatives. Not content with the vague language about revolution, Terry wanted people to talk about what it really meant. To provoke those discussions he would speculate on extreme possibilities of armed combat to see what people said. Diana always argued against it, but she was one of the few who did.

That winter, Terry began to work closely with the national collective, especially Bernardine, Bill, Mark Rudd and J.J., working on the Weatherman Paper even as the events at Kent continued to escalate.

BIBLIOGRAPHY

Albert, Judith Clavir and Stewart Edward Albert, eds. *The Sixties Papers: Documents of a Rebellious Decade*. New York: Praeger, 1984.

Alewitz, Michael. "The Legacy of Kent State." May 1970 speech at 30th anniversary of the shootings at Kent State.

Avorn, Jerry L., and members of the staff of the Columbia Daily Spectator, *Up Against the Ivy Wall: a History of the Columbia Crisis*. New York: Atheneum, 1970.

Ayers, William. *Fugitive Days*. New York: Beacon, 2001.

Bloom, Alexander, and Wini Breines, eds. *"Takin' It to the Streets": A Sixties Reader*. New York: Oxford University Press, 1995.

Breines, Wini. *Community and Organization in the New Left, 1962–1968*. New Brunswick: Rutgers University Press, 1989.

Brightman, Carol. *Sweet Chaos: The Grateful Dead's American Adventure*. New York: Pocket Books, 1998.

Brown, Elaine. *A Taste of Power: A Black Woman's Story*. New York: Anchor Books, 1992.

Burchett, Wilfred G. *Vietnam: Inside Story of the Guerilla War*. New York: International Publishers, 1965.

Callahan, Grace. Undergraduate thesis, Newcomb College, 2004.

Calvert, Gregory Nevala. *Democracy From the Heart: Spiritual Values, Decentralism, and Democratic Idealism in the Movement of the 1960s*. Eugene: Communitas Press, 1991.

Carmichael, Stokely. "What We Want," *New York Review of Books*, September 22, 1966, As quoted in Clayborne Carson, *In Struggle: SNCC and the Black Awakening of the 1960s*. Cambridge: Harvard University Press, 1981, 217.

Carmichael, Stokely, and Ekwueme Michael Thelwell, *Ready for Revolution: the Life and Struggles of Stokely Carmichael(Kwame Ture),* New York: Scribners, 2003.

Carson, Clayborne. *In Struggle: SNCC and the Black Awakening of the 1960s*. Cambridge, MA: Harvard University Press, 1981.

___, David J. Garrow, Gerald Gill, Vincent Harding, and Darlene Clark Hine, eds. *The Eyes on the Prize Civil Rights Reader: Documents, Speeches, and Firsthand Accounts from the Black Freedom Struggle*. New York: Penguin Books, 1991.

Chester, Pa. Jobs, Freedom Now: Community Organization in the Other America, Prepared by the Swarthmore College Chapter of SDS, in collaboration with the Committee for Freedom Now of Chester, Pennsylvania, and the Swarthmore Political Action Club. Distributed by Students for a Democratic Society, New York, 1964.

Churchill, Ward, and Jim Vander Wall. *The Cointelpro Papers: Documents from the FBI's Secret Wars Against Dissent in the United States.* Boston: South End Press, 1990.

Cleaver, Kathleen, and George Katsiaficas, eds. *Liberation, Imagination, and the Black Panther Party.* New York: Routledge, 2001.

Curry, Constance, et al. *Deep in Our Hearts: Nine White Women in the Freedom Movement.* Athens, GA: University of Georgia Press, 2000.

Cynosure. Abbott Academy, March 18, 1962.

Debray, Regis. *Revolution in the Revolution? Armed Struggle and Political Struggle in Latin America.* New York: Grove, 1967.

Dellinger, David. *From Yale to Jail: The Life Story of a Moral Dissenter.* Marion, SD: Rose Hill Books, 1993.

Di Prima, Diane. *Recollections of My Life as a Woman: The New York Years.* New York: Viking, 2001.

Dohrn, Bernardine, Bill Ayers, and Jeff Jones, eds., *Sing A Battle Song: The Revolutionary Poetry, Statements, and Communiques of the Weather Underground, 1970-1974.* New York: Seven Stories Press, 2006.

Dunbar-Ortiz, Roxanne. *Outlaw Woman: A Memoir of the War Years, 1960–1975.* San Francisco: City Lights, 2001.

Echols, Alice. *Daring to be Bad: Radical Feminism in America, 1967–1975.* Minneapolis: University of Minnesota Press, 1989.

Evans, Sarah. *Personal Politics: The Roots of Women's Liberation in the Civil Rights Movement and the Left.* New York: Vintage Books, 1979.

Fanon, Frantz. *The Wretched of the Earth.* New York: Grove, 1963.

Foner, Philip S., ed. *The Black Panthers Speak.* New York: Da Capo, 1995.

Forman, James. *The Making of Black Revolutionaries.* Washington, DC: Open Hand Publishing, 1985.

Fosl, Catherine. *Subversive Southerner: Anne Braden and the Struggle for Racial Justice in the Cold War South.* New York: Palgrave Macmillan, 2002.

Frost, Jennifer. *An Interracial Movement of the Poor: Community Organizing and the New Left in the 1960's.* New York: New York University Press, 2001.

Garvy, Helen. *Rebels with a Cause: A Collective Memoir of the Hopes, Rebellions and Repression of the 1960s*. Los Gatos, CA: Shire Press, 2007.

Gellhorn, Martha. "The Arabs of Palestine: A Case Study of the Refugees." *Atlantic Monthly*, October 1961.

Gitlin, Todd. *The Sixties: Years of Hope, Days of Rage*. New York: Bantam Books, 1987.

Grathwohl, Larry, and Frank Reagon. *Bringing Down America: An FBI Informer with the Weathermen*. New Rochelle: Arlington House, 1976.

Greene, Felix. *The Enemy: What Every American Should Know About Imperialism*. New York: Vintage Books, 1970.

Guevara, Che. "Message to the People of the World," speech to the Tricontinental, January 1967, Cuba. In *Venceremos! The speeches and writings of Ernesto Che Guevara*, edited by John Gerassi, New York: Macmillan, 1968.

Hayden, Tom. *Reunion*. New York: Random House, 1988.

Henig, Peter. "Manpower Channelers," *New Left Notes*, January 20, 1967.

Hilliard, David, and Lewis Cole. *This Side of Glory: The Autobiography of David Hilliard and the Story of the Black Panther Party*. Chicago: Lawrence Hill Books, 1993.

Isserman, Maurice, and Michael Kazin. *America Divided: The Civil War of the 1960s*. New York: Oxford Press, 2000.

Jacobs, Harold, ed. *Weatherman*. Los Angeles: Ramparts Press, 1970.

Jones, Thai. *A Radical Line: From the Labor Movement to the Weather Underground: One Family's Century of Conscience*. New York: Free Press, 2004.

King, Mary. *Freedom Song: A Personal Story of the 1960s Civil Rights Movement*. New York: William Morrow, 1997.

Krog, Antjie. *Country of my Skull, Guilt, Sorrow, and the Limits of Forgiveness in the New South Africa*. New York: Three Rivers Press, 1998.

La Farge, Phyllis. "Warm-hearted Guide to Certain Girls' Schools." *Harper's* April 1963.

Lerner, Jonathan. Unpublished manuscript.

Lewis, John. *Walking with the Wind: A Memoir of the Movement*. New York: Harcourt Brace, 1997.

Lloyd, Susan McIntosh. *A Singular School: Abbot Academy, 1828–1973*. Andover, MA: Phillips Academy, 1979.

Lorde, Audre. *Sister Outsider: Essays and Speeches*. Trumansburg, NY: Crossing Press, 1984.

Lynd, Staughton. *Living Inside Our Hope*. Ithaca: Cornell University Press, 1997.

Mao Tse-Tung, *Quotations from Chairman Mao Tse-Tung*. Peking: Foreign Language Press, 1966.

McMillan, John, and Paul Buhle, eds., *The New Left Revisited*. Philadelphia: Temple University Press, 2003.

Michener, James A. *Kent State: What Happened and Why*. New York: Random House, 1971.

Morgan, Robin. *Sisterhood is Powerful: An Anthology of Writings from the Women's Liberation Movement*. New York: Vintage, 1970.

Nicosia, Gerald. *Home to War: A History of the Vietnam Veterans' Movement*. New York: Crown Publishers, 2001.

Oglesby, Carl, and Richard Shaull. *Containment and Change: Two Dissenting Views of American Foreign Policy*. New York: Macmillan, 1967.

Olson, Lynne. *Freedom's Daughters: The Unsung Heroines of the Civil Rights Movement from 1830–1970*. New York: Scribner, 2001.

Pardun, Robert. *Prairie Radical: A Journey Through the Sixties*, Los Gatos, CA: Shire Press, 2001.

Pearson, Hugh. *The Shadow of the Panther: Huey Newton and the Price of Black Power in America*. Reading, MA: Addison-Wesley, 1994.

Polletta, Francesca, *Freedom is an Endless Meeting: Democracy in American Social Movements*. Chicago: University of Chicago Press, 2002.

Powers, Thomas. *Diana: The Making of a Terrorist*. New York: Houghton Mifflin, 1971.

Raskin, Jonah. ed. *Weather Eye: Statements of the Weather Underground*. New York: Union Square Press, 1975.

Raskin Jonah. "[TK]." *Dissent Magazine*,

Sale, Kirkpatrick. *SDS*. New York: Vintage Books, 1973.

Shiva, Vandana. *Earth Democracy: Justice, Sustainability, and Peace*. Cambridge, MA: South End Press, 2005.

Stein, Annie. "Strategies of Failure." *Harvard Education Review*, 41 (1971) 158-204.

Thompson, Becky. *A Promise and a Way of Life: White Antiracist Activism*. Minneapolis: University of Minnesota, 2001.

Untermeyer, Louis, ed. *A Treasury of Great Poems*. New York: Simon and Schuster, 1955.

Varon, Jeremy. *Bringing the War Home: The Weather Underground, the Red Army Faction, and Revolutionary Violence in the Sixties and Seventies*. Berkeley: University of California, 2004.

Walker, Daniel, ed. *Rights in Conflict: The Violent Confrontation of Demonstrators and Police in the Parks and Streets of Chicago During the Week of the Democratic National Convention of 1968.* Chicago Study Team Report to the National Commission on the Causes and Prevention of Violence, Rights in Conflict. Philadelphia: Braceland Brothers, 1968. (Known as the Walker Report).

Wells, Tom. *The War Within: America's Battle Over Vietnam.* Berkeley, University of California Press, 1994.

Wittman, Carl. *Students and Economic Action.* New York: Students for a Democratic Society, 1964.

PERIODICALS

National Guardian, 1967–1969.

New Left Notes. Students for a Democratic Society, January 1966–September 1969.

Washington Free Press, January 1967–September 1969.

FILM

De Antonio, Emile, Mary Lampson, Haskill Wexler, et al. *Underground.* New York: First Run Features, 1976.

Garvey, Helen, and Emiko Omori. *The Demise of SDS: Students for a Democratic Society, 1968-70.* Los Gatos, CA: Shire Films, 2003.

INTERVIEWS

Between the fall of 2001 and the summer of 2005, I had conversations with each of the following people about the period covered in this book. Some exchanges were casual conversations in the midst of social events, others were phone calls, and others informal interviews, scheduled ahead of time. I did not use recording equipment. In the handful of instances in the book where I directly use what someone said, it is paraphrased from my notes and acknowledged either in the text or in a footnote. I am grateful and indebted to all of these people for the invaluable information and insights I gleaned from those conversations.

Charles Beard
Paul and Heather Booth
Tom Bradley
Carol Brightman
Connie Brown
Lisa Meisel Burlingham
Greg Calvert
Ken Carpenter
Lyndon Comstock
E. G. Creighton
Rob Cunningham
Larry Davidson
Julie Diamond
Bernardine Dohrn
Deborah Drysdale
Susan Mallory Dunn
Nick Egleson
Howie Emmer
Linda Evans
Pam Fadem
Corinna Fales
Elizabeth Fink
John Fournelle
Peter Freedman
Jeanne Friedman
Elaine Fuller
Helen Garvey
David Gilbert
Dr. Hy and Ruth Gold
Andrew Goldman
Susan Hammond

Dr. Ann Hathaway
Phoebe Hirsch-Dubin
Naomi Jaffe
Eduardo Joly
Eleanor Stein Jones
Jeff Jones
Linda and Michael
   Josephowitz
Ted Kaptchuk
Peggy Klein Nelson
Colin Neiburger
Candy Erickson Knox
Liz Probasco Kutchai
Mary Lampson
Jonathan Lerner
Haven Logan
Dickie Magidoff
Charlotte Marchant
Marilyn McNabb
Delia Mellis
Marthe Osborne Norwick
Ann Wilkerson Olson
David Palmer
Wendy Panken
Robert Pardun
Mary Comstock Porter
John and Kathy Roberts
Wally Roberts
Barbara Robbins
Mark Rudd
Professor Alan Silver

Dr. Mark Smith
Michael Spiegel
Margie Stamberg
Linda Stark
Eleanor Stein
Jane Reynolds Swain
Laurie Tanenbaum
Allan Troxler
Marilyn Webb
Nick Wechsler
Sarah Wilkerson Wilde
Laura Whitehorn
Leni Wildflower
Robin Wilkerson
Jamie (Bill) Willet
Adrienne Yurick
Abbott Academy reunion
Georgetown University
   SDS reunion
SDS reunion at Simon's
   Rock
Swarthmore College
   reunion

NOTES

CHAPTER ONE

1. Letter from my father to his first grandchild, Eric, 1979.

CHAPTER TWO

1. Phyllis La Farge, "A Warm-hearted Guide to Certain Girls' Schools." *Harper's Magazine*, April 1963.
2. In the school newspaper I later wrote: "It is very simply time to wake up and assimilate what is going on in the world around us; to form a constructive opinion instead of always leaving the action to the other fellow....The people cannot know what they want unless they are constantly aware and have an active concern for the world at large." (*Cynosure*, March 18, 1962.)

CHAPTER THREE

1. John Lewis, *Walking with the Wind: A Memoir of the Movement*, 195.
2. "Letter from a Birmingham Jail," April 16, 1963, in *The Eyes on the Prize Civil Rights Reader: Documents, Speeches, and Firsthand Accounts from the Black Freedom Struggle*, ed. Clayborne Carson et al.
3. Lewis, John, *Walking with the Wind*, 199.
4. Jobs and Community Organization, Nick Egelson, Chester, PA.
5. The local chapter of the NAACP had been trying to develop an active movement in Chester for several years, but their efforts to organize legal cases concerning employment and housing issues had failed to break through the dispirited passivity that paralyzed the community after years of poverty and previously unsuccessful attempts to organize. A few Swarthmore students, including Carl, had occasionally attended the NAACP meetings, searching for a way to help the NAACP develop a more active relationship with the broader community. In the summer of 1963, after Carl had led trips down to Cambridge, Maryland, he and several other Swarthmore students continued to work in Cambridge, along with Stanley Branch, a leader of the Chester NAACP. Once on their way back from Cambridge, Carl and several others decided that the way to involve more Swarthmore students *and* more Chester residents was to do a large-scale survey in Chester, modeled on one done in Cambridge. The just-completed Cambridge survey had resulted in a seventy-page report on economic, social, and political conditions, and a chronology of the movement there. In Chester, Carl hoped a similar survey could identify which issues and problems most concerned the residents who were poor, a significant portion of whom were black. The activity would also provide an opportunity for Swarthmore students to familiarize themselves with the community and learn about the people and the conditions in which they lived. It was during the course of the survey the following fall that Chester activists became increasingly aware of parents' extreme dissatisfaction with the Franklin School. Carl Wittman, SDS pamphlet, Students and Economic Action.
6. In fact, by the following summer, the mayor, the city council and the school board had reneged on the board's promises. No new school was built, nor were most of the improvements made in the old building.
7. For an in-depth description of this early period see *Reunion* by Tom Hayden.
8. Kirkpatrick Sale, *SDS* (New York: Vintage, 1973), 40.

411

9. Judith Clavir Albert and Stewart Edward Albert, *The 60s Papers: Documents of a Rebellious Decade* (New York: Praeger, 1984), 179–181.

10. Judith Clavir Albert and Stewart Edward Albert, *The 60s Papers: Documents of a Rebellious Decade* (New York: Praeger, 1984), 122.

11. Sara Evans, *Personal Politics: The Roots of Women's Liberation in the Civil Rights Movement and the Left* (New York: Vintage Books, 1979), 154.

12. Sara Evans talks about how older ERAP women like Connie Brown, Carol McEldowney, and Sharon Jeffreys brought in younger women, such as Heather Tobis, Vivian Rothstein, and Cathy Barret. (Sara Evans, *Personal Politics*, 156.)

13. Sara Evans, *Personal Politics*, 163.

14. Robert Pardun, *Prairie Radical: A Journey Through the 60s* (Shire Press, Los Gatos, CA 2001).

15. As paraphrased by Paul Booth in his report on the December NC, *New Left Notes*, January 21, 1966.

16. Todd Gitlin, *The Sixties: Years of Hope, Days of Rage*. Bantam Books, New York. 1987. In this memoir, Gitlin argues that Weatherman and the women's movement were the two primary forces that destroyed SDS, implying that SDS would have continued growing without the challenges raised by these parts of the movement.

17. These included Peter Countryman (*NLN*, August 5, 1966), a white organizer from New Haven; Ivanhoe Donaldson, a SNCC member who spoke at the spring national council meeting about the black power position; Greg Calvert, Paul Booth, and Donald Jackson (*NLN*, August 5, 1966), from Chester, PA CORE (formerly SDS/ERAP); and Frank Joyce (*NLN*, August 5, 1966) of the Northern Student Movement in Detroit.

18. *New Left Notes*, June 24, 1966.

19. Statement of Congressman Bob Kastenmeier on the Resolution Providing Increased Funds for House Un-American Activities Committee, March 1, 1961.

CHAPTER FOUR

1. Greg Calvert, *Democracy from the Heart*, chapter 6, "Resistance and the War."

CHAPTER FIVE

1. For his own words on this period, see Greg Calvert, *Democracy from the Heart*, chapter 5.

2. Selective Service System Kit, as quoted in Henig.

3. Researchers into the corporate and university connections to foreign policy trained a generation how to use Standard and Poor's business directory, how to trace the boards of directors for corporate/government connections, and how to follow the money and to marvel over the many tentacles of the biggest and most powerful individuals and corporations. Many of these researchers went on to work with NACLA, Middle East Research and Information Project (MERIP), Africa Now, and other media that have continued to document and analyze the effects of US economic and military expansion and the movements against it.

4. Oglesby, *Containment and Change*, chapter 4, especially 104–106.

5. Oglesby, *Containment and Change*, 157.

6. Oglesby, *Containment and Change*, 147.

7. See Calvert, *Democracy from the Heart*.

8. Sara Evans, *Personal Politics*, 191.

CHAPTER SIX

1. Volunteers in Service to America, known as the domestic Peace Corps.
2. Gitlin, *The Sixties*, 252.
3. Quoted in Tom Hayden, *Reunion*, 204.
4. Jonathan Lerner, unpublished manuscript.
5. *Washington Free Press,* November 7, 1967.
6. Dave Dellinger, *From Yale to Jail.*
7. *New Left Notes*, Dec. 18, 1967.
8. "The Front considers a territory liberated when the Saigon administration is no longer able to exercise any power over the population of an area; instead the population operates with the principles articulated by the Front. [The NLF] elects by universal suffrage a village council, it elects representatives to the various district and regional governing bodies—for instance, the Federation of Workers, Union of Students, Federation of Women, Agricultural Committees and the like. In addition, land reform is carried out and the peasants finally obtain the freedom to till their own land. If a landlord has supported the Front and continues to remain in the area after it has been liberated he is usually allowed to maintain his status as a landlord but the rent rates are dropped from an average of 60 percent or more to 15 percent of the total crops." (Wilkerson, *New Left Notes,* January 15, 1968.)
9. *New Left Notes*, November 13, 1967, 2.

CHAPTER SEVEN

1. Jeannette Rankin was the first female congresswoman.
2. Alice Echols, *Daring to be Bad: Radical Feminism in America, 1967–1975*, 55–56.
3. Ibid., 69–70.
4. *Washington Free Press*, February 29, 1968
5. Stokely Carmichael, "What We Want," *New York Review of Books*, September 22, 1966, as quoted in Clayborne Carson, *In Struggle: SNCC and the Black Awakening of the 1960s*, 217.
6. Barry's work was hindered by the repeated loss of his unpaid or ill-paid organizers to the better-financed federal antipoverty program (Carson, *In Struggle,* 233). By June 1967, when he was interviewed by Sue Orrin for the *Washington Free Press*, Barry himself had left SNCC to become a consultant to the United Poverty Office (UPO), part of the antipoverty program. Orrin raised concerns that Barry was abandoning SNCC's old model for change based on mobilizing masses of people to participate in decisions, and Barry acknowledged the validity of those concerns. He believed, however, that UPO's programs could engage young black people in meaningful work. (*WFP*, July 1967.)
7. *WFP*, June 1967.
8. Carson, *In Struggle*, 249–250.
9. Carmichael, *Ready for Revolution* (New York: Scribner, 2003), 641.
10. Philip S. Foner, ed. *The Black Panthers Speak*, (New York: Da Capo Press, 1995), 214.
11. David Hilliard, and Lewis Cole. *This Side of Glory.*
12. Ward Churchill and Jim Vander Wall. *The Cointelpro Papers*, 393.
13. Sanders Bebura (managing editor, *Howard University Hilltop*), and Brenda Adams (*Hilltop* reporter), reprinted in the *Washington Free Press*, March 27, 1968.
14. Cindee Marshall, *The Hilltop*, March 29, 1968.
15. Ibid.
16. *NLN*, April 8, 1968.

17. *Washington Free Press*, April 22, 1965.
18. Ibid.
19. Peter Novick, *Washington Free Press*, April 22, 1968.
20. David Hilliard and Lewis Cole, *This Side of Glory*, chapters 14 and 15.
21. Churchill and Vander Wall, *The Cointelpro Papers*, 91.
22. Ibid., 92.
23. Ibid., 110.
24. Ibid. See pages 165–66 for multiple instances.
25. Ibid., 172, FBI memo of February 1966.
26. Ibid., 172.
27. Churchill and Vander Wall, *The Cointelpro Papers*, 177.
28. See Antjie Krog, *Country of My Skull*. The brave efforts and severe difficulties encountered by contemporary South Africans when they attempted to do this in postapartheid South Africa speak to these challenges.
29. See Greg Calvert, *Democracy from the Heart*, 198 and 209.
30. In an eloquent letter to Kirk several days later, Rudd wrote:

    > You might want to know what is wrong with this society, . . . We can point to the war in Vietnam as an example of the unimaginable wars of aggression you are prepared to fight to maintain your control over your empire. . . . We can point out your mansion window to the ghetto below you've helped to create through your racist University expansion policies, through your unfair labor practices, through your city government and your police. We can point to this University, . . . which trains us to be lawyers and engineers and managers for your IBM your Socony Mobil, your IDA [the Institute for Defense Analysis, which was contributing to the war effort with research on both weapons and mechanisms of social control], your Con Edison. We can point, in short, to . . . our revulsion with being cogs in your corporate machines as a produce of and reaction to a basically sick society.
    >
    > . . . You call for order and respect for authority; we call for justice, freedom, and socialism.

    (Mark Rudd, open letter to Grayson Kirk, April 22, 1968. As quoted in *Up Against the Ivy Wall*, Jerry L. Avorn et al, Boston: Atheneum, 1970, 25–26.)

31. Che Guevara, "Message to the People of the World," speech to the Tricontinental, Cuba, January 1967, in *Venceremos! The speeches and writings of Ernesto Che Guevara*, ed. John Gerassi.
32. His real name has been lost to my memory.
33. Robert Pardun, *Prairie Radical: A Journey Through the 60s*, 255–256.
34. *New Left Notes*, July 29, 1968.
35. *New Left Notes*, October 7, 1968
36. *New Left Notes*, November 11, 1968.
37. Ibid.
38. I am indebted to Grace Callahan for her insightful discussion of coolness in her undergraduate thesis "Women of Weatherman," Newcomb College, (2004).
39. Candy Knox, interview with author.
40. Alice Echols, *Daring to be Bad*, 104.
41. Previous attempts to do this, largely in the form of a few Movement for a Democratic Society (MDS) chapters, had gained only a little momentum. As presently constituted, SDS provided no national forum for MDS members.

CHAPTER EIGHT

1. Letter to Bernardine Dohrn, December 1968.
2. Jonathan Lerner, unpublished manuscript. See also Jeremy Varon, *Bringing the War Home: The Weather Underground, the Red Army Faction, and Revolutionary Violence in the 60s and 70s*.
3. Elaine Brown, *A Taste of Power: A Black Woman's Story,* 160-165.
4. Years later it would come out that these shootings had indeed been instigated by COINTEL-PRO, with Bunchy Carter and John Huggins as specific targets. See the FBI memorandum, November 25, 1968, as quoted in Churchill and Vander Wall, *The Cointelpro Papers,* in which the FBI states that "a serious struggle is taking place between the Black Panther Party (BPP) and the [United Slaves] US organization. . . . In order to fully capitalize upon BPP and US differences as well as to exploit all avenues of creating further dissension in the ranks of the BPP, recipient offices are instructed to submit imaginative and hard-hitting counterintelligence measures aimed at crippling the BPP." False letters and cartoons, which specifically targeted Carter and Huggins, as well as national BPP leaders Seale, Hilliard, and Newton, were sent as part of this program. One message sent to the Panthers contained the false information that since Carter and Huggins intended to kill Karenga, US had a plan to "ambush" BPP leaders, for the possible purpose of encouraging defection from the BPP to US. This was intended to provoke a US retaliation, very similar to what happened. (Churchill and Vander Wall, *The Cointelpro Papers*, 131). Additional evidence that the killings directly to the FBI came in 1995 from FBI agent M. Wesley Swearingen, on the Panther Squad during the time of the two killings. (Churchill in *Liberation, Imagination, and the Black Panther Party*, ed. Kathleen Cleaver and George Katsiaficas, 93.)
5. The Panthers themselves had a central committee led by a politburo, although in fact national leadership came from a tight knot around the few officers of the party: Huey Newton, Bobby Seale, Eldridge Cleaver, and David Hilliard, and those close to them. In LA, Chicago, and, later, New York, local leaders held sway.
6. Harold Jacobs, ed., *Weatherman,* 70.
7. Carl Oglesby, *Containment and Change* (New York: MacMillan, 1967), 146.
8. Richard H. Crossman, ed., *The God that Failed,* (New York: Columbia University Press, 1950). In this book several reknowned leftists criticized policies of the Communist Party USA and many embraced the tenets of anticommunism.

CHAPTER NINE

1. Interview with David Gilbert.
2. Celeste McCullough, "Goodbye, Columbus," *New Left Notes,* August 1, 1969, 1.
3. Kathy Boudin, Bernardine Dohrn, and Terry Robbins, SDS National Action Staff, *New Left Notes,* August 23, 1969. Italics added.
4. *New Left Notes,* August 29, 1969.
5. Ibid.
6. Ibid.
7. Jeremy Varon, *Bringing the War Home.*
8. The conference was originally scheduled as a national interim committee meeting, a vestigial remnant of SDS's old structure.
9. *New Left Notes,* September 12, 1969.
10. Ibid.
11. Ibid.
12. Ibid.

13. Kirkpatrick Sale, *SDS* 515, 632.
14. In fact the clergy at one of the churches that served as centers was assured that the demonstrations would be nonviolent. When police conducted a 2 a.m. raid on the demonstrators the third day, there were many injuries, and blood was left on the walls. Many outraged congregants turned on the clergy, and the membership declined steadily until the church finally closed in 2005.
15. Varon, *Bringing the War Home*, chapter 3.
16. Letter to the editor, *Liberation Magazine*.
17. Varon, *Bringing the War Home*.
18. Churchill and Vander Wall, *The Cointelpro Papers*, 211.
19. Varon, *Bringing the War Home*, 155.
20. Andy Kopkind, as quoted in Jonathan Lerner, unpublished manuscript, chapter 8.
21. Harold Jacobs, ed., *Weatherman*, 444.
22. Bernardine Dohrn, interview with author.
23. Dohrn, as quoted in Jeremy Varon, *Bringing the War Home*, 160.
24. Ibid., quote by John Jacobs.
25. Sale, *SDS*, 632.
26. It was never clear to what extent the leadership themselves shared this opinion, or whether they believed that the fate of the Seattle collective, like all others, lay in the hands of its members. It is likely that, already, a post-Flint split in leadership priorities was emerging between the coasts, and the thinking about the mission of the collectives might indeed have begun to diverge.

CHAPTER ELEVEN

1. As quoted by Mike Alewitz, in his speech, "The Legacy of Kent State: May 1970," at the 30th anniversary of the shootings at Kent State.
2. For statistics and a detailed summary of events during May 1970, see Kirkpatrick Sale, *SDS*.
3. Jeremy Varon noted that this procedure, which became the standard for all future Weather Underground actions, had been modeled by Sam Melville's group in New York when they carried out several symbolic bombings at corporate and government offices in 1969, before Melville and others were arrested. Melville, however, was an engineer, and successfully set out to achieve substantial structural damage, as opposed to Weatherman's more symbolic, albeit messy, damage of bathrooms and hallways. (Interview with Elizabeth Fink.)
4. "New Morning—Changing Weather," December 1970.
5. See appendix A for list of WUO bombings.
6. From "Women's Lament," in *Sing a Battle Song: The Revolutionary Poetry, Statements, and Communiqués of the Weather Underground, 1970-1974*, 100.

ACKNOWLEDGMENTS

My thanks to the community at El Puente Community Organization and High School for Peace and Justice, where I have shared hard work and hopeful visions of the future, especially with the class of 2002. Thanks also to my colleagues at Bank Street College Mathematics Leadership Program, with whom I continued to learn and puzzle about questions of change and problem solving.

Tamiment Library at New York University; Ron Grele, Director, Columbia Oral History Project, Columbia University; Roz Payne, who gave me generous access to her Newsreel film archives; Howard University Library; Matt Meyers who generously donated several original Weatherman materials when my own files were lost in an automobile mishap. Special thanks to Dickie Magidoff who shared his letters from Terry Robbins with me.

Two women had a profound influence on this book and on me. Susan Hammond was the first to suggest this project twenty years ago and then gave me insightful structural and content suggestions for each chapter as I pulled the manuscript together. Amy Scholder, editor in chief of Seven Stories Press, sought me out at the beginning of this project and has been an enthusiastic supporter, editor, and advisor at critical points.

Heartfelt gratitude also to Elizabeth Fink, my lawyer and invaluable friend; the Supper Club; Jim Monsonis and Lenore Gensburg, who fed me and took in the dog during the height of my writing and interviewing; my mother, father, and stepmother; my sisters, Robin Wilkerson, Ann Olson, and Haven Logan; Paul and Heather Booth, for their contribution; Dr. Hy and Ruth Gold; Barbara Robbins; and Marilyn Webb, who each corrected early versions of particular sections; all of those who took the time to give me interviews and who provided me with invaluable information and insights; and those, too numerous to name, who answered one or two questions along the way to confirm an impression or, dare I say, fact. Thanks, too, to Carol Hill and her writing group for not laughing me out of the room when I first started.

Finally and essentially, thank you to Delia Mellis, the first to read through the earliest drafts and offer both content and editorial suggestions; and to the readers of a later version of the text who gave me critical feedback, generous suggestions, and encouragement: Robert Cunningham, Jeanne Friedman, Marilyn McNabb, Jim Monsonis, Ann Olson, Joe Treasure, Leni Wildflower, and Robin Wilkerson.

And to my immediate/extended family who have loved me and challenged me to keep on growing and hoping: Bessie Wilkerson, Vicky Taylor, Eleanor Black, Crystal Hayes, and Myaisha Hayes. I especially thank my partner, Susan Tipograph, for supporting me in every conceivable way, even though she would never read the manuscript.

INDEX

..